Global Reflections on Children's Rights and the Law

Thirty years after the adoption of the UN Convention on the Rights of the Child, this book provides diverse perspectives from countries and regions across the globe on its implementation, critique and potential for reform.

The book revolves around key issues including progress in implementing the CRC worldwide; how to include children in legal proceedings; how to uphold children's various civil rights; how to best assist children at risk; and discussions surrounding children's identity rights in a changing familial order. Discussion of the CRC is both compelling and polarizing and the book portrays the enthusiasm around these topics through contrasting and comparative opinions on a range of topics.

The work provides varying perspectives from many different countries and regions, offering a wealth of insight on topics that will be of significant interest to scholars and practitioners working in the areas of children's rights and justice.

Ellen Marrus is the Royce Till Professor of Law at the University of Houston Law Center (UHLC) and founder and director of the Center for Children, Law & Policy in Houston, TX, USA.

Pamela Laufer-Ukeles is Professor of Law and Healthcare Administration at the Academic College of Law and Science in Hod Hasharon, Israel.

Routledge Research in Human Rights Law

Domestic Judicial Treatment of European Court of Human Rights Case Law
Beyond Compliance
Edited by David Kosař, Jan Petrov, Katarína Šipulová, Hubert Smekal, Ladislav Vyhnánek, and Jozef Janovský

Hate Speech and Human Rights in Eastern Europe
Legislating for Divergent Values
Viera Pejchal

Collective Punishment and Human Rights Law
Addressing Gaps in International Law
Cornelia Klocker

Executive Clemency
Comparative and Empirical Perspectives
Edited by Daniel Pascoe and Andrew Novak

International Human Rights Law and Crimes Against Women in Turkey
Legislation on So-Called Honour Killings
Ayşe Güneş

Rights of the Child, Mothers and Sentencing
The Case of Kenya
Alice Wambui Macharia

For more information about this series, please visit: www.routledge.com/Routledge-Research-in-Human-Rights-Law/book-series/HUMRIGHTSLAW

Global Reflections on Children's Rights and the Law

30 Years After the Convention on the Rights of the Child

Edited by
Ellen Marrus and
Pamela Laufer-Ukeles

Routledge
Taylor & Francis Group
LONDON AND NEW YORK

First published 2022
by Routledge
2 Park Square, Milton Park, Abingdon, Oxon OX14 4RN

and by Routledge
605 Third Avenue, New York, NY 10158

Routledge is an imprint of the Taylor & Francis Group, an informa business

British Library Cataloguing-in-Publication Data
A catalogue record for this book is available from the British Library

Library of Congress Cataloging-in-Publication Data
A catalog record has been requested for this book

ISBN: 978-0-367-67386-4 (hbk)
ISBN: 978-0-367-67388-8 (pbk)
ISBN: 978-1-003-13114-4 (ebk)

Typeset in Galliard
by codeMantra

We dedicate this book to all the children in the world.

Contents

Foreword xi
Introduction xiii
ELLEN MARRUS AND PAMELA LAUFER-UKELES
Acknowledgments xix
List of contributors xxi

PART I
Struggles, challenges, and successes in implementing and ratifying the CRC worldwide 1
A. Worldwide

1 **How to ensure wider implementation of the CRC** 3
OLGA KHAZOVA

B. European Union

2 **The European Union and the United Nations Convention on the Rights of the Child: towards a fully-fledged European Union child rights strategy** 17
AIDA KISUNAITE AND SIMONE DELICATI

C. Africa

3 **Thirty years of the CRC in Africa** 30
JULIA SLOTH-NIELSEN

D. Israel

4 **Thirty years later: the CRC's influence on Israeli law, taking stock and moving forward** 46
TAMAR MORAG

E. United States

5 Forever owned: children as possessions in the CRC 59
JAMES G. DWYER

6 Family obligations and socio-economic rights under the Convention on the Rights of the Child 73
BARBARA STARK

PART II
Children's Participation Rights and Child-Friendly Justice 87

7 My voice must be heard too: why children need a voice in custody hearings 89
ELLEN MARRUS, MALIKAH MARRUS, AND RIFQA SA'AADAT

8 Child-friendly justice: a malleable catalyst for the promotion of child and human rights 103
PHILIP D. JAFFÉ

9 Family group conferences in child protection: a communitarian implementation of children's participation rights 115
TALI GAL

10 The unheard voices of young girls at risk 128
SHIRAN REICHENBERG

PART III
Children's civil rights: rights to free speech, health, religious freedom, and privacy 141

11 Childhood, speech, and the right to free speech 143
NICHOLAS HATZIS

12 Upholding children's civil rights as relational rights: the example of childhood circumcision 157
PAMELA LAUFER-UKELES

13 Protection of the child's right to privacy in the Convention on the Rights of the Child, the General Data Protection Regulation and the Polish law 171
AGNIESZKA OGRODNIK-KALITA

14 Children's digital rights: realizing the potential of the CRC 183
KATHARINA KAESLING

PART IV
Children's right to identity 197

15 The child's right to know their biological origin in comparative European law: consequences for parentage law 199
GORDANA KOVAČEK STANIĆ

16 Québec's (out)law concerning medically assisted procreation: a plea for access to origins 211
JOHANNE CLOUET AND VALÉRIE P. COSTANZO

PART V
Protecting children at risk 223

17 Suffering at the hands of caregivers: the mandatory duty of caregivers to report child abuse and neglect from a South African perspective 225
MILDRED BEKINK

18 The journey from ignorance to acknowledgement of child sexual abuse in India 238
NAMRATA MISHRA

19 Dutch strategies for combating child poverty: a child rights-based approach 251
MEREL JONKER, JET TIGCHELAAR, CATRIN FINKENAUER, KIRSTEN VISSER, AND GONNEKE STEVENS

Index 265

Foreword

The faculty of the Academic College of Law and Science in Israel ("College"), where the International Society of Family Law's (ISFL) Regional Conference on the subject of Children's Rights and Interests took place, and upon which the chapters in this volume are based, includes the highest concentration of family law researchers in Israel and houses a Center for the Rights of the Child and the Family ("Center"), which is unique in Israel in its commitment to children's rights. The United Nations Convention on the Rights of the Child (CRC) Conference reflects the College's goals of promoting research and serving as a platform for discussion of current issues relating to the rights of all family members, and the Center's mission, which is based on the belief that every child is entitled to human rights by way of *right*. The College's collaboration with the ISFL expresses its conviction that the insights which can be gleaned from academic discussion between scholars from different States can provide benefits to children and families throughout the world.

The Israeli appointment of the Rotlevy Committee, which proposed a wide variety of reforms to Israeli legislation to ensure compliance with the CRC, may be seen as demonstrating Israel's genuine commitment to the interests of children and to implementing the CRC. The origin of this commitment may perhaps be traced to Jewish tradition, which was in many ways ahead of its time in recognizing the interests of children. Perusal of Jewish law sources reveals the sensitivity of the Sages to the vulnerable position of children and their need for protection and care. For example, Jewish law imposed a legal obligation on fathers to sustain their children until the age of six and a moral obligation to support older children. In the Talmud (compiled in the 4th century C.E.), we find severe criticism and denouncement of fathers who didn't take care of their children's welfare and reference to the Rabbinical Court as the "father of orphans." This phrase, which describes the protection provided by that court for helpless minors, expresses concern and compassion for those children who don't have anyone to ensure that their voices are heard and prevent their rights being violated. More generally, recognition of each child as a unique and independent individual is reflected in the Biblical advice to "educate a child according to his way" (Proverbs, 22:1).

In modern times too, Israel may be seen as a pioneer, especially in relation to the recognition of the child's right to participate. For example, further to the recommendations of the Rotlevy Committee, regulations now provide that children over the age of 6 have the right to have their voice heard in Family Court proceedings concerning them. In addition, a Child Representation Unit has been set up in the Legal Aid Department of the Israeli Ministry of Justice, which has recently conducted a campaign, called "A Lawyer of My Own," publicizing the right of minors to legal aid.

However, as recognized by all speakers at the conference, including the President of the Israeli Supreme Court, Justice Esther Hayut, there is still much more to be done in order to ensure that children have full access to justice and that their rights are properly protected. Accordingly, the most appropriate way to celebrate 30 years of the CRC is to focus on how we can build on what has been achieved so far. This book is a highly significant contribution to this quest.

Prof. Rhona Schuz, Prof. Ayelet Blecher-Prigat,
and Dr. Tehila Alon.

Introduction

Ellen Marrus and Pamela Laufer-Ukeles

The year 2019 marked the 30th anniversary celebration of the United Nations Convention on the Rights of the Child (CRC), the first international instrument that recognized children as rights holders. The CRC, however, did not intend to secure rights, but to create those rights and then lead a fight toward implementing and protecting those rights in a continuous manner. Putting children front and center is a work in progress that should be continuously discussed to be furthered. In the US, the only country not to have ratified the CRC, debates still rage about whether children's rights are worthy of separate and focused attention. Across the globe countries struggle with implementation of the CRC and how to best protect children's rights, even when recognizing their importance. It is a struggle and success worthy of capturing and discussing in classrooms and political debates worldwide.

Children's rights have been controversial for their potential conflict with parental rights, and for the way children's rights may be different from adult rights. Indeed, calling children's rights "rights" at all is controversial, as rights are usually entitlements that are demanded with one's own voice, and children's voices are often muted and without legal capacity. Nonetheless, rights need not depend on full autonomy. The state can establish children's rights, international treaties can grant such rights, and parents and other adults can respect those rights, even if children are not fully autonomous. Children's rights advocates focus on how children – without full liberty and constitutional rights – still maintain human, civil, and constitutional rights that deserve to be protected from interference.

Scholars also complain that rights talk creates unnecessary tension with parental rights. It is argued that protecting "interests" are a more accurate description of children's necessities and requirements. Interests are broader than rights but are also considered more flexible, as they are often balanced against other individual and societal interests, while rights make a more demonstrative claim. Accordingly, in order to balance with and preserve space for children, and to insure their rights against parental rights and state interests, rights language is used to provide a stronger flag for children to wave in their own advocacy.

Reflecting the struggle for terminology, the uniqueness and importance of children's rights originated from the need to balance the triangle of child, parent, and state. This confluence of interests is addressed throughout the book.

Contending with overlapping and at times competing rights and interests, the state must respect, support, and oversee a fragile interplay between parental discretion and authority and children's own voices and participatory rights. In general, the state at first gives discretion to parents, but upon an indication or complaint in the matter, the state must step in to insure children's well-being and the upholding of specified rights. This triangle involves a delicate dance, and it is easy for the state or parents to overwhelm the child. And too often the state and parents are caught in a power struggle instead of being jointly focused on promoting the rights and interests of children.

There are four guiding principles of the CRC that are continuously recognized as providing the conceptual anchor for the treaty and for efforts to implement the CRC: equality and non-discrimination, survival and development, best interests, and the right to participation. In addition, the evolving capacity of children, their right to maturity and development, and their need to have their own civil rights protected can be added. These themes are raised by many authors in this book.

The CRC provides particular focus on the best interests standard, a standard which is exceedingly hard to apply, and leaves vague how much of children's rights should be governed by parental discretion as opposed to children's own voices or state intervention. There are so many factors that can be considered in determining the outcome of the standard, many of which may be weighed against each other, such that the standard can be considered more of a normative goal as opposed to practical standard that can be applied. When used in this book by authors from different corners of the globe, each engrained in different language and cultures, professionally trained as lawyers, social workers, advocates, and academics, it is no surprise that the term will have different meanings in different contexts. However, the primary ideology that it represents is that it is children's interests, to the greatest extent possible, as far as such interests can be clarified, and not adult interests that are to be the focus of attention. While some authors complain that the treaty does not place enough emphasis on children's expressed interests as opposed to adult interests, and others are more concerned about the impact of the CRC on state and parental interests in various contexts, all the authors in this book seek, in their different ways, to promote interests central to children, and this development is remarkable.

Despite the fear of potential burdens or at times the amorphous "damage" it may do to children, the right to participate in legal proceedings that concern them, and more generally the right of children to have their voices heard in all matters of children's rights, from how to implement the treaty, to the right to demonstrate and the right to influence public policy, is central to promoting children's rights. While such participation is not the sole arena of children's rights as is sometimes misunderstood, the CRC clarifies that it is an important element of promoting the rights of children. Children's direct participation is slow to develop because it is perhaps the most progressive part of the CRC, but, in the future, more conferences on children's rights need to continue to ensure the involvement of children themselves, just as the CRC Committee and policy reforms need to include children's own opinions and perspectives in ongoing work.

Furthermore, it must be taken into account that children range in their capabilities. Infants and adolescents are profoundly different in their capacities – and of course within lies everything in between. The CRC, in addressing the substantive rights of children, perhaps does not do enough to distinguish between the different developmental stages that children experience. The application of these rights for an adolescent, particularly one who lives largely independent of one's parents, can be addressed in ways vastly different from an infant's rights.

As we develop increasingly sophisticated children's rights, such as digital rights, privacy rights, the right to know one's genetic origin and the right to participate in policy reforms, we must continue to stress the mere right of survival – the necessities. When local or world-wide disasters put people in difficult situations, children usually suffer even more extraordinary challenges. Children's daily lives will be disrupted, and any overall economic slowdown across the globe may push parents and their children into greater poverty and greater financial struggles.

This has certainly occurred during the current pandemic, and while the original ideas and concepts for this book were initiated prior to its onslaught, we do want to recognize the effect the pandemic has had on children. As the world reels from the effects of the pandemic on the health care system, the economy and mental health, children often bear the brunt of such hardships. Many children are facing homelessness, poverty, lack of health care, abuse, lack of education, and missing out on childhood socialization. Furthermore, although COVID-19 threatens all of us, it is not an equal opportunity disease. Communities of color and low-income neighborhoods face inequality in medical treatment, levels of exposure, underlying preexisting health risks, lack of resources to maintain a decent standard of living during the economic crisis, and the inability to have access to internet and on-line learning.

Implementation of all the rights enumerated in the CRC, in all their varieties, is a distinct concern from generation of the rights themselves. Creating and enforcing rights are very different endeavors, involving different means and measures, and we must continuously strive for the latter even while improving our efforts at the former. Challenges of implementation include monitoring without infringing on sovereignty, integrating varied perspectives and participants, educating and promotion, among other challenges that are discussed throughout the book.

The distinct sections in this book reflect core interests of the ISFL Conference celebrating the 30th Anniversary of the enactment of the CRC, but in no way are meant to suggest that they are the only areas of the CRC that are relevant. The first section brings together children's rights advocates from across the globe, reporting on the progress attained since the signing of the CRC and the successes and challenges in implementing its principles and standards. The book begins with the chapter of Olga Khazova, a Russian national who, has significant insight from her time as a member of the CRC Committee, imparting guidance as to how the CRC is to be implemented and child rights monitored, as well as providing updates regarding challenges in successes in implementing the CRC worldwide. Aida Kisunaite conveys the fascinating EU perspective and discusses the challenges and benefits of regional European Union implementation and support for children's rights, arguing that a children's rights culture that extends beyond national borders is necessary to secure progress. Julia Sloth-Nielson reports from the African continent, providing a range of statistics and distinct national challenges and successes faced in Africa, sharing a wealth of insight with considerable range. Tamar Morag discusses the particular challenges faced by Israel, which has succeeded with well-meaning adoption of the CRC's provisions, but faces considerable challenges incorporating its principles. Finally, in the last two chapters of this section, we hear from the lone dissenter country, the US. Accounting for the range of perspectives on the CRC in the US, and the many faces of US exceptionalism, we felt it was essential to provide different positions on the advisability of the US adoption of the CRC that would reflect both the lack of support and active advocacy on behalf of the CRC in different constituencies in the US. To this end, James Dwyer explains what he believes makes the CRC unappealing as an international treaty and why the US, despite its general support for children's rights, is better off without adopting it. Following, Barbara Stark offers a drastically different perspective, arguing that adoption of the CRC is sorely needed in the US where children suffer, despite the wealth of the country as a whole, in a disproportionate manner due to the lack of social welfare rights.

The right to be heard, to contribute one's own perspectives and insights to proceedings that affect them, to participate, are all fundamental and relied on for the implementation of all other rights. Although this right is supported through the CRC, its implementation and effectuation are challenging. In the second section, this right is discussed in depth, bringing in sociological and legal perspectives on how the judicial system should include children and examples of models that can guarantee participation without causing unintended consequences or harm. In their chapter, Ellen Marrus, Malikah Marrus, and Rifqa Sa'Aadat bring the child's voice to the book in the context of a custody dispute which also reflects their call for a collaborative model of child representation. The model involves an advocate and social worker, working together with the child, to enable effective child participation at any age. They emphasize the importance of the child's voice being heard in the decision-making process and the harm that can be caused if this does not occur. Philip Jaffe discusses the concept of child-friendly justice, an increasingly popular concept which has helped and encouraged judicial systems to provide children with access to justice and to adapt to their needs. Like the collaborative model discussed in the previous chapter, child-friendly justice emphasizes meaningful child participation while improving the way the professionals collaborate with each other and communicate with children. Tali Gal provides a range of frameworks in which to capture and support children's voices from the Israeli context in which such frameworks have been attempted. With a focus on child participation in the area of child protection and relying on the Israeli experience, she presents the distinct liberal and communitarian paradigms, which form the basis for completely different applications of the right of children to participation. The section concludes with a chapter by Shiran Reichenberg, discusses the right to participation by young girls at risk in care and supervision proceedings in Israel's youth court. Again, bringing in the voices of young girls who have been in the system and felt their voices were ignored, the chapter emphasizes the need for the girls' participation and the importance of this life skill in their ability to exercise their rights.

In section three, we explore children's civil rights more broadly – rights to free speech, health, to practice their religion, and privacy. These rights model adult civil rights. However, in the context of children, these rights are necessarily encapsulated and muted by children's own legal and physical immaturity. While they will one day be full, legal citizens, and require education and development in order to do so, in the context of children these rights must be monitored and implemented by parents in addition to the state. In this context, children are the primary rights holders, but need adult assistance and guidance, and ultimately, when parents fail or are unable to protect and support children; the state must be there to supplement and fulfill children's rights and protections. Nicholas Hatzis discusses children's civil rights to speech, why it is so crucial for children and explores how it can be best supported and protected. As children spent much of their time in school, protecting their rights in the educational environment is of crucial importance. Pamela Laufer-Ukeles describes the tension that arises between competing claims on children from state and parents. In order to balance tension and discord between parents, state and children themselves, and in light of children's developing capacities, she argues for a relational approach to promoting children's civil rights, one that focuses on advancing children's rights within the context of dependency on ongoing care relationships. Demonstrating the approach in the context of male and female circumcision, she argues for an approach that takes into account the extent of harm to the child, the age of the child and the impact on familial life when determining whether to ban or merely educate regarding juvenile circumcision. Agnieszka Ogrodnik-Kalita discusses the constantly developing right to privacy, from its most basic form to online rights, and from sharenting to the rights of embryos. The multiple forms and contexts to which the right to privacy applies creates a maze of challenges under the Polish law that she describes and beyond. Katharina Kaesling discusses modern digital rights of children, in all their vast varieties and complexities. With a glance to the future, she attempts to provide a framework for managing the intangible.

Section four discusses children's right to identity and how this right can come in conflict with the rights of others such as their legal or biological parents' desire to remain anonymous. Gordana Stanić compares legal solutions on children's right to know their biological parentage in contemporary European family laws, especially in the field of artificial reproduction technologies (ART), considering the theoretical bases for these differing legal perspectives. Countries differ widely on their approach to these matters, with some ascribing the right to know to the child explicitly, and others considering biological parentage to be an absolute secret. Johanne Clouet and Valérie P. Costanzo discuss the right of children born from medically assisted procreation to know their origins under the legal framework in existence in the Province of Québec, Canada, and compare the lack of such a right to the right to identity that is enjoyed in Quebec by adopted children. They examine the provisions of the CRC, as well as case law, to examine the legal factors that weigh in favor of children born from assisted procreation to know their identity.

The last section, section five, discusses children at risk of abuse, neglect, and poverty and their need for protection and support. Mildred Bekink starts the section by discussing the need for state intervention in detecting the maltreatment that children face by those who should be protecting them. Bekink examines South Africa's current reporting statutes and whether they comply with the protection principles of the CRC. Namrata Mishra's chapter turns to a discussion of child sexual abuse in India both before and after India's ratification of the CRC. She discusses the issues, challenges, and solutions facing India in its attempts to secure the safety of its children and evaluates the ability of the Protection of Children from Sexual Offences Act of 2012 to adequately protect Indian children. This section concludes with a chapter by Merel Jonker, Jet Tigchelaar, Catrin Finkenauer, Kirsten Visser, and Gonneke Stevens that takes an interdisciplinary approach to evaluating the Danish strategies for combating child poverty. Over the years, rather than taking a material approach aimed at the family, the Netherlands have moved to a child rights approach. In addition to taking into consideration the four principles of the CRC to develop policies to reduce child poverty, the authors assess how successful these policies are in not only reducing poverty, but also increasing child participation in the process.

Despite all the varied controversies, obstacles, and problems we have raised, much progress has been made globally and domestically in prioritizing and emphasizing children's rights since the enactment of the CRC. And, most important, in centering the discussion as children as stakeholders and right bearers as opposed to objects and possessions. And yet, there is much work that still needs to be done. The editors and authors all hope that this book can be part of that progress.

Acknowledgments

This book would not have come together if the International Society for Family Law had not held a dedicated conference in December 2019 at the Academic College of Law and Science in Hod Hasharon, Israel to celebrate the 30th anniversary of the initial signing of the Convention on the Rights of the Child (CRC). The organizing committee of the regional ISFL Conference, led by Dean Ayelet Blecher-Prigat and Prof. Rhona Schuz, and supported by President Aviad Hacohen, Dr. Tehila Alon, and the rest of the faculty, staff, and students at the Academic College of Law and Science, solicited abstracts from children's rights scholars and advocates from all over the world. From this collection, along with invited guests, the College hosted a two-day conference that brought together speakers from over twenty-five countries that presented, participated, and attended the many keynote lectures by distinguished judges and authors, panel discussions, roundtables, and celebratory events surrounding the conference. This book represents a small subsection of those contributions. It is our hope that the publication of these works will ignite a new generation of scholars and advocates that continue the work of expanding children's rights and the view society holds of children and youth.

The enactment of the CRC and its recognition by almost all the world's countries, the work of advocates from all corners of the world, the child-led activism that has surged through many countries, have generated a revolution that has reshaped the way society and our legal systems have come to think of children. They are no longer just objects to be dictated to, but rather, children have come to be recognized as their own and individual rights' holders. We publish this book as a contribution to that revolution.

We are extremely appreciative of all the contributors to this book who put in endless hours to write and finely tune these remarkable chapters in a relatively short period of time. Without their dedication, this book would not have come to be. We are also thankful to Alison Kirk, our editor at Routledge Publishing who recognized the importance of this work. We wish to thank the Irene Merker Rosenberg Child Advocacy Scholars from the Center for Children, Law, & Policy (CCLP) at the University of Houston Law Center (UHLC) for their countless hours reviewing and formatting each and every chapter. A grateful thank you to John LaPorte '21, Nicholas Guillory '21, and Mykal Peterson '22.

A special thanks to Kristen Guerra Dorton '20, UHLC Public Interest Fellow at the Center for Children, Law & Policy who also contributed to the review and formatting of the chapters. Ellen also wishes to thank UHLC's Dean Leonard Baynes for his continued support for CCLP's work in improving the status of children and his recognition of the significance of children's rights. I also thank UHLC for financial support to travel to Israel for the conference, for the support and time to work on the editing of this book, and for summer research funds to complete the book. Pamela thanks the Academic College of Law and Science, under the leadership of President Aviad Hacohen and CEO Yehuda Lieberman, for its continuous support of her research and her efforts in preparing this book for publication, as well as its support of the study of the family and children's rights generally, and in arranging the ISFL 30th Anniversary Conference. Special appreciation goes to Dean Ayelet Blecher-Prigat for her tireless work in bringing us all together in celebration of children's rights.

Contributors

Editors

Ellen Marrus is the Royce Till Professor of Law at the University of Houston Law Center (UHLC) and founder and director of the Center for Children, Law & Policy. She came to UHLC in 1995 after serving as a public defender in California. Professor Marrus directed the clinical programs at UHLC, including child advocacy clinics. She currently teaches juvenile law, children and the law, street law, and professional responsibility. Professor Marrus concentrates her scholarship in the areas of children's rights, juvenile law, race, and professionalism, with a focus on representing children's express interests and the intersection of juvenile justice with race and gender. She has presented at various conferences on these topics in the United States and internationally. In addition to numerous law review articles, she has written a casebook entitled *Children and Juvenile Justice* third edition and co-edited *Rights, Race, and Reform 50 Years of Child Advocacy in the Juvenile Justice System,* and *Children, Sexuality and the Law.* Professor Marrus received her JD from the University of San Francisco and her LLM from Georgetown University Law Center.

Pamela Laufer-Ukeles is Professor of Law and Healthcare Administration at the Academic College of Law and Science in Hod Hasharon, Israel. Her fields of expertise include torts, family law, bioethics, feminist theory, and elder law. Her research and writing, which has been published in dozens of law reviews and books, focuses on the legal analysis of complex and collaborative family-making through surrogate motherhood, gamete donations and adoption as well as legal analysis of children's rights, caregiving, informed consent, and relational autonomy. She is originally from the US where she was Professor of Law at the University of Dayton. She has also visited in several law schools, including Bar-Ilan University and the University of Montreal. Prof. Laufer-Ukeles received her BA, *Magna cum Laude,* in philosophy and economics at Columbia College, Columbia University, and her JD from Harvard Law School. She was a Fulbright Fellow and Harvard, Kennedy Traveling Fellow at Bar-Ilan University, as well as an Equal Justice Fellow at the Hale and Dorr Family Law Clinic at Harvard Law School.

Contributors

Mildred Bekink is currently an associate professor at the University of South Africa in the College of Law. She is an admitted Advocate of the High Court of South Africa, a member of the Legal Practice Council of South Africa and member of the South African Professional Society on the Abuse of Children. Her multidisciplinary academic qualifications and experience enable her to engage meaningfully in her primary research field, child law. Her LLD thesis is entitled *The Protection of Child Victims and Witnesses in a Post-Constitutional Criminal Justice System With Specific Reference to the Role of an Intermediary: a Comparative Study*. She has published widely in journals on aspects relating to the protection and promotion of children's rights, child victims, and witnesses within the justice system. She received her BA in Law from North West University, BA (Hon), LLB, and LLD (child law) (University of South Africa), LLM (child law) (cum laude) (University of Pretoria).

Johanne Clouet is a Professor at the Faculty of Law of the Université de Montréal Master's program in Notarial Law, director of the master's program, and faculty in the Bachelor of Law program. She is also an associate professor at the Institute of Science, Technology and Advanced Studies in Haiti. Her teaching and research activities focus on family law and human rights and have been the subject of her numerous national and international publications and presentations. In keeping with her interest in alternative dispute resolution and access to justice, she collaborates as a researcher on a project which studies the human and financial costs of justice. Prior to joining the Faculty of Law of the Université de Montréal, she led a postdoctoral project on the judicial protection of the elderly. Professor Clouet received a LLM from McGill University and a LLD from the Université de Montréal.

Valérie P. Costanzo is a trained lawyer, having practiced mainly in family litigation, representing both parents as well as children. She holds a Bachelor's degree and a Master's degree from the Faculty of Law of Université de Montréal and is currently pursuing doctoral studies at Ottawa University. Passionate about family law and access to justice, her master's thesis focused on the failed efforts to establish a unified family court in the Province of Quebec. Her doctoral thesis will present an ethnographic study of children's voices in courts, as articulated by their attorneys. In addition to her research, Miss P. Costanzo is a lecturer at the Faculty of Law of Université de Montréal. She is also an advisor to the Quebec Institute for Law and Justice Reform.

Simone Delicati is a researcher in the project "CRIMG – Mainstreaming of children's rights: multi-level governance perspective" at the department of Political Science, Law and International Studies of the University of Padua. He holds a Master's degree in "Human rights and multi-level governance" and a Bachelor's degree in "Political sciences, international relations and human rights" from the University of Padua and has been an Erasmus student at the University of Reading (United Kingdom) and the University of Antwerp (Belgium). His research activity focuses on children's rights and refugee rights with a particular focus on the EU legal and political system.

James G. Dwyer holds the Arthur B. Hanson chair at the William & Mary School of Law, where he teaches Family Law, Youth Law, Trusts & Estates, and Law & Social Justice and has three times received the university's Plumeri Award for Faculty Excellence. He received his law degree from Yale Law School and a Ph.D. in political and moral philosophy from Stanford University. Professor Dwyer has authored half a dozen books and dozens of articles on child-welfare related topics, and he is the editor of the Oxford Handbook of Children and the Law. Before entering academia, he worked as a family court Law Guardian in New York State, in addition to spending three years as an associate in Washington, D.C. law firms.

Catrin Finkenauer is a Professor of Youth Studies at Utrecht University and scientific director of Dynamics of Youth. Dynamics of Youth is an interdisciplinary research institute designed to foster research collaborations within and between Utrecht University and society to accelerate research and education that helps all youth to thrive and become constructive, engaged citizens actively contributing to solving present and future societal challenges.

Tali Gal is Senior Lecturer at the University of Haifa, where she is Head of the School of Criminology. Her scholarship integrates legal, criminological, and psycho-social knowledge and involves restorative justice, children's rights, and therapeutic jurisprudence. Dr. Gal is the author of the book *Child Victims and Restorative Justice: A Needs-Rights Model* (OUP, 2011), and co-editor (with Benedetta Faedi-Duramy) of *International Perspectives and Empirical Findings on Child Participation* (OUP, 2015). She has published extensively in peer-review as well as law-review journals on the areas of her expertise. Prior to joining academia, Tali Gal was the Legal Adviser of the Israel National Council for the Child.

Nicholas Hatzis is senior lecturer in law at City, University of London. Previously he was research fellow at Lady Margaret Hall, University of Oxford and referendaire at the Court of Justice of the European Union in Luxembourg.

Philip D. Jaffé is a Full Professor at the University of Geneva, Switzerland, and the founding former Director of its Centre for Children's Rights Studies. In 2018, he was elected to the United Nations Committee on the Rights of the Child. A clinical and a forensic psychologist trained in Switzerland and in the USA, he is still a practicing licensed psychotherapist and a court-appointed expert witness. He was a member of the group of experts drafting the 2010 Council of Europe Child-Friendly Justice Guidelines. Beyond the traditional "teach, research, publish or perish missions" required by a leading university, his vision of academic life is to branch out in the community at large as a science practitioner and an educator.

Merel Jonker is an Associate Professor of Family Law at the Utrecht Centre for European Research into Family Law and is involved in the interdisciplinary research group Dynamics of Youth – Youth got Talent at Utrecht University (NL). She specializes in Dutch and comparative family law, with a focus on intergenerational (financial) obligations. She is also interested in family-law related topics that concern minorities and have a huge impact on the family members involved, e.g. international child abduction, missing persons, and the right of contact with grandchildren.

Katharina Kaesling is Research Coordinator at the Käte Hamburger Center "Law as Culture", University of Bonn, Germany. She concentrates her scholarship on digital transformation in the areas of children's rights and New Media as well as intellectual property in the 21st century. Her research profile encompasses the legal fields of family law, data protection law, platform regulation, intellectual property, and property law, including international and comparative law perspectives. She holds degrees from the College of Europe as well as the University of Bonn and passed the German Judiciary and Bar Exam in 2017. Her research has received several awards, including the Doctoral Prize of the Law Department of the University of Bonn and the Prize of the Foundation for Fundamental Research in Family Law. In 2020, she was appointed a Young Member of the North Rhine-Westphalian Academy of Sciences, Humanities, and the Arts.

Olga Khazova is currently with the Moscow School of Social & Economic Sciences and the Private Law Research Centre (Moscow). Olga had worked as a legal scholar at the Institute of State & Law within the Russian Academy of Sciences, where she received her Ph.D. She received a LLM from Cornell University Law School. Her expertise is in international/comparative family law and child law. Olga serves as a consultant on family law matters, including cross-border disputes and human reproduction and matters related to children's rights. Olga is the author of *Marriage and Divorce in Western Family Law* and *The Art of Legal Writing*, as well as of numerous scholarly articles. She is a speaker at international conferences. She is a Vice-President of the International Society of Family Law (ISFL), a Fellow of the International Academy of Family Lawyers (IAFL), and in 2013 was elected as a member of the UN Committee on the Rights of the Child and was Vice-Chair in 2017–2018.

Aida Kisunaite is a researcher at the University of Padua (Italy) at the department of Political Science, Law, and International Studies and the principal investigator in the project "CRIMG – Mainstreaming of children's rights: multilevel governance perspective" (2018–2020) at the University of Padua. She is a former Director of Interdisciplinary Research Center for Children Rights (IRCCR). Dr. Kisunaite is an academic lawyer and political scientist working in the field of human rights with the particular attention on groups of the most vulnerable children and youth. Dr. Kisunaite has participated in various international multi-disciplinary research teams working on European policy issues with the major focus on social and health policies and the role of different stakeholders in the policy cycle. Her work for this book was funded by the University of Padova under the STARS Grants program (CRIMG – Mainstreaming of children's rights: multilevel governance perspective, funding: Euros 140.000).

Malikah Marrus is a professor of social work and director of Field Education at the University of Colorado at Colorado Springs. Prior to that, she taught social work and was director of Field Education at Hood College and taught at Missouri State University. She teaches human rights, introduction to social work, juvenile justice, forensic social work, and child abuse and neglect. Prior to teaching, she was a research fellow and social worker for the Southwest Juvenile Defender Center. In this role, she worked as part of the team of local attorneys representing youth in delinquency and abuse and neglect cases. Professor Marrus received her BA in history with honors from Fisk University in 1992 and her MSW from University of Houston's Graduate College of Social Work in 2003 where she was a Hartford AGIFT Fellow. She is currently a doctoral candidate at the University of Southern California.

Namrata Mishra (LLB, LLM) is an Independent Senior Legal Practitioner who dons many hats including that of a Company Director, Writer, Mediator, Trainer, Speaker and Humanitarian. Namrata is a leading face in India imparting legal awareness on laws related to women and children having conducted 216 pro bono workshops attended by over 150,000 children over the past few years. Her role in introducing the Postal POCSO Safety box in rural Agra (India) with the aid of Post Master General, Agra and Senior Superintendent of Police, Agra has been widely appreciated. Her articles and views on the topic are widely published in numerous journals, proceedings, and the International Bar Association newsletter. She is the recipient of the prestigious 'Karamveer Award' by Rex Foundation in association with the United Nations and the 'Global Goodwill Ambassador' award amongst others. You can connect with Namrata via her twitter handle: @namratamishra.

Tamar Morag is the academic director of the Child Advocacy Clinic at the Hebrew University Law School and lectures at the Hebrew University Faculty of Law and the family studies programs at the College of Management Academic Studies and the Tel Aviv-Yafo Academic College. Her research and teaching interests are family law, child law, clinical legal education, and law and social change. She is the editor of *Children's Rights and Israeli Law* (Ramot—Tel Aviv University Press) and has published numerous articles in leading law reviews in Israel and abroad. She was the first legal director of the Israel National Council for the Child and the founding director of its Center for the Child and the Law. Later she served as vice-chair of the Israeli legislative committee appointed to reevaluate Israeli child law in light of the UN Convention on the Rights of the Child.

Agnieszka Ogrodnik-Kalita is a lecturer at the Institute of Law and Economics of Pedagogical University in Cracow, Poland. She specializes in family and civil law. She is the author of the monograph *Alcohol Addiction as a Reason of the Breakdown of Marriage* and about 40 articles, opinions, and glosses on marriage and child issues. Ogrodnik-Kalita concentrates her research in the areas of protection of personal rights of the child and legal aspects of early parenthood. She has participated in many national and international conferences. She was the head of postgraduate studies and the Data Protection Officer for the protection of personal data in public administration units. She holds degrees in law and canon law.

Shiran Reichenberg is a clinical teacher in the Faculty of Law, Hebrew University, Jerusalem, Israel, in the 'Youth at risk Rights Clinic'. She represents youth at risk in different legal proceedings, and advocates for their rights in the Knesset and relevant official government offices. Her doctoral dissertation subject was *The Right to Participation and Care Proceedings in Youth Court* and was supervised by Prof. Dafna Hacker from Tel-Aviv University and Prof. Michael Karayyani, Faculty of Law, the Hebrew University. Shiran received an L.LB and L.LM from the Faculty of Law, the Hebrew University, and received the prestigious Leonard Sainer Chevening Scholarship (2007–2008) for L.LM studies at UCL. She wrote her dissertation on the subject: *What is the Optimal Modal for Child Representation in Civil Proceedings?*" supervised by Prof. Michael Freeman. In her dissertation, she developed a comparative holistic model for child representation in care and supervision proceedings.

Rifqa Sa'Aadat is a 23-year-old college student who had been attending Agnes Scott College, a woman's liberal arts college in Decatur, Georgia. For the past three years, Rifqa has been out on medical leave and hopes to return to school in the Fall 2021 to finish her degree. During this time, Ms. Sa'Aadat has been working with young children in an educational setting. As a result of her own experiences and not having her voice heard in court proceedings concerning her life, she recognizes the importance for children to have their voices and concerns heard. Upon graduation, her goal is to continue working with children, giving them a voice, and helping them strengthen their own identities.

Julia Sloth-Nielsen is a senior professor at the University of the Western Cape, Faculty of Law, and holds a Chair in Children's Rights and the Developing World at Leiden University, Netherlands. She served as Dean at UWC from 2009–2013. Her major research contributions are in the field of Children's Rights. She was a member of the SA Law Reform Commission Project Committee that drafted the Children's Act 38 of 2005 and the Child Justice Act 75 of 2008, the lead consultant of the regulations to the Children's Act of South Africa, and a member of the African Committee of Experts on the Rights and Welfare of the Child from 2011 to 2016. She has also worked on children's legislation in Namibia, Mozambique, Botswana, Tanzania, Zanzibar, Kenya, and South Sudan. Professor Sloth-Nielsen has published more than 150 articles and chapters on children's rights and has been appointed to the editorial board of Chronicle, a journal published by the International Association of Child and Youth Court magistrates and judges.

Gordana Kovaček Stanić is a Professor of law at the University of Novi Sad, Serbia. She teaches courses in Family Law, Comparative Family Law, and Comparative Child Law. She is a member of the Executive Board of Directors of the International Academy for the Study of the Jurisprudence of the Family, a member of Academic Network on Family Law in Europe, and a member of the International Society of Family Law. She was a director of Scientific Project of Faculty of Law, University of Novi Sad: Biomedicine, Environmental protection and Law 2011–2019. She is the author of the following books in Serbian: *Legal Aspects of Parenthood 1994*; *The Right of a Child to Know His/Her Origins* (1997), *Comparative Family Law* (2002), *Family Law: Partnership, Child and the Guardianship Law* (2014), and *Legislation on Human Reproduction with Biomedical Assistance* (2008). She is also the author of over 100 academic papers published in national and foreign journals.

Barbara Stark, Professor of Law and Hofstra Research Scholar, has published dozens of law review articles. Her books include *International Family Law* (2005); *Global Issues in Family Law* (with Ann Estin, 2007); *Family Law in the World Community* (with Marianne Blair et al., 2015); *International Law and Its Discontents* (ed. 2015, Cambridge); *Family Law in New York* (with Joanna Grossman, eds. 2016); *Human Rights and Children* (ed. 2017); and *Routledge Handbook on International Family Law* (with Jacqueline Heaton, eds. 2019). Professor Stark has made invited presentations throughout the world. She has taught at the Aix-Marseille University Law School in Aix en Provence, France and Doshisha Law School in Kyoto, Japan. She is a former Chair of the AALS Family Law Section and the Family Law Committee of the International Law Association. She is a lifetime member of the American Society of International Law and has served on its Executive Council.

Gonneke Stevens is an Associate Professor of Interdisciplinary Social Science at Utrecht University, the Netherlands. In her research, she focuses on understanding the association between social group membership (particularly socioeconomic status, immigration background and gender) and adolescent and young-adult mental health, well-being and risk behaviors. In doing so, she investigates processes from the individual to society. Her research integrates complementary methods: large-scale, cross-sectional, internationally comparative research, clinical interview studies, longitudinal research, and experimental and qualitative research.

Jet Tigchelaar is an Assistant Professor of Legal Theory at the Utrecht Centre for European Research into Family Law and is also involved in the interdisciplinary research group Dynamics of Youth - Youth got Talent at Utrecht University (NL). Her research entails the role of the state regarding identity-issues such as registration of gender and name change, non-discrimination law on the ground of sexual orientation, informal marriages, and parental religious upbringing.

Kirsten Visser is an Assistant Professor in Urban Geography at the Faculty of Geosciences at Utrecht University, the Netherlands. Her research activities focus on geographies of children and youth, urban inequalities and urban diversities. Her recent projects focus on young people's experiences with neighborhood deprivation and diversity, young people's experiences with state-led gentrification and forced relocation, and children's outdoor play in different urban neighborhoods.

Part I

Struggles, challenges, and successes in implementing and ratifying the CRC worldwide

A. Worldwide

1 How to ensure wider implementation of the CRC

Olga Khazova

Introduction: setting the scene

The UN Convention on the Rights of the Child (CRC), widely recognized as the most comprehensive, holistic, and inclusive international instrument on the protection of children's rights, marked its 30th Anniversary in November 2019. Looking back 30 years and comparing where children's rights and their protections were then and now, it is clear that the progress achieved, without exaggeration, is tremendous. The years during which the CRC has been implemented have brought significant improvements in the lives of millions of children. In particular, the CRC informed the perception of the child as an autonomous rights-holder and brought tremendous changes in understanding the part that children should play in society. For many, taking children's rights seriously,[1] acknowledging that a child is not an object, not the property of the parents but an autonomous subject, required a serious change in mindset. Changes that were brought about by the CRC, with its focus on the best interests of the child, the child's right to be heard, and the child's evolving capacities, were revolutionary.

However, it is still a serious challenge for many, whether parents or governmental officials, to accept that a child is a rights-holder to the same extent as adults and that children have the right to express their opinion on all matters that concern them, irrespective of age. It remains a challenge to accept that children's evolving capacities and immaturity should not be interpreted as an excuse for restricting children's autonomy and self-expression.[2]

Thus, despite huge improvements in the lives of children throughout the world over the last 30 years, there is still a lot to be done. Indeed, countries differ in the level of promotion of children's rights and the degree to which they have implemented the CRC; some are at the forefront and others lag behind. Indeed, there is no country in the world that could claim that it has fully implemented the CRC. There are considerable challenges to implementing children's rights, and to a certain extent, these challenges concern all States parties to the CRC. Poverty and discrimination, criminalization, violence, and armed conflicts are some of the many problems that continue to hamper children's full enjoyment of their rights. Regrettably, despite all the progress achieved, children are still too often left behind. Therefore, for all States parties, implementation of the CRC is a work in progress.

Moreover, "there are worrying signs that some of the gains that children achieved under the Convention are at risk of stagnation – and even reversal in a few cases," as was rightly noted in one of the recent UNICEF publications.[3] For example, vaccination of children, one of the greatest successes in public health that saved millions of children's lives, has recently stalled. The results are devastating. What has occurred recently in the Pacific region, where many countries have been plagued by the measles epidemic,[4] is a clear sign that additional efforts are required to overcome backsliding. Clearly, "it is time for a renewed commitment to the Convention and to the world's children, particularly the most disadvantaged," as UNICEF suggests.[5]

The States' obligations under the CRC and the mandate of the CRC Committee

There is no precise, clear answer to the question of how to ensure a wider implementation of the CRC. It is a multi-faceted undertaking, consisting of different activities, actions, and strategies, that involves a variety of actors and close cooperation between them.

On a practical level, the most important article of the CRC on the issue of implementation is Article 4, which "pledges [S]tates to translate all the rights set out in the CRC into reality."[6] As explained in the Committee's General Comment No. 5, ratification of the CRC means that a State "takes on obligations under international law to implement it."[7] Implementation, as the General Comment further explains, "is the process whereby State parties take action to ensure the realization of all rights in the Convention for all children in their jurisdiction."[8]

The two main characteristics of the mandate of the CRC Committee (hereinafter, "Committee") may be described as examining the progress made by States parties in realizing the obligations under the CRC and fostering its effective implementation.[9] While carrying out its mandate, the Committee performs many different activities. Among the different ways in which the Committee can approach the States directly or indirectly on particular issues of concern, three main forms of activities can be identified.

First, one of the most important activities performed by the Committee is a reporting and examination process that monitors the States' implementation of the provisions of the CRC and the progress that has been made. It is a long, "multi-layered and dynamic process,"[10] that includes an examination of a State's report, reports of UNICEF and other specialized UN agencies and bodies, and alternative and supplementary reports presented by NGOs and other competent bodies. The review of a national periodic report and other related documents and a dialogue with a State party are followed by the adoption of concluding observations that finalize the reporting process.[11] The second activity is the Committee's work on developing general comments. The third major activity performed by the Committee is the consideration of individual communications under the framework of the Optional Protocol to the CRC on a communications procedure.[12]

Thus, as a result of each of these three main activities, the Committee produces three written documents: concluding observations, general comments, and views adopted as a result of a consideration of individual communications. What these documents have in common is they are seen as the Committee's jurisprudence.[13] Therefore, they should be considered as recommendations that States parties should follow.[14]

Concluding Observations

"Concluding Observations" is a document that is adopted as a result of a constructive dialog with a State party and where the Committee, while performing its monitoring function, directly addresses that State party on a range of issues related to children's rights. To facilitate a more structured discussion with the States parties, the Committee's Reporting Guidelines grouped the CRC articles in clusters, according to content and in a logical order.[15] Based on concerns raised by States parties and NGOs, the Committee decided to indicate, as a separate issue, the main areas of concern with regard to a particular State party.[16] This innovation aims to provide guidance to the States on how to approach the Committee's recommendations and to make implementation easier. In this special paragraph titled "Main areas of concern and recommendations," the Committee highlights the issues that it considers the most burning for that particular State and which urgent measures should be taken.

Thus, the first cluster of the concluding observations is "General Measures of Implementation (Articles 4, 42, and 44.6)," and it is present in all concluding observations.[17] In this cluster, the Committee explains what is missing and gives certain recommendations that are necessary to ensure proper implementation of the CRC.

The Committee's recommendations to the States parties regarding the general measures of implementation of the CRC can be summarized in four important points. First, it is important to have legislation upon which to base governmental decrees and other types of regulations that set up the legal framework for children rights necessary to ensure their adequate protection. While there has been an overall increase in legislation related to children's rights, it remains limited or fragmented in many countries. If there is no national legal regulation that fully incorporates all the provisions of the CRC, it is usually very difficult, if not impossible, to contemplate implementation of children's rights.[18] As the Committee stresses, it is also important to introduce a children's rights impact assessment procedure for all legislation adopted at the national level.[19]

Second, it is absolutely crucial to have policies, strategies, action plans, and to identify the bodies responsible for the implementation of the CRC. Experience demonstrates that the existence of effectively functioning interdepartmental and multidisciplinary bodies, which ensure cooperation of all the actors in the area of children's rights, is a key to success.

Third, the CRC implementation measures should be supported by the allocation of appropriate financial, human, and technical resources. It is important to structure budgets in a way that would make allocations for the realization of children's rights transparent, identifiable, and traceable. It is also important to have properly functioning monitoring and impact assessment procedures that would provide an understanding of where the money goes, whether it is efficiently spent, whether it brings results, and what results specifically.

The fourth guideline is education, which is absolutely crucial for better implementation of the CRC, although it is not necessarily properly reflected in the cluster on the general measures of implementation. This includes dissemination not only of the CRC itself, but also the Committee's concluding observations, general comments, and making "the principles and provisions of the Convention widely known, by appropriate and active means, to adults and children alike," as the CRC Article 44 (6) and Article 42 require.[20] Dissemination is not just a technical requirement; rather, it should be accomplished by including specialized children's rights courses in the mandatory curriculum for children in school and by regular training seminars on how the CRC should be understood and applied for professionals working with children. However, this is often a problem.[21]

There are, of course, other necessary conditions that are important for effective implementation of the CRC, such as the availability of a data collection system[22] and effective independent national human rights institutions (NHRIs) that are entrusted with the mandate to receive, investigate, and address complaints by children.[23] To make everything that has been mentioned work effectively, political will is necessary, which is precisely what is often lacking. To make progress, children's rights should be at the forefront of any political agenda. Conferences, such as the International Society of Family Law's 30th Anniversary Celebration of the CRC at the Academic College of Law and Science in Israel, which inspired the creation of this book, can hopefully further raise awareness and interest in improving implementation of the CRC and respecting children's rights generally.

General comments

In accordance with the Committee's Rules of Procedure,[24] the Committee may prepare general comments based on the provisions of the CRC, with a view to further promoting their implementation and assisting States parties in fulfilling their reporting obligations. General comments also aim at stimulating "the international organizations and the specialized agencies... in achieving progressively and effectively the full realization of the rights recognized in the Convention."[25] This is consistent with the practice of other UN Treaty bodies, which publish their interpretation of the provisions of their respective human rights treaties in the form of "general comments" or "general recommendations."[26] General comments or general recommendations "cover a wide range of subjects," including "the comprehensive interpretation of substantive provisions" of a respective treaty.[27] This means that general comments are "topical," and not "country-specific."[28]

For instance, two of the Committee's recent general comments were dedicated to the problems related to the protection of the rights of *Children in Street Situations*,[29] and the rights of adolescents.[30] In 2019, the Committee adopted the general comment on *Children's Rights in the Child Justice System*, which reflected the developments that occurred during the last decade as a result of the promulgation of international and regional standards, the Committee's jurisprudence, new knowledge about child and adolescent development, and evidence of effective practices, including those relating to restorative justice.[31]

Among the most recent are two joint general comments adopted by the Committee together with the Committee on the Protection of the Rights of All Migrant Workers and Members of Their Families that covered a broad range of issues related to children's rights in the context of international migration.[32] They reflect on a critical problem common to many countries, and also a huge, international problem, which can only be solved through strong international cooperation among States parties, UN Treaty bodies, NGOs, and all those involved in the protection of children's rights.[33]

As noted above, the general comments should be considered the Committee's jurisprudence.[34] The general comments set standards based on the Committee's experience in monitoring the implementation of the CRC by the States parties. They serve as the guidelines on how to more efficiently implement the provisions of the CRC in a specific area; they provide "authoritative guidance" to States on developing comprehensive national strategies on the protection of children's rights.[35] Although it is generally accepted that "general comments do not legally bind" the States parties,[36] it is hard to overstate their importance. The legal status of general comments "has grown beyond a mere technical recommendation into an authoritative source of interpretation;"[37] they became documents "with interpretations of the provisions of the treaty and their implications for the measures of implementation to be taken by the States parties."[38] The Committee regularly refers to the general comments in its concluding observations when making recommendations on a specific issue.[39] In other words, these are documents that "should be taken into account" by the respective State party when implementing the concluding observations addressed to that State party.[40] Therefore, it can be reasonably expected that the States parties should follow the recommendations contained in the general comments, i.e. the CRC Committee's "authoritative interpretation."[41]

As a rule, a general comment should be widely disseminated within government, legal, and administrative structures, to children, parents and caregivers, professional organizations, communities, the private sector, and civil society.[42] Regrettably, "there is very little information on the use of General Comments by the States parties," and "[a] systematic follow-up on the impact of General Comments does not exist."[43] Experience also suggests that general comments are not properly heeded; sometimes people who are supposed to ensure implementation of the CRC are not even aware of their existence at all. In sum, with regard to dissemination, there is definitely room for improvement, both for the States parties and for the Committee itself.

What is lacking in the work of the CRC Committee?

The CRC Committee, as other UN treaty bodies, faces many different challenges,[44] and there are, undoubtedly, certain shortcomings in its work.[45] Most importantly, probably due primarily to financial obstacles,[46] the Committee does not have a systemic follow-up procedure that would allow it to check the progress that has been made since the last revision of the State report in the middle of a reporting cycle. Visits to States parties could allow Committee members to meet with government authorities, with NHRIs, NGOs, and other national actors in children's rights, and children themselves to discuss problems and challenges in the implementation of the CRC and the Committee's recommendations.[47] Research demonstrates that when the States are engaged in an ongoing dialogue with the treaty bodies, they "improve" their human rights practices and better "perform relevant indicators of rights outcomes."[48]

Communication procedure

A communication procedure under the Optional Protocol allows the Committee to respond to a concrete complaint regarding the violation of a certain article or articles of the CRC (or other Optional Protocols).[49] To date, the Committee has received over 300 individual communications, and there are over 100 registered cases.[50] The most significant number of cases received so far has been linked to the mass influx of migrants into Europe. They include issues related to non-refoulement, age determination, administrative detention of migrant children, separation of children from parents, family reunification, and access to asylum proceedings. Among other issues raised in registered cases are those concerning child abduction, custody and visitation rights, surrogacy, juvenile justice, corporal punishment, and male circumcision. If the Committee finds a violation of the rights of the child by a State party, it adopts the Views,[51] in which, taking into account the context and circumstances, it reminds the State party that it is under an obligation to prevent similar violations in the future.

A good example is the Views adopted by the Committee in the case of *C.E. v. Belgium* (informally known as the "*kafalah* case"), where the Committee found a violation of the CRC Articles 3, 10, and 12 because a Moroccan child taken in under *kafalah*[52] by a Belgian-Moroccan couple was denied an entry visa to Belgium.[53] Besides expressing its views on the violations of the child's rights,[54] the Committee also reminded the State party that it was "under an obligation to do everything necessary to prevent similar violations from occurring in the future."[55] In its follow-up submission, the State party informed the Committee not only about the measures taken to remedy the situation that was the ground for the complaint, but also about several measures aimed at the prevention of similar violations in the future. Among other measures, Belgium committed to examine visa requests for children taken in under *kafalah* expeditiously and that due weight would be given to the family life that developed between the child and their guardians.[56]

Child participation

Under the CRC Article 12, the child has the right to express their views freely in "all matters affecting the child," and those views are to be given due weight.[57] This right highlights the role of the child as an active participant in the promotion, protection, and monitoring of their rights, and applies to all measures aimed at implementing the CRC.[58] The child's right to be heard constitutes one of the fundamental values of the CRC. "What makes it valuable is both that there is a point to making one's views known and, further, that making one's views known makes a difference."[59]

The Committee highlights that in order to make child participation effective and meaningful, "it needs to be understood as a process, not as an individual one-off event."[60] Children should be encouraged and supported in expressing their views and discussing their rights; their participation should become part of the ongoing monitoring process.[61] Methods of children's participation in the reporting process are different and include children's submissions containing revision of States parties reports, either their own or through NGOs (Children's Reports), oral presentation during the pre-sessional, private meeting with the Committee, and participation in videoconferencing and plenary sessions.[62] In 1999, children took part in the pre-sessional working group meeting of the CRC Committee for the first time. Three years later, in 2002, the first Children's Reports on Belgium and the United Kingdom were submitted to the Committee.[63] In 2018, the Committee dedicated its Day of General Discussion to the topic of "Protection and Empowering Children as Human Rights Defenders"; this was the first global discussion that focused on these issues. Children participated as speakers, moderators, and audience members alongside adults. In addition, for the first time, children played a central role in the planning, implementation, and follow-up to an event of the Committee.[64]

Indeed, child participation is growing and becoming more visible. The child's right to have a say on all matters that affect the child is increasingly on the agenda. Interestingly, while national governments are thinking about how to take children's rights seriously, children themselves have been trying to exercise their rights more actively. Moreover, children themselves claim their rights in the areas that the States parties may find very challenging to address. It is, no doubt, a new phenomenon.

The following three examples illustrate children's increasing activism on their own behalf. First, children's participation in political and anti-violence protests is increasing.[65] Second, children seek the right to vote and they have obtained this right in Austria, Greece, and Malta, and at the local levels in Scotland and some other countries.[66] Third, children filed communications to the Committee under the Optional Protocol of communication procedure claiming that several States parties to the CRC are liable for lack of government action on the climate crisis.[67] Accordingly, children themselves are increasingly pushing governments to reconsider their vision of children's rights. This brings us hope that the child's rights movement may soon undergo a qualitative shift – perhaps, to a significant extent, thanks to children themselves.

Life is not static…

Life is not static; things are constantly developing, and new advances bring new challenges, including for those involved in the protection of children's rights and the implementation of the CRC. The provisions of the CRC, adopted 30 years ago, have proven to be in line with new realities, which the drafters could not even imagine. The CRC is indeed a living document. Two examples support this statement.

First, assisted reproductive technologies and, in particular, surrogate motherhood were almost non-existent in the 1980s when the CRC was drafted. The Committee has had to respond to the challenges that the States parties face in this regard in the context of the implementation of the CRC provisions. The Committee has had to address such issues as (1) the right of a child born through assisted reproduction, including through international surrogacy arrangements; (2) non-discrimination; (3) the right to identity; and to get access to the information about the child's origin, such as children's legal status, including citizenship; as well as (4) the misuse of surrogacy that may lead to the sale of children and other violations of children's rights.[68]

Second is the need to protect children's rights in the digital environment as modern children live both offline and online. This is a new phenomenon that emerged after the CRC was adopted. It turns out, however, that the CRC relates to all the issues arising from such new developments as digital media and Information Communication Technologies (ICTs) that did not exist 30 years ago. Among those CRC articles that directly relate to children in the digital environment, there are: the right of a child to have access to information, the right to freedom of expression, the right to freedom of assembly, the right to privacy, the right to education, and the right to leisure and play. However, these are also articles that aim to protect the child against violence, exploitation, and other harms. Thus, the digital environment in relation to children's rights raises a whole range of serious questions, concerns, and challenges for governments, businesses, NGOs, children's rights organizations, professionals working with and for children, parents, and children themselves that need to be urgently addressed. Moreover, two different, though interconnected, dimensions of the children's rights in the digital environment should be stressed: on the one hand, the right of a child to have access to digital technologies and the right to enjoy all their benefits and opportunities, and, on the other hand, the right to be protected against the risks associated with the digital environment. Additional challenges relate to the transnational nature of the digital environment and the networks, services, and businesses it is based on, making international cooperation vital to the effective protection of children's rights in this area. These and other related issues are addressed in the Committee's draft on General Comments on *Children's Rights in Relation to the Digital Environment* that was adopted in February 2021.[69]

Conclusion

In conclusion, I would like to return to my comments in the beginning regarding children as autonomous rights-holders. For adults, it may not be easy to treat children as equals; it requires many different qualities and skills. Most importantly, it requires respect for children and their rights; it requires building "a culture of respect" for children's views,[70] and such a culture is too often missing. A few quotations from a book by Janusz Korczak, *A Child's Right to Respect*, first published in 1928,[71] may be educative in this regard:

> Children make up a large percentage of the human race, the population, the nation, its inhabitants, our fellow-citizens – they are permanent comrades. They have been, they will be, they are...
> [Children] require:
> Respect for their lack of knowledge...
> Respect for the work acquiring knowledge...
> Respect for failures and tears...
> Respect for children's possessions and their budgets...
> Respect for the secrets and doubts of the hard work of growing...
> Respect for the current hour, for today...
> Respect for each individual moment, for these will pass and never come again.

The child's right to respect is not explicitly stipulated in the CRC, but you may read it between the lines in each and every article. If there would have been a better understanding and acceptance of the child's right to respect at many different levels, from parents to governmental officials, we may have achieved better and wider implementation of the CRC.

Notes

1 *See* Michael Freeman, *Why It Remains Important to Take Children's Rights Seriously*, 15 Int'l J. Child. Rts. 5, 5 *et seq.* (2007).
2 *See* Gerison Landsdown, *Innocenti Insight: The Evolving Capacities of the Child*, 28 (Florence, UNICEF, 2005).
3 UNICEF, For Every Child, Every Right: The Convention on the Rights of the Child at a Crossroads (New York, UNICEF, 2019).
4 *Measles – Pacific Island Countries*, World Health Org. (WHO), https://www.who.int/csr/don/15-december-2019-measles-pacific-island-countries-and-areas/en/ (last visited August 14, 2020).
5 For Every Child, Every Right, *supra* note 3, at 13. The CRC Committee, while getting prepared for the 30th Anniversary events, asked the States parties to renew their commitments by pledging to take one specific and measurable action for the promotion, protection, and realization of children's rights. Many States sent their pledges, which were displayed in Geneva, at Les Nations, where the CRC 30th Anniversary events took place in November 2019.
6 Michael Freeman, *Introduction: Children as Persons, in* Children's Rights: A Comparative Perspective 4 (1996). (Under Article 4, "States parties shall undertake all appropriate legislative, administrative, and other measures for the implementation of the rights recognized in the present Convention. With regard to economic, social and cultural rights, States parties shall undertake such measures to the maximum extent of their available resources and, where needed, within the framework of international co-operation.")
7 UN Committee on the Rights of the Child, *General Comment No. 5, General Measures of Implementation of the Convention on the Rights of the Child* (arts. 4, 42 and 44, para 6), § 12, U.N. Docs. CRC/GC/2003/5, para. 1 (Nov. 27, 2003).

8 *Id.* para 1.

9 As it follows from the CRC arts. 43 (para 1) and 45. *See* Nevena Vučković Šahović et al., *The Right of the Child in International Law* 336 (2012).

10 *Id.* at 342.

11 The reporting process is often described as a "reporting cycle." *See* Child Rights Connect, Global Status of Engagement in Reporting to the UN Committee on the Rights of the Child, 10–13 (2019), https://www.childrightsconnect.org/wp-content/uploads/2020/05/global_status_report_final.pdf (last visited Aug. 14, 2020).

12 There are three Optional Protocols to the CRC. The Optional Protocol on communication procedure (often called the 3d Optional Protocol) was adopted in 2011 and came into force in 2014. Currently, it has 46 ratifications and 18 signatories. Two other optional protocols are: the Optional Protocol to the Convention on the Rights of the Child on the sale of children, child prostitution, and child pornography and the Optional Protocol to the Convention on the Rights of the Child on the involvement of children in armed conflict; both were adopted in 2000.

13 See, e.g., David Weissbrodt et al., *The Role of the Committee on the Rights of the Child in Interpreting and Developing International Humanitarian Law*, 24 Harv. Hum. Rts. J. 115, 118 (2011).

14 *See* discussion *infra* under States' Obligations Under the CRC and the Mandate of the CRC Committee.

15 UN CRC Committee, *Treaty-specific Guidelines Regarding the Form and Content of Periodic Reports to be Submitted by States Parties under Article 44, paragraph 1 (b), of the Convention on the Rights of the Child*, U.N. Docs. CRC/C/5/Rev.3. (Mar. 3, 2015), https://digitallibrary.un.org/record/789762?ln=en#record-files-collapse-header.

16 UN Convention on the Rights of the Child, GAOR Supplement No. 41, U.N. Docs. A/73/41 (2018).

17 See, e.g., Trevor Buck, *International Child Law* 118 *et seq.* (Routledge, 3rd ed., 2014).

18 See, e.g., UN CRC Committee, *Concluding Observations, Denmark* § 6, U.N. Docs. CRC/C/DNK/CO/5 (Oct. 26, 2017)

19 See, e.g., UN CRC Committee, *Concluding Observations, Bahrain* § 6, U.N. Docs. CRC/C/BHR/CO/4-6 (Feb. 27, 2019) *See also* UN CRC Committee, *Concluding Observations, Bulgaria* § 6–7, U.N. Docs. CRC/C/BGR/CO/3-5 (Nov. 21, 2016).

20 The CRC Article 42 is considered as "simultaneously one of the most important and most overlooked provisions in the CRC." Jonathan Todres, *Making Children's Rights Widely Known*, 29 Minn. J. Int'l L. 109, 112 (2020). In this paper, the author discusses the CRC Article 42 mandate and its correlation, in particular, with the human rights education mandate under the CRC Article 29; the author criticizes the CRC Committee for giving insufficient attention to the implementation of Article 42, considering this as "a significant factor in the failure to achieve widespread acceptance of children's rights." *Id.* at 111.

21 See, e.g., UN CRC Committee, *Concluding Observations, France*, §§ 19–20, U.N. Docs. CRC/C/FRA/CO/5 (Feb. 23, 2016); UN CRC Committee, *Concluding Observations, Costa Rica*, U.N. Docs. CRC/C/CRI/CO/5-6 (Mar. 4, 2020).

22 See, e.g., UN CRC Committee, *Concluding Observations, Côte d'Ivoire*, § 10–11, U.N. Docs. CRC/C/CIV/CO/2 (Jul. 12, 2019).

23 UN CRC Committee, *General Comments No. 2 The Role of Independent National Human Rights Institutions in the Promotion and Protection of the Rights of the Child*, §§ 1 and 7, U.N. Docs. CRC/GC/2002/2 (Nov. 15, 2002); UN CRC Committee, *Concluding Observations, Norway* §§ 7–8, U.N. Docs. CRC/C/NOR/CO/5-6 (Jul. 4, 2018); UN CRC Committee, *Concluding Observations, Haiti* §§ 15–16, U.N. Docs. CRC/C/HTI/CO/2-3 (Feb. 24, 2016).

24 U.N. Docs. CRC/C/4/Rev.5. Rule 77.

25 UN CRC Committee, *Working Methods*, part IX, https://www.ohchr.org/EN/HRBodies/CRC/Pages/WorkingMethods.aspx.

26 *Human Rights Treaty Bodies – General Comments*, OHCHR, https://www.ohchr.org/EN/HRBodies/Pages/TBGeneralComments.aspx.
27 *Id.*
28 Weissbrodt, *supra* note 13, at 118–119.
29 UN CRC Committee, *General Comment No. 21 on Children in Street Situations*, U.N. Docs. CRC/C/GC/21 (June 21, 2017).
30 UN CRC Committee, *General Comment No. 20 on the Implementation of the Rights of the Child During Adolescence*, U.N. Docs. CRC/C/GC/20 (Dec. 6, 2016).
31 UN CRC Committee, *General Comment No. 24 on Children's Rights in the Child Justice System*, § 1, U.N. Docs. CRC/C/GC/24 (Sep. 18, 2019).
32 UN Committee on the Protection of the Rights of All Migrant Workers and Members of Their Families (CMW), *Joint General Comment No. 3 (2017) of the Committee on the Protection of the Rights of All Migrant Workers and Members of Their Families and No. 22 (2017) of the Committee on the Rights of the Child on the General Principles Regarding the Human Rights of Children in the Context of International Migration*, 16 November 2017, CMW/C/GC/3-CRC/C/GC/22; *Joint General Comment No. 4 (2017) of the Committee on the Protection of the Rights of All Migrant Workers and Members of Their Families and No. 23 (2017) of the Committee on the Rights of the Child on State Obligations Regarding the Human Rights of Children in the Context of International Migration in Countries of Origin, Transit, Destination and Return*, U.N. Docs. CMW/C/GC/4-CRC/C/GC/23.
33 According to the UNICEF statistical data, of all children who arrived in Europe in 2018, a total of 12,700 children were unaccompanied or separated, what constituted 42% UNICEF, *Refugee and Migrant Children in Europe*, https://www.unicef.org/eca/sites/unicef.org.eca/files/2019-05/Infographic%20Children%20and%20UASC%202018%20FINAL.pdf (last visited Aug. 14, 2020).
34 A detailed analysis of this issue is beyond the scope of this chapter. See, e.g., Paula Gerber et al., *General Comment 16 on State Obligations Regarding the Impact of the Business Sector on Children's Rights: What Is Its Standing, Meaning and Effect? 14 Melb. J. Int'l L. 93, 96–103 (2013); Weissbrodt, supra note 13, at 118–123.*
35 See, e.g., General Comment No. 21 (2017) on *Children in Street Situations, supra* note 29, at § 2.
36 Paula Gerber, *supra* note 34, at 99.
37 *Id.* at 101.
38 Vučković Šahović, *supra* note 9, at 355.
39 Amongst the most recent, See, e.g., UN CRC Committee, *Concluding Observations, the Cook Islands, §§ 11, 12, 21, 23, 26, 28, 32, 38, 40, 43 and 50*, U.N. Docs. CRC/C/COK/CO/2-5) (Apr. 2, 2020); UN CRC Committee, *Concluding observations, Austria, §§ 10, 11, 14, 19, 22, 23, 27, 31, 32, 38 and 42*, U.N. Docs. CRC/C/AUT/CO/5-6 (Mar. 6, 2020).
40 Vučković Šahović, *supra* note 9, at 355.
41 Buck, *supra* note 17, at 95.
42 See, e.g., *General Comment No. 21 (2017) on Children in Street Situations, supra* note 29, § at 62.
43 Vučković Šahović, *supra* note 9, at 356.
44 *See* U.N. Docs. A/RES/68/268 (Apr. 21, 2014); Olivier de Frouville, *The Committee System: 2020 and Beyond: The Treaty Body System Has Been in Crisis for at least Thirty Years. Will the Year 2020 Bring Change?* OpenGlobalRights (Nov. 19, 2019), https://www.openglobalrights.org/the-committee-system-2020-and-beyond/.
45 See, e.g., Jonathan Todres, *supra* note 20, at 112.
46 *See* Cosette D. Creamer & Beth A. Simmons, *The Proof Is in the Process: Self-Reporting under International Human Rights Treaties*, 114 Am. J. Int'l L. 1, 21 (2020).
47 Although this work of the Committee is considered as "indispensable to guarantee a better application of the Convention," there were just occasional trips as a follow-up

to concluding observations in a number of countries upon invitation from States, civil society organizations, and UNICEF (*Report of the UN Committee on the Rights of the Child*, *supra* note 16). Regrettably, during the past eight years, there was only one formal follow-up visit of a Committee member to a State party by Morocco in 2015.

48 Creamer, *supra note* 46, at 2–3.

49 The Optional Protocol on communication procedure came into force in 2014. Currently, it has 46 ratifications and 18 signatories.

50 UN CRC Committee, *Recent Developments in the Individual Communications received under the Optional Protocol to the Convention on the Rights of the Child on a Communications Procedure (OPIC-CRC)*, Note on OPIC-CRC Trends, https://www.ohchr.org/EN/HRBodies/CRC/Pages/CRCIndex.aspx.

51 The Committee adopts the Views as a result of consideration of a case on the merits. *See* UN CRC Committee, *Rules of Procedure under the Optional Protocol to the Convention on the Rights of the Child on a Communications Procedure*, U.N. Docs. CRC/C/62/3 (Oct. 2, 2020).

52 In most of the Muslim States, *kafalah* is defined as "a voluntary undertaking to provide for a child and take care of his or her welfare, education and protection." *See Harroudj v. France*, Eur. Ct. H.R., App. No. 43631/09, judgement of 4 October 2012, para. 16. *Kafalah* is different from adoption. See, e.g., 358–362 Olga A. Khazova & Benyam Dawit Mezmur, *UN Committee on the Rights of the Child. Continued Reflections on Family Law Issues in the Jurisprudence of the CRC Committee: The Convention on the Rights of the Child @ 30, in* International Survey of Family Law 358–362 (M. Brinig ed., 2020).

53 UN CRC Committee, *Views adopted by the Committee under the Optional Protocol to the Convention on the Rights of the Child on a Communications Procedure, Concerning Communication No. 12/2017*, U.N. Docs. CRC/C/79/D/12/2017 (Nov. 5, 2018).

54 In its Views, the CRC Committee noted that the State party is under an obligation to urgently reconsider the application for a visa for *C.E.* in a positive spirit, while ensuring that the best interests of the child are a primary consideration and that *C.E.*'s views are heard. In considering the best interests of the child, the State party should take account of the family ties that have been forged de facto between *C.E.* and the authors.

55 The Views, *supra* note 51, at para. 9.

56 UN CRC Committee, Complaints Procedure. Follow up, *Follow-up Progress Report on Individual Communications, C.E. v. Belgium*, U.N. Docs. CRC/C/79/D/12/2017, U.N. Docs. CRC/C/82/82/R.1., https://www.ohchr.org/EN/HRBodies/CRC/Pages/CRCIndex.aspx.

57 Apart from the CRC Article 12, children's participation rights are set out in arts. 13, 14, 15, and 17.

58 UN CRC Committee, *General Comment No. 5*, *supra* note 7, § 12.

59 David William Archard, *Children's Rights, in* The Stanford Encyclopedia of Philosophy (Winter 2018 Edition E.N. Zalta ed.), § 8, https://plato.stanford.edu/archives/win2018/entries/rights-children/

60 UN CRC Committee, *General Comment No. 12 The Right of the Child to be Heard*, § 133, U.N. Docs. CRC/C/GC/12 (Jul. 20, 2009).

61 UN CRC Committee, *Working Methods for the Participation of Children in the Reporting Process of the Committee on the Rights of the Child*, § 4, U.N. Docs. CRC/C/66/2 (Oct. 16, 2014).

62 *Id.* Para 8. *See also* Child Rights Connect *supra* note 11, at 30.

63 Child Rights Connect *supra* note 11, at 37, In 2016, when the CRC Committee considered the combined third, fourth, and fifth periodic reports of Sierra Leone at its 2136th and 2137th meetings, a 15-year-old boy, who was at that time the Secretary General of the Children's Forum Network of Sierra Leone, was included in the

official Governmental Delegation, *Consideration of Sierra Leone – 2136th Meeting 73rd Session of Committee on Rights of the Child*, UNWebTV (Sep. 14, 2016), http://webtv.un.org/search/consideration-of-sierra-leone-2136th-meeting-73rd-session-of-committee-on-rights-of-the-child/5124933636001/?term=crc%20sierra%20leone%202016&sort=date&page=40 (last visited Aug. 14, 2020).

64 UN CRC Committee, *Protecting and Empowering Children as Human Rights Defenders* (2018), https://www.ohchr.org/Documents/HRBodies/CRC/Discussions/2018/crc_dgd_2018_outcomereport_en.pdf.

65 *See*, Aoife Daly, *Demonstrating Positive Obligations: Children's Rights and Peaceful Protest in International Law*, 45 Geo. Wash. Int'l L. Rev. 763 (2013); Verna Yu, *Children of the Revolution: the Hong Kong Youths Ready to Sacrifice Everything*, Guardian (Dec. 15, 2019), https://www.theguardian.com/world/2019/dec/15/children-of-the-revolution-the-hong-kong-youths-ready-to-sacrifice-everything; Ruth Michaelson, *Egypt: Children Swept Up in Crackdown on Anti-Sisi Protests*, Guardian (Oct. 8, 2019), https://www.theguardian.com/world/2019/oct/08/egypt-children-swept-up-in-crackdown-on-anti-sisi-protests; *Russia: Children, Students Targeted after Protests*, HRW (Jun. 11, 2017), https://www.hrw.org/news/2017/06/11/russia-children-students-targeted-after-protests; https://www.thehindu.com/opinion/op-ed/protecting-childrens-right-to-protest/article30846374.ece; *UNICEF Calls for the Protection of Children Involved in Indonesia's Protests*, UNICEF (Oct. 1, 2019), https://www.unicef.org/press-releases/unicef-calls-protection-children-involved-indonesias-protests (last visited Aug. 14, 2020).

66 See, e.g., UN CRC Committee, *Concluding Observations, the United Kingdom of Great Britain and Northern Ireland*, §§ 32–33, U.N. Docs. CRC/C/GBR/CO/5 (Jul. 12, 2016).

67 UN CRC Committee, Communications No. 104/2019 against Argentina, No. 105/2019 against Brazil, No. 106/2019 against France, No. 107/2019 against Germany, No. 108/2019 against Turkey, https://www.ohchr.org/Documents/HRBodies/CRC/TablePendingCases.pdf.

See also Child Petitioners Protest Lack of Government Action on Climate Crisis, UNICEF (Sep. 23, 2019), https://www.unicef.org/press-releases/16-children-including-greta-thunberg-file-landmark-complaint-united-nations.

68 *See*, Olga A. Khazova & Benyam David Mezmur, *UN Committee on the Rights of the Child. Reflections on Family Law Issues in the Jurisprudence of the CRC Committee*, Int'l Surv. of Fam. L. 322–326 (M. Brinig ed., 2019).

69 The Committee's work on the draft General Comment no. 25 has attracted a lot of interest, and it has received more than 130 submissions on the draft that was placed for public consultations at the UN CRC webpage in August 2020. https://www.ohchr.org/EN/HRBodies/CRC/Pages/GCChildrensRightsRelationDigitalEnvironment.aspx.

70 UN CRC Committee, *General Comment No. 12*, *supra* note 60, at § 134.

71 Janusz Korczak, *A Child's Right to Respect* 27–33 (Warszawa, 2017).

B. European Union

2 The European Union and the United Nations Convention on the Rights of the Child

Towards a fully-fledged European Union child rights strategy

Aida Kisunaite and Simone Delicati

Introduction

In the wake of the 30th anniversary of the United Nations Convention on the Rights of the Child (CRC), children's rights protection in the European Union (EU) is expected to undergo a phase of great change. In her inaugural address as the newly elected President of the European Commission on July 19, 2019, Ursula von der Leyen identified the creation of a comprehensive EU child rights strategy as a priority for her mandate. Accordingly, she also entrusted Commissioner Nicolas Schmit and Vice President Dubravka Šuica with developing and coordinating the implementation of the European Parliament's proposal for a European Child Guarantee scheme to secure free healthcare, education, early childhood education and care, decent housing, and adequate nutrition for vulnerable categories of children living in the EU.[1]

In this chapter, we aim to evaluate the EU's success in implementing the children's rights protections guaranteed by the principles and standards of the CRC to which the EU has committed itself to upholding. We conclude that the CRC has been increasingly referenced and used as a legal and ideological framework for shaping EU child law and policy-making. However, failings in the way children's rights measures are concretely applied denote a mismatch between "children's rights theory" and "children's rights practice." This mismatch in EU policy versus practice demonstrates a lack of dedication to the child rights culture underpinning the CRC at the level of EU institutions and Member States. We argue that in order to address this mismatch, it is essential for the EU to prioritize its actions along three dimensions relevant to children's rights protection: creation of political leverage, generation of ownership at the level of institutions and stakeholders, and promotion of child participation.

The analysis in this chapter is interdisciplinary, combining a legal approach and a political science perspective to these issues, and is divided into three sections. The first part traces the main developments in children's rights protection in the EU, emphasizing the pivotal role played by the Lisbon Treaty in shifting EU intervention towards a more child-centred and CRC-based approach. The second part presents the mismatch between how the CRC's principles and provisions are endorsed and routinely incorporated into EU measures and the more limited manner in which these measures are implemented in practice and evaluates the reasons behind the mismatch. The third part suggests how the EU can effectively address this mismatch within the forthcoming comprehensive announcement of an EU child rights strategy, which is intended to integrate policy measures across the continent. The final section offers a conclusion.

The two phases of children's rights protection in the EU before and after the Lisbon Treaty

The identification of the EU as an actual, rather than a potential, "children's rights actor" within the international community is only a recent development.[2] The incorporation of children's rights protection into the EU agenda has been a slow and interrupted process that has undergone two distinct phases. During the first phase, beginning in the 1960s throughout the 2000s, children's rights protection was advanced by the EU in a very occasional and indirect manner, through piecemeal provisions addressing children's rights issues by relating to specific economic, commercial, and political priorities.[3] During the second phase, beginning with the enactment of the Lisbon Treaty, EU efforts for safeguarding children are more unitary, complex, and value driven, focused specifically on incorporating the provisions of the CRC.[4]

In the 1960s, children benefited indirectly as part of workers' families from the rights granted to EU workers by the EU free movement laws, which allowed families the freedom to move between Member States and benefit from different social guarantees.[5] These measures were instrumental to the promotion of migrant work across the EU rather than directed at improving children's socio-economic status.[6] Employment equality legislation, which included maternity and paternity leave benefits to support parents in harmonizing their work and child-rearing responsibilities, also benefited children indirectly.[7] At the end of the following decade, more direct actions were taken to protect children through EU Council Directives, such as the regulation of television advertising activities and the safeguarding of children and young people at work.[8] Further children's rights provisions were later adopted around the turn of the millennium in the fields of EU migration law and cross-border family justice, where the EU had extended its competence. From the mid-2000s onwards, the Directorate-General for Justice, Freedom, and Security of the European Commission took the lead in establishing a common framework for the protection of children at the EU level.[9] The first major step was taken in 2006 with the adoption of the Commission's Communication: "Towards an EU Strategy on the Rights of the Child." This communication set out, for the first time, the EU's intention to establish a comprehensive EU strategy "to effectively promote and safeguard the rights of the child in the EU's internal and external policies and to support Member States' efforts in this field" on the basis of the principles and the provisions of the CRC.[10] The need to better safeguard children's rights had gathered momentum because of the political attention focused on Romania's abandoned children. The Commissioner for Freedom, Security, and Justice, Franco Frattini, took the opportunity to begin incorporating the protection of children within the fundamental rights agenda of the EU.[11]

However, it was only with the enactment of the Lisbon Treaty in 2009 that an actual child rights strategy began to emerge, opening up the possibility of achieving a "more ethical and ideologically robust approach to the development of children's rights measures."[12] Indeed, the Lisbon Treaty brought about two major changes to the constitutional structure of the EU, greatly impacting the EU's potential in advancing children's rights. First, the Lisbon Treaty amended the fundamental treaties of the EU, positioning the protection of children's rights among the general objectives of the EU (Article 3(3) TEU) and of its external policy (Article 3(5) TEU), as well as providing a specific legal basis for legislation combating human trafficking and sexual exploitation of children under two new distinct provisions (Articles 79 and 83 TFEU).[13] Second, the Lisbon Treaty conferred to the EU Charter of Fundamental Rights (CFR) the same binding legal status of the fundamental treaties, unlocking the potential of its child-related provisions, such as Article 14, envisaging the right to receive free compulsory education; Article 21, prohibiting any form of discrimination on the ground of age; and Article 32, protecting children from exploitative labour or harmful working conditions. Other important provisions that came into force include Article 7, prohibiting undue interference in private and family life, home, and communications and Article 33, requiring legal, economic, and social protection for the family. Even more impactful, Article 24 of the CFR provides children with substantive rights directly, building on the standards and principles of the CRC. As described in the text, children have the right to such protection and care as is necessary for their well-being, the opportunity to express their views freely and a guarantee that such views are taken into consideration on matters which concern them in accordance with their age and maturity (Article 24 (1)), the right to have their best interests taken as a primary consideration in all actions concerning them (Article 24 (2)), and the right to maintain on a regular basis a personal relationship and direct contact with both parents, except when it is contrary to their interests (Article 24 (3)). Building off of the CRC, the CFR recognizes children's rights as fundamental rights at the EU constitutional level, independently and separately from the ones of EU adult citizens and of the family in general. Moreover, with regard to the implementation process, the enactment of the Lisbon Treaty made it possible for the EU institutions to hold the EU Member States legally accountable for their failure to protect children's rights, establishing direct obligations vis-à-vis children.[14]

Despite these constitutional changes, which seemed to herald a new era in children's rights protection, the protection of children by the EU institutions has remained fragmental. There has been a significant failure to legislate children's rights protection within a single policy framework under the oversight of the EU institutions. In fact, the EU's actions remain limited due to the competence boundaries set out in the EU fundamental treaties, granting the EU only a subordinate legislative power in relation to the Member States' own legislation based on the principle of conferral. Where it does not have "exclusive competence" (Article 3 TFEU), the EU may have a "shared competence" (Article 4 TFEU) or an even more limited competence to only integrate, namely to "support, coordinate or supplement" (Article 6 TFEU) the action of the Member States and it must abide by the principles of subsidiarity and proportionality stipulated under the TEU.

Indeed, two trends may be observed in the way the EU has been pursuing its commitment to children's rights protection generally and in implementing the CRC in particular. At the level of policy discourse, the EU has increasingly used official documents and communications to present its commitment to children's rights as fundamentally guided by the CRC.[15] At the normative level, the EU has accordingly developed a growing body of hard-law and especially soft-law measures addressing children's rights through targeted and comprehensive instruments, aiming to progressively incorporate the CRC's principles and standards at the EU level.

Nonetheless, despite the EU's normative commitment to furthering children's rights, the effective implementation of EU measures aimed at protecting children's rights within its Member States lags, accentuating a mismatch between the expectations raised and the reality on the ground. The next sections of this chapter aim to present this mismatch, evaluate the reasons behind it, and suggest how the EU can more effectively promote children's rights.

An incomplete process of maturation: evaluating the mismatch between EU children's rights theory and practice in light of the CRC

There is no doubt that by endorsing children's rights in line with the provisions of the CRC, "the EU has set itself a challenging task."[16] Nevertheless, as widely recognized by the European Court of Justice (ECJ), despite not being a party to the CRC, the EU is obliged to adhere to the principles and provisions set out in international human rights instruments, such as the CRC, which has been ratified by all EU Member States. International human rights instruments are considered an integral part of the "general principles" of EU law, binding the EU institutions in formulating, implementing, and interpreting the law of the EU.[17] Therefore, the task of the EU, in relation to its Member States, is not to reinvent children's rights, or to incorporate them indirectly, but rather to reinforce children's rights obligations as expressed by the CRC through a process of direct incorporation.[18]

The incorporation of the CRC into EU laws and policies

Accordingly, the EU *acquis* and the policy framework for the protection of children's rights aim to directly incorporate the principles and provisions of the CRC, with special regard to the four "general principles" of the

CRC: non-discrimination (Article 2 CRC), best interests of the child (Article 3 CRC), the rights to life, survival, and development (Article 6 CRC), and the right to be heard (Article 12 CRC).[19] Notably, the EU has also gradually incorporated the human rights principles of interdependence, indivisibility, and interrelatedness into EU laws and policies, stressing the need to integrate children's rights protection strategies based on intersectoral policy coordination, which is particularly effective in implementing the CRC.[20] In line with Articles 5 and 7 of the CRC, EU measures have emphasized the central role of the family in advancing the well-being and development of children, requiring respect for parents' guidance in helping children exercise their rights in line with their evolving capacities.[21]

Even though the EU has not undertaken a comprehensive and systematic legal and policy review in assessing the progress made by incorporating the CRC's provisions in its laws, the children's rights measures implemented by the EU are summarized and updated by the EU Commission through the "EU *Acquis* and Policy Documents on the Rights of the Child" initiative.[22] Over the last decade, many EU legislative and policy measures incorporating the CRC's principles and provisions have been adopted in the fields of the EU free movement and family law, immigration and asylum law, criminal justice and protection of children from violence, abuse, and exploitation, as well as in the fields of child poverty and social exclusion.[23] For example, EU measures adopted in the context of cross-border criminal activities and immigration and asylum include binding legislation requiring the implementation of children's rights to have their best interests taken into account as a primary consideration, to be heard and to appropriate representation during proceedings, to protect and to provide access to social, education, and health services as well as to reunification with family members.[24] Similarly, the CRC's standards have been directly incorporated into EU legislation protecting children from violence, abuse, and exploitation.[25]

The process of incorporating the CRC's principles and standards at the EU level has also been accomplished through wide-ranging soft-law instruments and policy strategies aimed at combating child poverty and discrimination through furthering child participation and children's access to basic social, education, and health services. Prominent examples of such soft-law measures include the 2011 Agenda for the Rights of the Child ("Agenda"), the 2013 Recommendation on "Investing in Children: Breaking the Cycle of Disadvantage" ("Recommendation"), the 2017 European Pillar of Social Rights, and the wide range of more targeted policy documents and action plans aimed at improving the conditions of children belonging to vulnerable groups (e.g. Roma children, unaccompanied minors, children with disabilities, migrant children).[26] In particular, the Agenda and the Recommendation have established the "blueprint for the EU's normative and methodological approach to children's rights law" in a manner that is fundamentally based on the CRC, reinforcing an "ethic of child protection, participation and non-discrimination."[27] The Agenda identifies the CRC as guiding the development of children's rights protection at the EU level.[28] The Recommendation, adopted as part of the Social Investment Package within the Europe 2020 strategy, proposed a "rights-orientated holistic and integrated approach to child poverty," stressing the indivisibility of all children's rights as established by the CRC and aiming to improve the conditions of children by increasing access to adequate resources, affordable quality services, and mechanisms of child participation.[29]

The EU has thereby increasingly and consistently carried out its normative responsibilities to protect children's rights, as enshrined in the principles of the CRC, through binding legislation and soft-law measures. Consequently, the protection of children's rights by the EU has gained increased significance and legitimacy within a more coherent and robust framework.[30] Nonetheless, the extent to which the EU *acquis* and the policy framework for the protection of children's rights are actually implemented by EU Member States and EU institutions themselves continues to be insufficient and inadequate.

Challenges in making children's rights concrete

First, despite being the object of concerted strategies and targeted actions by the EU, child poverty remains at worrying levels. According to the latest data, 23 million, or about one out of four, children in the EU are at risk of poverty and social exclusion, making it the age group at the greatest risk of experiencing poverty. Remarkably, a recent follow-up analysis to the 2013 EU Recommendation has demonstrated low levels of implementation with only four EU Member States making significant improvements, and all the others, especially the ones with already high or very high levels of child poverty and social exclusion, achieving very limited progress or even weakened protection in most areas under review.[31] As a consequence, millions of children, particularly the ones belonging to vulnerable groups, continue to have great difficulty accessing basic services such as education, health, housing, nutrition, sanitation, and water. Moreover, actions to combat child poverty and social exclusion have not been given the necessary priority by the monitoring framework of the European Semester,[32] and the use of EU funds has been inefficient and thus unable to provide added value to the actions of EU Member States.[33] Remarkably, following the proposal by the European Parliament and Commission to ensure adequate funding at both the EU and Member State levels to support a future Child Guarantee, the EU leaders have not earmarked resources for combating child poverty under the European Council Conclusions on the EU's Recovery Package and the EU's budget for the 2021–2027 Multiannual Financial Framework.[34]

Lack of implementation of EU child-protective measures does not only apply to soft-law instruments, but also to binding legislation where the EU has repeatedly sanctioned EU Member States. Among the most recent examples, the EU initiated infringement procedures against several of its Member States for failing to incorporate the "Procedural Safeguards Directive," granting children who are suspects or accused persons in criminal procedures the right to be informed and heard in a child-friendly manner, into their national legislation.[35] Currently, the incorporation of the revised Audio-Visual Media Services Directive into Member States law, due in September 2020, has made little to no progress. Moreover, even in the sensitive context of online sexual abuse, the European Commission had to begin sanctioning procedures against 23 EU Member States due to their persistent failure to implement the rules set out by the Sexual Abuse Directive.[36]

Inadequate implementation of EU children's rights measures is also present at the level of EU institutions. Despite being the most active among the EU institutions for the protection of children's rights, the EU Commission has been subject to criticism for failing to effectuate its formal commitments and for "paying lip service" rather than "allegiance" to the principles of the CRC.[37] In particular, EU institutions have been criticized for being unable to promote genuine and meaningful child participation in shaping and claiming their rights.[38] Similarly, the principle of the best interests of the child is ineffectively implemented despite a myriad of references to the concept in EU formal legislative and policy texts.[39] At the judicial level, the ECJ seems to be particularly reluctant to address child protection and to engage with the principles enshrined in the CRC.[40] In fact, the ECJ has dealt with only a few cases concerning children's rights and a closer analysis reveals that CRC principles are sparingly taken into account in the ECJ judgements.[41]

A question of a child rights culture

The mismatch between the expectations raised by the EU's endorsement of the CRC and the incorporation of its principles and standards into the EU's measures and the extent to which the CRC is implemented in practice suggests two considerations about children's rights protection at the EU level. First, it reinforces the idea that the EU's competence to adopt child-related binding legislation does not ensure implementation and effectiveness of the measures themselves. Binding legislation and related enforcement mechanisms are not necessarily the most effective tools, especially keeping in mind that children, by nature, "face additional barriers to making legal claims."[42] Moreover, emphasizing the discourse of enforcement can be detrimental by providing EU institutions with a scapegoat or a "defensive narrative" through which ineffectiveness or inaction on the part of the EU can be easily attributed to its limited powers.[43]

Second, the discrepancy between "children's rights on paper" and "children's rights in practice" at both the level of EU Member States and EU institutions highlights a lack of attachment to a child rights culture and the deepest values underpinning the CRC.[44] Indeed, the CRC's power lies in its potential educational impact, which by recognizing children as autonomous persons capable of having and exercising rights has caused a "paradigm shift" towards considering children as both "beings" and "becomings."[45] Research demonstrates how the absence of a child rights culture can impact the capacity and effectiveness of governments, institutions, and other stakeholders in implementing child-related policies and practices.[46] In other words, effective implementation of children's rights – be it at the legislative, political, judicial, service, or programme level – depends on the degree of perception of children as autonomous rights-holders entitled to "exert influence on their own lives."[47] The failure to encourage meaningful child participation in the EU law and policy-making processes reflects this lack of emphasis on children's rights in society. Without a culture of respect for children's rights and a robust ideological thread to link individual measures together, the growing number of soft-law instruments and policy strategies risks being ineffective.[48] Indeed, true belief in the value of children's rights is essential for "even the most explicit, binding measures relating to children's rights, to be truly effective in stimulating positive change in children's lives."[49]

Incorporating the CRC at the EU level: towards a full-fledged EU child rights strategy

To effectuate real progress in furthering children's rights, "genuine allegiance" to the child rights culture of the CRC is required, and this entails the need to embrace the "entire process, investment and ideology" underpinning the CRC and not only incorporating its principles and standards in formal texts.[50] In order to fundamentally improve the implementation of children's rights protections in practice, we suggest that three elements should be emphasized in establishing the forthcoming EU comprehensive child rights strategy.

The first element is creating political leverage through the appointment of a European commissioner for children's rights, taking advantage of the window of opportunity created by the current favourable political momentum at the EU institutional level. As empirical research has demonstrated, the most significant achievements in implementing the CRC come from support by a particular political champion.[51] At the Member States level, the Commissioners' actions have been critical to effectively monitoring the implementation of children's rights measures over time, holding governments to account, and ensuring the coherent implementation of the CRC in times of political change.[52] At the EU level, political commitment and political leadership within the Council, Commission, and Parliament have been essential for advancing EU child-related laws, policies, and funding instruments, with positive consequences for encouraging further action on the part of Member States.[53] The nomination of an *ad hoc* high-level political figure within the European Commission, working exclusively on children's rights, would strongly contribute to making children's rights a priority on the ground.

The second element involves widespread cooperation and integration in the form of the adoption of a comprehensive child rights strategy along the lines of the General Measures on Implementation of the CRC as expressed by *General Comment No. 5*.[54] Based on the recognition that "children and their rights cannot be separated from the society of which they are an integral part," such a strategy would not only entail *ex ante* integration of children's rights provision into formal texts, but also effective *ex post* enforcement of children's rights through coordinated action capable of creating ownership, responsibility, and action among all the actors working directly with children.[55]

The third element involves the need for placing child participation at the heart of EU institutions. The goal should be to build a robust culture of child participation at all levels – including family, community, local, regional, national, and European – as required by the Bucharest EU Children's Declaration. The promotion of child participation is a central tool for shaping children's rights protection and can contribute to transforming the EU approach to children to be more rights-based. The transformation would ensure for children the same claims to dignity as autonomous adults, in accordance with the values underpinning the CRC.[56] The EU institutions should be running focus groups with children and include their conclusions in policy documents and legislative measures affecting their future. An example of good practice in the emphasis on child participation is the feasibility study for the establishment of a European Child Guarantee, which includes consultations with four groups of children. Despite being carried out as an *ex post* "reality check" to the official study, the consultations demonstrated the need for incorporating children's voices to enrich and shape the development of effective children's rights protection.

A key step for the EU would be to accede to the CRC through a unilateral declaration of adhesion or through the conclusion of an international protocol in accordance with Article 216 of the TFEU, which states that the EU can accede to international treaties "where the conclusion of an agreement is necessary to achieve, within the framework of the Union's policies, one of the objectives referred to in the Treaties." Such an approach was taken by the EU in its accession to the UN Convention on the Rights of Persons with Disabilities in 2006.[57] Even if such a step would not change EU formal responsibilities, powers, and competence on children's rights, it would most likely act as a "boost" to all the three elements identified as necessary to further the implementation of children's right by the EU. In fact, EU accession to the CRC would carry a strong symbolic value in furthering the very child rights culture we have argued is lacking. Such an action would also encourage a more consistent EU approach to the protection and fulfilment of children's rights, further establishing EU's obligations and commitment to children's rights protection through the external supervision of the UN Committee on the Rights of the Child.[58] Most importantly, once acceded to the CRC, the EU would become subject to its monitoring mechanism and reporting obligations, thereby obligating itself to carry out systematic, periodic reporting of progress against the General Measures of Implementation of the CRC across all its institutions and develop specific implementation priorities and goals concerning the protection of children's rights.[59]

Conclusion

The EU has made great strides in the protection of children's rights over the last decades, especially after the enactment of the Lisbon Treaty, which permits the EU to embed children's rights protection into a framework of fundamental rights. In particular, by endorsing the CRC as its fundamental guide and incorporating its principles and provisions into EU measures, the EU has achieved a broader and more unitary children's rights approach. However, the process of implementing children's rights protection at the EU level remains incomplete, preventing the EU from providing a decisive added value to the child-related actions of its Member States. In fact, the lack of implementation reflects a mismatch between how children's rights are protected and promoted "on paper" and "in practice." This mismatch emphasizes a general lack of attachment to the child rights culture underpinning the CRC. In order to address this discrepancy, in this chapter, three elements that should be prioritized within the forthcoming EU comprehensive child rights strategy have been suggested: creating political leverage, improving coordination, and ensuring child participation. It is also argued that the EU accession to the CRC would act as a boost to all the elements identified, sending out a highly symbolic message about the EU's commitment and belief in the values underpinning the CRC and obliging the EU to monitor its child-related action against the General Measures of Implementation of the CRC.

Notes

1 European Parliament Resolution 2014/2237(INI), 2015, O.J. (C 366) 19–30.
2 Ingi Iusmen & Helen Stalford, *Conclusion: How Can the EU Be A Better Children's Rights Actor? in* The EU as a Children's Rights Actor: Law, Policy and Structural Dimensions, 311 (Verlag Barbara Budrich, 2016).
3 European Union Agency for Fundamental Rights & Council of Europe, Handbook on European Law Relating to the Rights of the Child, 20 (2015).
4 *Id.*
5 Helen Stalford & Eleanor Drywood, *Using the CRC to Inform EU Law and Policy-making, in* The Human Rights of Children From Visions to Implementation, 200 (Antonella Invernizzi ed., 2011).
6 *Id.* at 201.
7 *Id.*
8 European Council Directive 89/552/EEC, 1989 O.J. (L 298) 23, 30; European Council Directive 94/33/EC, 1994 O.J. (L 216) 12, 20.
9 In 2010 the Directorate-General Justice, Freedom and Security was then Split into the Directorate-General Justice and the Directorate-General for Home Affairs.
10 European Commission Communication, COM(2006) 367 final (Apr. 7, 2006).
11 Jean Grugel & Ingi Iusmen, *The European Commission as Guardian Angel: The Challenges of Agenda-Setting for Children's Rights*, 20 J. of Eur. Pub. Pol'y 77 (2013).
12 Helen Stalford, *The CRC in Litigation Under EU Law, in* Litigating the Rights of the Child, 211 (Ton Liefaard & Jaap E. Doek eds., 2014).
13 TEU stands for the Treaty on European Union, TFEU stands for the Treaty on the Functioning of the European Union as it was renamed the Treaty establishing the European Community.
14 Helen Stalford & Mieke Schuurman, *Are We There Yet? The Impact of the Lisbon Treaty on the EU Children's Rights Agenda*, 19 Int'l J. of Child. Rts. 381 (2011).
15 Ingi Iusmen, *How Are Children's Rights (Mis)Interpreted in Practice? The European Commission, Children's Rights and Policy Narratives, in* Narrative Policy Analysis, 97 (R.A.W. Rhodes ed., 2018).
16 *Id.* at 100.
17 Stalford & Drywood, *supra* note 5, at 202–203.
18 Stalford, *supra* note 12, at 229.
19 *Id.* at 212–213.
20 Aida Kisunaite, *Children's Rights Protection in the EU: The Need for a Contextual Perspective*, 3 Peace Hum. Rts. Governance 177 (2019).
21 European Parliament & European Council Directive (EU) 2019/1158, 2019 O.J. (L 188) 79, 93.

22 European Commission, EU Acquis and Policy Documents on the Rights of the Child, JUST.C2/MTF, https://ec.europa.eu/info/sites/info/files/eu_acquis_and_policy_documnets_rights_of_the_child_march_2019.pdf (last visited Sep. 16, 2020).
23 Stalford, *supra* note 12, at 212.
24 European Council & European Parliament Directive 2013/32/EU, 2013 O.J. (L 180) 60, 95; European Parliament Directive 2013/33/EU, 2013 O.J. (L 180) 96, 116; European Council Directive 2003/86/EU, 2003 O.J. (L 251/12) 12, 18; European Parliament & European Council Directive (EU) 2016/800, 2016 O.J. (L 132) 1, 20; Stalford, *supra* note 12, at 220.
25 European Parliament & European Council Directive 2011/93/EU, 2011, O.J. (L 335/1) 1, 14; European Parliament & European Council Directive 2011/36/EU, 2011 O.J. (L 101) 1, 11; European Parliament & European Council Directive 2012/29/EU, 2012 O.J. (L 315) 57, 73.
26 European Commission Communication, COM(2011) 60 final (Feb. 15, 2011); European Commission Recommendation, 2013/112/EU, 2013 O.J. (L 59) 5, 16; European Commission Communication, COM(2017) 250 final (Apr. 26, 2017).
27 European Union Agency for Fundamental Rights & Council of Europe, *supra* note 3, at 22.
28 Stalford, *supra* note 12, at 212.
29 European Union Agency for Fundamental Rights, Combating Child Poverty: An Issue of Fundamental Rights, 29 (2018).
30 Stalford, *supra* note 12, at 212.
31 Hugh Frazer & Eric Marlier, European Commission, Progress Across Europe in the Implementation of the 2013 EU Recommendation on 'Investing In Children: Breaking the Cycle of Disadvantage,' (2017).
32 The European Semester is a cycle of economic and fiscal policy coordination between the European Commission and Member States during which these latter align their budgetary and economic policies with the objectives and rules agreed at the EU level. Its focus is on the 6-month period from the beginning of each year. It was established by European Commission Communication COM(2010) 367 final, 30.6.2010.
33 Hugh Frazer et al., European Commission, Feasibility Study for a Child Guarantee: Final Report (2020).
34 The proposal requires the allocation of at least € 5.9 billion of the European Social Fund Plus (ESF+) for the programming period 2021–2027 and that every EU Member State invests at least 5% of ESF+ resources under shared management to support the Child Guarantee.
35 European Union Agency for Fundamental Rights, Fundamental Rights Report, 165 (2020).
36 *Id.*
37 Iusmen, *supra* note 15, at 14.
38 *Id.* at 107; Iusmen & Stalford, *supra* note 2, at 313.
39 Iusmen, *supra* note 15, at 112.
40 Stalford, *supra* note 12.
41 *Id.*
42 Stalford & Schuurman, *supra* note 14, at 402.
43 Iusmen, *supra* note 15.
44 *Id.*
45 Michael Freeman, *The Value and Values of Children's Rights*, *in* The Human Rights of Children: From Visions to Implementation, 7 (Antonella Invernizzi & Jane Williams eds., 2011).
46 Laura Lundy et al., *Incorporation of the United Nations Convention on the Rights of the Child in Law: A Comparative Review*, 21 Int'l J. of Child. Rts. 442 (2013); Sandy Ruxton, Governance Fit for Children: To What Extent have the General Measures of Implementation of the UNCRC been Realised in Five European Countries? 13 (2011).

47 *Id.* at 10.
48 Ingeborg Odink, *Children's Rights in the EU Marking 30 years of the UN Convention on the Rights of the Child* (European Parliamentary Research Service, 2019); Stalford & Drywood, *supra* note 5, at 202.
49 Iusmen & Stalford, *supra* note 2, at 313.
50 Stalford & Drywood, *supra* note 5, at 214.
51 Lundy et al., *supra* note 46, at 14.
52 *Id.* at 12.
53 *Id.* at 14; Frazer et al., supra note 33, at 183.
54 U. N. Children's Right Commission, *General Comment No. 5 (2003): General Measures of Implementation of the Convention on the Rights of the Child*, U.N. Doc. CRC/GC/2003/5.
55 Olivia Lind Haldorsson, *Save the Children Sweden, Governance Fit for Children. To What Extent Have the General Measures of Implementation of the UNCRC Been Realised in the EU Institutions?* 21 (2011); Stalford, *supra* note 12, at 228.
56 Iusmen, *supra* note 15, at 99.
57 Stalford, *supra* note 12, at 14.
58 Haldorsson, *supra* note 55, at 18.
59 *Id.*

C. Africa

3 Thirty years of the CRC in Africa

Julia Sloth-Nielsen

Introduction and context

This chapter will review the 30 years of the Convention on the Rights of the Child (CRC) on the African continent. It will not be confined to the family law domain, but will traverse child protection, health, education, and juvenile justice, amongst others, as well. In 1990, Ghana was the first African country to ratify the CRC, and the most recent country to ratify was the African provenance, Somalia, in 2015. Ratification of the CRC in Africa is now universal.

To contextualise this chapter, by 2055, Africa's child population will reach one billion children, making it the largest population of children anywhere on the globe.[1] Since 2017, sub-Saharan Africa has been recording the highest number of new births annually, with no decrease in population growth rates, and this trend will likely continue for the rest of the century.[2] Mortality rates of children under five years decreased by 57% between 1990 (the date of coming into force of the CRC) and 2017,[3] which can likely be attributed largely to the Millennium Development Goals (MDG), which has as one indicator the reduction of under-five mortality rates. Nevertheless, more than half of the 5.4 million deaths of children below five years of age in 2017 across the globe occurred in Africa.[4] And while mortality rates have declined across all age groups in Africa, they tend to be concentrated among the younger age groups, with 85% of all deaths of children under the age of 15 occurring in the under-five age group.[5] More specifically, in 2016, pneumonia, malaria, and diarrhoea accounted for 36% of all deaths of children under five in Africa. A total of 31 million under-five deaths will occur between 2018 and 2030.[6] There is a long way to go, therefore, in implementing Article 24 of the CRC,[7] insofar as it relates to preventable childhood diseases.

Another key MDG was to achieve universal primary education across Africa by 2015. Although it is widely accepted that this goal was met, it was achieved at the expense of quality education in many places.[8] It has been estimated that more than 6.3 million primary school educators are still needed in sub-Saharan Africa by 2030 to meet optimal teacher-pupil ratios.[9]

Africa is the fastest growing Muslim region in the world and by 2060, it is estimated that 37% of the population of Africans in sub-Saharan Africa will practice the Muslim faith.[10] Currently, it is estimated that as many as 40% of African children are raised in the Muslim faith, which in turn can have implications for the fulfilment of CRC rights. Several African countries entered reservations to the CRC upon ratification, arguing that they would not accede to provisions that they regarded as incompatible with Islam.[11]

Drawing from the 2019 Report "Getting Girls Equal,"[12] the following summary findings can be recorded. Despite the gains made in achieving access to education, 23% of all girls remain outside of school. Sexual abuse of girls at school is as high as 83% (Botswana), 55% (Cameroon), and 50% (Rwanda). Moreover, 40% of girls in sub-Saharan Africa marry before the age of 18,[13] and in some places, such as Niger, this rises to 60–70% of all girls. Female genital mutilation/cutting is rampant in some regions, with up to 94% of girls subjected to this harmful practice. Africa, worldwide, has the highest adolescent pregnancy rates,[14] which contributes to the huge continental population growth. One in ten girls misses school during menstruation, which effectively means losing 20% of the academic year. Some laws continue to discriminate directly against girls, for instance in relation to the transmission of nationality and laws relating to inheritance.[15] Girls are particularly at-risk when overlapping and intersectional causes of their vulnerability arise, such as when they are poor, employed in domestic work, living on the street, or have a disability.

Violence against children is another area of concern on the continent. As initially highlighted by the 2006 Report of the UN Special Rapporteur on Violence Against Children, the World Report on Violence against Children,[16] and consistently addressed by subsequent UN Special Rapporteurs on Violence Against Children, deeply rooted patriarchal and traditional cultural norms foster community beliefs that sanction acts of violence against children, which are then met with impunity. Nonetheless, by June 2020, the global movement to ban parental corporal punishment had already born fruit in the African context, with Togo, Benin, South Sudan, Kenya, Rwanda, Tunisia, Republic of Congo, and Cabo Verde having outlawed it.[17] But overall, cooperation and coordination need to be strengthened at all levels to improve responses to reports of violence and to provide victims with appropriate remedies, redress, and psycho-social support.

Sub-Saharan Africa has been disproportionately affected by HIV/AIDS, leading to increased rates of orphanhood amongst children. In Kenya, for instance, it is estimated that there are more than two million orphaned children.[18] Some collateral consequences include a sharp rise in the establishment of institutional care settings, such as orphanages,[19] and the abandonment of community care structures in favour of alternative care placements.

The role and impact of armed conflict on children's lives cannot be left out of the reckoning. In fact, UNICEF predicted 2016 to be "the worst year for children" due to the escalating insurrections and conflict that had occurred.[20] Some regions affected included North Africa (Libya), East Africa (Somalia, Northern Kenya), Central Africa (Democratic Republic of Congo, Burundi, Central African Republic), and West Africa (northern Nigeria, Mali). The impact extends far beyond children actually recruited into militias but also to those who are victims of attacks on schools, hospitals, and who are killed and maimed in crossfire and warfare.[21] Migration remains a significant opportunity.[22]

Impact of the CRC

Law reform

There has been significant upgrading and modernisation of child law throughout the continent, notably in child protection legislation, inspired by the norms and principles of the CRC.[23] This reform is generally aimed at setting up child protection systems, detailing how to respond to child abuse and neglect, and providing the basis for various forms of alternative care. Sporadically, juvenile justice laws have also been either included in overarching child protection laws or upgraded separately. Work on juvenile justice reform continues, for instance, in Namibia, Zimbabwe, and South Sudan.[24] In a significant number of countries, dedicated sectoral or issue-based legislation in the realm of trafficking, harmful cultural practices, and gender-based violence (or domestic violence) has additionally been adopted. Some countries – e.g., Mozambique – have amended the minimum age of marriage to exclude children, and South Africa, Kenya, Zimbabwe,[25] Malawi, and to some extent, Tanzania, have implemented meaningful constitutional guarantees for children's rights, inspired by the CRC. South Africa's constitutional jurisprudence on various facets of children's rights remains a leading example around the globe. Judgements spanning an array of issues, from banning corporal punishment in the home, to the maintenance of the privacy of both an accused child and child witnesses once they reach 18 have been decreed, and the flow of jurisprudence since the adoption of the constitution in 1996 can only be described as momentous.[26]

CRC-compliant law reform has served as a basis for further development of more in-depth regulation. "Second wave" law reform, building on initial child justice and protection statutes, has already begun to take shape. The revisionist or more detailed legislation builds on the strong basis created by earlier attempts to adopt legislation giving effect to the CRC. Some examples include Uganda, which, in 2016 adopted amendments to the Children Act, South Africa adopting amendments to the Child Justice Act 75 of 2008 in 2020 and this year is debating amendments to the Children's Act 37 of 2005), and Rwanda in 2016, adopting the law setting the age of majority at 18 years and the minimum age for marriage at 21 years.[27] Mozambique is currently supporting a review of the system for children's access to justice (although this has been somewhat delayed due to the lockdown put in place under COVID-19).[28] The Democratic Republic of Congo passed a new law in 2016[29] that seeks to comprehensively address the state's treaty obligations, including (by express reference) the CRC. Kenya is at an advanced stage of revision of its children's legislation and to regulate intercountry adoption, and steps are well underway to align the Zimbabwean 2001 children's law with the 2013 Constitution, as well as to modernise it.[30]

In the Seychelles, the Children Amendment Act 2020 was adopted by the National Assembly on May 12, 2020 to explicitly prohibit corporal punishment and repeal the defence of reasonable chastisement. The Children

Amendment Act 2020 amends the Children Act 1982 to insert a new Article 70B that states:

> (1) Notwithstanding any other law, no child shall be subjected to corporal punishment. (2) Any person who contravenes subsection (1) commits an offence and on conviction is liable to a fine of SCR25,000 or to imprisonment for not more than 2 years, or to both a fine and imprisonment, provided that the Court shall first consider other appropriate means of disposing of the matter, taking into consideration the relationship between the offender and the child.

The 2020 Act further states in its introduction that, in addition to repealing the statutory defence, it aims to abolish "any other defence with respect to assault against a child available to parents and persons acting *in loco parentis*" – leading to children having "the same legal protection from assault as adults."

Mozambique adopted legislation relating to child marriage in 2019. However, it has not yet been promulgated by the President and is, at the time of this writing, not yet in force.[31] In 2016, Burundi enacted legislation aimed at preventing and responding to gender-based violence. The chapeau refers amongst others to the CRC. The legislation also introduced measures aimed at combatting early marriage (*marriage precoce*).[32]

In general, the law-making function has become more detailed, with enhanced complexity drawing on CRC Committee jurisprudence and other guidance (such as the 2009 United Nations (UN) Guidelines on Alternative Care). It can be predicted that ongoing statutory revisions and elaborations in the children's rights sphere will continue to develop.

Systems strengthening for child protection

Systems strengthening was the topic of a General Comment issued by the African Committee of Experts on the Rights and Welfare of the Child in 2018. "Systems strengthening" refers to identifying, establishing, and strengthening the coordinated response to violations relating to abuse, neglect, maltreatment, and exploitation.

By implementing a system strengthening approach, States Parties address the full spectrum of the rights of the child just as a systems-wide approach would aim to protect the rights of all children including, in particular, the most vulnerable and marginalised. These include, but are not limited to, internally displaced or migrant and refugee children (including unaccompanied children) children with disabilities, girls, children affected by conflict or disaster, orphaned children, children with a disability, and those belonging to a minority group. It would also consider the different gender and age-based needs of girls and boys.

The systems approach differs from earlier child protection efforts, which have traditionally focused on single issues such as child trafficking, street children, child labour, emergencies, institutionalisation, or HIV/AIDS. This diffused approach often resulted in a fragmented child protection response, marked by numerous inefficiencies and pockets of unmet need.[33]

> Well-functioning systems pay particular attention to developing and fostering cooperation, coordination, and collaboration among all levels of stakeholders, from community level upwards. The coordination extends to managers and those involved in service delivery components. A systems approach entails that rather than treating each child protection issue separately, a holistic view of children and child protection is promoted, and all stakeholders who are involved in child protection responses are involved. Systems include both formal and informal local contexts, and the contours of the system should be deliberately mapped out: a silo approach to child protection should be avoided in favour of overarching systems which respond to all forms of vulnerability and which adopt a 'bottom up' approach.[34]

Crucially, child protection responses are heavily reliant on the availability of human resources, in whatever mix is appropriate and sufficient for the local context, and may include skilled social workforce, community-based auxiliaries, investigative, and forensic staff, etc.[35] All systems strengthening endeavours must be underpinned by the steady expansion and training of the necessary human resources to respond to violence against and abuse of children. Even in States where the primary response to child protection lies in the informal sector, or in the community, certain professionals are needed to undertake, for instance, assessments and onward referrals to professionals (medical or forensic personnel, mental health professionals, or prosecutors). Indeed, government spending on child protection systems remains far too low in relation to other expenditures and sustained advocacy is needed to ensure that it increases.

Notably, during the era of COVID-19, significant weaknesses and gaps in relation to child protection systems have been noted, including increases in child marriage, female genital mutilation/cutting, and the numbers of children who are victims of violence in the home. In some places, a near complete breakdown of response and referral services is evident. Rebuilding the required social welfare interventions to benefit children at the grassroots level is a matter currently occupying the child protection space.

Child participation and access to justice

In 2018, the African Child Policy Forum, a pan-African NGO based in Addis Ababa, together with Defence for Child International (DCI), launched "Spotlighting the Invisible: Access to Justice for Children in Africa."[36] This report reviews all aspects of children's contact with justice systems, including civil, administrative, and criminal proceedings. A dedicated chapter examines children's interactions with informal and traditional justice systems too, as these are the predominant ways in which disputes are resolved in rural areas (and sometimes transplanted to urban areas) in many parts of the continent. This is further discussed in the following section.

The Report concludes that considerable improvements in establishing more child-friendly justice systems can be detected. Often premised on law reform, but also on policy initiatives and administrative developments, these include greater access to legal representation for children (especially those in conflict with the law), the establishment of specialised police units to address victims of gender-based violence, the formation of dedicated forensic services to better collect evidence of survivors to improve prosecution practice (modelled on the South African *Thuthuzela* centres located at identified hospitals and medical centres),[37] and greater access to diversion away from formal criminal proceedings, as in South Africa,[38] Zimbabwe,[39] Ethiopia,[40] Mauritania,[41] Uganda,[42] Zambia,[43] and Malawi.

An increasing trend towards strategic litigation to further children's interests is attracting international attention and is illustrative of a growing trend towards access to justice for children becoming a reality. In Tanzania, a challenge to the provisions enabling child marriage were successfully brought in the High Court in 2016.[44] The appeal by the Attorney General to the Court of Appeal, which was finalised on September 19, 2019 failed.[45] The Court found that the Law of the Marriage Act, (Cap 20 R.E. 2002), which established a minimum age of marriage for girls at 15, and for boys at 18 years, violated the constitutional guarantee of equality and ordered that the Government amend the Law of the Marriage Act within a period of one year to render the age of marriage constitutional. Reliance was expressly placed on the fact that Tanzania had ratified the CRC.

In Zimbabwe, the Constitutional Court ruled child marriage in all forms to be contrary to the 2013 Constitution in *Madzhuru v Minister of Justice, Parliamentary and Constitutional Affairs* in 2016[46] and 2019 saw a judgement ruling that juvenile whipping was offensive to the Constitutional protection of dignity.[47] In Kenya, in the case of *MWK v Attorney General*,[48] a young girl was found guilty of possession of *cannabis sativa* (marijuana). Since the drugs were allegedly concealed under her clothes at the time of her arrest, the police took naked pictures of her and circulated these on social media, thereby violating her right to dignity and her best interests. The Court noted that section 53 of the Kenyan Constitution offers special protection to children in conflict with the law and accords them treatment that upholds human dignity and worth.

South Africa's children's rights jurisprudence based on the constitutional precepts of section 28 (the children's rights clause) has been lauded the world over.[49] Reliance has frequently been placed on international instruments, including the CRC, in interpreting the children's rights clause and its impact. As will be seen from the next section, children's access to justice has also been furthered through the development of dedicated courts with specialised personnel.

Specialised institutions, personnel, and courts

The development of dedicated children's courts, which benefit from social work staff and probation officers, has been ongoing for some decades now. Although in some places these courts are confined to capital or larger cities only, there are promising signs of a more widespread geographical reach, such as in Kenya where more than 30 districts are served by such courts. In Senegal, a juvenile court exists within each regional court.[50] In Mauritania, the authorities established the El Mina Centre for the Reception and Social Reintegration of Children in Conflict with the Law. The Centre falls under the Ministry of Justice and its mission is in line with the Children's Code.[51] Training has been conducted for juvenile justice practitioners, and diversion is well established.[52]

On December 4, 2018, the Judicial Service of Ghana, with support from UNICEF, inaugurated the first child-friendly court in Ghana. The Court, which is situated within the Gender Based Violence Courts, is aimed at addressing the needs of children using more age-appropriate procedures and tools. The child-friendly court includes facilities such as a waiting room designed to provide a friendly environment to child victims, witnesses, and children who for other reasons come into contact with the law. The facility is furnished with necessary technical equipment such as closed circuit television (CCTV), a small library, toys, and information, as well as literature on child protection for psychologists, lawyers, support persons, and parents.[53]

In South Africa, special rules for child witnesses have been in place for years, such as permitting them to give evidence through an intermediary. Recently, a spike in reported cases of gender-based and sexual violence has seen three new amendment bills introduced to Parliament. One of these substantially expands the form of proceedings in which intermediaries are appointed and also extends the use of audio-visual aids (such as one-way mirrors) designed to assist children give evidence.[54]

Several projects have been undertaken to develop specialised training for police units dealing with child victims. Namibia and Zambia provide examples of this, and Zimbabwe is shortly to follow suit.[55]

Although from a continental perspective, it cannot be claimed that child-friendly justice is routinely experienced by children who encounter formal justice systems, it can be demonstrated that pockets of excellence are to be found and these provide a useful launch pad for ongoing endeavours.

Intercountry adoption

There was a period after the turn of the millennium, reaching a peak around 2012, when Africa was set to become the new frontier for intercountry adoption. At the height, it was estimated that Ethiopia was one of the top sending countries in the world.[56] Then, when Ethiopia started to clamp down due to abuses and irregularities, the focus turned to Ghana and Uganda, and later to the Democratic Republic of Congo. An increasing number of African countries have ratified the Hague Convention on Intercountry Adoption of 1993, and started to put measures in place to exert some state control over intercountry adoption, including through legislation and by establishing Central Authorities as the Convention requires. At the time of writing, signatory states include Benin, Burkina Faso, Burundi, Cabo Verde, Congo, Cote d'Ivoire, Eswatini (formerly

Swaziland), Ghana, Guinea, Kenya, Lesotho, Madagascar, Mali, Mauritius, Namibia, Rwanda, Senegal, Seychelles, South Africa, Togo, and Zambia.[57]

There have been initial indications that some parts of Africa are becoming attractive international surrogacy destinations, including South Africa and Kenya.[58] The latter, along with Nigeria, is contemplating the introduction of legislation regulating surrogacy and South Africa already has such a regulation in the Children's Act 38 of 2005, which contains a dedicated chapter on this topic. In South Africa, in order to engage in surrogate motherhood legally, one commissioning parent must be domiciled in the country before the surrogate motherhood agreement can be confirmed in an attempt to block international reproductive tourism. Surrogacy in Ghana is reportedly growing, but unregulated. A website to profile prospective surrogate mothers in Botswana lists at least a dozen entries, some added as recently as July 2020.[59]

It is predictable that with the expansion of private and modern fertility clinics that offer less expensive services than in the global north, this trend might continue.

Child-sensitive social protection

Also known as social cash transfer schemes, child-sensitive social protection schemes have mushroomed in Africa as a response to the call for the eradication of absolute poverty and the attainment of the original MDG (replaced in 2015), and thereafter the Sustainable Development Goals, which were developed to steer global development from 2015 to 2030. These schemes often target the most marginalised – orphans who are being cared for by the elderly, pregnant women, or mothers immediately following the infants' birth – and can be on a small scale and of limited reach. Nevertheless, they have demonstrated efficacy in desirable social and health outcomes when the transfers are linked to requirements such as school attendance and immunisations or hospital check-ups. A wealth of supporting data and evidence has been collated by the World Bank, UNICEF, and other development agencies to this effect.[60] Although operative largely as development initiatives and without formal legal backing,[61] these expanding social safety nets can be rooted in the child's right to an adequate standard of living in Article 27 of the CRC. The African Committee of Experts Report on Agenda 2040, under aspiration five (every child grows up well-nourished and with access to the basic necessities of life), provides a list of almost all African countries in which a social cash transfer programme benefiting children now exists.[62]

The African Charter on the Rights and Welfare of the Child (ACRWC) and other treaties

The period being reviewed has also seen the coming into force of the ACRWC, a regional treaty promoting the rights of children,[63] which at the time of writing enjoys 48 ratifications (out of a possible 54 member states of the African Union). Many state parties have submitted initial and several periodic reports to the

African Committee of Experts on the Rights and Welfare of the Child, the monitoring body of the ACERWC, since the first report was submitted (by Egypt and Nigeria) in 2008. Apart from the ACRWC itself, African states have also ratified the Optional Protocols to the CRC on children and armed conflict, and on the sale of children, child prostitution, and child pornography. Only three countries appear to have ratified Optional Protocol Three on an individual complaints procedure. However, 54 African states have ratified International Labour Organization (ILO) convention 182 on the Worst Forms of Child Labour (1999). Ratification of the Palermo Protocol (Protocol to Prevent, Suppress and Punish Trafficking in Persons, Especially Women and Children, supplementing the UN Convention against Transnational Organized Crime of 15 November 2000) is universal amongst African states[64] and widespread adoption of domestic legislation on trafficking in persons has occurred to give effect to its provisions.[65] The law seeks to protect all victims, but children are singled out in the treaty as being especially vulnerable to exploitation and coercion; this is also the theme of Article 35 of the CRC.[66]

Monitoring and enforcement

There are any number of ministries, agencies, and departments within governments that are now tasked with monitoring and fulfilling children's rights, outside of education departments (which have children's education as a core objective) and health departments (which oversee the fulfilment of citizens' health rights generally, including children). In many African countries, there is an overarching and multi-sectoral National Committee for Children, which draws in civil society organisations. Kenya, Namibia, Egypt, Algeria, and Ghana provide further concrete examples of this trend.

Most national human rights commissions have identified children's rights as a focal point. There are three examples of independent and dedicated children's rights ombudspersons in Africa, pointing to a growing trend of establishing these institutions. While Mauritius' ombudsperson has been in existence since 2003,[67] Malawi's has only recently been established by law,[68] and in one South African province, the ombudsperson took office in June 2020.[69]

Role of non-state actors

Non-governmental organisations provide protection of children's rights in Africa in a variety of domains. These include the private sector, which has entered the education space as a provider of education as an alternative to state run schools,[70] charitable organisations providing child protection services to abused, neglected and abandoned children, and faith-based and other organisations providing alternative care to children.

The period since the CRC's rise in force has seen states tighten up on the regulation and registration of non-state actors working with children. Ethiopia introduced new laws on the operation of non-profit organisations in 2012, for instance, and Kenya is preparing a new legislation that will seek further to regulate charitable organisations. On the one hand, there have been cries that civilian space is shrinking under harsher regulatory regimes; on the other hand, few would contend that civilian organisations that undertake service delivery to children should operate without checks and balances of any kind, given children's vulnerability to becoming victims of sexual and other predators.

Reconfiguration of the family and urbanisation

The 30 years since the adoption of the CRC has seen rapid changes to family forms and to traditional notions of family structures on the continent. Amongst other reasons, this can be attributed to rapid urbanisation that continues to occur.[71] In addition, increasing access to education has no doubt played a role, as there is a demonstrated correlation between increased access to education for girls and lower fertility rates. The CRC has brought about changes in the way children born out of wedlock are treated under the law,[72] and in some places, recognition has been given to child-headed households by law.[73] A central thrust of African Union endeavours at present is campaigning to end child marriage (which is proscribed by the ACRWC).[74] It is predictable that the communal kinship structures of old are going to change in the growing urban economies of the future, which in turn will change the way that many children are raised in Africa.

Sexual and reproductive health rights

The clear guidance from the Committee on the Rights of the Child notwithstanding,[75] girls' access to sexual and reproductive health rights (SRHR) remains elusive in many quarters due to systemic patriarchy, pervasive cultural stereotypes, and conservative societal attitudes that deny that children engage in consensual sexual activity. The ACERWC is preparing a General Comment on sexual exploitation, which will include some discussion of access to SRHR. A controversial topic, the minimum age of sexual consent, is linked to this issue and the Committee is discussing the possibility of hosting a General Day of Discussion on both themes at its next meeting.

Pluralistic legal systems and restorative justice

It has been noted that the co-existence of pluralist legal systems – civil law alongside customary law – has proved surprisingly resilient, even in modern times. They continue to form the backbone of access to justice for citizens in an estimated 70–90% of instances.[76] Whereas it was once thought that informal and traditional justice forms would 'wither and die,' this has not transpired, for various reasons. These reasons include that formal justice systems are geographically inaccessible, operate with extremely limited infrastructure and resources, and resolution is characterised by long delays that are inimical to achieving justice for victims and those affected by disputes. Formal justice systems often appear to lack legitimacy, as cases are won by 'clever' lawyers who do the talking, as opposed to the truth-seeking approaches of the informal justice system.[77] One of the common characteristics of informal justice systems is that they approach dispute resolution from the perspective of the collective rather than the individual or in the case of criminal offences, from the vantage-point of the interests of the state. They embrace informal modes of information-gathering in contrast to the formal evidentiary rules of the state justice system. They are flexible, often entailing a high degree of public participation. That children are impacted – often directly[78] – goes without saying.

Recent advice suggests applying a holistic, integrated approach to justice sector reform. Support to informal justice systems should complement or be incorporated support to the formal justice system to enable everyone to access justice regardless of their education, class, ethnicity, gender, sexual orientation, or age.[79]

Much more research on children's involvement in informal justice systems has been advocated for recently.[80] This is not an easy endeavour, as informal justice systems are by their nature not systems of record and rely on oral tradition. Also, it is known that children often do not have a voice directly but are represented by other relatives. Nonetheless, there is some evidence from field work that a significant number of children in rural and urban areas have as their first contact with informal justice systems.[81]

Conclusions

This chapter has selectively reviewed specific themes and areas where the impact of the CRC has arguably been most visible. It is written with the background understanding that the socio-economic position of many children has not improved, that many children still suffer hunger, malnutrition, and stunting, that the number of preventable deaths of children should be decreasing much more rapidly, and that access to education for many African children is still out of reach. Discrimination against girl children in practice remains pervasive.

However, equally, much has changed in 30 years for the better. Children's issues are far more prominent on government agendas and periodic reporting processes[82] allow them to take stock and institute improvements. Certainly, law making has been crucially affected by children's rights principles and child-specific institutions and structures continue to be established. Children's voices are much more readily heard and courts have played an important role in giving effect to their best interests in a variety of domains. These factors all serve as important building blocks to improve African children's access to their rights over the next 30 years.

Notes

1 *See* UNICEF, Generation 2030 Africa 2.0: Prioritizing Investments in Children Toreap the Demographic Dividend, https://data.unicef.org/resources/generation-2030-africa-2-0/.

2 *Id.*
3 *Id.*
4 *See* UNICEF, Level and Trends in Child Mortality Report 2017, https://data.unicef.org/resources/levels-trends-child-mortality-2017.
5 *Id.*
6 *Id.*
7 UN Convention on the Rights of the Child (CRC), *General Comment No. 15 On The Right Of The Child To The Enjoyment Of The Highest Attainable Standard Of Health (Article 24)*, UN Doc. CRC/C/GC/15 (Apr. 17, 2013).
8 There was what was termed "access shock" with classrooms filled to overflowing with incoming learners.
9 UNESCO Institute for Statistics, *The World Needs Almost 69 million New Teachers to Reach the 2030 Education Goals*, https://unesdoc.unesco.org/ark:/48223/pf0000246124.
10 North Africa is already predominantly Muslim (Egypt, Algeria, Tunisia, Morocco, and so forth).
11 See, e.g., Algeria, Djibouti, Mauritania.
12 African Child Policy Forum and Plan International, Getting Girls Equal (2019); Note that the CRC is remarkably silent on the position of girls, except as regards the reference to harmful traditional practices prejudicial to the health of children in Article 24(3). Even so, the CRC formulation does not single out girls as the primary victims of these practices.
13 For instance Zambia (42%) and Malawi (40%).
14 Such as in Guinea where 40% of newborns are born to adolescents.
15 *Supra* note 12, at Chapter 9: Inheritance and Nationality.
16 U. N. General Assembly, *Report of the Independent Expert for the United Nations Study on Violence against Children*, U.N. Doc. A/61/299 (Aug. 29, 2006).
17 Global Initial to End All Corporal Punishment, *Countdown to Universal Prohibition*, https://endcorporalpunishment.org/countdown/.
18 Orphan Outreach, *Kenya* (Nov. 3, 2020), https://orphanoutreach.org/country/kenya.
19 In many places – Ghana, Kenya, Uganda – these are private institutions operated by charities or faith based organisations, or civil society groups.
20 https://www.unicef.org.au/blog/news-and-insights/january-2016/2016-predicted-to-be-worst-year-for-children (accessed Dec. 4, 2020).
21 African Committee of Experts on the Rights and Welfare of the Child (ACERWC), Continental Study on the Impact of Armed Conflict and Crises on Children in Africa (2016), https://www.acerwc.africa/studies-research/.
22 *See* ACERWC, *Mapping Children on the Move within Africa* (2018).
23 African Child Policy Forum, *Child Law Resources*, https://www.africanchildforum.org/clr/.
24 The author has been a consultant to the reform process in Namibia and Zimbabwe, which is ongoing at the time of writing.
25 There have been significant constitutional court decisions on child marriage and on corporal punishment of children emanating from the highest court in Zimbabwe. *See infra* 2.3 below.
26 Julia Sloth-Nielsen, *Children's Rights Jurisprudence in South Africa – A 20 Year Retrospective*, 52 De Jure 501 (2019), http://dx.doi.org/10.17159/2225-7160/2019/v52a29.
27 Law No 32/2016 Governing Persons and Family (2016).
28 The author is a member of the team that is undertaking this assignment.
29 A copy of this law and its full title could not be found. *See also* United States State Department, *Republic of Congo*, https://www.justice.gov/eoir/page/file/1323521/download (referencing its December 2019 adoption).

30 The author has been consulted in relation to both processes.

31 ACERWC, *Agenda 2040: Fostering an Africa Fit for Children – Assessment of the First Phase of Implementation (2016–2020)* 55 (forthcoming).

32 *Id.* at 66. *See also* Burundi, Portant Prevention, Protection Des Victimes et Repression Des Violences Basees Sur Le Genre [Protection and Prevention of Gender Based Violence] [Burundi], https://www.africanchildforum.org/clr/Legislation%20Per%20Country/2018%20Update/Burundi/burundi_preventionprotectionofvictimsandrepressionofgender-basedviolence_2016_fr.pdf.

33 ACERWC, *General Comment No. 5 on State Party Obligations Under the African Charter on the Rights and Welfare of the Child (Article 1) and Systems Strengthening for Child Protection* 31, par. 6.1 (2018).

34 *Id.*

35 *See* The Social Service Workforce, http://www.socialserviceworkforce.org/ (last visited Oct. 21, 2020).

36 The African Child Policy Forum (ACPF), Spotlighting the Invisible: Justice for children in Africa (2018), https://app.box.com/s/qchz99m0x9q0iz378a95upnh57nxcu2m.

37 These can be found in (for instance) Namibia, Zimbabwe, Malawi, and Tanzania.

38 Diversion is central to the Child Justice Act 75 of 2008, in operation from April 1, 2010.

39 Diversion has been piloted since 2009 and is now available in 16 districts. Although currently based on policy guidelines drafted by a steering committee headed by a Judge, legislation to formalise diversion is at an advanced stage of preparation. The author was a consultant at an earlier stage of the legislative drafting process.

40 *Children's Legal Protection Center*, African Child Policy Forum, https://www.africanchildforum.org/index.php/en/special-pages/children-s-legal-protection-center. This service now resorts under the Federal Supreme Court. The criminal justice policy of Ethiopia adopted by the Ministry of Justice in 2011 has a section that deals with the issue of young offenders. The policy in this section provides for the establishment of separate benches, police departments, and prosecutions. In addition, it envisages the need to have alternative disposition measures applicable for young offenders. Separate police divisions (Child Protection Unit, CPU) for juveniles are also operating (without legal basis) in Addis Ababa, and in regional states in Adama, Bahirdar, Dessie, Diredawa, Shashemene, Awassa, and Wolayta Sodo. The other de facto measure taken is the institutionalisation of diversion. Community Based Correction Centers (CBCCs) in Addis Ababa, Adama, Bahirdar, Dessie, and Dire Dawa. CBCCs were first introduced by Ethiopian based NGO, Forum for Sustainable Child Empowerment (FSCE) in conjunction with Addis Ababa City Police Commission in 2004. *See* Tsegaye Deda Baffa, Child Protection and Child Friendly Justice: Lessons Learned from the Program in Ethiopia 4 (2012).

41 ACPF, *supra* note 36, at 55.

42 On August 22, 2019 – The Uganda Police Force and UNICEF – United Nations Children's Fund – have launched Diversion Guidelines that allow children below 18 years who commit petty offences to be rehabilitated instead of being tried in court. According to the Justice, Law and Order Sector Annual Report 2017/18, the national diversion rate is 76.3%. Kampala, *Guidelines to Promote the Rights of Children in Conflict with the Law are Launched*, UNICEF Uganda (Aug. 22, 2019), https://www.unicef.org/uganda/press-releases/guidelines-promote-rights-children-conflict-law-are-launched.

43 Zambia adopted a National Diversion Framework to standardise principles and practices in diversion in 2018. *See* Republic of Zambia, Ministry of Community Development and Social Services, National Diversion Framework, 2018.

44 *Rebecca Gyumi v. Attorney General*, Tanzania Civil Cause 5 (2016).

45 Civil Appeal 204 of 2017.

46 *Mudzuru & Another v. Ministry of Justice, Legal & Parliamentary Affairs (N.O.) & Others* (Const. Application No. 79/14, CC 12-15) [2015] ZWCC 12 (Jan. 20, 2016);

Julia Sloth-Nielsen et al., *Mudzuru & Another v the Minister of Justice, Legal and Parliamentary Affairs & 2 Others: A Review*, 16 Afr. Hum. Rts. L.J 554 (2016).

47 *S v. Chokuramba*, Judgment No CCZ 10-2019 (2019); *See also* S. Mutsvara, *A New Culture for Juvenile Sentencing: S v Chokuramba and the End of Judicial Corporal Punishment in Zimbabwe*, SACJ (forthcoming 2020).

48 High Court of Kenya Constitutional and Human Rights Division Constitutional Petition No. 347 (2015). *See* Rongedzayl Fambasayi & Admark Moyo, *The Best Interests of the Child Offender in the Context of Detention as a Measure of Last Resort: A Comparative Analysis of Legal Developments in South Africa, Kenya and Zimbabwe*, 36 South African J. on Hum. Rts. 25 (2020), https://www.tandfonline.com/action/showCitFormats?doi=10.1080/02587203.2020.1775495.

49 Sloth-Nielsen, *supra* note 25. *See* Ann Skelton, *Child Justice in South Africa: Application of International Instruments in the Constitutional Court*, Int'l. J. on Child. Rts. 391–422 (2018).

50 Senegal, *State Party Reports*, https://www.unicefirc.org/portfolios/documents/436_senegal.htm.

51 U. N. Committee on Rights of the Child (CRC), *Combined Third to Fifth Periodic Reports Submitted by Mauritania under Article 44 of the Convention, due in 2013*, para 198, UN Doc. CRC/C/MRT/3-5 (Jan. 10, 2017).

52 ACFP, *supra* note 36.

53 UNICEF Ghana, *A New Child-friendly Court Established in Accra* (Dec. 4, 2018), https://www.unicef.org/ghana/press-releases/new-child-friendly-court-established-accra#:~:text=4th%20December%202018%20%2D%20The%20Judicial,age%20appropriate%20procedures%20and%20tools.

54 Criminal Law and Related Matters Amendment Bill 17 of 2020.

55 The author is a member of a team that has been awarded the assignment to develop training materials for the police college curriculum.

56 ACFP, Africa The New Frontier for Intercountry Adoption (2012), https://www.childwatch.uio.no/news/2012/africa---the-new-frontier-for-intercountry-adoption-en.pdf.

57 The Hague Convention on the Civil Aspects of International Child Abduction has been ratified by fewer African states, namely Burkina Faso, Gabon, Guinea, Lesotho, Mauritius, Morocco, Seychelles, South Africa, Tunisia, Zimbabwe, and Zambia. South Africa has an active Central Authority and dedicated domestic legislation to provide for Hague Abduction proceedings. By contrast, Zimbabwe has yet to identify its Central Authority.

58 J. Sloth-Nielsen, *Presentation to the Africa Conference on the Implementation of the Hague Conventions in Africa* (Mar. 2019)(unpublished manuscript). *See* Vanessa Cordeiro, *The Right of the Child Born Through a Surrogacy Agreement in Kenya* (Unpublished LLM dissertation, University of Leiden, 2019).

59 Find Surrogate Mother, https://www.findsurrogatemother.com/surrogate-mothers/botswana.

60 See, e.g., World Bank State of social safety nets 2018 report, https://openknowledge.worldbank.org/handle/10986/29115; UNICEF, *Towards Universal Social Protection for Children*, https://www.unicef.org/media/49401/file/Towards%20universal%20social%20protection%20for%20children.pdf.

61 An exception is South Africa, whose Child Support Grant (reaching 12 million children monthly through the application of the filter of a means test) is rooted in the Social Assistance Act 9 of 2004.

62 *See* ACERWC, *supra* note 30, at 99–100.

63 In 1999, once 15 ratifications had been achieved.

64 *See supra* note 45.

65 Countries that have adopted dedicated anti-trafficking legislation include Angola, Burkina Faso, Cameroon, Central African Republic, Djibouti, Egypt, Ghana, Guinea

Bissau, Kenya, Malawi, Mali, Mauritius, Morocco, Mozambique, Namibia, Niger, Nigeria, Senegal, Sierra Leone, South Africa, Sudan, Tanzania, Tunisia, Uganda, and Zambia. *See supra* note 45.

66 Article 35 provides that "State Parties shall take all appropriate national, bilateral and multilateral measure to prevent the abduction of, the sale of or traffic in children for any purpose or in any form."

67 The Ombudsperson for Children Act of Mauritius 2003. The main objectives of the ombudsperson for children is to ensure that the needs, interests, and rights of children are given full recognition by public authorities, private bodies, and individuals, to promote the best interest of the child, and to encourage the implementation of the CRC and ACRWC. The Office of the ombudsperson for children also has the capacity to receive complaints and take action. The Office of the ombudsperson for children is regarded as an important institution, with the budget for the Office being allocated directly from the Prime Minister and the Office also received increasingly more power. *See The Role, Powers and Functions of the Ombudsperson for Children*, Ombudsperson for Children's Office, www.oco.govmu.org.

68 National Children's Commission Act 12 of 2019 (Malawian Children's Commission Act).

69 The Western Cape Children's Commissioners Act, No. 2 of 2019.

70 Such as in South Africa and Kenya, to name two instances.

71 Nial Patrick Walsh, *Why Africa is the Future of Megacities*, Arch Daily (Nov. 6, 2019), https://www.archdaily.com/927842/why-africa-is-the-future-of-megacities.

72 *See* Julia Sloth-Nielsen et al., *Does the Differential Criterion for Vesting Parental Rights and Responsibilities of Unmarried Parents Violate International Law? A Legislative and Social Study of Three African Countries*, 55 J. of Afr. L. 203–229 (2011).

73 C Phillips, *Child-headed Households: A Feasible Way Forward, or an Infringement of Children's Right to Alternative Care?* (2007) (referring to South Africa, Namibia, and Uganda in this regard).

74 Article 21. The ACERWC has also released a General Comment on Child Marriage.

75 See, e.g., UN CRC, *General Comment No. 3 HIV Aids and the Rights of the Child*, UN Doc. CRC/GC/2003/3 par 20 (2003); UN CRC, *General Comment No. 4 Adolescent Sexual Health and Development*, UN Doc. CRC/GC/2003/4 par 28 (2003); UN CRC, *General Comment No. 20 on the Rights of the Child in Adolescence*, UN Doc. CRC/C/GC/20, par 33 (2016); UN CRC, *General Comment No. 18 on Children's Rights and Harmful Cultural Practice*, par 68, UN Doc. CRC/C/GC/18/REV.1/E (2019).

76 ACERWC, *supra* note 21, at 82.

77 *Id.*

78 *Id.* at 86.

79 *Id.* at 95.

80 *See* ACFP, *supra* note 36, at chapter 5: Children and informal justice systems (p 82 et seq).

81 *Id.*

82 To the CRC Committee, the African Committee of Experts on the Rights and welfare of the Child, via the Universal Periodic Review process, and in reporting processes to other relevant UN Treaty bodies.

D. Israel

4 Thirty years later

The CRC's influence on Israeli law, taking stock and moving forward

Tamar Morag

Introduction

Israel ratified the UN Convention on the Rights of the Child (CRC) in 1991,[1] an act that did not seem particularly significant at the time and was not accompanied by meaningful public discussion or controversy. The ratification appeared as a mainly symbolic and rhetorical affirmation of the obvious – Israel's commitment to children. Based on the lack of controversy, it would seem that few, if any, expected much by way of actual change on the ground as a consequence of Israel joining the CRC. The realization that the CRC bears a message that has resulted in profound changes in the way we think about children and act on matters affecting them has come gradually. In this chapter, I address both the significant change in Israeli law that has been tied to the CRC as well as the limits of this change. I will confine myself to the CRC's influence on Israeli law, even though its effects are discernible in social discourse, academic scholarship, and in the day-to-day practice of many professionals in Israel.

This chapter is divided into three parts. The first part discusses the recognition of the CRC as a new conceptual basis for the body of law relating to children in Israel. The second part addresses the scope and limits of the change through a critical examination of the implementation in Israeli law of the CRC's four guiding principles – non-discrimination, the child's best interests, the right to life survival and development, and the right to participation. In the third and last part, I take stock and look forward. In 1987, in response to an initiative of the Israeli National Council for the Child, the Ministry of Justice appointed a public committee charged with re-evaluating the entire body of Israeli child law in light of the CRC.[2] The extensive work of this committee is one of the most ambitious attempts of any legal system to promote the CRC's systematic implementation.[3] The six detailed reports submitted, which dealt with various spheres of children's life, created a platform for absorbing not only the CRC into Israeli law, but also the extensive body of interpretive work on its provisions developed by the UN Committee on the Rights of the Child. The work of this committee, which was chaired by Tel Aviv District Judge Savyona Rotlevi and of which I served as the vice-chair, significantly enhanced the CRC's influence on Israeli legislation and case law.

Recognition of the CRC as a new conceptual basis for laws on children in Israel

A series of legislative measures and judicial rulings adopted in Israel since the ratification of the CRC contains various declarations about its broad acceptance as a new comprehensive conceptual basis for laws affecting children. These statements convey the recognition that Israeli law is deeply committed to the spirit of the CRC and to the broad perceptual change it entails.

Several statutes refer explicitly to the CRC, as a whole, as providing the conceptual and normative basis for its provisions. For example, the Law on the Rights of Students states in section 1: "The purpose of this law is to set the principles for the rights of the student in the spirit of human dignity and of the UN International Convention on the Rights of the Child."[4] Similarly, section 1 of the Law on Foster Care for Children states, "The purpose of this law is to ground the rights of children in foster care and the duty of the state to protect their welfare and their rights according to the Convention on the Rights of the Child."[5] This law places children and their rights at the center and defines government actions on behalf of children in foster care through the lens of children's rights.

Another prominent piece of legislation that adopts the CRC as its normative foundation is the Law on Information about the Influence of Legislation on Children's Rights.[6] The law requires that the rationale accompanying every bill submitted to the Israeli Parliament detail its implications for the rights of children, their living conditions, and the services provided to them. The rationale, which is attached to the bill of this law, explicitly states that its purpose is to ensure that every bill takes into account its effect on children's rights "in the spirit of the CRC."[7]

The case law shows a similar commitment of Israeli law to the profound conceptual change conveyed by the CRC. For example, in a decision dealing with the custody of children whose mother had joined the Jehovah's Witnesses sect, former Chief Justice Meir Shamgar explicitly relied on the CRC in ruling, "The approach encapsulated in the concept of children's rights is this: the child is an autonomous creature, with rights and interests independent of those of his or her parents."[8]

A Supreme Court ruling issued in 2000 dealt with the legitimacy of parents using corporal punishment to discipline their child.[9] Chief Justice Dorit Beinisch referred to the period after the CRC's ratification as "a new era" and stated that "today, in the era after the legislation of Basic Law: Human Dignity and Liberty, and after Israel has ratified the UN Convention on the Rights of the Child,"[10] the corporal punishment of children could no longer be allowed. These and several other rulings issued in the 1990s after Israel's ratification of the CRC reveal a commitment to the new conceptual approach emerging from it.[11]

Both the legislation and the case law in Israel indicate a declarative adoption of the CRC as a whole and, as explicitly formulated in some cases, of the "spirit of the CRC." Israeli law thereby recognizes that the importance of adopting the CRC lies not only in endorsing its specific provisions, but also, and perhaps mainly, in endorsing a new approach regarding the status of children and their recognition as rights bearers. This declarative endorsement of children's rights according to the CRC and its spirit is extremely significant, even prior to and apart from the more detailed examination of the extent to which its specific principles were indeed adopted in Israeli law. The main import of such declarations is in their effect on broad areas of legislation, of life, and on the change in consciousness that they promote. Nevertheless, we must also examine the actual implementation of this new approach in the legal realm and the following section attempts to show that the four principles of the CRC are a suitable tool for this purpose.

Taking stock: the scope of the change in light of the CRC's four principles

The UN Committee on the Rights of the Child ("CRC Committee") is an independent expert body responsible for interpreting and implementing the CRC. The CRC Committee defined four sections in the CRC as general basic principles to be used as the lens for reading, interpreting, and implementing its provisions: non-discrimination, the best interests of the child, the child's life, survival and development, and participation. The CRC Committee pointed to these principles as mutually supportive, complementary, and as jointly conveying a holistic approach. The ongoing endeavor to interpret these principles is the main impulse behind the development of a comprehensive approach on the essence and characteristics of the rights of the child according to the CRC and for promoting changes in the child's status in the law and in society within its context. Seemingly, then, when considering the extent to which the spirit of the CRC has penetrated Israeli law and leveraged actual change, these four principles afford the best tool.[12] My discussion of these principles' effect on Israeli law proceeds in a downward progression. I will begin with the principle that has had the most significant effect on Israeli law and conclude with the one that has had the least effect.

The participation principle

The principle of participation is anchored in Article 12 of the CRC, which states:

1 States Parties shall assure to the child who is capable of forming his or her own views the right to express those views freely in all matters affecting the child, the views of the child being given due weight in accordance with the age and maturity of the child.

2 For this purpose, the child shall in particular be provided the opportunity to be heard in any judicial and administrative proceedings affecting the child, either directly, or through a representative or an appropriate body, in a manner consistent with the procedural rules of national law.[13]

The right to participation as formulated in Article 12 includes three main components: the right to express views, the right to do so freely, and the right to have those views given due weight. Accompanying this right is the right to receive information.[14] The right to participation was defined by the CRC Committee as a symbol of the change process in the perception of the rights of the child expressed in the CRC:

> The new and deeper meaning of this right is that it should establish *a new social contract*. One by which children are fully recognized as rights-holders who are not only entitled to receive protection but also have the right to participate in all matters affecting them, a right which can be considered as the symbol for their recognition as rights-holders.[15]

This right to participation is the principle that has been most widely and significantly implemented in Israeli legislation and case law. A series of legislative amendments designed to implement the right of children to participate in various realms of life was enacted following Israel's ratification of the CRC. All these amendments define participation as the minor's right, refer explicitly to the principle of participation in section 12 of the CRC, and formulate the amendment by relying on this section's wording. Most of these laws stipulate detailed provisions specifying the mode of hearing children and providing meaningful participation. For example, a comprehensive amendment of the Youth Law (Judgement, Punishment, and Treatment) 1971, dealing with delinquent youth, devotes a long chapter to the right of minors in criminal trials to information and participation in all decisions bearing on their punishment and treatment and to the explanation of all decisions affecting them.[16] An amendment to the Law on Working Youths 1953, authorizing the Minister of Labor and Welfare to grant permits allowing children to be employed in public performances, or in advertising, anchored the right of children to participate in the decision to grant a permit.[17] Another amendment concerns legislation dealing with children as witnesses. The Law on the Rules of Evidence (protection of children) 1955, allows minors who are victims of incest or of sex offenses to refuse to testify and enables a children's investigator to appear in court instead.[18] Special procedures were also determined for children who do testify in such cases.[19] According to an amendment to the law, no decision is to be made about the testimony of children on such offenses nor about the mode of their testimony before they are given an opportunity to express their view on these matters.[20]

Following the ratification of the CRC, the most comprehensive legislative reform furthering child participation adopted into Israeli law relates to children's participation in divorce proceedings. To enable the participation of children in these proceedings and in line with the public committee's recommendations, special regulations regarding child participation in family courts have been enacted.[21] According to these regulations, special welfare units staffed by social workers were established within the family courts. Children aged six and older involved in divorce cases are invited to attend a meeting with a social worker.[22]

At this meeting, children are given the opportunity to express their feelings, attitudes, and desires.[23] The children can choose whether to have their wishes conveyed by a social worker or meet personally with the judge dealing with the case.[24] Every child who wishes to meet with the judge has a right to do so.[25] Whatever the child says remains confidential, whether told to the judge or to the social worker.[26]

A series of Supreme Court rulings also show increasing recognition of the child's right to be heard on issues affecting them as an independent right that follows from the CRC. For example, Justice Arbel notes, "Hearing the child's wishes, a right that is also anchored in section 12 of the UN CRC, conveys the view of the child as an autonomous person, as a rights bearer."[27] In recent years, hundreds of decisions in lower judicial instances have increasingly included statements in a similar spirit.[28] A significant rise has also been recorded in the scope of children's hearings by the courts, particularly in proceedings conducted in family courts.[29]

And yet, despite the considerable influence of the CRC on the case law and on judicial practice, the participation principle cannot be said to have been fully endorsed, either in theory or in practice. Despite a significant increase in child participation in many cases, according to studies on the issue, children are still *not* heard.[30] The limited research that has been conducted so far in Israel suggests initial explanations for the gap between the declarative stance on children's right to participation and its actual implementation, including the ambivalent attitudes of social workers and judges towards it, as well as concerns about a heavier workload. One interesting finding that emerged in the study touched on some of the judges' avoidance of children's participation due to the emotional strains evoked by the hearings, where they faced the children's distress without any tools to help them.

The main difficulty, however, concerns the weight assigned to children's views when they *are* heard. Israeli case law – and Israeli jurisprudence does not appear to be exceptional in this regard – emphasizes the right of children to be heard but hardly touches on the weight to be accorded to their views.[31] The scant research on this topic indicates that children's views tend to be assigned little weight.[32]

The best interests of the child principle

The best interests of the child principle is anchored in section 3 of the CRC: "In all actions concerning children, whether undertaken by public or private social welfare institutions, courts of law, administrative authorities or legislative bodies, the best interests of the child shall be a primary consideration."[33] According to the CRC Committee, the child's best interests is a threefold concept: (1) a substantive right of the child to have his or her best interests assessed and taken as a primary consideration when various interests are being considered in order to reach a decision on the issue at stake; (2) a fundamental, interpretative legal principle if a legal provision is open to more than one interpretation; and (3) a rule of procedure for whenever a decision is to be made that will affect a specific child, an identified group of children, or children in general, the decision-making process must include an evaluation of the possible impact (positive or negative) of the decision on the child or children concerned. Assessing and determining the best interests of the child requires procedural guarantees.[34]

One of the main innovations of the CRC Committee on the Rights of the Child is the CRC's innovative holistic interpretation of the relationship between this principle and other rights. The CRC Committee has recurrently stressed that the CRC must be read as a whole.[35] Therefore, in determining the best interests of the child, the full range of child's rights should be considered. The child's best interests are not in tension or in contrast with specific children's rights, including children's liberties and their right to participation, which must all be considered when examining this principle. This holistic view was adopted and developed by the Israeli CRC committee,[36] which recommended redefining the best interests of the child principle in Israeli legislation and case law as "the range of the rights, the needs, and the interests of the child."[37] The committee thereby sought to adopt the holistic interpretation endorsed by the CRC Committee stating that, when considering the best interests of the child, all their rights and interests must be taken into account.[38]

The best interests of the child principle was recognized as significant in Israeli law prior to the CRC's ratification, but had been perceived in vague, subjective, and paternalistic terms.[39] After the ratification, attempts to imbue new meaning into the best interests principle are evident in both legislation and case law.[40] The new formulation of the best interests of the child as "the range of rights needs and interests" has been adopted in the foster care and adoption laws.[41] It is also well reflected in dozens of judicial rulings.[42] In the words of the Tel Aviv Family Court,

> Today, new meaning should be ascribed to the concept of 'best interest of the child,' shifting from the paternalistic perspective that had been at its focus to one that views the child as a whole person, as an independent and autonomous rights bearer.[43]

Rarely, however, do the courts go beyond references to the new conceptualization to actually examine and balance the full range of relevant rights.[44] Discussions are still mainly paternalistic and fail to address the relevant rights in any meaningful way, particularly those touching on participation and on children's liberties.[45]

When discussing the best interests of the child principle and the need to move away from amorphous and ambiguous uses of it, the Israeli CRC Committee considered proposing not only a change in the content of the best interests principle, but also a change in its name. It was decided to keep the name; however, this may have been a mistake as the courts' reliance on a long legacy, and even inertia in the way the best interests standard is applied, appear to be extremely difficult to change.

The life and survival and development principle

The life and survival and development principle is anchored in section 6 of the CRC, which states:

1 States Parties recognize that every child has the inherent right to life.
2 States Parties shall ensure to the maximum extent possible the survival and development of the child.[46]

Of the three elements joined in this principle – the right to life, survival, and development – the right to development has been acknowledged as a keystone in the recognition of children's rights as formulated in the CRC.[47] This right points to a fundamental difference between children and adults: children are in a process of swift and vulnerable growth that imposes special obligations on both the parents and the state to ensure its optimal development. The right to development imposes positive obligations on the state to ensure the optimal course for the child's transition from immaturity to maturity, while addressing broad and diverse aspects of children's lives and needs adopting a forward-looking perspective. In discussing this principle, I limit myself to the right to development. After the CRC, some allusions to the right to development can be found in Israel's legislation and case law. Thus, the Law on Children's Foster Care defined, for the first time, the right to personal development as a right of children.[48] Several court decisions have also referred to the right to development.[49] The Supreme Court defined the right to development as the right underlying the authority and obligation of the state to protect children at risk:

> The purpose of the law is to involve the authorities in the concern for minors in distress, to offer a helping hand to ensure their survival, to assist in their rehabilitation, and to enable them to grow in an environment where they can follow a natural course of development physically, mentally, intellectually, and socially, and realize their potential (section 6 of the CRC).[50]

In a ruling of the Jerusalem District Court on a case dealing with the corporal punishment of children, the Court relied on the CRC and on the reports of the public committee and stated,

> The right to development: childhood is a stage of constant growth, experimentation, learning, change, and exposure. It is an extremely dramatic and intensive process, vital and central to the child's development ... The gradual development process that minors undergo, involving the development of many personality aspects, compels fulfillment of the physical, mental, social, and cultural needs that they are entitled to.[51]

The Tel Aviv District Court, overturned the lower court's decision to place a 17-year-old girl illegally residing in Israel in a detention center.[52] In overturning the lower court's ruling, the court relied on the CRC, emphasizing the potential effect of the detention on her development.[53]

These legislative and judicial references to the right to development are extremely important because they attest to some percolation of its recognition as a right unique to children in Israeli law. Nevertheless, no breakthrough is yet discernible, either in the legislation or in the case law, concerning recognition of the state's positive obligations. Thus, for example, the right of children at risk to protection and the state obligations deriving from it have not yet been anchored comprehensively in the legislation. No Supreme Court ruling has yet determined that the state must be compelled to engage in specific actions or provide specific services to children due to the state's obligation to ensure the proper development of children.

The implementation of the right to development is not a simple task and will require complex thinking on the scope of the state's obligations. Yet, the very recognition that this right imposes clear and new obligations on society that have yet to be fulfilled is key to the potential for change in supporting this essential principle.

The non-discrimination principle

The equality principle is anchored in section 2 of the CRC, which states:

1 States Parties shall respect and ensure the rights set forth in the present Convention to each child within their jurisdiction without discrimination of any kind, irrespective of the child's or his or her parent's or legal guardian's race, color, sex, language, religion, political or other opinion, national, ethnic or social origin, property, disability, birth or other status.
2 States Parties shall take all appropriate measures to ensure that the child is protected against all forms of discrimination or punishment on the basis of the status, activities, expressed opinions, or beliefs of the child's parents, legal guardians, or family members.[54]

Not only does the CRC apply the non-discrimination principle to children, but it also seeks to protect them from specific forms of discrimination. Section 2(2) of the CRC prohibits discrimination of children based on the status, activities, expressed opinions, or beliefs of their parents or guardians. The main innovation of this section involves recognition of children's right to be accepted in society as separate persons and precludes discriminating against them in any way as a result of the actions by their parents or guardians. Beyond this, however, ensuring children's equality according to the CRC imposes enhanced obligations on the state. One of the main justifications for such enhanced obligations is the need to read the principle of non-discrimination together with the principle of development, based on the assumption that discriminating against children is potentially harmful to their development. Children who are victims of discrimination in the context of healthcare, education, or personal safety are children whose development could be irreversibly harmed.

This principle of non-discrimination, as articulated in the CRC, is adopted into some of the legislation, such as the law on foster care and the municipality ordinance.[55] And yet, its impact on Israeli law has so far been negligible. A review of all published Israeli case law finds no mention of Article 2 nor any discussion of the unique importance of non-discrimination for children. The case law referring to the discrimination against children focuses on education and special education. To explain the relevance of equality in those cases, the Supreme Court relies on its own precedents and on international conventions rather than on the equality principle in section 2 of the CRC.[56] In light of the great challenges confronting Israel regarding discrimination of many groups of children (Arab children, Ethiopian children, children from the periphery, girls, boys, children with disabilities, and many other groups), the CRC's lack of influence in this area is extremely troubling.

Summary

Attempts to sum up the influence of the CRC on Israeli law are confronted with a complex reality. On the one hand, the CRC had a profound impact on Israeli law relating to children. The CRC has served as a platform for leveraging a deep conceptual change in Israeli law, touching on the actual recognition of children as rights bearers and on the unique characteristics of children's rights. At the same time, the limits of the CRC's transformative effect on Israeli law are also evident.

What explains these limits, and what can be done to enhance the CRC's effects? I suggest three possible explanations for the limits of the CRC's influence on Israeli law. First, Israeli law is still in the process of transforming and improved implementation will come with time. This is an optimistic, possibly overly optimistic, explanation. A second potential explanation for the limits of the CRC's influence relies on its life cycle. After reaching a peak in its early years, and especially after the CRC Committee's reports, its impact has declined. Indeed, the number of Supreme Court cases mentioning the CRC, which peaked in 2005, two years after the CRC Committee submitted its reports in 2003, has since declined.[57] The third and final explanation focuses on the text of the CRC itself and its interpretation. The CRC presents a non-extreme, holistic approach. It is because of this moderation that the CRC could be adopted in Israel and in many other countries with little opposition. This approach has been key to its success. The downside of this moderate approach, however, is a limited ability to mobilize more transformative reforms.

What can be done to enhance the CRC's influence? Domestically, Israeli policy-makers, and society in general, should keep alive the discussion of its implementation, monitor its influence and possible infringements, and constantly endeavor to enlarge its impact. Internationally, a comparative analysis of the CRC's impact in various jurisdictions should be expanded. Lessons from successful implementation stories should be heeded. But, no less important, we should also use the comparative lens to locate and define common obstacles to the CRC's full enactment. Such insights can assist in the important interpretive work of the CRC Committee and, with time, may even lead to amendments in the CRC itself.

Notes

1 U.N. Convention on the Rights of the Child, opened for signature (Nov. 20, 1989), 1577 U.N.T.S. 3 (entered into force Sep. 2, 1990) [hereinafter *CRC*]. For a discussion of the CRC's influence on Israeli child law *see* Tamar Morag, *The Principles of the UN Convention on the Rights of the Child and Their Influence on Israeli Law*, 22 Mich. St. Int'l L. Rev. 531 (2014) [hereinafter *The Influence of the CRC*]; Tamar Morag, *The Recognition of Children's Rights in Israeli Case Law: A Spiral Progression*, 28 Isr. Stud. Rev. 282 (2013) [hereinafter *Spiral Progression*]; Tamar Morag, *The Case Law after Israel's Ratification of the UN Convention on the Rights of the Child: Indeed a New Era? in* Children's Rights and Israeli Law, 21 (Tamar Morag ed., 2010) (Hebrew) [hereinafter *The Case Law*].

2 Tamar Morag, *The Influence of the Committee for the Review of Basic Principles in the Realm of the Child and the Law on the Depth Perceptions of Israeli Case Law*, 3 Fam. L. 67 (2009) [hereinafter *The Influence of the Committee*].

3 Tamar Peled Amir, *The Report of the Israeli Public Committee* 31–39 (2003) (Isr.). The committee is known as the Public Committee for the Implementation of the CRC and its official name was: "The Committee for the Review of Basic Principles in the Realm of the Child and the Law and their Implementation in Legislation." The Committee was appointed by the then Minister of Justice, Tsahi Hanegbi, on June 27, 1997 (*Id.*, at 15–31). For the committee's reports see – The Israeli Justice Department, https://www.justice.gov.il/Units/YeutzVehakika/NosimMishpatim/HavaadLeZhuyot/Pages/DochKliali.aspx (Hebrew).

4 Rights of Students Law, 5761-2000, § 1, SH 1761 42 (Isr.).

5 Law of Foster Care for Children, 5776-2016, § 1, SH 2534 586 (Isr.).

6 Law on Information about the Influence of the Legislation on Children's Rights, 5762-2002, SH 1859 486 (Isr.).

7 *See* Draft Proposed Law on Information about the Influence of the Legislation on Children's Rights, 5762-2002, SH 3125 608 (Isr.).

8 CivA 2266/93 *Anonymous v. Anonymous*, 46 (1) PD 221, 248 (1995) (Isr.).

9 CivA 4596/98 *Jane Doe v. State of Israel*, 54(1) PD 145 (2000) (Isr.).

10 *Id.* at 185.

11 In turning to the CRC, Israeli case law relies on the presumption of a fit between Israeli legislation and the provisions of the Convention. For the first anchoring of this presumption in a judicial ruling, *see* CivA 3112/94 *Abu Hassan v. State of Israel*, 53(1) PD 422 (1999) (Isr.). For rulings linking Israel's ratification of the U.N. Convention on the Rights of the Child to the development of a deep conceptual change, *see also* Further Hearing CivA 7015/94 *State of Israel v. Jane Doe*, 50(1) PD 48 (1995) (Isr.) (Justice Dorner's ruling); CivA 6106/92 *Jane Doe v. State of Israel*, 48(4) PD 221 (1994). (Isr.).

12 *See* U.N. Committee on the Rights of the Child, *General Guidelines Regarding the Form and Content of Initial Reports to be Submitted by States Parties under Article 44, Paragraph 1(a), of the Convention*, U.N. Doc. CRC/C/5, para. 13 (Oct. 15, 1991); *see also* Comm. on the Rights of the Child, *General Guidelines for Periodic Reports*, U.N. Doc. CRC/C/58, para. 40 (Oct. 11, 1996). For the role of the four principles in the work of the Israeli CRC Committee, see Peled Amir, *supra* note 3, at 101–102. For a discussion of the principles and their interpretations see Tamar Morag, *20 Years Later: Children's Rights and Children's Image According to the U.N. Convention on the Rights of the Child*, *in* Child. Rts. and Israeli L., Hamishpat L. Rev (in collaboration with Ramot press) 15 (Tamar Morag ed., 2010) (Hebrew).

13 *Id.* at art. 12.

14 *Id.* at art. 32.

15 U.N. CRC Committee, *Day Of General Discussion On The Right Of The Child To Be Heard*, U.N. Docs. 11-29 (Sept. 29, 2006) (emphasis added) *available at* http://

www2.ohchr.org/english/bodies/crc/docs/discussion/Final_Recommendations_after_DGD.doc.

16 Youth Law (Trial, Punishment and Modes of Treatment), 5731-1971, § 1B, SH 2171 688 (Isr.).

17 Law on Working Youths, 5731-1973, § 4, SH 1673 256 (Isr.).

18 Amendment to the Law on the Rules of Evidence (Protection of Children), 5715-1955, § 2, SH 184 96 (Isr.).

19 *Id.*

20 Tenth Amendment of The Law of Evidence Revision (Protection of Children), 5764-2004, § 2(7), SH 1957 534 (Isr.). The bill and the explanatory note were published in the Tenth Amendment of The Law of Evidence Revision (Protection of Children), 5764-2004, HH 46 129 (Isr.).

21 Civil Procedure Regulations, 5744-1984, § 258-33(1)–258-33(12), SH 4685 2220 (Isr.).

22 *Id.* at § 258-33(4).

23 *Id.* at § 258-33(2).

24 *Id.* at § 258-33(6).

25 *Id.*

26 *Id.* at § 258-33(8).

27 FamA 5579/07 *Anonymous v. Anonymous*, Nevo Legal Database (Aug. 7, 2007) (Isr.).

28 *Spiral Progression*, *supra* note 1, at 291–292.

29 Rhona Schuz, *The Right of the Child to Participate: Theory v. Practice in the Family Courts*, 2 Fam. L. 207 (2008) (Isr.).

30 For discussion of the extent of child participation in divorce proceedings see: Tamar Morag, Dori Rivkin & Yoa Sorek, *Child Participation in Family Courts: Lessons from the Israeli Pilot Project*, 26 Int'l J. L., Pol'y & Fam. 1 (2012). Tamar Morag & Yoa Sorek, *Child Participation in Family Courts in Israel: An Account of an Ongoing Learning Process, International Perspectives and Empirical Findings on Child Participation from Social Exclusion to Child Inclusive Policies*, 157 (Tali Gal & Benedetta Faedi-Duramy eds., 2015). For discussion of child participation in child protection administrative proceedings, see Ravit Alfandari, *Evaluation of a National Reform in the Israeli Child Protection Practice Designed to Improve Children's Participation in Decision-Making*, 22 Child & Fam. Soc. Work 54 (2015).

31 *Spiral Progression*, *supra* note 1, at 290–291.

32 Morag & Sorek, *supra* note 30.

33 CRC, *supra* note 1, at Article 3(1).

34 U.N CRC Commitee, *General Comment No. 14 (2013) on the Right of the Child to Have His or Her Best Interests Taken as a Primary Consideration (art. 3, para. 1)*, CRC /C/GC/14 (2013), https://www.refworld.org/docid/51a84b5e4.html.

35 Peled Amir, *supra* note 3, at 39–43.

36 *Id.* at 137.

37 *Id. See Robert Licht–Petran, Deciding on the Case of a Girl: Toward Reconciliation between Her Best Interest and Her Rights, Child. Rts. and Israeli L. 429 (Tamar Morag ed., 2010) (Isr.).*

38 *Id.*

39 *Id.* at 436.

40 *Id.*

41 Eighth Amendment of the Adoption Law, 5771-2010, § 1(2), SH 2268 110 (Isr.). *See also* Law on Foster Care for Children, 5776-2016, § 4, SH 2534 586 (Isr.).

42 *See the Influence of the CRC*, *supra* note 1.

43 Fam C (DC TA) 54297/02 *John Doe v. John Doe*, ¶ 17 Nevo Legal Database (July 1, 2007) (Judge Juifman Isr.).

44 For a review of the Israeli case law relating to the principle of the best interests of the child after the ratification of the Convention, see *The Influence of the Committee*, *supra* note 1.

45 Geraldine van Bueren, *The International Law on the Rights of the Child* 45 (1995); Robert Mnookin, *Children's Rights: Beyond Kiddie Libbers and Child Savers*, 7 J. Clinical Child Psychol. 163 (1978).
46 CRC, *supra* note 1, at Article 6.
47 Manfred Nowak, *A Commentary on the United Nations Convention on the Rights of the Child, Article 6: The Right to Life, Survival and Development* (2005).
48 Law on Foster Care for Children, 5776-2016, § 7, SH 2534 586 (Isr.).
49 *See* court decisions discussed *infra*.
50 CivC 6041/02 *Anonymous v. Anonymous*, 58(6) PD 246, 270 (2004) (Isr.) (*citing* CRC, Sec. 6).
51 CrimC 113/03 (DC Jerusalem) *State of Israel v. Vullach*, Nevo Legal Database (July 29, 2004) (Isr.).
52 *Id.*
53 AdminA (DC TA) 000282/06 *Ajman v. State of Israel*, Nevo Legal Database (Jan. 30, 2006) (Isr.). For a similar decision see AdminA 282/06 (DC TA) *Ajman v. State of Israel*, Nevo Legal Database (Oct. 30, 2006) (Isr.).
54 CRC, *supra* note 2, at art. 2.
55 Seventy-Second Amendment of the Municipality Ordinance (New Version), 5724-1964, § 5(2), SH 1733 149 (2000) (Isr.).
56 A review of all published supreme court cases revealed no mention of Article 2 to the convention (Nevo December 2019) (Isr.). The case law, however, recurrently refers to section 28 of the CRC, which anchors the right to education and the right to equality in education. *See* for example HCJ 2599/00 *Yated: Children with Down Syndrome v. Ministry of Education*, 50(3) PD 834 (2003) (Isr.). *See also* HCJ 7245/10 *Adalah: The Legal Center for Arab Minority Rights in Israel v. Ministry of Social Affairs and Social Services*, 66(2) PD 442 (2013) (Isr.).
57 A review of all published Supreme Court cases was conducted in November 2019. In 1995–2003, there were 1–2 mentions of the Convention by the Israeli Supreme Court. In 2003, there were 5 mentions, and in 2005, 15 mentions. Since then, mentions have gradually declined (retrieved from Nevo Database).

E. United States

5 Forever owned

Children as possessions in the CRC

James G. Dwyer

The Children's Rights Convention (CRC) was, perhaps, a strategic mistake on the part of well-intentioned advocates for children. In the 1980s, they faced a choice, though they might not have recognized it. Disturbed by the suffering, mistreatment, and disrespect so many children around the world experienced, they could draft and promote a special charter of rights for children, or they could launch a campaign to enforce the rights that children already possessed as human persons under existing human rights conventions and domestic rights charters. Advocates chose the former, and in the process effectively obviated the latter possibility, by supplanting – in the minds of legal actors and scholars, though not in actual law – children's rights as humans with children's rights as children. And, the implicit conception of children reflected in the CRC's final version, after all the inevitable compromising, is not so much as persons in their own right but rather as valued appendages or, even, objects of possessory rights – of parents, of ethnic groups, of nations.

Whether children would, on the whole, have better lives today in a counter-factual world where they fully shared general human rights with other human beings, rather than having their own special set of rights, is likely impossible to calculate with confidence. This chapter simply points out troubling aspects of the CRC and concrete ways it makes children worse off, closing with the conclusion that the US refusal to ratify is likely, on balance, a good thing for children.

The special rights fallacy

An assumption prevails that if a government enacts a special charter of rights for a particular group, members of that group are thereby made better off. One might expect that historical counter-examples, such as the special "protections" wives had under coverture, would weaken that assumption. Having one's own special set of rights can mean having a very different set of rights, and whether having different rights is a good thing depends on whether those rights are stronger or weaker, better or worse, than rights others have. Specific ways special rights might actually make their holders worse off include:

- Special rights substitute for stronger general human rights.
- What special rights guarantee for rights holders is actually bad for them. For example, under coverture, wives might have been said to have a special

positive right, correlative to husbands' duty as head of household, to be physically chastised for their own good.

- Special rights invite *sui generis* "reasoning" about what the special rights holders are due, rather than extending to them the same principles developed in a similar context in adjudication of generally applicable human rights.
- Special rights relegate rights holders to a weaker enforcement mechanism.
- Special rights create the impression that the subject group has received all the protection it should receive; the work is done.

All these potential drawbacks of special rights are true of the CRC. One or more might also be true of special rights conventions for other groups, such as persons with disabilities; it is especially likely when many group members are non-autonomous and unable to challenge what convention-drafters formulate. The next section identifies specific problems with the CRC's content.

Specific deficiencies in the CRC

The CRC begins in a troubling way by prescribing a police power approach to all decisions concerning children. In its police power role, the state acts as an agent for all of society, aiming to serve collective ends and balance competing interests. This contrasts with a *parens patriae* role, in which the state acts as an agent for a dependent individual. In a *parens patriae* role, the state is a fiduciary for the individual, just like a guardian, trustee, or attorney, and therefore should be devoted exclusively to effectuating the rights and promoting the welfare of that individual, rather than balancing that individual's interests against interests of other individuals or the collective.

In dealing with non-autonomous persons, the state should act in its *parens patriae* role when deciding matters that, for autonomous persons, fall within the realm of rights-protected self-determination. For example, when prescribing what form of education or medical care non-autonomous persons will receive, from among alternatives practically available to them, or what intimate relationships they will be able to enter into with other willing persons – things autonomous persons are entitled to decide for themselves, the state should act solely to further children's interests.[1] The only justification for the state acting at all in regard to such matters is that children need an agent to act on their behalf. The state should use its police power in exerting control over children's lives only when deciding matters that ordinarily are not matters of self-determination even for autonomous adults, but rather matters as to which many or all members of society have a valid claim – for example, distribution of natural resources and regulation of inter-personal violence. Yet Article 3(1) of the CRC states: "In *all* actions concerning children… the best interests of the child shall be *a primary consideration*" (emphasis added). Making children's interests merely a *primary* consideration is wrong, morally offensive even, with respect to many of the most important decisions the state makes regarding children's lives. Article 3 should have said, instead or in addition: "In actions the state takes pursuant to its *parens patriae* authority, the best interests of the child shall be *the sole* consideration." That is the ostensible rule for some decisions US courts make regarding children, such as parenting plans at divorce or approval of adoptions. Were the US to ratify the CRC, Article 3 might be read to permit, even encourage, amending such rules so they instead explicitly prescribe a balancing of children's interests against other persons' interests or state interests – for example, rewarding people for past parenting efforts or military service, promoting feminist or other progressive aims, or compensating poor or disabled persons for their sufferings.

The next paragraph in the CRC endorses the morally offensive notion that children are appropriate objects of others' rights. Article 3(2) provides that state action to protect and nurture children is constrained by the rights of parents. Similarly, Article 14(2) commands state parties to "respect the rights … of the Parents… to provide direction to the child in the exercise of his or her rights." Why should rights of persons other than children appear in a charter of rights for children? Imagine, analogously, a charter of rights for disabled persons stating: "States will give elderly persons of diminished capacity protection and care, taking into account the rights of their children." As to both autonomous and non-autonomous adults, US law rejects the notion that direction of their lives should be a matter of anyone else's entitlement, because that would fail to respect their distinct personhood.[2] Ascription of such control rights, as opposed to duties and authority held as a matter of privilege, to caregivers or more powerful persons in a relationship misdirects moral attention and in many contexts will amount to sacrificing to some degree the interests of the subordinate persons.[3] In American law, analysis of parent-state conflicts over childrearing typically begins with a statement of parents' presumptive entitlement to do what they want and then balances children's welfare, and possibly (other) state interests, against that right, which has meant in some cases deeming parents entitled to deny their children medical care, education, or other benefits.[4] These CRC provisions would reinforce that approach.

Article 3 thus frames children as lesser persons, beings of inferior moral status, less worthy of state protection of their interests than are adults as to interests of the same sort. As discussed below, many other CRC provisions also suggest that the particular underlying, denigrating conception of children is as things owned – by parents, communities, or nations. There are numerous provisions about keeping children in custody and control of parents, but none that specify a child's right to separation from dysfunctional parents, from the outset of life or at any time thereafter.[5] Several provisions suggest kin and cultural or ethnic communities also have rights to hold on to "their" children, but there is little or nothing about a child's right to dissociate from a pervasively dysfunctional family or community or from an oppressive, invidiously discriminatory culture.

The CRC preserves this ownership structure under the guise of protecting an imputed, unqualified, grossly exaggerated interest of children in being and remaining connected to their origins – their biological parents and the parents' world, including the country where parents live and its culture. The CRC ascribes a need to partake in parents' religion and culture even to infants, and to have imposed at birth the nationality of the country where one is born, but no independent right to exit a country to secure a better life.

Following is a catalog of CRC Articles evidencing an ownership view of children. The point is not that these provisions are inherently bad; one can imagine circumstances where they would serve a true and compelling need of children, and even presume they were drafted with such circumstances in mind. But the emphasis on the child remaining in the possession of parents, kin, cultures, and nations is striking, and there is no clear acknowledgement of the potential downside to reifying such ties. At best, the CRC provides an occasional "unless that is not in the child's best interests" qualification, which merely gives nations permission to do otherwise for the sake of a child's well-being but does not require them to do so (i.e., does not accord children a right to separation from parents, kin, community, or nation when that is best for them).

First, the CRC is replete with provisions embodying the idea that children belong to and with their biological parents throughout childhood. Consider:

- Article 7(1): "right from birth ... to know and be cared for by his or her parents."
- Article 8(1): "right of the child to preserve his or her ... family relations as recognized by law."
- Article 9(1): "ensure that a child shall not be separated from his or her parents against their will, except when ... necessary for the best interests of the child."
- Article 9(3): "right of the child who is separated from one or both parents to maintain personal relations and direct contact with both parents on a regular basis, except if it is contrary to the child's best interests."
- Article 10(1): "applications by a child or his or her parents to enter or leave a State Party for the purpose of family reunification shall be dealt with by States Parties in a positive, humane and expeditious manner" [but not for the purpose of forming a new family].
- Article 10(2) "right of the child and his or her parents to leave any country, including their own, and to enter their own country..." [but no independent right of children to emigrate without parents].
- Article 11: "combat the illicit transfer and non-return of children abroad."
- Article 16(1): "No child shall be subjected to arbitrary or unlawful interference with his or her ... family ...."
- Article 21: "States Parties that recognize and/or permit the system of adoption shall ... ensure that ... the adoption is permissible in view of the child's status concerning parents ... and that, if required, the persons concerned have given their informed consent...."
- Article 22: "efforts ... to trace the parents or other members of the family of any refugee child in order to obtain information necessary for reunification with his or her family."
- Article 29(1): "the education of the child shall be directed to... development of respect for the child's parents."

These provisions heavily emphasize parental possession and control, and no provision states a right of children to avoid a relationship with biological parents who are incapable of adequate care or to exit harmful relationships.

The CRC also ascribes rights to extended family to possess a child and control the course of a child's life. Consider:

- Article 5: "respect the ... rights... of the extended family or community as provided for by local custom...."
- Article 21: "ensure that the adoption of a child ... is permissible in view of the child's status concerning ... relatives...."
- Article 22: "co-operation in any efforts ... to trace... other members of the family of any refugee child in order to obtain information necessary for reunification with his or her family."

It is certainly not inherently bad for kin to play a role in child rearing; it might usually be good for children when parents are absent or incapable. However, there is no recognition that staying with extended family could, for some children, be unimportant or bad – in particular, when dysfunctions or disadvantages pervade the family.[6]

Similarly, the CRC ascribes rights to communities and suggests an exaggerated, trumping value of culture for children that is unsupported by empirical research on child development.

- Article 8: "right of the child to preserve his or her identity."
- Article 20(3): "due regard shall be paid to the desirability of continuity in a child's upbringing and to the child's ethnic, religious, cultural and linguistic background."
- Article 29(1): "the education of the child shall be directed to... development of respect for... his or her own cultural identity, language and values."
- Article 30: "In those States in which ethnic, religious or linguistic minorities or persons of indigenous origin exist, a child belonging to such a minority or who is indigenous shall not be denied the right, in community with other members of his or her group, to enjoy his or her own culture, to profess and practise his or her own religion, or to use his or her own language."

The best evidence of the value of some cultures might be the multitudes of adults who wish to escape them – for example, women born into highly patriarchal cultures or independent thinkers born into cultures emphasizing rigid conformity – or who simply value the benefits of emigration, such as greater career or marriage opportunities elsewhere, more highly than remaining connected to the culture in which they were raised, given that the latter is likely to be less feasible in another country.[7] The CRC supposes all children need to acquire and preserve an identity imposed by parents' culture, and manifests no recognition that a child should perhaps have a right not to have an identity imposed, that some cultures impose on many children an identity that undermines their well-being, and that even positive aspects of culture might not be a significant factor in a child's life until later stages of development.[8] There are situations in which any of these provisions could serve children's true interests, but they are also easily manipulated to serve the interests of adult members of cultural or ethnic groups.

Finally, the CRC buys into the false notion that citizenship in some nation, any nation, is an unqualified good, and that statelessness is necessarily much worse for a child.

- Article 7(1): "The child shall be registered immediately after birth and shall have the right from birth ... to acquire a nationality."
- Article 8(1): "States Parties undertake to respect the right of the child to preserve his or her ... nationality."
- Article 29(1): "the education of the child shall be directed to... respect for... the national values of the country in which the child is living, the country from which he or she may originate...."
- Article 21: "inter-country adoption may be considered as an alternative means of child's care, if the child ... cannot in any suitable manner be cared for in the child's country of origin."

There is no recognition that some countries offer little or no benefits to citizens and that many nations claim power to impose duties on their citizens regardless of residence (e.g., military service, taxes) and to exercise dominion over their citizens (e.g., by prohibiting exit). Moreover, some countries provide many children with a highly adverse living environment, with little or no prospect for improvement by internal migration. Accordingly, for some children in some places, citizenship arguably is a net liability, and they would be better off stateless.

An example of CRC's harmful impact

One illustration of how the CRC embodies the trappings of what I have termed the Special Rights Fallacy is international adoption. Many countries from which international adoptees used to come in substantial numbers have shut down or severely limited the practice, some because their leaders considered it an affront to the nation's dignity, and many because UNICEF forced them to do so by threatening to withhold desperately needed aid if they did not: (a) give strong preference to domestic placements for children, e.g. by holding children in institutions for some years before making them available for international adoption and (b) ensure complete eradication of any illicit practices, such as misleading parents who drop off their children at orphanages to believe they can come back at any time in the future to reclaim their offspring.[9] The severe cutback in international adoption has denied millions of children an opportunity for a family and a flourishing life. And, it has likely exacerbated whatever illicit practices have existed; basic economic principles suggest that when fewer children are available for adoption, those who control their destiny can demand higher payments from those seeking to welcome a child into their families, and then bad actors have a greater financial incentive to secure additional children by any means possible.[10]

What does the CRC have to do with the drastic decline in international adoption? If the CRC did not exist, advocates for children would be more likely to assert rights of children under the International Convention on Civil and Political Rights (ICCPR) and other general human rights treaties, including the right of every person to exit their country of birth and to join a family that wishes to welcome them, when they or an appropriate proxy decides that is best for them among all available options. Any country that wished to stop children from leaving for this purpose would, under the jurisprudence that has developed in application of those charters when nations have prevented adults from emigrating, bear the burden of demonstrating a compelling rationale, backed by empirical evidence.[11] The flimsy rationales for shutting down international adoption offered by UNICEF, the Children's Rights Committee, and other international bodies would not come close to sufficing.

Some rationales are weak because they lack evidentiary basis, others because the underlying concerns are far less weighty than the harm of being deprived of family life and infinitely greater opportunities for flourishing. A closer look at these rationales reveals that most are adult-centered rather than principally about children's welfare. They are essentially of two types. One is that sinister forces seek to obtain children to exploit them in seriously harmful ways, i.e., trafficking for labor or sex. The second is that some unknown number of children enter into the adoption process because something illicit was done to their parents – namely, that their children were kidnapped or they were "tricked, coerced, or paid ... to relinquish children for adoption."[12]

As to the trafficking concern, although it points to scenarios in which the child clearly would be worse off as a result of an international adoption, there is little or no evidence of children actually being procured by traffickers through international adoption.[13] Traffickers of persons for labor certainly are not going to want infants at all, and traffickers of persons for sex also overwhelmingly are looking for older minors or adults. Thus, if trafficking via international adoption were common, it could be addressed by allowing inter-country adoption of only young children – the opposite of what some countries are doing. Moreover, traffickers for sexual exploitation, whether seeking older children or infants, are highly unlikely to seek to procure them through an adoption agency, one at a time, with a succession of individuals somehow posing as foreign nationals and alerting the central authority of receiving countries about the transaction. Thus, there is no evidence of sex-trade rackets using that means of obtaining victims. An individual pedophile might think of international adoption as an effective way to procure a victim and somehow conclude that this would be easier than attempting adoption or kidnapping in their own country, but it is implausible to think they would risk exposure by making a formal application in a foreign country and, again, inviting the scrutiny of their home country's central authority. Both traffickers and individual pedophiles would likely see far better prospects in the estimated 100 million children worldwide living in the streets. The counter-intuitive nature of this concern calls for greater evidence to substantiate it.[14]

As to the concern for illicit treatment of birth parents, the scenarios most people have in mind when they worry about how children in developing countries become available for international adoption are that profiteers:

- Kidnap babies from their homes.
- Kidnap teen girls and impregnate them while confining them on "baby farms," then coerce the mothers to relinquish their rights to the resulting children.
- Pay parents to hand over their baby.
- Place for adoption a baby who came into their custody legitimately by parental request, even though the parents think they can reclaim the child at any time.

All these scenarios are troubling in some way, even though some children might nevertheless be better off in the latter two scenarios. The first two scenarios are, in fact, horrific, entailing grave physical and psychological dangers for children and/or adults. It does not follow, however, that banning international adoption is a proper means of preventing any of these occurrences. Indeed, it is clearly counter-productive; all would be far less likely to occur in any given country that does permit international adoption if many other developing countries removed their bans of, or substantive restrictions on, international adoption, because this would dramatically increase the number of clearly unparented children in the world who are available for adoption, and thereby severely reduce the profit to be gained by securing a child through those illicit means.[15] In addition, in light of the high likelihood of developmental harm to children who remain parentless in developing countries as a result of the bans and substantive restrictions, such responses are utterly irrational from a child welfare perspective, undoubtedly causing far more harm than they avoid.[16] Far more sensible from that perspective would be for international bodies to change their purpose in reviewing local practices, to one of awarding certificates of ethical practice, rather than deciding whether countries may operate international adoption programs at all. Then the demand side would also be positively impacted; many people in developed countries seeking to adopt internationally, perhaps the vast majority, would likely be willing to pay some premium for that peace of mind and the confidence that they provided a family to a child who had no parents who could care for them.

Thus, arguing to limit or end international adoption for these reasons, by pointing to ways children are separated from birth parents, is not child-centered and is rarely expressed in terms of violations of children's rights; it focuses on the suffering of parents and for some critics also reflects an ideological distaste for the developed world's extraction of anything or anyone "valuable" from the developing world.[17] Such ways of thinking should have no place in the agenda-setting of international bodies that pretend to be guardians of the world's children, nor in law- and policy-making regarding an issue that should be driven by the rights and welfare of children. When children's interests coincide with those of parents, they might both be said to have rights at stake. Both, for example, might be said to have a right against any violent disruption of their relationship. This is sufficient basis for criminalizing and severely punishing kidnapping and for restoring the relationship, if the child is thereafter found, so long as that remains in the child's best interests. But to say that parents have rights that should control law and policy regarding international adoption, even to the point of banning the practice for all, should require a convincing normative argument that no one has provided. The CRC invites that way of thinking and sacrifice of children's welfare for the sake of supposed parent rights.

In contrast, analysis within the ICCPR framework and its conferral on children of a right to emigrate and to form healthy family relationships, or under other general human rights charters, would preclude a country from denying its children the possibility of emigrating for the purpose of joining a family on the grounds that some other persons (parents) might suffer as a result of their departure or that some very small percentage of them might be somewhat worse off on the whole as a result of emigrating and joining a new family. Yet there has been little legal challenge to this brute and illicit exertion of power by countries, effectively eviscerating some of children's most fundamental rights – to leave and to form intimate relationships.[18] Since the CRC was promulgated, the international child welfare community has become incapable of thinking outside of its bounds, as if the CRC completely supplanted every other source of rights for children.[19] The Hague Convention on Intercountry Adoption later supplemented the CRC in creating international standards for adoption, but it does not articulate *any* rights of children and appears intended principally to protect birth parents' interests.[20] Consider, for example, that there is no clear basis in the CRC or the Hague Convention for objecting to Russia's 2012 shutdown of its international adoption program with the US in a naked act of political retaliation.[21] American parents did challenge that action in court, but based on the European Convention on Human Rights rather than the CRC or the Hague Convention.[22]

Thus, in practice, the CRC clearly has, with respect to a voiceless and powerless group, substituted a lesser set of rights for the clear and robust rights set forth in pre-existing general human rights charters. As a matter of international law, the CRC actually does not and cannot diminish children's rights under general human rights conventions, but the international community appears oblivious to this fact.[23] Relatedly, because conversation/debate is artificially limited to the special rights framework, there is little reference in political advocacy on behalf of children or in scholarly discussion to the general principles developed in the adjudication of ICCPR rights. "Reasoning" about international adoption policies and practices is *sui generis* and *ad hoc*; international bodies and legal scholars can simply assert: international adoption raises certain concerns and therefore should be severely curtailed or entirely foreclosed. Such partial syllogisms, devoid of major premise, are rampant.

Further, what the CRC promises by way of enforcement is, even for nations that have ratified the Third Protocol, weaker than what the ICCPR provides.

For children in the majority of nations that have not adopted the Third Protocol, there is not even the possibility of individual "communication" to the CRC. Indeed, the Committee's infrequent reviews of country implementation are likely to encourage the very practices about which a child would complain.[24]

Lastly, the CRC creates the impression that it provides all that children deserve. There have been three protocols promulgated since the CRC was first issued – two expanding on children's rights in specific contexts, armed conflict and the sex industry, and the third providing for individual complaints. But otherwise, there has been little effort to expand children's rights, let alone consideration of redrafting the CRC.

Conclusion

I have emphasized negative features of the CRC. Others will extol its positive aspects, and there are many. Most of the clearly positive commitments States Parties have made are, however, quite vague, and the US could plausibly claim already to be doing or providing what they require. A couple of clearly positive provisions are more definite – for example, regarding children's "opportunity to be heard" in legal proceedings (Article 12) and "measures to protect the child from all forms of physical or mental violence" (Article 19(1)). But the US might also assert that it provides these things. As to currently lawful corporal punishment, it would contend this is not violence and, anyway, it is simply "taking into account the rights of parents" as Article 3 of the CRC instructs. A comprehensive ban on violence might better be secured by asserting general human rights for children.[25]

Whether it would be a good thing for American children that the US ratify the CRC would seem to depend on whether there are life-enhancing benefits to the CRC for children that could not be obtained at least as effectively by asserting children's rights under the ICCPR, the International Covenant on Economic, Social, and Cultural Rights (ICESR), the Universal Declaration of Human Rights (UDHR), or under the constitutional and statutory laws of the US, and whether those benefits outweigh the costs for children arising from the problematic provisions identified in Part II. I am far from convinced. To further rights of children in the US, I believe it preferable to mine the unrecognized potential of the US Constitution. For example:

- Substantive due process rights

  Against the state's forcing a child into relationships with dysfunctional parents
  Against the state's holding a child in foster care limbo without true child-centered justification
  Against the state's returning a child to the custody of still-dangerous parents
  Against state destruction of attachments to non-parent caregivers.

- Equal protection rights

  Against state denial of state-law rights to education and medical care because of parents' religious beliefs
  Against state authorization of private violence against persons under 18
  Against state authorization of nonconsensual alteration of boys' bodies

Many problems other contributors to this volume discuss are violations of equal protection, and if the discrimination is based on ethnicity, gender, or religious affiliation, or if the interest at stake is one the federal courts deem fundamental, then the US Constitution should provide adversely affected children ample protection. Some criticized state practices courts would also or instead view as violations of basic rights under the Due Process Clause of the US Constitution. By invoking this charter of rights that applies to all persons, advocates for children tap into a jurisprudence developed primarily in response to complaints about state action on behalf of adults, which is likely to provide stronger protection than a doctrine developed in an *ad hoc* fashion just for children.

Notes

1 *See* James G. Dwyer & Shawn F. Peters, *Homeschooling: The History and Philosophy of a Controversial Practice*, ch. 5 (2019); James G. Dwyer, The Relationship Rights of Children, ch. 5 (2006).
2 See, e.g., Va. Code §§ 64.2-2000 (defining "guardian"), 64.2-2019-20 (specifying guardians' duties and powers); Cruzan by Cruzan v. Dir., Missouri Dep't of Health, 497 U.S. 261 (1990) (rejecting the notion that parents of woman in persistent vegetative state have any right in connection with decision making about her life support).
3 *Id.*, 1411-20; James G. Dwyer, *Clarifying Questions About the Nature of Rights*, 11 Jurisprudence ___ (2020); Rowan Cruft, *Why Is It Disrespectful to Violate Rights?* 113 Proc.Aristotelian Soc'y 201 (2013).
4 See, e.g., In re Green, 448 Pa. 338, 292 A.2d 387 (1972) (holding child's interest in receiving surgery to correct spine curvature insufficient to override parents' rights, because his life was not in danger), *id.* at 393 (Eagen, J. dissenting) ("The Court's analysis presumes there are two primary interests at stake, that of the state to protect its citizens, and that of the mother to follow her religious convictions. The difficulty, and what I believe to be the fatal flaw in this reasoning, is that too little consideration and attention is given to the interests of the health and well-being of this young boy."). Cf. In re Guardianship of L.S. & H.S., 120 Nev. 157, 167, 87 P.3d 521, 527 (2004) (holding that because the child's life was in danger, "the child's interest in self-preservation and the State's interests in protecting the welfare of children and the integrity of medical care outweigh the parents' interests in the care, custody and management of their children, and their religious freedom. The combined weight of the interests of the child and the State are great and, therefore, mandate interference with Jason and Rebecca's parental rights. NRS 159.052 strikes an appropriate balance between the various interests."). *See also* Jeffrey Shulman, *Private School Regulation: Individual Rights and Educational Responsibilities, in* The Oxford Handbook of Children and the Law, 701–732 (James Dywer ed., New York: Oxford University Press, 2020) (describing U.S. states' deregulation of private schools and homeschools in the name of parental rights).
5 Art. 19 directs states to protect children from harm "while in the care of parent(s)," or when in the care of other guardians or caregivers, including by providing supports,

endeavoring to prevent maltreatment, and responding to maltreatment when it occurs, but it says nothing about separating a child from parents, let alone articulating any right of children against the state's putting them in danger of maltreatment by conferring legal parent status and custody on persons unable or unwilling to provide adequate care.

6 *See* James G. Dwyer, *Liberal Child Welfare Policy and its Destruction of Black Lives*, 79–83 (2018) (discussing the inter-generational cycle of dysfunction and the commonality of dysfunction pervading families of parents who maltreat children).

7 *See* Marie McAuliffe & Binod Khadria, eds., World Migration Report (2020) International Organization for Migration, at 19 ("there were around 272 million international migrants in the world in 2019… The overwhelming majority of people migrate internationally for reasons related to work, family and study… those who have been displaced, such as refugees and internally displaced persons, comprise a relatively small percentage of all migrants"). An example especially pertinent to thinking about international adoption is the explosion in the number of Eastern European, Asian, Latin American, and African women joining international marriage agencies following the advent of the internet. See, e.g., Olga Oksman, *Mail-Order Brides: Old Practice Still Seen as New Chance for a Better Life-for Some*, The Guardian (Jan. 11, 2016); Harriet Zurndorfer, *Escape from the Country: The Gender Politics of Chinese Women in Pursuit of Transnational Romance*, 25 Gender, Place & Culture 489 (2018). There are also multitudes who do not attempt to emigrate *despite* their native country's culture, rather than because of it. See, e.g., Nesrine Malik, *Escape—Or Betrayal: Why Muslim Women Who are Oppressed by their Families are Often Reluctant to Break Free*, The Guardian (July 24, 2008).

8 Cf. Elizabeth Bartholet, *Permanency Is Not Enough: Children Need the Nurturing Parents Found in International Adoption*, 55 N.Y.L. Sch. L. Rev. 781, 783 (2011) ("Those attacking such adoption as in conflict with children's heritage rights are speaking a language of a past in which it was common to see people as essentially defined by their race and national origin.").

9 *See generally* Elizabeth Bartholet, *International Adoption: The Human Rights Position*, 1 Global Policy 91–100.

10 The financial aspect of international adoption leads some critics to characterize it as "baby buying," but there is no evidence of international adopters viewing the situation as such or children as commodities. It is, rather, the critics who are wont to treat children as market goods. See, e.g., Shani King, *Challenging Monohumanism: An Argument for Changing the Way We Think About Intercountry Adoption*, 30 Mich. J. Int'l L. 413, 436 (2009) ("Little attention is paid in legal scholarship … to the argument that industrialized countries are exploiting developing countries and stealing their national resources, i.e., their healthy children."); Kathleen Ja Sook Bergquist, *International Asian Adoption: In the Best Interests of the Child?* 10 Tex. Wesleyan L. Rev. 343, 349 (2004) (similarly characterizing international adoption of children by wealthier countries' citizens as colonialist acquisition of national resources); Barbara Yngvesson, National Bodies and the Body of the Child: "Completing" Families through International Adoption, in Cross-Cultural Approaches to Adoption, 216–217 (citing authorities in developing countries who refer to children as a nation's resources). For fuller response to these critics, see James G. Dwyer, *Inter-Country Adoption and the Special Rights Fallacy*, 35 U. Pa. J. Int'l L. 189, 239–241, 244–245, 251–252 (2013).

11 *See id.* at 210–237.

12 Judith L. Gibbons, *Human Trafficking and Intercountry Adoption*, 40 Women Ther. 170–189 (2017), at 178.

13 The prevailing definition of "trafficking" limits it to "obtaining a person for compelled labor or commercial sex acts." (U.S. Department of State, 2013b). Books

devoted to the topic of trafficking make no mention of international adoption. See, e.g., Ryszard Piotrowicz et al., *Routledge Handbook of Human Trafficking* (2017); Segrave et al., *Sex Trafficking and Modern Slavery* (Routledge, 2018). Scholars and legal actors who devote their lives to combatting trafficking, bemoan the overuse of the term "trafficking" and related concepts like slavery, because it makes their work harder. See, e.g., id., at 9–10.

14 Cf. Susan Otuoma, *To Link International Adoption in Kenya to Trafficking is Ignorance*, The Star (Kenya) (9/14/15).

15 See UNICEF, *Orphans*, UNICEF Press Center (June 15, 2015), www.unicef.org/media/media_45279.html. (estimating that in 2015 there were 15.1 million children in the world who have lost both parents); Johanna Oreskovic & Trish Maskew, *Red Thread or Slender Reed: Deconstructing Prof. Bartholet's Mythology of International Adoption*, 14 Fuff. Hum. Rts. L. Rev. 71, 106–109 (2008) (describing "a remarkably consistent and predictable cycle" in which international adoption agencies learn "fast, easy placements of infants and toddlers" have become possible in a particular country and so rush in, but then increased demand leads to abuses such as financial inducements to birth parents, which in turn results in the country's shutting down its international adoption program, and then agencies wait for some other country to open up). Critics of international adoption point out that most of the estimated eight million children in orphanages worldwide have at least one living parent. See, e.g., id. at 79. But having a living parent is not the appropriate criterion for adoption availability; the vast majority of domestic adoptions in the US occur in situations where the child has one or two living biological parents. What is relevant is whether a child is being parented or likely could be adequately parented by a birth parent within a reasonable period of time, which for a baby is a short period of time. *See* James G. Dwyer, *Liberal Child Welfare Policy and Its Destruction of Black Lives*, 70–77 (2018).

16 *See* Christopher Balding, *International Child Adoption Law and Empirical Analysis*, 13 Whittier J. Child & Fam. Advoc. 51, 61–68 (2014).

17 See, e.g., King, *supra* note 10, at 413.

18 For exceptions, *see* A.H. and Others v. Russia, European Court of Human Rights (2017) (asserting right to family life in Art. 8 of the European Convention on Human Rights); Hearing on Human Rights of Unparented Children and Related International Adoption Policies, Inter-Am. Comm'n H. R., 137th Ordinary Period of Sessions (2009) (written testimony of Delegation), http://www.law.harvard.edu/programs/about/cap/ia/testimonyfullnov09.pdf (describing how Professor Elizabeth Bartholet led an appeal to the Inter-American Commission on Human Rights, on the basis of provisions in the American Convention on Human Rights, for assistance in getting Latin American nations to reopen international adoption, citing the universally applicable "right of every person to a family"); Paulo Barrozo, *Finding Home in the World: A Deontological Theory of the Right to be Adopted*, 55 N.Y.L. Sch. L. Rev. 701, 704–705 (2010–2011) (urging the right to family life as a normative basis for opposing restrictions on inter-country adoption).

19 There is language in the CRC preamble that one could cite in support of such a right, but no Art. of the CRC actually establishes such a right. *See* CRC preamble, para. 7 ("the child, for the full and harmonious development of his or her personality, should grow up in a family environment, in an atmosphere of happiness, love and understanding").

20 *Hague Convention on the Protection of Children and Co-operation in Respect of Inter-Country Adoption*, May 29, 1993, 343 U.N.T.S. 89, *reprinted in* 32 I.L.M. 1134-46 (1993). The Convention begins in its preamble by "[r]ecognizing that inter-country adoption may offer the advantage of a permanent family to a child for whom a suitable family cannot be found in his or her State of origin." However, Art. 4, which is more directive, states:

> An adoption within the scope of the Convention shall take place only if the competent authorities of the State of origin… have determined, after possibilities for placement of the child within the State of origin have been given due consideration, that an intercountry adoption is in the child's best interests.

So, with respect to whether international adoption ought to be available to a child, the Hague Convention contains an inert factual observation and a normative constraint that can be read – and has been read by UNICEF and the Hague Conference – as giving lexical priority to domestic placements regardless of whether that is in children's best interests. *See* Hague Conference on Private International Law, *The Implementation and Operation of Hague Intercountry Adoption Convention: Guide to Good Practice*, Guide No. 1, sect. 2.1.1 'Subsidiarity', 29–30 (2008).

21 *See* Masha Lipman, *What's Behind the Russian Adoption Ban?* The New Yorker (Dec. 21, 2012).

22 *See A.H. v. Russia, supra*. note 18.

23 *See* United Nations Convention on the Rights of the Child, Art. 41, Nov. 20, 1989, http://www.ohchr.org/en/professionalinterest/pages/crc.asp (hereinafter CRC). ("Nothing in the present Convention shall affect any provisions which are more conducive to the realization of the rights of the child and which may be contained in … (b) International law in force for that State."); Hague Convention, Art. 1: (providing that States must "ensure that intercountry adoptions take place in the best interests of the child and with respect for his or her fundamental rights as recognized in international law"); ICCPR, Art. 5(1) ("Nothing in the present Covenant may be interpreted as implying for any State, group or person any right to engage in any activity or perform any act aimed at the destruction of any of the rights and freedoms recognized herein or at their limitation to a greater extent than is provided for in the present Covenant.").

24 *See* UNICEF, UNICEF's position on Inter-country adoption, https://www.unicef.org/media/media_55412.html. ("inter-country adoption should only be envisaged for a child [when] stable in-country solutions are not available. This position is shared by UNICEF, UNHCR, the UN Committee on the Rights of the Child…").

25 *See* Susan H. Bitensky, *The Mother of All Human Rights: The Child's Right to Be Free of Corporal Punishment As Hard International Law*, 36 Ohio N.U. L. Rev. 701 (2010).

6 Family obligations and socio-economic rights under the Convention on the Rights of the Child

Barbara Stark

Introduction

This chapter is part of a larger project that explores and begins to map the complicated relationship between family obligations, which bind us all, and human rights, i.e., universal norms set out in multiple legal instruments, ratified by most of the world's states, but familiar to relatively few of the world's people. My thesis is that these systems are interdependent; neither works without the other. As a corollary, we need both to thrive; at this point, many of us need both to survive.

This project is important in a world still reeling from a global pandemic and staggering economic inequality, in which capital moves freely and people do not, in which, as political theorist Wendy Brown puts it, "neoliberalism transmogrifies every human domain and endeavor, along with humans themselves."[1] Almost everything – national politics, clean water, leisure time – is commodified, bought, and sold, subject to the rules of the marketplace. Family obligations and human rights, despite their own transmogrification, remain vibrant sites of resistance to the abuses of global capitalism because at the core of each is the affirmation of our relationships, our interdependence, and our responsibility for each other and the living world we share. Both reject neoliberalism's reduction of individual human beings to "specks of human capital,"[2] in Brown's words.

The Convention on the Rights of the Child (CRC) is a particularly appropriate focus now for several reasons. First, children are disproportionately poor and disproportionately vulnerable. Even if they are not targeted by the coronavirus, their basic needs cannot be met as their parents lose their income.[3] Many now lack adequate food, care, and education, which may well affect them for life. They cannot afford that, and neither can the rest of us. Resilient, healthy, well-educated children are our best collective hope for the future.

This chapter focuses on children's socio-economic rights, specifically, the right to health set out in Article 24 of the CRC, the right to an adequate standard of living set out in Article 27, and the right to education set out in Articles 28 and 29. Part I of this chapter explains how these Articles require states to support families.[4] It draws on the work of the Committee created by the CRC to oversee its implementation (CRC Committee), as well as recent country reports to show how countries throughout the world support their children. It also shows what the lack of such support costs American children and their families. Part II explains how family obligations support human rights. First, families assume responsibility for assuring certain human rights for their members, especially children. The right to an "adequate standard of living,"[5] for example, is usually assured for children by parents or other family members who feed, house, and clothe them. Second, preparing children to participate in the community, and the larger society of which it is a part, is at the core of the family's obligation to children. Children first learn about respect, equality, tolerance, and human dignity in their families. It is in families that human rights take root.[6]

But not all families accept these basic human rights precepts. Part III considers the options when family obligations and human rights conflict. This part focuses on the child's right to education and whether the right to education can be met by homeschooling. While the privatization of education, the questionable quality of that education, and its profitability are increasingly urgent international concerns, homeschooling is not.[7] But in the United States, where experts estimate that 1.7 million children may be homeschooled, it is a subject of ongoing, intense debate.[8] Part III shows how the components of the child's right to education, set out in the CRC, which neither prohibits homeschooling nor requires states to allow it, clarifies this debate and exposes what is really at stake. In addition, the CRC situates the discussion in the world we now live in, where 1.05 billion children are not in school,[9] and the United States is the only country that has not yet ratified the CRC. Ratification – good faith ratification, without the usual caveat that it would be non-self-executing[10] – would bring the United States closer to this world, and closer to an understanding of what we owe our children and all children.

Why families need human rights

The CRC requires States to recognize – and assure – the child's socio-economic rights, including the rights to health and an adequate standard of living. This often takes the form of state support for the child's parents, or other caregivers. This part shows how the CRC Committee has helped states interpret these rights and how some wealthy democracies have implemented them. It concludes by describing how the United States' rejection of these rights affects American children.

The child's right to health

Article 24 requires States to "recognize the right of the child to the enjoyment of the highest attainable standard of health." The specific measures to be taken by the States are spelled out. They include measures to reduce infant and child mortality; assure that all children receive necessary medical assistance and health care, adequate nutritious food, and clean drinking water; and assure pre-natal and post-natal health care for mothers. States are also required to provide guidance for parents, and family planning education and services.

In its General Comment on children's right to health, the CRC Committee notes that "most mortality, morbidity and disabilities among children could be prevented" if States made doing so a priority.[11] The States' obligation to reduce infant and child mortality, for example, can be effectively addressed by "scaling up simple, safe and inexpensive interventions ... such as ... promotion of breast-feeding practices."[12] The obligation to "assure pre-natal and post-natal health care for mothers," similarly, is within the capacity of most States: "Pregnancy and child birth are natural processes, with known health risks that are susceptible to both prevention and therapeutic responses, if identified early."[13] In Iceland, for example, free prenatal care is available at every primary health clinic.[14]

The CRC Committee repeatedly reminds States that under the CRC, their obligations with respect to socio-economic rights are as important as their obligations with respect to civil rights.[15] As the CRC Committee observes, "Preventable maternal mortality and morbidity constitute grave violations of the human rights of women and girls."[16]

The CRC requires States to do more than meet basic requirements regarding children's right to health. Rather, the CRC Committee quotes with approval the Constitution of the World Health Organization, in which "States have agreed to regard health as a state of complete physical, mental and social well-being and not merely the absence of disease or infirmity."[17] Iceland provides free health-care up to the age of six.[18] Monitoring is not limited to the health of the child, but looks also to the general welfare of the child and the family in order to enable early intervention, if needed, so that "the child will reach its greatest potential."[19]

The child's right to an adequate standard of living

Article 27.1 of the CRC explicitly requires States parties to recognize the "right of every child to a standard of living adequate for the child's physical, mental, spiritual, moral and social development." While the child's parents or guardians have the primary responsibility, States "shall take appropriate measures to assist [them]... and shall in case of need provide material assistance."[20] As the CRC Committee warns States, "These prescriptions leave no leeway for [their] discretion ... [rather, the obligation extends] to the maximum extent of [its] available resources."[21] This includes entitlements for families. In 2006, for example, Canada enacted the Universal Child Care Benefit (UCCB), which provides parents with $100 per month for each child under six.[22] This affected up to 1.5 million Canadian families with over 2 million children.[23] In addition, the 2009 budget included non-taxable payments to low- and middle-income families, lifting roughly 500,000 children out of poverty.[24] Also in 2009, Canada passed the Fairness for the Self-Employed Act, which extended benefits to self-employed people who opted in.[25] As economist Paul Krugman noted, "Most advanced countries devote substantial sums to benefits for families with children; in Europe, these benefits average between 2% and 3% of G.D.P. The corresponding number for the United States is 0.6% of G.D.P."[26] In addition, every developed country except the United States has enacted a national paid family leave policy.[27] Child poverty was high even before the pandemic: 13.1% of children in the 36 countries of the Organization for Economic Cooperation and Development (OECD) lived in relative income poverty in 2019.[28] While total global wealth increased from the 1980s until 2018, most of the benefit went to the already rich. Global inequality grew until 2015, when the top 1% owned 47.5% of it.[29] As Christine Lagarde, the then Managing Director of the International Monetary Fund (IMF), pointed out in 2014, "There has been a staggering rise in inequality – 7 out of 10 people in the world today live in countries where inequality has increased over the last three decades."[30] As Thomas Piketty has shown, birth predicts wealth as certainly as it did during the Gilded Age.[31]

Children – everywhere – are disproportionately poor.[32] Children make up nearly half of the almost 900 million people living on less than $1.90 per day; ten million of the 21 million people who have been forcibly displaced from their homes are children.[33] Fifty-nine million children, between 6 and 11, are out of school.[34] Then in early 2020 the coronavirus arrived.

Economists' projections about the pandemic's effect on the global economy are grim. As the IMF notes in its June 2020 World Economic Outlook (WEO) Update, "[t]he adverse impact on low-income households is particularly acute, imperiling the significant progress made in reducing extreme poverty in the world since the 1990s."[35] Since the available data on the economic impact of the pandemic are not disaggregated by age, UNICEF and Save the Children collaborated to develop models under various scenarios. They concluded that between 86 and 106 million additional children could be pushed into monetarily poor households by the end of 2020. The total number of children living in such households globally would then be between 670 and 692 million.[36] The CRC Committee issued a statement in April 2020 urging States to take measures to

> ensure that children are fed nutritious food during the period of emergency...as many children receive their only nutritious meal through school feeding schemes... [and] [d]efine core child protection services as essential and ensure that they remain functioning...[since] [c]onfinement may expose children to increased physical and psychological violence at home...protect children...living in poverty and lacking access to adequate housing.[37]

The CRC Committee's warning seems prescient, according to the limited data available.[38]

How America's rejection of the CRC affects children

The US refusal to recognize children's rights, reflected in its rejection of the CRC, has been costly. US infant and maternal mortality rates, as well as its child poverty rates, are higher than those of other wealthy countries; its social and economic mobility is lower. America is no longer the "land of opportunity."[39]

Infant mortality

A recent study shows that babies born in America are less likely to survive their first year than babies born in other wealthy countries.[40] Higher poverty rates and a weak social safety net are responsible for the surprisingly high rate of infant mortality.[41] As the National Center for Health Statistics notes, the infant mortality rate (IMR) – the ratio of infant deaths to live births in a given year – is a good indicator of the overall health of a population.[42] In 2017, the IMR in the United States was 5.8 per 1,000 live births.[43] In 2016, the IMR for non-Hispanic blacks was 11.4; for American Indian/Alaskan Native, 9.4; Native Hawaiian or other Pacific Islander, 7.4; Hispanic, 5.0; non-Hispanic whites, 4.9; and Asian, 3.6.[44] The three leading causes of infant death in the United States in 2017 were birth defects, preterm birth and low birth weight, and maternal pregnancy complications.[45]

Maternal mortality

Maternal mortality, similarly, is higher in the United States than in other wealthy countries, especially for black women, whose risk of death from pregnancy-related causes is three to four times that of white women.[46] More than 700 women die in the United States every year from pregnancy-related causes and more than half of these deaths are preventable.[47]

Paul Farmer and Ophelia Dahl, founders of the non-profit Partners In Health (PIH), have explained how maternal mortality in Haiti has been reduced by more than half in the past 25 years. First, PIH worked closely with the Haitian government to strengthen public health infrastructure, by rebuilding clinics and hospitals, and training personnel, including "more than a thousand community health workers."[48] Second, confronted with evidence that maternal mortality was higher where fees were higher, the health commissioner for central Haiti announced that prenatal care and emergency obstetrical care would be free. Third, prenatal and obstetric care were linked to an "all-out effort to improve access to primary health care."[49] The failure of wealthy countries like the United States to take similar measures to prevent maternal mortality, as the CRC Committee notes, is a "grave violation of women's human rights."[50]

Child poverty

According to the National Center for Children in Poverty, 43% of children in the United States live in families that struggle to meet their most basic needs.[51] Between December 2017 and June 2019, one million lower-income American children lost health insurance.[52] UNICEF defines poverty as households whose disposable income is less than 50% of the national median. Under this standard, of the wealthiest 41 countries, the bottom five countries overall for children were Chile, Bulgaria, Romania, Mexico, and the United States.[53] Barbara Bennett Woodhouse has compared child poverty in the United States and Canada. Before factoring in government programs, the two countries had roughly the same rate of child poverty in 2009–2011; 25.1% of both countries' children were poor.[54] After factoring in government assistance, however, child poverty in the United States went down only 2%, to 23.1%, while child poverty in Canada was reduced by more than 10%, to 13.3%.[55]

As Nancy Dowd explains, "Poverty affects where and how children live, including nutrition, family well-being, safety, and community well-being."[56] The links between parental poverty and outcomes for children are clear and negative: "Family, instead of being a resilience factor, becomes a risk factor."[57] What Dowd calls "developmental equality" is particularly crucial from birth through age three, because of the "explosion of neurological growth" during that period.[58] Achievement gaps appear at 18 months. Universal high-quality pre-kindergarten, accordingly, is especially important for poor children.[59]

Again, this was before COVID-19. While programs such as the CARES Act, the March law that sent one-time checks to most Americans and a weekly bonus to the unemployed, enabled millions to avoid poverty, these programs have expired.[60] Other programs, such as Pandemic Electronic Benefit Transfer, aimed at the 30 million children who rely on subsidized meals at school, have been less effective because of the massive efforts required to coordinate thousands of school districts and other difficulties reflecting the lack of national infrastructure. Only 15% of those eligible have received benefits as this program, too, runs out of funds.[61]

The CRC, along with other human rights instruments and compliance mechanisms, are not the only reason that other developed countries provide more and better support for their families. But they are a major factor, structuring and maintaining a culture of support. They are symbolically important, a public statement to the rest of the world, as well as to their own people, that families matter, that the well-being of all families is a matter of concern for the whole society as well as for the State.

Why human rights need families

This part explains how the CRC depends on families for two critical functions: first, implementation of human rights on the ground; and second, teaching children about human rights. These functions may overlap; some family members may try to model respect, equality, tolerance, and human dignity while taking care of children.[62]

Human rights on the ground

Families, including extended families,[63] traditionally take care of each other, especially their most vulnerable members, providing food, clothing, and shelter for children, the elderly, and the disabled. In fact, care work is overwhelmingly provided by families throughout the world.[64] Even where governments have assumed significant responsibility for education and healthcare, for example, families make sure that their children go to school, that they are dressed appropriately, get there safely, and that they have whatever books and school supplies are not provided by the school. Family members take each other to the doctor, or to Urgent Care, and pick up prescriptions at the pharmacy.

Families are not just the means to achieve human rights; the right to a family is *itself* a human right. The Preamble of the CRC sets out that States parties are: "[c]onvinced that the family, as the fundamental group of society and the natural environment for the growth and well-being of all its members..." The Preamble further provides, "that the child, for the full and harmonious development of his or her personality, should grow up in a family environment, in an atmosphere of happiness, love and understanding." The child's right to a family is affirmed in Article 7, which provides that the child "shall have the right from birth to a name, the right to acquire a nationality and, as far as possible, the right to know and be cared for by his or her parents."

Teaching children about human rights

Parents teach their children about human rights by modeling the behavior they want their children to emulate, by taking care of them, and by assuring that their basic needs are met. Parents teach children respect for other people by treating them with respect; they teach children about tolerance and equality by treating people who are not of their religion, race, or ethnic group with respect, as equals. They teach children about gender equality by avoiding gender stereotypes in parenting and other work within the home.[65]

Some parents may not teach their children about human rights law. Others may reject its basic precepts. Parents may be racist, misogynist, or believe that people who follow religions different from their own are damned. Assuming that their attitudes do not result in "mental violence" to their children under Article 19.1, which may trigger other forms of state intervention,[66] human rights education at school, as required under the CRC, is intended to compensate for the lack of parental education and expose their children to other perspectives.

When family obligations and human rights conflict: children's education

A family's values, and the obligations grounded in those values, may violate the rights of the child. The CRC Committee notes that discrimination against children with disabilities is pervasive in families, for example, although it violates Article 2 of the CRC, which prohibits discrimination, and Article 29.1(a), which requires that education be directed to the development of the child's "fullest potential."[67] It is the State's responsibility to "formally incorporate [the principles of article 29.1] into their education policies and legislation at all levels" as well as to develop a "national plan of action to promote and monitor realization of … article 29.1."[68]

The United States, in contrast, defers to parents' often idiosyncratic views about their children's education or to the standards, however minimal, set by states (such as California or Florida), even when doing so violates the child's rights. In the context of education, the United States falls short of the requirements of Articles 28 and 29 in three important ways. First, Article 29.2 safeguards the "liberty of individuals," such as homeschoolers, to establish alternatives to public schools, "*subject always*" to "the principles set forth in article 29.1" and such "minimum standards as may be laid down by the State" (emphasis added). The "principles" referred to in Article 29.1 require that the school curriculum be infused with *values*, including tolerance, respect for the principles set out in the UN Charter, and respect for the environment. The United States has historically shied away from such requirements.[69]

Second, as noted above, Article 29.1(a) requires that education be directed to the development of the child's "*fullest potential.*" In *San Antonio Independent School District v. Rodriguez*, however, the US Supreme Court concluded that because there is no fundamental right to education, a state need not provide more than an "adequate" education.[70] As a corollary, Article 29.2 requires that alternatives to public schools be subject to "minimum standards as may be laid down by the state." The holding that public schools must merely be "*adequate*" fails to meet this requirement as well.

Third, both of the differences set out above suggest that the CRC would require significant investment in education by the federal government. It would be expensive, for example, to assure that the 50% of public school students living in poverty[71] had access to education that was equal to that available to public school students who lived in wealthy districts. This would probably be the most significant difference in a country that does not recognize socio-economic rights.

The heart of the CRC

Article 29 "promotes, supports and protects the core value of the CRC: the human dignity innate in every child and his or her equal and inalienable rights."[72] The aims of education set out in Article 29.1 are "all linked directly" to this core value. These aims are "[t]he holistic development of the full potential of the child, including development of respect for human rights, an enhanced sense of identity and affiliation, and his or her social interaction with others, and with the environment."[73]

Some of these principles may be compatible with the law of the 50 states.[74] Article 29.1(c), for example, requires that education be directed to the "development of respect for the child's parents... for the national values of the country in which the child is living, the country from which he or she may originate, and for civilizations different from his or her own." As the CRC Committee observes, "[T]his article underlines the importance of respect for parents... and the fact that most children's rights, far from being externally imposed, are embedded within the values of local communities."[75] Comparing state laws and the CRC, Anna Dolinsky notes, "Virtually every state requires that school children study national and state history."[76] While no state statute directly contradicts this provision, Dolinsky concludes that "some may raise doubts about the state's commitment [to 'respect for civilizations different from [its] own.]'"[77]

David Smolin suggests that Article 29.1(b), which provides that education "develop respect for human rights… and the principles enshrined in the Charter," may be challenged as unconstitutional because "[u]nder Supreme Court case law, there is in effect a constitutional right for private schools to foster a negative view of the United Nations."[78] But disrespect for the "principles of the UN Charter" is quite different from criticism of the international organization. Similarly, while conceding that "respect and tolerance do not require a doctrine of religious relativism," Smolin argues that "the stark elevation of a particular religion could easily be seen by some as violating article 29."[79] As the CRC Committee explains, this would be a mistake. Article 29.1 is intended to serve as an "antidote" to "racism and related phenomena [which] thrive where there is ignorance … unfounded fears of … racial, ethnic, religious… or other forms of difference."[80] Students can be taught that their religion is superior, as long as they are also taught that others feel the same way about *their* religions, and that their views must be respected. Again, as Dolinsky notes, no state statutes directly contradict either of these requirements.

"Minimum standards as may be laid down by the State"

The CRC, like all human rights treaties, makes the State responsible for assuring its people's human rights. Education in the United States, like family law, is governed by the laws of the 50 states. Opponents of ratification have argued that the CRC would undermine federalism as well as parental rights.[81] The states, however, are subject to the federal Constitution[82] and treaties of the United States.[83] As Louis Henkin pointed out, "The federal Government exercises jurisdiction over all matters covered in a human rights convention, if only by making the treaty."[84]

Despite the states' responsibility for education, the United States would remain responsible for any violations under the CRC. There are several. First, the United States has not established *any* minimum national standards beyond the requirement that public education must be "adequate." In addition to the facial deficiencies of such a standard under the CRC, homeschooling – which is permitted in every state – shows how the lack of a federal standard, and oversight, risks additional violations of children's rights, and hides them at the same time.

Ten states require parents to notify education officials that they intend to homeschool their children.[85] This is the only requirement in these states, and it is only required once.[86] Roughly 12 states do not even require notification. Only about ten states require that parent teachers have any qualifications, generally a high school diploma.[87] Several states exempt parents from teaching anything that conflicts with their religious beliefs.[88] As Fineman shows, textbooks designed for such parents contain statements such as "Evolution is false," and "Noah's Ark was real."[89] In addition, as Woodhouse shows, the ability of parents to completely isolate their children exposes some to life-threatening abuse.[90]

For these reasons, and others, homeschooling is rare in the rest of the world and prohibited by some countries.[91] As the German court noted in upholding such a prohibition, "The social integration required for a tolerant society c[an] only be achieved through [school attendance]."[92] Where homeschooling is permitted, registration, regulation, and periodic monitoring is generally required.[93]

The right to education is a socio-economic right

Unlike the US Constitution, Article 2 of the CRC prohibits "discrimination of any kind," explicitly including discrimination on the basis of property or wealth. Under the CRC, accordingly, it would be discriminatory for a state to base the resources available to a public school on the local property taxes of the community in which the school is located, especially where this leaves some children in overcrowded, underfunded schools.

Although this was upheld by the Supreme Court in *San Antonio Independent School District v. Rodriguez*,[94] parents, students, and growing numbers of Americans have continued to demand the truly "equal" education promised by *Brown*.[95] The CRC would become the "supreme law of the land" if ratified under Article 6 of the US Constitution, and would pick up where the Constitution leaves off. Because socio-economic rights are the obligations of the State, the State is required to devote its "maximum available resources" to their realization.[96] The State can fund poor schools by raising taxes, for example. This would be the major change in US law if the CRC was ratified in good faith and it would undoubtedly be contentious.

Conclusion

The pandemic has changed the world. The United States, with more coronavirus cases and deaths than any other country, has learned the real cost of the lack of a national healthcare system. While the other wealthy democracies have invested in healthcare infrastructure, the United States is winging it.[97] The pandemic's impact on the economy has forced the federal government to subsidize unemployment benefits, impose moratoria on evictions and foreclosures, and distribute trillions in aid to failing small businesses, jobless Americans, and millions of children. The crisis is not over. Too many American children lack healthcare, an adequate standard of living, and access to quality education. As the CRC – and every other country – recognizes, a country's children are its future; committing wholeheartedly to their well-being is a matter of our collective survival.

Notes

1 Wendy Brown, *Undoing the Demos: Neoliberalism's Stealth Revolution*, 9 (2015).
2 Wendy Brown, *Political Theory is Not a Luxury: A Response to Timothy Kaufmann-Osborn's "Political Theory as a Profession"*, 63 Pol. Res. Q. 680, 682 (2010).
3 *Children in Poor Households to Soar by Millions due to Covid-19*, UNICEF (June 2020), http://data.unicef.org/topic/child-poverty/covid-19.
4 They do so in conjunction with a broad network of human rights treaties, including: the International Covenant on Economic, Social, and Cultural Rights (ICESCR)

(Jan. 3, 1976), 993 U.N.T.S. 3; the International Covenant on Civil and Political Rights (ICCPR) (Mar. 23, 1976), 999 U.N.T.S. 171; the Convention on the Elimination of All Forms of Racial Discrimination (CERD or the Race Convention) (Jan. 4, 1969), 660 U.N.T.S. 195; the Convention on the Elimination of All Form of Discrimination Against Women (CEDAW) G.A. Res. 34/180, 34 U.N. GAOR, Supp. No. 46, U.N. Docs. A/34/46, at 193 (Dec. 18, 1979). (hereinafter CEDAW or the "Women's Convention") "States," as used in this article, generally refer to nation states, such as Mexico and China, rather than the constituent political entities joined in a federal union, such as Idaho and Maine. The context will indicate when 'states' refer to the latter, such as the discussion of the law of the 50 states in Part III.

5 CRC, *supra* note 1, at art. 27.

6 As Eleanor Roosevelt put it, "Where, after all, do universal human rights begin? In small places—close to home." Mary Ann Glendon, *A World Made New: Eleanor Roosevelt and the Universal Declaration of Human Rights* 9 (2001).

7 UN Human Rights Council (HRC) Committee, *The Implementation of the Right to Education and Sustainable Development Goal 4 in the Context of the Growth of Private Actors in Education*, U.N. Docs. A/HRC/41/37 (Apr. 10, 2019).

8 Compare Elizabeth Bartholet, *Homeschooling; Parental Rights Absolutism vs. Child Rights to Education and Protection*, 62 Ariz. L. Rev. 1 (2020); Martha Fineman & George B. Shepherd, *Homeschooling: Choosing Parental Rights Over Children's Interests*, 46 U. Balt. L. Rev. 57 (2016); Barbara Bennett Woodhouse, *Speaking Truth to Power: Challenging 'The Power of Parents to Control the Education of Their Own,'* 11 Cornell J.L. & Pub. Pol'y 481 (2002) (urging prohibition or strict regulation of homeschooling); Brian D. Ray, *Worldwide Guide to Homeschooling: Facts & Stats on the Benefits of Homeschool* (2005) (describing benefits of homeschooling.); *See generally* James G. Dwyer & Shawn F. Peters, *Homeschooling: The History and Philosophy of a Controversial Practice* (2019).

9 UNESCO, *Covid-19 Education Response*, *see* http://en.unesco.org/covid19/educationresponse (last visited July 17, 2020).

10 *See* Linda A. Malone, *The Effect of U.S. Ratification as a 'Self-executing' or as a 'Non-self-executing' Treaty*, in The U.N. Convention on the Rights of the Child 33 (Jonathan Todres et al. eds. 2006).

11 UN CRC Committee, *General Comment No. 15 On the Right of the Child to the Enjoyment of the Highest Attainable Standard of Health* (art. 24), U.N. Docs. CRC/C/GC/15 (Apr. 17, 2013).

12 *Id.* at para. 35.

13 *Id.* at para. 51.

14 UN CRC Committee, *Combined Fifth and Sixth Periodic Reports Submitted by Iceland*, U.N. Docs. CRC/C/ISL/5-6, at para. 56. (Feb. 7, 2019).

15 General Comment No. 15, *supra* note 12, at para. 7.

16 *Id.*

17 *Id.* at para. 4.

18 Iceland's Report, *supra* note 16, at para. 56.

19 *Id.*

20 Art. 27.4 further requires the state to secure maintenance from any other responsible person.

21 UN CRC Committee, *General Comment No. 21 on Children in Street Situations*, U.N. Docs. CRC/C/GC/21 (Jun. 21, 2017).

22 UN Committee on Economic, Social and Cultural Rights, *Concluding Observations on the Sixth Periodic Report of Canada*, U.N. Docs. E/C.12/CAN/6 (Mar. 23, 2016).

23 *Id.*

24 *Id.*

25 *Id.* at 25.

26 Paul Krugman, *Why Does America Hate Its Children?* N.Y. Times (Jan. 17, 2020), at A22.
27 Benjamin Ryan, *Paid Family Leave is a Game Changer for New Parents' Health, Not Just Their Economic Security*, The Nation (Aug. 12, 2019).
28 This refers to the percentage of children with an equivalized household disposable income below the poverty threshold of 50% of the median disposable income in each country, *see* http://www.oecd.org/els/soc/CO_2_2_Child_Poverty.pdf (last visited Feb. 27, 2020).
29 Credit Suisse, Res. Inst. Global Wealth Rep. (2018), at 9.
30 Christine Lagarde, *The IMF at 70: Making the Right Choices—Yesterday, Today, and Tomorrow* (Oct. 10, 2014), www.imf.org/external/am/2014/speeches/pr02e.pdf at 3.
31 Thomas Piketty, *Capital in the Twenty-First Century*, 408–409, 421 (2014).
32 Philip Alston et al., *Laying the Foundations for Children's Rights: An Independent Study of Some Key Legal and Institutional Aspects of the Impact of the CRC*, UNICEF, 5, 32 (2006).
33 UNICEF, State of the World's Children (2016), https://www.unicef.org/sowc2016/.
34 UNICEF, Fixing the Broken Promise of Education for All (2016).
35 IMF, *A Crisis Like No Other, An Uncertain Recovery*, WEO (June 2020).
36 UNICEF, *Children in Poor Households to Soar by Millions Due to Covid-19* (June 1, 2020), https://www.unicef.org/nepal/press-releases/covid-19-number-children-living-household-poverty-soar-86-million-end-year.
37 CRC Committee, *Warns of the Grave Physical, Emotional and Psychological Effect of the Covid-19 Pandemic on Children* (Apr. 8, 2020), https://www.ohchr.org/EN/HRBodies/Pages/COVID-19-and-TreatyBodies.aspx (last visited July 27, 2020).
38 *See* nn. 61–62, infra.
39 *See* Barbara Bennett Woodhouse, *The Ecology of Childhood: How Our Changing World Threatens Children's Rights*, 133 (2019) (the World Bank, using the Gini coefficient, which measures inequality, ranks the United States 94th in terms of "an individual's opportunity to move up the economic ladder.").
40 David Johnson, *American Babies are Less Likely to Survive Their First Year Than Babies in Other Rich Countries*, Time (Jan. 9, 2018).
41 *Id.*
42 Sherry L. Murphy et al., Mortality in the United States, 2017, NCHS Date Brief No. 328, fig.4 (2018), https://www.cdc.gov/nchs/products/databriefs/db328.htm.
43 *Id.* at fig.5 In Iceland, the rate is 1.8. Iceland's Report, *supra* note 12, at para. 57.
44 Center for Disease Control (CDC), *Infant Mortality Rates by Race and Ethnicity* (2016), https://www.cdc.gov/reproductivehealth/maternalinfanthealth/infantmortality.htm Reproductive Health.
45 *Id.*
46 CDC, *Meeting the Challenges of Measuring and Preventing Maternal Mortality in the United States* (2017), https://www.cdc.gov/grand-rounds/pp/2017/20171114-maternal-mortality.html; *See also* Emily Bobrow, Black, Pregnant and in Greater Peril, N.Y. Times (Aug. 9, 2020), at MB1 (noting that, "In New York City, however, black women are 8–12 times more likely to die.")
47 *Id.*
48 Paul Farmer & Ophelia Dahl, *Keeping New Mothers Alive*, Wash. Post (May 11, 2008).
49 *Id.*
50 *See* text accompanying note 17, *supra*.
51 Amy Rothchild, *Is America Holding Out on Protecting Children's Human Rights?* The Atlantic (May 2, 2017).
52 Abby Goodnough & Margot Sanger-Katz, *Medicaid Covers a Million Fewer Children. Baby Elijah was One of Them*, N. Y. Times (Oct. 25, 2019), https://www.nytimes.com/2019/10/22/upshot/medicaid-uninsured-children.html (noting that "more

than a million children disappeared from the rolls of the two main state-federal health programs for lower income children … between December 2017 and June.").

53 UNICEF, *supra* note 34 (noting that other indicators in the wealthiest countries – income inequality, self-reported adolescent mental health, and obesity – were all on a downward trend.).

54 Woodhouse, *supra* note 39, at 137.

55 *Id.*

56 Nancy E. Dowd, *Reimaging Equality: A New Deal for Children of Color* 12 (2018).

57 *Id.* at 14.

58 Dowd, *supra* note 56, at 11.

59 *Id.* at 15.

60 Jason DeParle, *Buoyed by U.S. Virus Aid, Millions Avoided Poverty*, N. Y. Times (June 22, 2020), at 8.

61 Jason DeParle, *Millions of Children Face 'Dire' Wait for Hunger Aid*, N. Y. Times (May 27, 2020), at A1. The program helped reduce hunger, according to the Brookings Institution. Jason DeParle, *Program Helped Rescue Child Hunger, Study Says*, N. Y. Times (July 31, 2020).

62 As set out in the Preamble to the CRC: "Considering that the child should be … brought up in the spirit of the ideals proclaimed in the Charter … [in particular] peace, dignity, tolerance, freedom, equality and solidarity."

63 *See* Moore v. City of East Cleveland 431. U.S. 494 (1977).

64 Most of this work is done by women. See, e.g., Veerle Miranda, Cooking, Caring and Volunteering: Unpaid Work Around the World, 14 OECD Social, Employment and Migration Working Papers, Working Paper No. 116 (2011).

65 See, e.g., CEDAW, *supra* note 5, at article 5.

66 Art. 19–22 are discussed in Part VI of this volume, infra.

67 UN CRC Committee, *General Comment No. 1, Article 29.1 The Aims of Education*, U.N. Docs. CRC/GC/2001/1, para. 10 (Apr. 17, 2001).

68 *Id.* at paras. 17 and 23.

69 The mission of the US Department of Education is to "promote student achievement and preparation for global competition by fostering educational excellence and ensuring educational access." U.S. Dept. of Educ., https://www2.ed.gov/about/overview/mission/mission.html (last visited Aug. 8, 2020).

70 San Antonio Independent School District v. Rodriguez, 411 U.S. 1 (1973).

71 *See* Fineman & Shepherd, *supra* note 9, at 79.

72 General Comment No. 1, *supra* note 67.

73 *Id.* at para.1.

74 Anna Dolinsky, State Education Law Compared to Rights Under the CRC, in Todres et al., *supra* note 11 at 251, 256.

75 General Comment No.1, *supra* note 67 at para. 7.

76 Dolinsky, *supra* note 74, at 256.

77 *Id.*

78 David M. Smolin, *Overcoming Religious Objections to the CRC*, 20 Emory Int'l L. Rev. 81, 104 (2006).

79 *Id.*

80 General Comment No.1, *supra* note 67, at para. 11.

81 Luisa Blanchfield, Congressional Research Service, The UN Convention on the Rights of the Child (Apr. 1, 2013), at 6–7.

82 Brown v. Board of Education, 347 U.S. 483, 493 (1954) (holding that segregated public schools are unconstitutional).

83 Missouri v. Holland, 252 U.S. 416 (1920).

84 Louis Henkin, *U.S. Ratification of Human Rights Conventions: The Ghost of Senator Bricker*, 89 Am. J. Int'l L. 341, 346 (1994).

85 Bartholet, *supra* note 9, at 36.

86 *Id.*
87 *Id.*
88 *Id.* at note 226.
89 Fineman, *supra* note 9, at 81.
90 Woodhouse, *supra* note 9, at 499.
91 Bartholet, *supra* note 9, at 62–64.
92 *Id.* at 63.
93 *Id.*
94 *See* note 71, *supra.*
95 Dana Goldstein, *Lawsuit Says Rhode Island Failed to Teach Students to Be Good Citizens*, N.Y. Times (Nov. 29, 2018); Dana Goldstein, *U.S. Students Have Right to Literacy, Court Rules*, N.Y. Times (Apr. 28, 2020), at A17.
96 ICESCR, *supra* note, 5 at art. 2.1.
97 Michelle Goldberg, *Too Broken To Fight the Coronavirus*, N.Y. Times (June 23, 2020) (noting that, "No other developed country is doing as badly as the United States.").

Part II

Children's Participation Rights and Child-Friendly Justice

7 My voice must be heard too

Why children need a voice in custody hearings

Ellen Marrus, Malikah Marrus, and Rifqa Sa'Aadat

Introduction

Many legal proceedings significantly affect children's lives. In this chapter, we focus on custody and visitation decisions of the US family law courts and consider how the Convention on the Rights of the Child (CRC) can strengthen the US legal system, providing more protection for children. The CRC, although not a perfect document, does enumerate 42 rights that provide a broad framework for ensuring children's rights. Compliance by state signatories is determined through yearly reports submitted to the United Nations (UN) to denote their observance and protection of these rights. However, enforcement mechanisms do not exist to guarantee that countries comply with the provisions.[1] Still, every country, except the US, has ratified the CRC.[2]

The reality is that too many children have no voice in their parent's custody battles.[3] Through one child's story and the model we suggest for child representation, we hope to encourage the legal system to give children a voice that will be heard.[4]

Rifqa's story

From the age of 6 months until 21 months old, I did not see my father. He had moved away; my mother filed for divorce, and by the time my father started to visit me, he was a stranger. Additionally, when the visits started, he was abusive to me, physically and emotionally. I had difficulty handling the visits and would cry when I had to see him. One time I cried so loudly that a neighbor came to see what was wrong. Even at a young age, I would try to postpone the inevitable and find reasons to stop frequently on the one-hour drive to the visits.

I started to see a child therapist. When things did not get any better, she did family therapy with everyone. The therapist believed my father and I had not bonded and was not sure we would in the near future. She based this on her in-person observations of our interactions and by viewing a videotape he prepared for her. The therapist concluded he displayed poor parenting skills and recommended visits should be discontinued if there was no improvement. The court did not follow her recommendation. During one therapy session she asked if I knew my father loved me. I told her that he would say that, but he didn't act like he did. I sensed the way he treated me did not show parental love.

I repeatedly told my parents I did not want to go for visits. My father did not listen to me. My mother listened to my apprehensions and had her own concerns. However, I did not give her any additional information that may have assisted her in having visitation modified. My mother tried to talk with my father to help improve the visits. He would not listen to any of her suggestions or ideas.

My father was abusive in every possible way – emotionally, physically, and sexually. He threatened that if I told anyone, he would kill my mother and grandmother. I believed him. During visitations he used drugs and would often take me along on his drug deals. I knew he had a gun and believed he would use it. I felt I had nowhere to turn.

When I was about five years old, he started to sexually abuse me. After one visit, my mother noted a discharge from my vagina. Usually, I was a happy and talkative child but following a visit I would not be. My mother and grandmother attempted to talk to me about the visits, inquiring if anyone had touched my private areas. I said nothing happened because I was too scared to tell the truth. My mother also spoke with my pediatrician about her concerns and the doctor asked about the visits, but I would not tell her either.

During another visit, we had stayed at a hotel. My father got three rooms. One for him and his wife, a connecting room for their other children, and I was by myself, making it easier for him to come in and rape me. I went to the reception area and asked the woman to call the police because I was in a room by myself. She told me to go back to my room. After he started sexually abusing me, I learned to deal with it by shutting down and putting a cocoon around myself, forcing me to block out what was happening. It was not until I was in college that my memory of the sexual abuse returned.

The neighbor who heard me crying didn't want to get involved. My mother talked to my father to try and improve things, but he would not listen. She had concerns and tried to decrease the time for visitation. The court did not listen to her. The therapist recommended that the visits cease as my father and I had not bonded. The court did not listen to her. The hotel receptionist would not listen to me nor get involved.

Despite all the trauma I experienced, the visitations continued. I asked several times to speak to the judge and was not able to. I wanted to tell the judge my story and that I never wanted to visit with my father. I trusted that if the judge heard me, he would help. The judge made decisions about where a child lives and the extent of visitation for the noncustodial parent. I knew he could keep me from having to go visit with my father. I perceived the judge as a powerful person who made decisions about people's lives. I am not exactly sure why I thought the judge would decide differently if he heard my voice, but it was my expectation. I am sure it would have been beneficial for the judge to hear my voice prior to making his ruling. How can a judge make decisions about what is best for the child without hearing from the child? To me, my dad was, and still is, a monster that caused multiple tribulations in my life, including physical ailments that doctors say are a result of the sexual abuse.[5]

The law: in the US and the CRC

One of the most important rights for a child is for their voice to be heard and to tell their story in one's own words. The CRC in Article 12 clearly protects this right stating:

> State Parties shall assure to the child who is capable of forming his or her own views, the right to express those views freely in all matters affecting the child, the views of the child being given due weight in accordance with the age and maturity of the child.[6]

Even without being a signatory, the CRC principles can influence legal proceedings in the US. In *Roper v. Simmons*,[7] the US Supreme Court found that the death penalty is unconstitutional when applied to acts committed by persons when under the age of 18.[8] The Court based its opinion on several factors including their immaturity, their susceptibility to peer pressure, and their still malleable character.[9] The Court also referenced the international consensus against the juvenile death penalty, with Justice Kennedy stating, "[t]he opinion of the world community, while not controlling our outcome, does provide respected and significant confirmation for our own conclusions."[10] In *Graham v. Florida*,[11] the Court again referred to customary international law and the CRC.[12] The CRC can provide guidance for lower court judges, attorneys, and policy makers in the US to develop best practices and meet the best interests of the children involved.[13]

Having the right to express their opinion is crucial for children in all matters, particularly when other individuals express their positions and the outcome affects the child. Allowing children's positions to be heard not only provides decision makers with essential information,[14] but it helps children practice a decision-making process that will influence their lives.[15] Furthermore, research has shown that if the parties are not directly involved with the terms of a decision, they are less likely to be invested in the matter, and orders are less likely be complied with.[16] For example, mediations often bring about longer lasting and more beneficial results when the parties have a voice in the process and are involved in creating solutions.[17] This is true for adults and children alike.[18] However, US children are rarely given the opportunity to have their voices heard or to be consulted on matters that affect them. If Rifqa's voice had been heard during the divorce proceedings, the abuse she suffered may have been avoided or at least curtailed, mitigating its long-lasting effects.

Custody and visitation arrangements for the noncustodial parent, control of decision-making responsibility regarding education, health care, residency, religion, legal matters, and finances for the child are all matters that particularly concern the child,[19] and yet, the child's voice is rarely heard in these contexts.[20] Even in cases adjudicating parentage, the child is not a mandatory party to the action,[21] and is not automatically represented by counsel in custodial issues. It may be within the court's discretion to appoint a lay advocate,[22] who informs the court about best interests, but no one is mandated to express the child's own interests to the court. The child's opportunity to consult with the judge is generally discretionary and non-binding.[23] Most courts rely on the belief that parents look after their child's best interests.[24] Furthermore, by state statute, the court is asked to consider the best interests of the child when making its ruling.[25] However, even when considered by the judge or presented by a lay advocate, the best interests standard does not consider that the child's own expressed interests may be different from what the court, the lay advocate, or the parents consider to be in the child's best interests. Oftentimes, judges and guardians ad litem use their own values, beliefs, and biases in making their determinations in cases.[26] Moreover, statutes and case law are often nebulous in defining best interests and what the court takes into consideration when making decisions for the child.[27] As such, it is difficult to comprehend how a judge can make decisions that will be in a child's best interests without even hearing from the child. Who better to explain the circumstances than the child who has to live with the consequences of the decisions?

A framework for representation: lawyers and social workers working together

We propose this framework for representation of the child in an effort to improve the family court process and incorporate the requirement within the CRC that children's voices be heard in all legal proceedings that affect them. Without a child having a platform to tell their story, decisions are made without all the necessary information. We suggest that family courts ensure that all children have lawyers to represent them when their parents are in court for custody or visitation matters. The child's attorney should take a holistic approach and work with other professionals to provide the type of representation that will help the child's voice be heard.[28] For this to work effectively, all interested parties, parents, third parties, and children alike, should be on equal footing in the proceedings. All their opinions should be presented, and the child's interests should be given full consideration based on their age and maturity. Even very young children can demonstrate their feelings. If a child constantly cries with one caregiver or constantly turns to the same person to take care of their needs, they are demonstrating who they believe cares for them. Our proposal attempts to enable direct child participation in custody proceedings through integration of the child, child-advocate, and social worker into a collaborative team that supports the child's own voice.

In custody decisions, parents or third parties, such as stepparents or grandparents, are typically represented by an attorney or they may decide to proceed pro se. However, to allow children to fully engage with the process and have their views voiced, it is important for them to have an advocate. It should be someone other than the parents who may be in conflict with each other and/or the child over these matters.[29] This is also true, if a third party, such as a grandparent, is seeking visitation. The parent, child, and grandparent may also be at odds with each other.[30] A lawyer advocate would be the best, but whether the advocate is a lawyer or a lay person, it should be clear that the person is advocating for the child's point of view, not their own understanding of the child's best interests.[31] In a holistic model, there would be a lawyer advocate that has a clear understanding of the law, working with a lay advocate, such as a social worker. The social worker should be trained in child development and family dynamics in order to create a trusting relationship with the child and to gain the respect of the court.[32]

The Model Rules of Professional Conduct (MRPC) sets guidelines for attorneys to follow in their representation of clients. Lawyers, as advocates, should zealously represent the goals and wishes of their clients[33] in a diligent and timely manner.[34] This is true whether the client is an adult or a child. Even when representing a client with diminished capacity, the rules are clear that age alone does not determine a client's ability to make decisions regarding representation.[35] Furthermore, even if the client cannot make decisions on all matters, the attorney can still represent their wishes and should still treat the client with respect, maintain communication, and explain legal proceedings in a manner that the client would be able to understand.[36] To accomplish effective communication between the attorney and client, both parties need to listen to one another. It is important for the attorney to keep the client informed about the case and the proceedings,[37] just as it is important for the client to be clear about his or her interests.[38] The attorney decides the strategy used to help the client reach his or her goals.[39] The attorney is the tool for the client to obtain what they want within the confines of the law and realistic possibilities. It can be helpful to have other professionals involved who are well trained in communicating with a child and can aid the attorney-client relationship.[40]

An attorney is not just an advocate, but also an advisor.[41] It is not the attorney's place to decide what the client wants, but it is his or her role to explain the advantages and consequences of various decisions.[42] The lawyer can also help a client recognize alternative options. Social workers are excellent professionals that can help attorneys accomplish their client's goals because, like attorneys, they work to help their clients become empowered and to reach their own goals. This is done by building on the client's strengths. If Rifqa had her own attorney that worked with a team and that team listened to Rifqa and gained her trust, things may have been different. The team would have learned information about Rifqa's life that no one else was able to obtain, and even if Rifqa did not testify or talk to the judge, the lawyer would have been able to provide the court with additional facts that would have helped with visitation decisions. Rifqa's life may have been very different.

Just as the MRPC provides ethical rules for attorneys to follow, the Code of Ethics from the National Association of Social Workers specify the ethical standards for social workers.[43] The social work profession is based on human rights principles, and in some ways, even more so than attorneys, social workers may think of their obligations to a client in respect to social justice.[44] Social workers advocate for individual rights within a just society. Beyond working towards obtaining the basic human rights of food, water, shelter, and health care for their clients, social workers work to ensure their clients live in a just society and help develop policy changes towards this goal.

The International Federation of Social Workers (IFSW) states in their principles and in the International Code of Ethics that social workers must respect the dignity and worth of others and believe in self-determination.[45] Section 1.02 of the National Association of Social Workers (NASW) Code of Ethics states that the client has a right to self-determination. The dignity and worth of others and clients applies to all individuals, regardless of age. One way this is accomplished is to help clients have a voice in actions that are occurring in their lives.

Although children may be influenced by one of their parents, it is worth taking the chance to try and determine what the child truly wants. The child's social worker and attorney can effectively enable child participation. The social worker's education also has components of child development and family dynamics,[46] while most attorneys lack this knowledge. The lawyer, while having some experience with children, does not necessarily have the degree of training that a social worker would have. The lawyer will know the law and what may be able to be done to protect the child, but the social worker would have been more adept at getting the story from Rifqa in spite of her fear because of the threat of harm to herself and to family members. Although Rifqa was young during the early decisions on visitation, she still had valuable input to provide to the court that was missing in the decision-making process.

The social worker, along with the lawyer, can also help prepare the child for court. This may include the child testifying in court or talking with the judge in chambers.[47] If the child does not feel secure, it is unlikely that they will be able to tell their story or speak the full truth. By working together, the inter-professional team can go over the questions that may be asked in court or by the judge. Social workers cannot do this entirely on their own; they need to be part of an inter-professional team, ensuring the child understands the questions and will be able to provide truthful answers.

The social worker can arrange a time for the child to visit the courtroom, explain where everyone will be, what the child will be doing, and put the child at ease for being in court,[48] erasing some of the fear the child might have about appearing in court. If the social worker sees that the child will not be able to testify in court, she will be able to help the attorney prepare arguments to allow the child to speak to the judge privately in chambers. Rifqa, as a young child would in all likelihood not be comfortable talking about the abuse in open court in front of her abuser. The social worker could have acted as a support for Rifqa and arrange with the judge for her to have a comfort/lovie item to help calm her nerves while in the courtroom or chambers.[49]

In Rifqa's case, she did not have a lawyer or a collaborative team to represent her. Although her mother was concerned about what was happening during the visits, she did not have any proof of abuse.[50] There was an attorney representing Rifqa's mom and he was allegedly trying to represent Rifqa's interest in court. However, he never met or spoke to Rifqa and did not know all the pertinent information. It is difficult to try and protect someone when you do not have the facts necessary to do so. A professional team working on Rifqa's behalf may have been able to acquire the information and provide it to the court.

If the judge is not willing to listen to the child or let the child tell her own story, the social worker would be able to speak for the child in court. The attorney cannot testify as a witness, but the social worker on the team could do so. It would be important to make sure the social worker has the proper credentials and training in order for the judge to give her testimony credence,[51] and would need to be clear when she was expressing the voice and wishes of the child versus when she was testifying from her professional opinion. By speaking for the child and keeping that separate from the social worker's perspective, the social worker is still following good social work practices by having the child practice self-determination.[52] The lawyer and social worker would carefully go over the expressed wishes of the child and together they could make sure that the court would have the proper information to make an informed decision that would also meet the child's wishes. They could also go over the plan with the child to confirm that they are expressing the client's desires. This allows for the child to have some voice in the court proceedings. It is not best practices as the child is not expressing herself to the court, but it does allow for more information to be available.

In Rifqa's case, a child therapist did prepare a report for the court. The therapist did not have the information of the abuse but was able to observe interactions between Rifqa and her father and believed it was in Rifqa's best interest to end the visits if they did not improve. In the therapist's opinion, a bad relationship between Rifqa and her father could be worse than none at all. This proved to be true. The judge did not give much weight to the report in her decision making, but at least her mother's attorney was able to include it. We cannot second guess if Rifqa had told her entire story to the therapist if it would have had more of an impact on the judge, but it may have made Rifqa feel empowered and given her more control over her future. Although many years later, telling her story at the conference and in this chapter has helped the healing process more than therapy. It is important for people, including children, to be able to tell their stories publicly and be acknowledged in a positive manner.[53]

An inter-professional team of a social worker and an attorney or lay advocate can provide the support and means to help the child tell their story. Each professional has different skills and techniques to help in this process, and although they have different ethical professional rules, there is also much similarity between the two professions. Both want to give a voice to their clients and to have their clients have a sense of empowerment and enfranchisement. Prior to the forming of the collaborative team, all the professionals should meet to discuss how children's cases should be handled and clarify the roles and responsibilities for all team participants. It is important for the collective team to have a clear direction and to be on the same page. When the holistic approach was used at a university clinic, the supervising attorney, supervising social worker, social work interns, and law students would meet to agree on the process. The social work portion of the team was able to assist with client meetings and interviews bringing another perspective to the case and another validation to the client's voice, conduct home visits, home studies, finding resources and connecting clients to the resources, and appearing in court. The lawyer team was able to explain the legal process to the interns and clients, determine how the facts and law could work to the benefit of the client, provide validation for the client, and supply a mechanism for the client's voice to be heard.

In Rifqa's case, if there had been an attorney assigned to represent her and a team approach was used, maybe they would have discovered why Rifqa wanted to talk to the judge and felt that the judge was the only person who could help. Rifqa might not have told the team her truth either as she was afraid, but the team approach and the time the professionals could have taken with her may have alleviated some of her fears and enabled her to open up. The team could have also advocated for her to have time with the judge, even though the statute did not call for it. None of us are sure if the court heard her story, the judge would have believed her and put in protections for Rifqa's well-being. However, we do know that without her story being told, there was no chance for that to happen.

As much as we believe in this approach, some people would disagree with our position that the child's voice should be heard. Critics argue it could put a child in a difficult position to have to choose between two parents and state the preference in front of the parents.[54] Some professionals believe that children should not have to make this choice at all and, therefore, do not even want to listen to the child.[55] This can be resolved by (1) not having the child testify in court, but rather arrange for the child to have an individual meeting with the judge, (2) not asking the child directly with whom they want to live, but rather having the child describe the relationship that exists with each parent and the things that the child does with the parent, and (3) forcing the child to talk to the judge so their opinion could be heard. If the child is represented by a collaborative team, the team will have extensive communication with the child and can help the judge proceed with the interview in such a way that does not put pressure on the child, or the team can provide the information directly to the judge.

Another concern is that the parent will manipulate a child to tell the court particular things that may or may not be true.[56] Again, this can be determined during the interview process if it is conducted by a seasoned interviewer or judge. It is also argued that children do not have an understanding of the family law system and would not understand the questions being asked of her or him.[57] The team would explain the proceedings to the child in such a way that the child has a better understanding of what is happening at home and in the court. Finally, there is a concern that children will feel traumatized by the experience, particularly if the judge is not trained in family law, child development, and family dynamics. However, there are no studies that indicate that a child is traumatized by being a part of the process. Rather, they show the opposite. The child is happier with the results and better decisions are made by the court.[58] Children may be nervous about the interview process prior to meeting the judge, but if it is conducted in a child-friendly manner, the child is more likely to be satisfied with the process and the results.[59]

Besides helping to get the child's story heard, social workers and attorneys experienced in collaborating on behalf of children can advocate for policy changes to systematically allow children's voices to be heard. This needs to be done on all levels – beginning locally with family court judges and local court rules to a national level with support for the CRC and children's voices being heard. On local and state levels, individuals can work to make sure that, either by election or appointment, family court judges understand child development, family dynamics, appropriate ways to interview children, and that they go through suitable training. Attorneys who are going to represent children in these matters should also receive appropriate training that will help them relate to their child clients. When developing the team, the attorney should ensure that the social worker and other members of the team view the child's right to have a voice in the same way. Social workers, lawyers, and others can advocate for changes in local rules and state laws to permit, or even mandate that, children be represented in divorce proceedings or custody battles, not just by a lawyer, but to follow best practices and allow for a collaborative team.[60] The statute should also call for the judge to hear either directly from the child or from the team to confirm that the child's expressed interests are being heard. Although social workers and attorneys can advocate for their individual clients, it is important to make these changes on a larger scale to ensure that all children can be heard. On a national level, training can be provided for judges through the National Council for Juvenile and Family Court Judges (NCJFCJ).[61] There are also child advocate groups that can provide continuing education for lawyers and social workers,[62] and advocacy groups can encourage the ratification of the CRC by Congress. To accomplish this, there needs to be an educational campaign to help voters understand that the CRC will not infringe on parental rights. Finally, there is a need for research in the US that will show the benefit to children and their families when the child's voice is heard. There is data from other countries that can be used, but it would be helpful to collect documents and statistics in the US to sway public and elected officials' opinion to accept the CRC. Children deserve a chance to tell their story, have their voices heard as loudly as the adults involved, and for consideration to be given to their wishes and interests.

Conclusion

One of the most important empowerment rights enumerated in the CRC is the child's right to participation and the right to have their voices heard. When parents are fighting over custody, visitation, and who will be making decisions for the child about their education, health, and religion, the child seldom has a voice in the proceedings. These decisions greatly affect the child, but he or she is likely left out of the process. Under the model we have proposed, the child would participate in the proceedings by having a holistic representation approach with social workers and lawyers working together to provide the child with the best opportunity to have their voice heard by the court and parents. For this standard to work, proper training of all players – judges, attorneys, and social workers – must occur and the players should be committed to the process. This training can begin during the educational process for lawyers and social workers but should continue through continuing education. Additionally, if this process is going to be implemented in the US family courts, attorneys and social workers will have to advocate for children to be part of the process. It will have to become a normal part of practice with support from state laws and court rules.

Although some children may not wish to tell their story to the court or to have their voice heard through a social worker's testimony, this model would allow children who want to do so, to have a way to do it. Having an attorney and social worker, working directly for and with the child, would enable the court to have more information in its decision-making, even if the child does not speak to the court.

Would it be worse for Rifqa, or any child, to have been able to tell her story and for the judge to have ignored her? Maybe. She certainly would not have a belief in the system working for children, but she did not believe the system worked for children without her voice being heard. Having a voice at least lets the child know that someone may be listening, and it can improve future outcomes for the child.

Notes

1 Implementing and monitoring the Convention on the Rights of the Child, UNICEF https://www.unicef.org/child-rights-convention/implementing-monitoring. *See also*, Howard Davidson, *Does the U.N. Convention on the Rights of the Child Make a Difference?* 22 Mich. St. Int'l l. Rev. 497, 510 (2014) ("Despite what the CRC fear mongers say … no international police force or punitive sanctions exist to enforce provisions of any international human rights treaty.").

2 Carol M. Stern, *Obama Should Take Action to Protect the World's Children*, Time, Apr. 19, 2016, https://time.com/4293977/convention-on-the-rights-of-the-child/.

3 24 Am. Jur. 2d *Divorce and Separation* § 197 (2019) ("Generally, the husband and wife are the only proper parties to a divorce action. A child is not a party to a marriage dissolution, or ancillary custody proceedings, nor do minor children have a common-law right to intervene in their parents' divorce.").

4 The model we propose of holistic lawyering and a collaborative approach among professionals could be used in any legal setting and be advantageous for youth.

5 Sadly, according to RAINN, Rape, Abuse, and Incest National Network, I was not by myself in this predicament. I was only one of the 34% of people whose sexual abusers are family members. Children and Teens: Statistics, RAINN, https://www.rainn.org/statistics/children-and-teens (out of the yearly 63,000 sexual abuse cases substantiated, or found strong evidence, by Child Protective Services (CPS), about 80% of the perpetrators were parents).

6 United Nations Convention on the Rights of the Child, Nov. 20, 1989, http://www.ohchr.org/en/professionalinterest/pages/crc.asp (hereinafter CRC).

7 Roper v. Simmons, 543 U.S. 551 (2005).

8 *Id.* at 571.

9 *Id.* at 569–570.

10 *Id.* at 578.

11 Graham v. Florida, 560 U.S. 48 (2010), as modified (July 6, 2010).

12 *Id.* at 80. ("The Court has looked beyond our Nation's borders for support for its independent conclusion that a particular punishment is cruel and unusual.").

13 *See generally* Maria Grahn-Farley et al., *New York's Compliance with the Convention on the Rights of the Child: Student Contributions*, 12 N.Y. City L. Rev. 473 (2009).

14 *See* Ann O'Quigley, *Listening to Children's Views: The Findings and Recommendations of Recent Research*, Joseph Roundtree Foundation 1 (2000) (listening to children in court proceedings can lead to better decisions).

15 Child-Friendly Justice, European Union Agency for Fundamental Rights, 112 (2017) ("In custody cases, children mentioned that parents' rights, such as visitation rights, restricted fulfilment of their best interests. Some children reported efforts by parents to manipulate them, deeming these contrary to their best interests."). *See also* O'Quigley, *supra* note 14, at 27. ("Where children do not want contact with a parent this view needs to be taken very seriously. Research shows that rigid adherence to contact arrangements can be very distressing for children. Human relationships cannot be forced; [for example,] children who have been forced to maintain contact with fathers have poor relationships."). In Rifqa's case, her being forced to visit with her father caused long term harm and went against her wishes and the recommendation of her therapist.

16 *See generally* Robert M. Emery et al., *Child Custody Mediation and Litigation: Custody, Contact, and Coparenting 12 Years After Initial Dispute Resolution*, 69 J. of Consulting & Clinical Psych. 323, 331 (2001) ("The most important findings were that nonresidential parents who mediated maintained more contact and involvement with their children in comparison with nonresidential parents who litigated child custody. Significant differences were found on four key measures of nonresidential parent involvement in childrearing, specifically, visitation frequency, telephone contact, influence on the residential parents' decision making.").

17 *See generally* Emery et al., *Divorce Mediation: Research and Reflections*, 40 Fam. Ct. Rev. 22 (2005); Pauline H. Tesler, *Collaborative Family Law*, 4 Pepp. Disp. Resol. L.J. 317, 328 (2004) ("The process invites maximum client involvement and control over outcome, while maximizing privacy and creativity.").

18 O'Quigley, *supra* note 14 ("Listening to children involved in these situations and taking their views into account will lead to better decisions which will be more likely to be adhered to in the longer term.").

19 24 Am. Jur. 2d *Divorce and Separation* § 197 (2019) ("Even though a child is not a party to a divorce action, the child nevertheless has an interest in the divorce and child custody matters.").

20 *See, e.g.*, Soo Jee Lee, *Note: A Child's Voice vs. a Parent's Control: Resolving a Tension Between the Convention on the Rights of the Child and U.S. Law*, 117 Colum. L. Rev. 687, 713 ("Courts have therefore generally prioritized parental authority over a child's right to make decisions; again, it is only when parental rights do not directly conflict with the views of children that their participation rights are recognized.").

21 All states have adopted some version of the Uniform Parentage Act (UPA) (1973). The UPA was updated in 2000 and includes § 612. Child as Party; Representation., Unif. Parentage Act (2000) ("A minor child is a permissible party, but is not a necessary party to a proceeding under this [article].").

22 Tex. Fam. Code Ann. § 160.612; Wis. Stat. Ann.§ 767.407 (West 2008); ("A guardian ad litem shall be appointed for the child *only if* child abuse or neglect is alleged, or if the child is named as a defendant, or if the court determines that the interests of the child and his or her next friend are in conflict.") (Emphasis added).

23 See, e.g., GA ST § 19-9-3; Tex. Fam. Code Ann. § 153.009; Ohio Rev. Code Ann. § 3109.04 (West); Colo. Rev. Stat. Ann. § 14-10-126 (West); Ky. Rev. Stat. Ann. § 403.290 (West).

24 Troxel v. Granville, 530 U.S. 57, 65–66 (2000). ("It is cardinal with us that the custody, care and nurture of the child reside first in the parents, whose primary function and freedom include preparation for obligations the state can neither supply nor hinder.").

25 For a complete guide to state statutes, *see* US Child Welfare Information Gateway, *Determining the Best Interests of the Child*, Department of Health and Human Services, Children's Bureau (Washington, DC, 2020), https://www.childwelfare.gov/pubPDFs/best_interest.pdf#page=2&view=Guiding%20principles%20of%20best%20interests%20determinations.

26 O'Quigley, *supra* note 14, at 6 (citing Murch et al., *Safeguarding Children's Welfare in Uncontentious Divorce: A Study of s.41 of the Matrimonial Causes Act Report to the Lord Chancellor's Department*, Cardiff University, p. 68) ("[T]he district judges were not able to provide any clear idea of their concept of 'children's welfare' … the whole process depends upon the district judges exercising some sort of 'sixth sense' which enables them to identify cases which may call for some sort of intervention but which defies definition.").

27 While each state statute provides a laundry list of factors to be considered in "best interests" (including history of abuse, preferences of each parent, current residence), none are identical in language or application or weight of factor. See, e.g., La. Civ. Code Ann. art. 134; Del. Code Ann. tit. 13, § 722 (West); Mont. Code Ann. § 40-4-212; Colo. Rev. Stat. Ann. § 14-10-124 (West). Some statutes even include more nebulous features such as "factors as determined by the court." See, e.g., Tenn. Code Ann. § 36-6-106 (West); Mich. Comp. Laws Ann. § 722.23 (West).

28 Holistic lawyering requires a team approach that allows for the lawyer to act as a lawyer zealously advocating the client's expressed interests, while having other professionals that can provide additional assistance to the client and the attorney. *See* Ellen Marrus, *Best Interests Equals Zealous Advocacy: A Not So Radical View of Holistic Representation for Children Accused of a Crime*, 62 Md. L. Rev. 288, 334–345 (2003). Although this article speaks to holistic representation for children in delinquency court, the same model could be used to provide quality representation to children in any setting. Other professionals have used a holistic approach for a long time. For example, the medical profession uses a team approach when treating patients, as does social service agencies. For information about these models see, *id.*, fn. 272–276 and accompanying text.

29 O'Quigley, *supra* note 14 ("It is dangerous to assume that parents will always act responsibly with regard to their children. Yet, where parents are in agreement about arrangements post-divorce, then these will rarely be subject to judicial scrutiny and children's views will not be ascertained.").

30 *See generally*, Ellen Marrus, *Over the Hills and Through the Woods to Grandparents' House We Go: Or Do We, Post-Troxel?* 43 AZ. L. Rev. 751 (concluding that representation for the child is necessary in third party visitation hearings).

31 Michael E. Lamb et al., *Children and the Law, in* 3 Handbook of Child Psychology and Developmental Science, 498 (Richard M. Lerner & Michael E. Lamb eds., 7th ed., vol. 3, Hoboken, NJ: Wiley, 2015) ("Exactly how children's voices should be heard varies depending on their ages, characteristics, and circumstances, with various options (including legal representation, and informal or formal interviewing by judges or mental health professionals) … In many cases, a mental health professional or custody evaluator interviews affected children and considers their preferences and best interests which are conveyed in reports prepared for the court.").

32 Courts often appoint a social worker to do a home study. However, this person is typically paid for by the parents and conducts the home study from the parent's perspective rather than the child. The social worker on the child's representation team would be there for the child and may be able to reveal additional information to the court to aid in the decision-making process.

33 Model Rules of Prof'l Conduct r. 1.3 cmt. 1 (Am. Bar Ass'n 2013) ("A lawyer must also act with commitment and dedication to the interests of the client and with zeal in advocacy upon the client's behalf.").

34 Model Rules of Prof'l Conduct r. 1.3 (Am. Bar Ass'n 2013) ("A lawyer shall act with reasonable diligence and promptness in representing a client.")
35 Model Rules of Prof'l Conduct r. 1.14 (Am. Bar Ass'n 2013).
36 Model Rules of Prof'l Conduct r. 1.14 cmt. 2 (Am. Bar Ass'n 2013).
37 Model Rules of Prof'l Conduct r. 1.2 and 1.4 (Am. Bar Ass'n 2013).
38 Model Rules of Prof'l Conduct r. 1.2 (Am. Bar Ass'n 2013). Although attorneys are bound to work toward their clients' objectives as long as it is not criminal or fraudulent, this cannot happen unless the client communicates their wishes.
39 Model Rules of Prof'l Conduct r. 1.2 cmt.1 and 2 (Am. Bar Ass'n 2013).
40 *See* Marrus, *supra* note 28, at 334–337. Although this article discusses holistic lawyering in delinquency cases, the same principles would apply to the representation of children in other settings, including child custody and visitation. *See also* Model Rules of Prof'l Conduct r. 2.1 cmt. 4 (Am. Bar Ass'n 2013).
41 Lawyers are called attorney at law, but also counselor at law because there is a dual role. Certainly, we advocate for our clients, but to do this properly we must also advise and counsel clients on options, advantages, and consequences. *See* Model Rules of Prof'l Conduct r. 2.1 (Am. Bar Ass'n 2013).
42 Model Rules of Prof'l Conduct r. 2.1 (Am. Bar Ass'n 2013).
43 *Seegenerally*, *CodeofEthics*, NationalAssociationofSocialWorkers(2019), https://www.socialworkers.org/about/ethics/code-of-ethics/code-of-ethics-english (last visited Feb. 10, 2020).
44 *See id.* (The preamble to the Code of Ethics lists the core values of the profession: service, social justice, dignity and worth of the person, importance of human relationships, integrity, and competence.).
45 *Id. see also* IASSW, *Global Social Work Statement of Ethical Principles*, https://www.ifsw.org/wp-content/uploads/2018/07/Global-Social-Work-Statement-of-Ethical-Principles-IASSW-27-April-2018-1.pdf (expanding on the ethical principles adopted by the IFSW).
46 Council on Social Work Education, *Educational Policy and Accreditation Standards (EPAS) for Baccalaureate and Master's Social Work Programs Council on Social Work Education* (2015), https://www.cswe.org/getattachment/Accreditation/Accreditation-Process/2015-EPAS/2015EPAS_Web_FINAL.pdf.aspx. (Undergraduate programs have a liberal arts background ensuring that students are exposed to a variety of subject matters that will help them in the profession. Master's programs look for a well-rounded undergraduate education and in addition have courses on human development and group/family relationships and interactions.).
47 A good workbook to use as a reference with young children is *What's Happening in Court? An Activity Book for Children Who Are Going to Court in California*, Center for Families, Children, and the Courts (2012), https://www.courts.ca.gov/documents/CAB_English_web.pdf.
48 In Green County, MO, the court has a monthly program where children can come to the courthouse to see the building, the courtroom, and learn what is going to happen when they go to court. Children meet the judge, a bailiff, and attorneys. They are treated to a pizza dinner and a certificate of completion.
49 Green County, MO also makes sure a child has something to offer security while in court and the child will either be given a comfort or a lovie or bring one with her.
50 One case that we were involved with in the clinic, the mother came to court talking about the child being abused by the father. The judge told her to come back when the child had a broken arm or leg. When parents hear about things like this happening, it is hard for them to believe they can be any concerns to the court and be heard. Rifqa's mother did bring a concern about where the father was living. She had tried to have him served at the address he had given to her and the court. When the sheriff went to the apartment to serve him, he was told no one lived there by that name. When they

were in court because Malikah did not want Rifqa to go for a visit without knowing the correct address, the judge asked Rifqa's father if the address given to the court was correct, he said it was. The court asked to see his license, but he did not have one from the state that he claimed he was living in nor did it have a correct address. The judge told Malikah that if she had a concern she could go to the address and check it out.

51 The social worker who is going to be testifying should be a master level. The attorney needs to be aware of the social worker's training, both in school and continuing education, and any previous employment that would add to the social worker's credibility.

52 This is also following the NASW Code of Ethics of self-determination for clients.

53 *See* David K. Androff, *Narrative Healing among Victims of Violence: The Impact of the Greensboro Truth and Reconciliation Commission* 38 (2012) ("Victims' testimonies are expected to result in a cathartic release along with a public acknowledgement of their abuses by sympathetic witnesses, thereby benefiting individuals' recovery from violent trauma. Findings from narrative interventions with victims of violence suggest that there is a benefit to telling one's story to a supportive audience.").

54 Nicholas Bala et al., *Children's Voices in Family Court: Guidelines for Judges Meeting Children*, 47 Fam. L. Q. 379, 381 (2013).

55 Gillian Douglas et al., *Safeguarding Children's Welfare in Non-Contentious Divorce: Towards a New Conception of the Legal Process?* 63 Mod. L. Rev. 177, 190–191 (2000). Their study indicated that the judges and solicitors did not believe the child's views should be part of the legal process and most solicitors stated they never spoke to children. They were concerned that allowing the child to have a voice would place undue pressure on the child. The solicitors also felt that "lawyers are neither trained to deal directly with children, nor the appropriate channel through which children's views should be communicated." *Id.* at 191. They suggested that welfare officers should talk to the child and communicate the information. *Id.* Under our model we suggest a social worker who is working with the child's attorney. This would leave no doubt about the role of the social worker and the attorney who are working with the child. They would be there to help the child's voice and interests be heard.

56 Bala, *supra* note 54.

57 *Id.*

58 *Id.* at 382.

59 *Id.* at 401–407. This article includes suggestions for the interview structure and questions that would be beneficial to the child and would help the court in its decision making.

60 The question always arises who will pay for this collaborative team. In some cases, there may be a nonprofit community agency that represents children in this way and is funded by foundations and individual donations. Some attorneys may do this occasionally on a pro bono basis. Some jurisdictions may require parents to split the costs of the child representation team, if they can afford to do so. Finally, the state might pick up the cost as they do in child abuse and neglect cases where children are represented by counsel in many, if not most jurisdictions.

61 *The National Council of Juvenile and Family Court Judges*, https://www.ncjfcj.org/ (last visited Feb. 7, 2020). The NCJFCJ is the oldest organization in the U.S. to provide training and knowledge to judges and court personnel in the juvenile, family, and domestic violence areas. The organization maintains publications for judges, court personnel, and families. They also provide technical assistance to individual states and in addition to providing national trainings the organization also train judges in individual states.

62 The National Association of Counsel for Children (NACC) holds a yearly conference to inform lawyers, social workers, and court personnel of best practices. The National Organization of Forensic Social Work (NOFSW) also does yearly conferences to better prepare social workers to work on behalf of children.

8 Child-friendly justice

A malleable catalyst for the promotion of child and human rights

Philip D. Jaffé

Introduction

Since the Guidelines of the Committee of Ministers of the Council of Europe on child-friendly justice ("Council of Europe Guidelines") were adopted in November 2010 and widely disseminated,[1] the concept of child-friendly justice has flourished and gained significant popularity. Child-friendly justice has been promoted at national and supranational levels as a central strategic objective to encourage judicial systems to provide access to children and to adapt to their needs. The underlying principles of child-friendly justice have also percolated up into influential jurisprudence and legislative initiatives, as well as down into research projects and training programs for legal and psychosocial professionals on how children react to and fare within the justice system as a whole. Indeed, in the field of family law, this has led to an emphasis being placed on child participation and modifying structures and procedures, improving how professionals interact and communicate with children, listen to and harvest children's views and opinions to boost their relevance to the proceedings. Even more remarkable has been the degree to which the concept of child-friendly justice has become a malleable catalyst for the promotion of child rights as a whole, as enshrined in the Convention on the Rights of the Child (CRC).[2] Indeed, the present contribution seeks to illustrate this process by way of a personal reflection, at times more testimonial than scholarly, and by sharing in a customized child-rights approach a conceptual "smoothie" on child-friendly justice. For this, I will draw on personal experience as a clinical psychologist, a designated court evaluator, and a child rights advocate. I will also share a vignette to promote the notion that child-friendly justice can only become a substantive reality in children's lives when adults working with and for children in the justice system, envisioned holistically, are willing to adopt and implement a child rights culture. But I will begin with a brief reminder of the history, definition, and scope of child-friendly justice.

The origin and the core of child-friendly justice

As the leading regional governmental organization tasked with the promotion of democracy, the protection of human rights and the rule of law, the Council of Europe has been a driving force behind the notion of child-friendly justice within the 47 member states and beyond.[3] Since its inception in 2005 in the ongoing Council of Europe's transversal human rights program, ***Building a Europe for and with children***, child-friendly justice has been an integral component and one of its most resounding successes, effecting significant changes in almost all national systems of justice. It has sprouted many training programs, conferences, and research initiatives and become somewhat of an overarching concept that transcends national boundaries. It is almost a fundamental principle of what constitutes justice and how the judicial system should strive to operate when children are involved directly or indirectly in any capacity.

The Council of Europe Guidelines were drafted over the course of two years by a group of experts (of which I was a member) with the full support of a dedicated secretariat. In retrospect, it is remarkable how the definition of child-friendly justice retained in the Council of Europe Guidelines is consensual and obvious at its core. The guidelines

> [...] refers to justice systems which guarantee the respect and the effective implementation of all children's rights at the highest attainable level, bearing in mind the principles listed below and giving due consideration to the child's level of maturity and understanding and the circumstances of the case. It is, in particular, justice that is accessible, age appropriate, speedy, diligent, adapted to and focused on the needs and rights of the child, respecting the rights of the child including the rights to due process, to participate in and to understand the proceedings, to respect for private and family life and to integrity and dignity.[4]

The Council of Europe guidelines were also written in a way that is fully compatible with the provisions and principles of the CRC and are referred to in much of the UN Committee on the Rights of the Child's (Committee) subsequent work, including in its Concluding Observations to States Parties as part of its monitoring mandate or in its most recently adopted General Comment.[5] In particular, child-friendly justice is predicated on the respect for the rule of law and it explicitly upholds ***inter alia*** the principles of child participation, non-discrimination, and the best interests of the child.

Most importantly, the Council of Europe Guidelines are intended to be all encompassing and to apply to children in whatever capacity they are brought into contact with competent bodies and services involved in implementing criminal, civil, or administrative law. Indeed, the situations in which children are likely to encounter the justice system can be classified into four broad categories: the criminal justice system (when in conflict with the law or as victims and witnesses); the civil justice system (such as when in need of care, protection, judicial review of removal or placement; in custody and access disputes; in guardianship issues; and as unaccompanied or separated foreign children); the administrative justice system (such as school disciplinary proceedings and aspects of the care and protection system); and in the customary system traditional courts, or informal alternatives. Despite the comprehensive objective of the Council of

Europe Guidelines, it should be underscored that, at its origin and in practice, substantial emphasis has been on civil justice and the criminal justice system. Less attention has been paid, for example, to school disciplinary proceedings and to customary traditional courts or settings in which decisions of a quasi-judicial nature are made and implemented.

Another major explanation for the success of the Council of Europe Guidelines is the fact that they embrace complexity and do not attempt to reduce child-friendly justice to a set of rules or procedures by defining strict legal standards. In fact, the Council of Europe Guidelines explicitly widen the scope of application beyond the actual justice system and court proceedings and are holistically aimed at all professionals dealing with children in and outside traditional judicial proceedings. Sectors such as law enforcement, social welfare, health services – both physical and mental – are also considered responsible for contributing to making the justice system, as a whole, more child friendly. Furthermore, child-friendly justice is viewed as a dynamic process, made of many moving parts that unfold over time, in many instances long before children come into contact with the law in any shape or form. Child-friendly justice applies during more traditional formal proceedings within the judicial system, but also well after as, for example, when children need the necessary programmatic support for community reintegration and care. This evolving process is well captured by the specific main sections within the Council of Europe Guidelines dedicated to and entitled *before*, *during*, and *after judicial proceedings*.

While the Council of Europe Guidelines have elevated the concept of child-friendly justice, one should also mention similar constructs that promote access to and participation of children in the court system. For example, the UN Economic and Social Council Guidelines on Justice in Matters Involving Child Victims and Witnesses of Crime define the notion of *child-sensitive* as "an approach that balances the child's right to protection and that takes into account the child's individual needs and views."[6] Another influential entry, *child focused justice*, was crafted by the International Association of Youth and Family Judges and Magistrates which produced Guidelines on Children in Contact with the Justice System.[7] These guidelines were developed on the basis of the child-friendly justice guidelines and its equivalents in Africa and Latin America. In some circles, a more neutral expression has taken root which refers to *child-centered justice*. Irrespective of the labels that are put forward – friendly, sensitive, focused, or centered – it is difficult to pinpoint any major rivalry, as there are no significant differences in their meaning and in terms of their implication. Indeed, whatever minimal differences could be highlighted by purists dissipate entirely if one takes into account the communality that unites them, that is the concept of multidisciplinarity, if not interdisciplinarity.

Interdisciplinarity at the heart of child-friendly justice

The reader will no doubt wonder how, in the introduction to this chapter, the reference to a "smoothie" is germane to child-friendly justice and to family law. The reason is that child-friendly justice requires the justice system as a whole, as well as its main actors, to move away from traditional views that favor the involvement of jurists and rely on legal procedures. Rather, it must move to include theory, expertise, and practice from other disciplines. This includes, but is not limited to, social science, ethics, human rights, and many more theories and fields of practice. While made up of a majority of jurists of different stripes, the drafting group of experts welcomed several influential representatives from law enforcement and the social sciences, a mixture that provided for a broader and richer perspective. In many ways, the Council of Europe Guidelines offer an illustration of interdisciplinary activity, both with regard to the drafting process itself and, more importantly, to outcome and influence in terms of how they should be adopted in practice and promoted by a wide circle of professionals from a variety of disciplinary horizons.

Fittingly, the term "smoothie" is borrowed from the seminal article of Nissani, intriguingly entitled *Fruits, Salads, and Smoothies: A Working Definition of Interdisciplinarity.*[8] In his contribution to the field of education, Nissani convincingly demonstrates that, whereas distinct whole fruits represent individual disciplines and a fruit salad can be conceived as multidisciplinarity, the smoothie is the ultimate image that reflects how various disciplines can blend together and reach a structure and a flavor that has dramatically evolved from its constituent ingredients. In the same way, interdisciplinarity brings together various disciplines that operate on a new and different plane with regard to knowledge, research, education, theory, and professional practice.[9] To a great extent, child-friendly justice's popularity and strength stems in part from the fact that it is an extremely malleable notion, a conceptual Rorschach inkblot that accommodates many moving parts, concepts such as dignity, participation, best interests, access to justice, procedural autonomy, emotional tort, ethics, professional attitudes and practice, to cite just a few.

Additionally, in thinking about the concepts of child-friendly and child-sensitive approaches, and how they are meant to transform the justice system, I am reminded of the debate on the evolution from integration towards inclusion that pertains to the education of children with disabilities. Inclusive education has gained considerable momentum and the concept as a whole has, and still is, transformative for the education system in a way similar to what child-friendliness is for the justice system. On the one hand, integration refers to the necessary adaptation of children who are considered different to the classrooms as they exist to serve so-called mainstream children. In this regard, for children with disabilities, integration requires assimilation, uniformity and loss of differences. By comparison, according to the principles of integration, children who come into contact with the justice system should adapt to the greatest extent possible to what exists and how the system operates (as it was conceived by adults for adults). The process of inclusion, on the other hand, occurs when the education system and school operations bend, change, and adapt to the diversity of its pupils, transforming itself in depth to welcome greater diversity despite the many challenges that this generates. In a similar fashion, with the notion of child-friendly justice, the justice system bends, changes, and adapts to the full spectrum of its users, including children (as well as children with disabilities), and provides them with pathways to access the system and to participate as children. Even more importantly, a child-friendly justice system seeks to empower children with the objective of promoting authentic and meaningful justice in a way that children are not discriminated against in any fashion. In this sense, it could be argued that the inclusive foundation of child-friendly justice is the only pathway to meeting Target 16.3 of the Sustainable Development Goals,[10] which calls for ensuring equal access to justice for all.[11]

Lofty goals and real consequences

One major hurdle that the Council of Europe Guidelines face is the same that confronts many important guiding texts, be they national laws and policies or supranational recommendations and even binding conventions. While these documents may be diligently studied by administrative and political entities and guide public policy strategies and decisions to a significant extent, it remains an almost palpable challenge to bring them to be adopted and implemented by frontline professionals who operate in the trenches of the activities that they cover. From experience, I am often amazed at how few European practitioners and colleagues, stemming from a plurality of disciplines and working with and for children, candidly admit, when informally polled, that they have not read the full text of the CRC and are unfamiliar with the Council of Europe Guidelines on child-friendly justice.[12] One may wonder what is the usefulness of these lofty texts if they are not known to the professionals tasked with applying them in real-life situations?

It is always challenging to be involved in judicial proceedings that deal with high-conflict parental separations impacting children in which parental competence must be determined, as well as, depending on the particulars of the actual case, guardianship, and visitation modalities. In a vignette that is discussed later, none of the professionals emerge deserving much praise. I usually serve in the capacity of a designated court evaluator, but in this case, I was involved as a child therapist that got drawn into the judicial proceedings and was confronted with the reprehensible professional conduct of the court evaluator. Despite the inadequate behavior of this particular court evaluator, court evaluators play central, impactful roles in custodial decision-making. Indeed, in family proceedings, this role commands the best seat in the house, providing the practitioner with an unadorned intimate look at how a given judicial conflict plays out and getting to examine most, if not all the data of a given case. If the court evaluator is able to operate within the necessary court deadlines and if they experience some passion for this particular line of work, it is an incredibly stimulating professional endeavor. The court evaluator must be diligent, fair, and very thorough in all their actions; but unless they seriously botch the entrusted judicial mission, the court evaluator is not responsible for the decisions that are ultimately taken. Whether the court's decisions are deemed good or bad – those are the judicial authority's problem. Even better, usually nobody really tells the court evaluator how to conduct the evaluation and the methodology that they implement is rarely fundamentally challenged, although there are manuals and some sensible specialized guidelines that should be conformed to. Furthermore, in line with the satisfaction of conducting these evaluations, generally the participants, be they children, parents, or professionals, do their best to collaborate. In fact, the parents often compete to volunteer at the court evaluator's standing request to share with the evaluator what matters to each of them in terms of parental responsibility, visitation, guardianship, the other parent's behavior, and his or her meanness, the horrible judge and social workers, and so on. To put it mildly, outside of forensic evaluations that take place in the context of criminal procedures, court evaluators are privy to the best and worst human behaviors and cognitions as well as to the best and worst professional practices.

In the following vignette, the notion of dignity lies at the forefront. As a reminder, the Council of Europe Guidelines spell out the significance of considering the child's dignity as follows:

> [C]hildren should be treated with care, sensitivity, fairness and respect throughout any procedure or case, with special attention for their personal situation, well-being and specific needs, and with full respect for their physical and psychological integrity. This treatment should be given to them, in whichever way they have come into contact with judicial or non-judicial proceedings or other interventions, and regardless of their legal status and capacity in any procedure or case.[13]

Indeed, I would argue that in many situations, but even more so in situations where professionals are called in to examine high-conflict parental separations, the child's dignity is paramount and represents the ultimate test of the notion of child-friendly justice – that the child who goes through a judicial process should not come out of it worse off in terms of their well-being in the broadest sense than when they enter. Put differently, in these instances, it is absolutely clear that all professionals involved, but especially judges and other forms of judicial authority, have a special responsibility under the notion of child-friendly justice, whether they are properly trained or even if they are not. It is the judicial authority's ultimate responsibility to protect the child as much as possible from secondary harm associated with the judicial process. This should be straightforward. If the judge is informed of, or if they catch a whiff of, a child being maltreated in some form or fashion, even mildly, by the process or a professional's actions, they must act under a foreseeability expectation, call it out and modify the process. In addition to any single professional's actions, an individual judge should also be held accountable for emotional abuse if a child is maltreated during the course of the proceedings carried out under his or her judicial authority.

This illustrative vignette goes beyond established, child-friendly justice thinking and touches on reprehensible professional behavior and ethical parameters for practice. A few years ago, while sharing a long period in a waiting room of a courthouse (communal for all professionals involved), before being called in to testify in an explosive custody case, the psychiatrist appointed as court evaluator shared with me, as the child's therapist, that he was very satisfied with the fact that he had been able to extract everything he had sought from the child regarding the father's negative attitude towards the mother. This came as a major surprise for me given that, in therapy, the young boy had demonstrated a strong and passionate wish to remain neutral and had explicitly expressed caring feelings towards both parents. Being particularly curious to discover how the court appointed expert had obtained this information, I faked admiration for his professional capacity and expressed my wish to learn from his productive methods. Barely prompted, the colleague proudly explained how he had become progressively more menacing towards the child until he formulated a stark threat that, should the child not confirm some of the hearsay accounts of the father's negative attitudes/behavior towards the mother, it would be in his power, as a court appointed evaluator, to recommend that the child be placed in foster care until he became more cooperative.

Obviously, no reference to this highly questionable method was mentioned in the report that had been filed with the court nor was it later expressed in oral court testimony by the court evaluator. It was revealed only as part of an informal moment of professional banter, this particular colleague sharing information with the pride of a diligent professional! Fortunately, the child himself was subsequently called in to testify, in a restricted hearing without his parents' presence, and the astute judge had no trouble noticing a complete disconnect between the child's views and what the court evaluator had reported in his report and in person. However, despite some hints, the full extent of the court evaluator's unethical method never officially surfaced. Hypothetically, had the judge been cognizant of any significant details of the methods used by the court evaluator and chosen to ignore the unethical behavior, the judge could be considered liable for allowing the child to experience emotional distress under his authority and be held accountable, possibly cautioned by the judicial hierarchy. In reality, this would not have happened, as in most jurisdictions the judge suffers no consequences in situations such as these. What actually occurred in this case is that the judge basically ignored the expert's findings and recommendations (which in itself is a rare occurrence in this particular Swiss jurisdiction where there is a strong mandated deference to experts' opinions). However, neither did he confront the expert regarding the discrepancies between the child's testimony and his own, nor did he report him.[14] For that matter, most if not all court actors may also be responsible for bringing the evaluator's behavior to the court's attention, including the child therapist or the attorneys if they had learned of the evaluator's methods.

Child-friendly justice: a long road ahead

It is unquestionable that child-friendly justice is complex in terms of implementation because it faces numerous barriers. It is not as if there is a lack of legal guidance. A quick read of the CRC suggests that child-friendly justice should harmoniously resonate with the principles of best interests and participation. In fact, the CRC is very clear:

> In all actions concerning children, whether undertaken by public or private social welfare institutions, courts of law, administrative authorities or legislative bodies, the best interests of the child shall be a primary consideration.[15]

General Comment 14, which provides the Committee on the Rights of the Child's guidance on Article 3 of the CRC, states unambiguously that:

> [E]very "action" relating to a child or children has to take into account their best interests as a primary consideration. The word "action" does not only include decisions, but also all acts, conduct, proposals, services, procedures and other measures. Inaction or failure to take action and omissions are also "actions."[16]

In addition, for the best interests of the child to be fully and respectfully ascertained and assessed, the child's participation is unavoidable and should be compulsory except in the most unusual of circumstances. Indeed, Article 12 of the CRC states that:

1 States Parties shall assure to the child who is capable of forming his or her own views the right to express those views freely in all matters affecting the child, the views of the child being given due weight in accordance with the age and maturity of the child.
2 For this purpose, the child shall in particular be provided the opportunity to be heard in any judicial and administrative proceedings affecting the child, either directly, or through a representative or an appropriate body, in a manner consistent with the procedural rules of national law.[17]

With regard to the latter paragraph, it is important to put to rest the controversy regarding whether a child should be heard directly or whether indirect participation should be deemed sufficient. In other words, in the instance of a divorce case, particularly in high-conflict situations, should a judge hear the child directly or is it enough to hear the child indirectly via a social worker's account of a meeting or a specialized lawyer or a court-appointed guardian. The Committee on the Rights of Child has taken a clear position on this matter in its General Comment 12 on the right of the child to be heard and has been rather forcefully recommending "that, wherever possible, the child must be given the opportunity to be directly heard in any proceedings."[18]

The only reasonable exceptions in parental divorce and separation cases would be if the child does not wish to be heard directly, or indirectly for that matter; or if the process of participating and being heard could have a foreseeable and reasonably demonstrable detrimental effect on the child.[19] In other words, protection concerns for the child should rightly kick in, but only when necessary.[20]

In addition, directly hearing the child should also take place when it is known beyond doubt that the child is parroting a parental talking point or position. With the guidance of a trained mental health professional, it provides an opportunity for the judicial authority to introduce a reality check on the child and the manipulative parent's omnipotence. Conversely, not hearing the child would not necessarily provoke a positive change in the child or for their situation. After all, adults are never excluded from being heard on the basis of a perceived lack of sanity or truthfulness of the testimony. Finally, in the same vein, hearing the child should take place even when the parents' divorce is by mutual consent (so-called faceless divorces) and, as a precaution in the child's bests interests, not be ignored because it is not picked up by any of the adult actors of the judicial procedure.

Child-friendly justice, predicated on respect for the child's dignity, the child's bests interests, and their right to meaningful participation, does often crash into some serious barriers that deny children access to justice and make participation into just a slogan. The obstacles are numerous and draw for the most part from tradition and the sempiternal adult-centric perception of children as mostly lacking competence, ability, and maturity. Referring more specifically to protection cases, Skivenes pointedly asks, "Why don't children participate?" and stresses the traditional adult mindset that children are vulnerable and should be protected "from potential re-traumatisation and to relive pain they have experienced. Furthermore, decision-makers do not want to place the child in a difficult conflict of loyalty, or further burden the child."[21] This argument often resonates with many professionals as a prime reason for maintaining children at bay and resisting honoring their participatory rights. Of course, a benevolent protective attitude should always be at the forefront of all instances of children's participation before, during, and after judicial proceedings of any nature. Yet, protection and participation also should not be viewed as mutually exclusive, an assertion that research continues to validate.[22] Indeed, from my professional experience, there are very few exceptions in which participation is harmful to children if a child-friendly system is set up by taking the necessary steps and adopting the prescribed adaptations, including stringent procedural safeguards for the child's protection.

This precise recommendation is one of several highlighted in research conducted by the European Union's Agency for Fundamental Rights (FRA), drawing from the perspectives and experiences of professionals on children's participation in civil and criminal judicial proceedings[23] and from the perspectives and experiences of children involved in judicial proceedings as victims, witnesses, or parties.[24] Based on the analysis[25] of structural (legal provisions and policies), process (implemented legal and policy provisions), and outcome indicators (actual improvement of the situation of child rights), the main areas for action are clearly delineated. While it is beyond the scope of this chapter to summarize these findings, which should be viewed holistically and as interdependent by nature, it is my view that three nonetheless stand out, two of which were already discussed at length. First, the conceptual framework of a child-friendly justice system should resolutely draw from the main principles of the CRC, be set in law, and implemented in practice: best interests, non-discrimination, protection, and participation. Second, there is a clear need for advanced training of all professionals working with and for children within any justice system aiming to become or remain child-friendly. And, in training and practice, multidisciplinary cooperation should be favored based on the premise that the situation of any given child within the justice system is too complex to be handled by a single discipline.

Third, but by far not least, is the right to information. Child-friendly justice is nothing less than an empowerment of children to exercise their rights and contribute themselves to the enforcement of their rights. Legal empowerment of children by providing them with procedural autonomy requires specialized courts, child focal points, and accessible complaint mechanisms, specialized child lawyers and professionals from social, psychological, and medical fields who are paid decently. However, it also requires extensive sources of information including child-friendly online applications and resources, dedicated staff with lots of time and being able and willing to inform children of the full extent of their rights and how to exercise them. In other words, child-friendly justice should be about providing children with a sense of agency. On this level, there is no doubt that great progress is being achieved to provide child-friendly information and there are many best practices that are innovative both in communicating with children of different ages[26] and integrating digital technology. Yet, for most children almost everywhere, Stalford, Cairns, and Marshall's assessment that "attempts to develop child-friendly information have yet to progress beyond adult-driven, largely tokenistic and superficial re-branding exercises" still rings true to a great extent.[27]

Child-friendliness is about professional ethics, moral advocacy, and human rights

At its core, a child-friendly justice system is all about respect for the child as a person and their human rights considered equal to any other person. Skivenes explains that participation is a right of every individual to be involved in a process without necessarily dictating the outcome.[28] This also holds true for adults taking part in judicial procedures. The difference for children is that, for them to be involved, the justice system must reinvent itself. To be equal, children require specialized assistance to access and navigate the justice system in a secure fashion. Procedures must be adapted and information redesigned to fit with children's evolving cognitive and emotional capacities.

But it is not only the justice system that must strive for friendliness. Children also need friends that lend a helping hand. Indeed, it is my view that wherever one sits, at the edge of the justice system looking in (for example, conducting research) or in its midst operating as professionals coping with its complexity, we not only have an obligation to comply with moral expectations and ethical guidelines, but also a duty "within [our] practice to contribute to a society of [professionals] that are caring and practicing in line with fundamental human rights, without any discrimination and prejudice."[29] Hence, we are transformed into child rights advocates, defenders of children's rights, challenging the system with novel ideas and best practices, but also denouncing untoward professional conduct of colleagues. In this sense, child-friendly justice is also a catalyst for the promotion of human rights of all members of society.

Notes

1 Council of Europe, Guidelines of the Committee of Ministers of the Council of Europe on Child-friendly Justice, (Strasbourg, France Council of Eur. Publ'g 2010).

2 United Nations (U.N.) Convention on the Rights of the Child (Nov. 20, 1989), www.ohchr.org/en/professionalinterest/pages/crc.aspx.

3 In addition to traditional continental Europe, the Council of Europe's membership extends to Ukraine, the Russian Federation, and Turkey (only the Republic of Belarus is not a member). Additionally, Canada, the Holy See, Israel, Japan, Mexico and, the United States of America are active associate members.

4 *Supra* note 1, at § II(c).

5 U.N. Convention on the Rights of the Child (CRC), General Comment No. 24 Children's Rights in Juvenile Justice, U.N. Doc._CRC/C/GC/24 (2020).

6 United Nations Economic and Social Council (ECOSOC), U.N. Economic and Social Council 2005/20: Guidelines on Justice in Matters involving Child Victims and Witnesses of Crime, U.N. Doc. E/RES/2005/20 (July 22, 2020), https://digitallibrary.un.org/record/558183?ln=en.

7 Int'l Ass'n of Youth and Family Judges and Magistrates, Guidelines on Children in Contact with the Justice System (2016), http://www.aimjf.org/download/Documentation_EN/AIMJF/Guidelines_-_ENG_-_Ratified_17.04.26.pdf.

8 Moti Nissani, *Fruits, Salads, and Smoothies: A Working Definition of Interdisciplinarity*, 29 J. of Educ. Thought 119 (1995).

9 Moti Nissani, *Ten Cheers for Interdisciplinarity: The Case for Interdisciplinary Knowledge and Research*, 34 Soc. Sci. J. 201 (1997).

10 U.N. Dept. of Econ. & Soc. Aff., Sustainable Development Goals (2015), https://sdgs.un.org/goals.

11 This chapter adopts the view that child-friendly justice includes the more traditional legal notion of access to justice, in of itself a comprehensive construct, and should not be reduced to how children fare once they have gained access. *Id.*

12 I routinely poll gatherings of professionals and classes of students in human rights or helping professions as to their degree of familiarity with fundamental human rights texts, a habit borrowed from the late Jonathan Mann, professor of epidemiology, whose theoretical mantra was that health cannot be dissociated from human rights and conversely human rights are a health issue. Prof. Mann made a habit of polling medical students as to whether they had read the U.N., Universal Declaration of Human Rights, G.A. Res. 217 (III) at 71 (Dec. 10, 1948), https://www.un.org/en/universal-declaration-human-rights/.

13 Council of Europe (2011), p. 18.

14 It would also be fair for the reader to question the attitude and the professional cowardice of the child's therapist, i.e., the author of this article. After discussing the situation with several experienced colleagues, it was decided to not intervene expressly in the case at hand, but to pool various observations concerning the peculiar methods of this particular court evaluator with the intent of informing the judicial authorities. However, this somewhat controversial step was not taken as the shady court evaluator dropped off the professional radar shortly thereafter for reasons that to this day remain mysterious.

15 CRC, *supra* note 2, at art. 3, para. 1.
16 U.N. CRC., General comment No. 14 On the Right of the Child to Have His or Her Best Interests Taken as a Primary Consideration (art. 3, para. 1), U.N. Doc. CRC/C/GC/14, para. 17 (2013).
17 CRC, *supra* note 2, at art. 12.
18 U.N. CRC, General Comment No. 12. The Right of the Child to be Heard, U.N. Doc. CRC/C/GC/12, par. 35 (2009).
19 Different views exist on the cut off age of a young child to participate directly. Under the age of six is often cited in practice in progressive jurisdictions. However, in some cases, and if thought out and well managed, it may in the bests interests of the child to participate at a younger age for its symbolic effect on the parental conflict.
20 In these situations, protective measures, once implemented, should not preclude the child's participation and right to be heard at a later stage.
21 Marit Skivenes, *Why Don't Children Participate?* Ctr. for Research on Discretion and Paternalism, Aug. 27, 2020, https://discretion.uib.no/why-dont-children-participate/.
22 See Jessica Jacobson & Penny Cooper, *Participation in Courts and Tribunals Concepts, Realities and Aspirations* (2020); Aline Schoch et al., *Participation of Children and Parents in the Swiss Child Protection System in the Past and Present: An Interdisciplinary Perspective*, 9 Soc. Sci. 148.
23 Eur. Union Agency for Fundamental Rts., Child-friendly Justice. Perspectives and Experiences of Professionals on Children's Participation in Civil and Criminal Judicial Proceedings in 10 EU Member States (2015), https://fra.europa.eu/sites/default/files/fra-2015-child-friendly-justice-professionals_en.pdf.
24 *Id.*, Child-friendly justice Perspectives and Experiences of Children Involved in Judicial Proceedings as Victims, Witnesses or Parties in Nine EU Member States (2017), https://fra.europa.eu/sites/default/files/fra_uploads/fra-2017-child-friendly-justice-children-s-perspective-annexes_en.pdf.
25 The analysis relies on the United Nations (2012) model for human rights measurement implementation. U.N. Hum. Rts. Off. of the High Comm'r, Human Rights Indicators: A Guide to Measurement and Implementation (2012), www.ohchr.org/Documents/Publications/Human_rights_indicators_en.pdf.
26 For example, writing judgements for children (Stalford, 2020), a most challenging practice for just about every judicial authority, perhaps even an unachievable goal for most. Helen Stalford & Kathryn Hollingsworth, *"This Case is About You and Your Future": Towards Judgments for Children*, 83 Mod. L. Rev. 1030 (2020).
27 Helen Stalford et al., *Achieving Child Friendly Justice through Child Friendly Methods: Let's Start with the Right to Information*, 5 Soc. Inclusion 207 (2017).
28 *Supra* at note 20.
29 Geoff Lindsay et al., *Ethics for European Psychologists*, 79 (2008).

9 Family group conferences in child protection

A communitarian implementation of children's participation rights

Tali Gal

Introduction

How can children be allowed to exercise their right to participation in decision making without endangering their well-being? This question arises often, especially when it comes to charged and complex issues, as in the case of children at risk. Some of the arguments are prompted by fears of exposing children to difficult and painful content, of placing a burden greater than they can bear on their shoulders, and of exposing them to explicit and implicit pressures. These arguments are weighty and warrant an in-depth discussion of ways to implement the children's right to participation.

The purpose of this chapter is to present the distinct liberal and communitarian paradigms, which form the basis of completely different applications of the right of children to participation. The discussion focuses on the area of decision making in cases of children at risk, which is one of the most fateful situations imaginable in the lives of children. Implementation of the right to participation within the framework of the liberal paradigm is exemplified by the Planning, Treatment, and Assessment Committees (PTACs). The application of the right to participation within the communitarian framework is exemplified by the Family Group Conference (FGC) model. Relying on the Israeli experience implementing the two alternatives, a comparison between the models amplifies their distinct characteristics. The purpose of this chapter is not to delve into the practical expressions of each model, but to delineate the theoretical contours of the two paradigms and the "applied archetype" of the practical models derived from them.

UNCRC and the right to participation

The adoption of the United Nations (UN) Convention on the Rights of the Child (CRC) three decades ago by the UN General Assembly marked a watershed in the discourse concerning the rights of children. Laws were enacted worldwide, judgements handed down, organizations established, and projects developed with the aim of enshrining various children's rights and implementing them in practice. The participation right symbolizes more than any other of the

CRC's articles the change in the social construction of children, having created a framework for treating children as citizens, community members with their own interests, desires, and opinions. The right to participation has established a duty for parents, guardians, educators, social workers, and political leaders to take into account children's viewpoints and to ascribe to them appropriate weight, even when they themselves are entrusted with representing the best interests of the children.[1]

The participation right does not create an obligation to act in accordance with the child's wishes, nor is it satisfied by providing children with opportunities to present their positions unilaterally. Instead, the CRC requires that children be included in dialogue on the subject under discussion. Academic writing has emphasized the interpersonal nature of the discourse of rights that the CRC makes possible.[2]

The centrality of the principle of participation in the CRC, and the challenges that emerge in its implementation while realizing the other guiding principles (those of the best interests of the child, of equality, and of development), compelled the development of new and creative mechanisms for joint decision making. Since the CRC came into force in 1989, the meaning of the principle of participation and the ways in which it has been implemented have been the subject of discussion and constant development by academics, practitioners, and policy makers.[3] This vibrant discourse reflects the difficulties in reaching the full realization of the participation right in the real world. Together with the desire to enable children to participate in a safe, development-compatible, and egalitarian manner, other challenges emerge owing to built-in power disparity resulting from differences in age, experience, role, socio-economic status, language, and more. These challenges are particularly pronounced when it comes to children at risk. How is it possible to overcome the many barriers facing these children when they seek to participate in decision-making processes that affect their destiny?

The following analysis offers a distinction between the liberal and the communitarian paradigms of children's rights, which lead to a different application of the right to participate and offer different ways of dealing with the challenges mentioned.

The liberal paradigm and its effect on the children's rights discourse

The Age of Enlightenment, which began in the late 17th century, marked the rise of liberalism as a leading political philosophy. Under liberalism, people are entitled to basic freedoms, such as the right to property, freedom of conscience and religion, and freedom of association.[4] Liberal theory assumes the existence of an autonomous and rational subject capable of making decisions independently. Legal and administrative mechanisms have evolved to balance competing rights and to resolve conflicts between individuals or between individuals and the state. Decisions are made based on equal competition between the parties, each side bringing its best arguments. Children, especially young ones, challenge the liberal paradigm because they do not realize the premise of full autonomy and rationality.[5] To overcome this difficulty, many systems have designed competency and rationality tests to determine who could be considered a rights-holder (including the possibility of participating in the decision-making process) and who remains an object of protection. Two key features of the liberal paradigm are revealed here. One is the centrality of the competency test as a condition for gaining entry into the legal or administrative process; the second is adherence to procedural rights, such as the right to representation, the right to remain silent, and the right to argue and to appeal the decision. Presumably, if the procedural rights are maintained and all those who are capable of making rational decisions are then allowed to express their views, the procedure will be a fair one, leading to the best decision.

The discourse on children's rights has developed against the background of the liberal approach. In most cases where attempts have been made to regulate children's right to participation, emphasis has been placed on the opportunity to participate. The right to participate is usually established through procedures that give children and their parents an opportunity to express a position before a decision is made on their case. At best, children and their guardians were provided the right to receive early information about the forthcoming decision, adequate invitation to the process, and a requirement was included to provide an explanation of the decision. As a result, in many countries, the right of children to participate in decisions concerning their lives is implemented in a way that can be called liberal: formalistically, adversarially, and individually.[6]

One of the problems with the liberal model is that it is based on the assumption that it is possible to conduct a consultation between the decision makers (state representatives) and children using the same decision mechanism that exists in consultation with adults, provided that some modifications are allowed. Yet, the existing liberal decision-making mechanisms are fundamentally unsuitable for dialogue with young participants. One explanation for this structural difficulty is that, for many children, the condition for participation is a certain type of relationship with the relevant adults. Children value an ongoing and respectful relationship based on personal acquaintance and genuine interest in them. They respond with resistance, disengagement, or indifference to encounters that lack these qualities.[7]

Another key feature of the liberal paradigm is the emphasis on family and individual privacy. Because the premise is one of autonomy and rationality, the project at the heart of liberalism is the prevention of over-intervention by the state in the lives of individuals and families. Accordingly, decision-making processes concerning child protection include only the child and parents, and where relevant, additional potential custodians. Extended family members, community members involved in the child's life, and family friends are not part of the process. The price of protecting the privacy of the family unit is the missed opportunities for support and involvement of people from the natural circles surrounding the family.

Admittedly, in recent decades, there has been a shift from the "pure" liberal paradigm in favor of efforts to overcome the children's inherent inferiority.

Procedures for age-appropriate explanations and preparation have been established for children, and models have been developed for the representation and guidance of children by trained lawyers and other adults, making special accommodations with the help of counselors from the therapeutic professions. Nevertheless, these efforts do not deviate from the prevailing paradigm in which capability tests constitute the key for joining the procedure and affecting its outcomes. Indeed, without a paradigm shift, no real change can be accomplished in the way children are legally allowed to take part in decisions concerning their fate.

The communitarian paradigm and its effect on the children's rights discourse

The communitarian paradigm considers the individual as part of a close fabric of reciprocity and interdependence.[8] The modern communitarian paradigm does not relinquish the rights of the individual but holds that it is the mutual responsibility of all members of the community to ensure that situations of inferiority to another are minimized (non-domination).[9]

Restorative Justice (RJ) provides a practical framework for implementing the communitarian paradigm in decision making.[10] RJ was born out of frustration with both the punitive and the rehabilitative approaches and offered a "third lens."[11] Crime, according to RJ, harms people and relationships, and creates a duty to repair the harms caused by it. Social and family ties are a powerful source of condemnation of the act and of support for the victim, but they are also the ones who have been harmed and need to be repaired.[12] Justice, therefore, must include the offender, the victim, and the community in the search of ways to heal the harm that has been created and to restore security.[13] The RJ approach seeks to ensure equal and safe participation of all involved, in an effort to achieve results that promote the social and emotional rehabilitation of the perpetrators and victims, all out of respect for their human rights.[14]

RJ has been implemented in recent years in other contexts outside the criminal arena.[15] "Restorative practices" are applied and explored, among others, in schools,[16] in child protection cases,[17] and in the context of international and inter-ethnic conflicts.[18] RJ can therefore be viewed not only as a social response to crime, but also as an approach for interpreting and applying human rights in a way that transforms power relations between community and state and shifts decision-making power to natural stakeholders: those directly affected by the act and those around them.[19]

With respect to children at risk, RJ constructs an egalitarian discourse in which the nuclear and extended family members play a key role in decision making. Weaknesses resulting from differences in gender, age, and social status may be reduced through the participation of supporters and through a strength-based approach.[20]

Communitarianism can also be found in the CRC itself. Reading it from a communitarian perspective outlines a vision of a utopian reality where children are at the center of the various communities that surround them, active and involved in decision making, with conditions around them individually tailored for them according to their desires, well-being, and interests. The child's family, immediate community, culture, and nationality are all key and active variables in shaping this utopian reality.[21] The aspiration of communitarianism to eradicate or at least minimize domination and coercion, together with the centrality to relationships, creates a theoretical and ideological framework for equal treatment of children, in the deep and essential sense of the term.[22]

Planning, treatment, and assessment committees: liberal implementation of the right of children at risk to participation

The PTACs constitute a central mechanism in the child protection system in Israel. They are a forum that includes all the relevant professionals dealing with cases of children at risk of harm and neglect, and their purpose is to allow the various professionals to exchange information, make an assessment of the child's level of risk, consider various alternatives for treatment, and formulate a recommendation for a detailed treatment plan. In 2006, a comprehensive reform was launched, which regulated the activity of the PTACs, and established the principles of partnership with parents, stakeholder empowerment, and reliance on strengths as guiding principles. In practice, the reform has resulted mainly in procedural changes that regulate the way children and parents participate in these committees. The reform formulates age-based assumptions regarding the participation of children in committees; concerns about their personal safety may prevent them from taking part in the process. Nevertheless, all children are given the opportunity to voice their position, whether before the entire committee, the case worker, or the committee chair. Children who participate physically in the process receive preparation guidance and information in advance, and are accompanied by someone from their immediate environment. All children receive information about the decision that was ultimately reached.[23]

The reform has significantly strengthened the status of children (and of their parents) in the decision-making process, at least in the formal sense.[24] An in-depth look, however, reveals that at the core of the reform are the assumptions inherent in the liberal paradigm, of competency, rationality, and autonomy. Those evaluating the child's competency to make a rational decision are the very professionals who are authorized to make decisions in the child's case. This raises the question whether a child can be perceived as having "rationality" when the professionals know that the child has a different opinion from theirs.[25] The best interest of the child trumps the right of children to participation in the PTACs; when the parents or professionals think that the child's participation may be detrimental to the child's well-being, participation may be prevented, even if the child has expressed a desire to participate in the PTAC.[26]

The PTACs act as a tool for exercising the authority of the state to intervene, even by force, in family autonomy.[27] In light of the great power of the state to remove children from parental custody or to instruct parents to behave in a certain way, the emphasis in the PTACs regulations is to ensure the procedural rights of parents and children. The liberal paradigm implemented in this framework creates an adversarial and formalistic reality. At the end of the process, it is the state representatives who make the decision about the child's fate, while the parents and children are able, at most, to try to influence this decision.[28] Even close adherence to the values of "partnership" and "listening," as the guidelines demand, does not change the existing divide and unequal balance of power between state representatives, on the one hand, and the child and the family, on the other.

FGC: communitarian implementation of the participation right of children at risk

FGCs are one of the widely known models of RJ in the context of child protection. FGC processes include the child, the parents, other family members, and any other person with significant ties to the family such as friends, teachers, and spiritual leaders. The facilitator is responsible for a meaningful preparation process and for bringing together everyone involved in a face-to-face meeting. Relevant professionals may participate in the discussion, but their role is limited to providing information. To the extent possible, the reins are held by the direct stakeholders. Many programs include a "family private time," in which non-family members leave the room and allow the family to put together an intervention plan based on the concerns, resources, and goals presented earlier. This plan needs to be approved by all participants in the meeting. If there is no agreement, the family reconvenes to make changes, until a consensus is reached.[29]

In Israel, an FGC operated for a short time in the early 21st century, and recently began operating again as an alternative to the PTACs.[30] Evaluation studies point to the potential of FGC processes to serve as child-friendly forums as far as the inclusion of the children in the decision-making process is concerned.[31] The success of these processes seems to lie, at least in part, in the ability to adapt each procedure to the needs, wishes, and abilities of each and every child. Much less is known about the long-term outcomes of these processes, and their ability to improve the situation of children at risk.[32] To determine unequivocally whether FGC processes are a more efficient way of treating children at risk than are PTACs, there is a need for assessment studies based on rigorous protocols, which are difficult to conduct for ethical and practical reasons.[33] Instead of arguing for the superiority of either approach in achieving desirable results for children at risk, the analysis below conceptualizes the differences in how each of the paradigms constructs, achieves, and enables the implementation of children's participation right.

Comparison

The following table identifies three differences in the modes of construction of children's right to participation under the liberal and the communitarian paradigms regarding children at risk:[34]

	Liberal paradigm	Communitarian paradigm
1. Depth of participation	Children as invited guests	Children as partners
2. Breadth of participation	Children and parents	Natural support circles
3. Conditions for participation	Competency tests	Meaningful tie with the family

Regarding the **depth of participation**, the liberal approach perceives the professional state representatives as the decision makers, because only a qualified representative is authorized to intervene in the family cell. Procedural rights of participants legitimize the state power. Conversely, the communitarian approach perceives the private stakeholders as key players in child protection decisions because they also bear the collective responsibility for the well-being of community members. Thus, family members, supporters, and professionals jointly engage in a process of deliberative democracy,[35] in which the issue is debated until a common agreement is reached. This does not necessarily mean an equal partnership, but rather that all partners contribute their perspective according to their wishes and abilities and are enriched by the perspectives of other partners.

A special challenge is posed by the concept of partnership with young children. Partnership means a willingness to share power and change one's original viewpoint. Treating children as partners means perceiving them as potentially contributing to an optimal decision, and therefore their opinions, feelings, and desires are sought not as a favor to them, but due to its significance. Treating children as partners also expresses the recognition of children's dependence on their environment, as the right to participation cannot exist in a vacuum, without the presence of other decision partners who listen to them respectfully and engage in dialogue with them.[36]

More broadly, partnership with children at risk is based on a triangle of interdependencies and shared interests, whose vertices are the children, the parents, and the state.[37] At the center of the triangle lies the common interest in protecting the safety of the child. Children depend on their parents to fulfill their basic needs, and on the state to help them in this endeavor. The state and parents need children to cooperate and adapt to new and often difficult situations. How can each side help the other? Beyond the search for common solutions, the transition to seeing each side as a partner conveys a message of equality, reciprocity, and respect.

The second distinctive characteristic relates to the **breadth of participation**. Reflecting a liberal paradigm, the 2006 PTACs regulations have enshrined the right of children and their parents, and them only, to participation. Other people with significant relationships with the child have no legal standing. The extended family is excluded from the process because their involvement ostensibly infringes on the privacy of both the nuclear family and of themselves. According to the communitarian perception, in contrast, the circles surrounding the nuclear family are seen as powerful resources that may help the family in crisis, and which, if requested, will willingly come closer and help their family members, with whom in many cases the relations have weakened over the years.

The third distinguishing feature concerns the **threshold conditions** for substantive participation in the decision-making process in the case of children at risk. The liberal conception imposes an entrance test, however minimal, of competence, to meet the expectation of rationality underlying the liberal rights theory. Child protection procedures impose a threshold test for participation in proceedings, whether through an age limit or by means of maturity tests. Even where the threshold conditions do not sweepingly prevent children from participating, their maturity and ability limit the extent to which they are allowed to participate and influence the decision.[38] One reason for this is that a liberal system requires that individuals contribute their consolidated and final position to the process, so that it can be either accepted or rejected as is.

A communitarian approach does not invite stakeholders to deliver final positions, but to participate in a dynamic, deliberative dialogue. Naturally, differences in experience, maturity, and ability may affect how one participates in such decision-making processes, but the ongoing deliberative discourse allows diverse communication styles and allows participants with different levels of understanding to take an active part in the discussion.

The proposed analytical distinction is not so categorical in reality. Some of the procedures in the PTACs may be understood as reflecting a communitarian approach, such as the call for partnership of children in the committees, the opportunity given to children and parents to be accompanied by a support person, and the importance ascribed to the children's indirect statements. At the same time, the discussions that take place in the FGCs do not always live up to the communitarian ideal. Supporters beyond the nuclear family do not always participate actively in the process, young children are not always involved in it, and there is a possibility that professionals would "guide" family members to reach what they consider a desirable solution.[39] In fact, one can argue that it is the liberal approach that ensures a wider realization of children's participation right because it contains more guarantees through clear procedures and the right of appeal. The communitarian perception, by contrast, is characterized by the transfer of power to the natural circles surrounding the child, which may result in silencing the children. Indeed, neither model guarantees full implementation of the participation right. Both approaches rely on systemic support through legislation, training, and budgeting that encourage meaningful participation of children in decisions.[40] The argument here is that proceedings within the liberal paradigm are limited in their ability to maintain "inclusive participation." By contrast, although procedures conducted from a communitarian perspective do not guarantee inclusive participation in every case, they at least potentially allow such sharing of power.

What, then, is the desired relationship between the liberal and the communitarian paradigms, and accordingly, between the different modes of application of children's participation rights? Ostensibly, it may be concluded that these are two alternative and opposing paradigms. A full implementation of the communitarian approach means a comprehensive reform and a transition to permanent use of FGCs, or of some similar model, in all cases of children at risk. A fully liberal approach means continued application of the right to participate in PTACs, with continuous improvement of the tools for deciding who can be allowed to actively participate and who is to participate indirectly.

A preferable alternative is a combination of the two paradigms into a one-tiered system. As a starting point, whenever a concern arises for the safety of a child, a deliberative procedure should take place, based on the FGC or similar model, in cooperation with the nuclear family and others surrounding them. Family members control the decisions aimed at ensuring the safety of the children, in accordance with the concerns raised by them and by the professionals. The latter are also providers of information and guidance, and help the family reach the assistance services they request. The state does not abdicate its responsibility toward the family and children. In addition to training, funding, and development of such processes, the state also delineates rules designed to prevent silencing, manipulations, and pressure by the litigants. If the procedure or the treatment plan fail, the case moves up on the "enforcement pyramid," to a liberal model, where decision-making power passes to professionals, for example, to the PTAC.[41] The default, as noted, should be based on the community model that promotes self-regulation of the family in coordination with professionals. The authority of state representatives to intervene serves to motivate families to design and implement the intervention plan themselves.[42]

Conclusion

PTACs operating in Israel in cases of children at risk are required to allow children to make their voice heard as much as possible. However, it seems that in practice the committees find it difficult to genuinely involve children of different ages in their deliberations.[43] The conceptualization of the PTACs as derivatives of the liberal paradigm provides an explanation for this difficulty. In the liberal paradigm, "minors" are held to be different from rational participants.[44] Any attempt to make minors participate is based on a weaker starting point than that of the "ideal" participant.[45] Participation in the liberal paradigm means the right to express a position vis-à-vis the authorities which have the power to make decisions. The emphasis on family privacy excludes from the decision-making process additional participants who know the child and the family, emphasizing the dichotomy between the rational and irrational, between private stakeholders and state representatives, and between children and adults.

The communitarian paradigm, by contrast, is based on a conception of shared responsibility of the community toward all the individuals in it, especially toward children.[46] In doing so, it expands the definition of participants in decision-making processes beyond those who are legally responsible for the children. For children, the advantage inherent in the communitarian paradigm is that it dispels the dichotomy between the rational and the irrational, between the capable and the incapable, and between the incidental guest and the decision maker. In communitarian processes such as FGCs, "weak" or "disempowered" participants, such as children, minority groups, and people with disabilities can be empowered in various ways, such as personal guidance, intensive preparation, and an individually tailored process.[47] The communitarian conceptualization of children's right to participation emphasizes the possibility of treating children as partners in the decision-making process, through sharing knowledge and decision-making power between state representatives and family members.[48]

Naturally, there are risks in the processes derived from the communitarian paradigm. The transfer of power to the community, even in the presence of state supervision, can lead to the silencing of weak voices, to pressure participants to "sweep problems under the carpet," and to solutions that could aggravate the situation of children. These are real risks faced by programs worldwide.

Without taking a position on the superiority of one approach over another, the comparison conducted in this chapter makes it possible to advance the discussion on the communitarian alternative. Current discourse is far from having exhausted the potential of this paradigm for inclusive participation of children at risk in decision-making processes. Arguably, the communitarian approach and FGC processes as its practical expression are not suitable for all children and all families. Nevertheless, such processes should at least be considered as an alternative for many children at risk. Indeed, comparing the FGC and the PTAC models creates an artificial antithesis that does not fully correspond to reality. The comparison between the "pure" characteristics of each model highlights their structural potential for real and meaningful participation of children at risk in decision-making processes. This analysis may also assist in the development of future models that deviate from accepted patterns of procedural rights, promoting personal well-being, respect, and equality for children.

Notes

1 Gerison Lansdown, *The Realisation of Children's Participation Rights: Critical Reflections*, *in* A Handbook of Children and Young People's Participation, 11–23 (Barry Persy-Smith & Nigel Thomas, eds., 2010).

2 *E.g.*, Robyn Fitzgerald et al., *Children's Participation as a Struggle Over Recognition Exploring the Promise of Dialogue*, *in* A Handbook of Children and Young People's Participation, 293–305 (Barry Persy-Smith & Nigel Thomas, eds., 2010).

3 *See* Roger A. Hart, *Children's Participation: From Tokenism to Citizenship*, *in* Innocenti Essays, 4 (1992) (proposing the 'Ladder of Participation'); Harry Shier, *Pathways to Participation: Openings, Opportunities and Obligations*, 15 Child. & Soc'y 107 (2001) (proposing a matrix of five levels of participation and three levels of institutional support); Laura Lundy, *'Voice' is not Enough: Conceptualizing Article 12 of the United Nations Convention on the Rights of the Child.* 33 Brit. Educ. Rsch J. 927 (2007) (proposing four conditions for full implementation of the participation right: space, voice, audience, and influence).

4 John Locke was the first to formulate the principles of liberalism comprehensively in his book on political government, published in 1689: John Locke, *Two Treatises of Government* (1689).

5 H. L. A. Hart, *Essays on Bentham: Jurisprudence and Political Philosophy* (1982).

6 *See* Eran Uziely, ***Pupils' Participation in Placement Committees in Israel Implementing the Principle of Child Participation***, *in* International Perspectives And Empirical Findings On Child Participation: From Social Exclusion To Child-Inclusive Policies, 59 (Tali Gal & Benedetta Faedi Duramy eds., 2015) (showing that despite the legal obligation to involve children in the decisions of placement committees regarding their placement in special education, there is a considerable gap between the degree of participation desired by young people and their actual participation in these discussions).

7 Tali Gal, *From Social Exclusion to Child-Inclusive Policies: Toward an Ecological Model of Child Participation*, *in* International Perspectives and Empirical Findings on Child Participation: From Social Exclusion to Child-inclusive Policies, 451 (Tali Gal & Benedetta Faedi Duramy eds., 2015).

8 Hughes Gordon, *Communitarianism and Law and Order*, 16 Critical Soc. Pol'y 17 (1996).

9 John Braithwaite & Philip Pettit, *Not Just Deserts: A Republican Theory of Criminal Justice* (1992).

10 John Braithwaite, *Shame and Modernity*, 33 The Brit. J. of Criminology 1–18.

11 Howard Zehr, *Changing Lenses: A New Focus for Criminal Justice* (1990).

12 John Braithwaite, *Crime, Shame and Reintegration* (1989).

13 Zehr, *supra* note 11, at 181.

14 John Braithwaite, *Principles of restorative justice*, *in* Restorative Justice and Criminal Justice: Competing or Reconcilable Paradigms? 1 (Andrew von Hirsch et al. eds., 2003).

15 Declan Roche, *Dimensions of Restorative Justice*, 62 J. of Soc. Issues 217 (2006).

16 B. Morrison, *Bullying and Victimization in Schools: A Restorative Justice Approach*, 219 Trends and Issues in Crime and Crim. Just. 1 (2002).

17 Joan Pennel & Gale Burford, *Family Group Decision Making: Protecting Children and Women*, 79 Child Welfare 131 (2000).

18 John Braithwaite, *Pre-Empting Terrorism*, Current Issues in Crime and Crim. Just. 96 (2005).

19 Jennifer Llewellyn & Brenda Morrison, *Deepening the Relational Ecology of Restorative Justice*, 1 Int'l J. of Restorative Just. 343–355 (2018).

20 Joan Pennell, *The Personal is Political: The Restorative Dialectic of Child Inclusion*, 1 The Int'l J. of Restorative Just. 413–427 (2018).

21 Tali Gal, *Child Victims and Restorative Justice: A Needs-Rights Model* (2011).

22 Martha Minow, *What Ever Happened to Children's Rights?* 80 Minn L. Rev. 267 (1995).

23 Ministry of Welfare and Social Services, Planning, Treatment and Assessment Committees: Principles and Working Routines, Inclusion of Parents and Children, the Computerized System – The Research, Planning, and Training System (2014) (hereinafter, Planning, Treatment, and Assessment Committees, 2014).

24 Shani Oppenheim-Weller, Ella Schwartz & Asher Ben-Arieh, *Child Involvement in Treatment Planning and Assessment in Israel*, 22 Child & Fam. Soc. Work 1302 (2017) (although many children received preparation in advance of the PTACs meetings, their actual influence on the decisions was insignificant. Parental involvement and their ability to influence decisions were described as higher).

25 Planning, Treatment, and Assessment Committees, 2014, *supra* note 23, at 28 ("From the age of 9, children can be brought to participate in committee discussions of their case. The family social worker **must assess the child's ability to appear before the committee**, taking into account all the data: age, physical and mental condition, developing skills, too many participants, the desire of the parents, the desire of the child. If **the family social worker, in consultation with the committee chair**, decides not to bring the child to the hearing, care must be taken to document the decision, and its reasons must be described in detail") (emphasis added).

26 *See* State of Israel, Ministry of Labor, Welfare and Social Services, Instructions and Announcements: Planning, Treatment and Assessment Committee: Its Role and Work Methods 6 (January 2017).
27 Clare Huntington, *Rights Myopia in Child Welfare*, 53 UCLA L. Rev. 637 (2005).
28 See Oppenheim-Waller et al., *supra* note 24, at 1307.
29 Jeanette Elizabeth Schmid & Shoshana Pollack, *Developing Shared Knowledge: Family Group Conferencing as a Means of Negotiating Power in the Child Welfare System*, 21 Prac. Soc. Work in Action 175–188 (2009).
30 See Amir Kashi, *Planning, Treatment, and Assessment Committees within the Partnerships Space*, 16 Meeting Point 28–31 (Heb.).
31 *See* Paul Nixon et al., A Survey of International Practices, Policy and Research on Family Group Conferencing and Related Practices 35 (2005) (A survey of FGC programs in 17 countries revealed that the degree of participation of children in these processes varied, but in places where proper preparation and planning were conducted, and where children were accompanied by a supporter, their participation was satisfactory).
32 *See* Stephanie Cosner Berzin et al., *Does Family Group Decision Making Affect Child Welfare Outcomes? Findings from a Randomized Control Study*, 87 Child Welfare 35 (2008) (No differences were found in children's personal safety and the number of placements between control and study groups); Knut Sundell & Bo Vinnerljung, *Outcomes of Family Group Conferencing in Sweden: A 3-Year Follow-up*, 28 Child Abuse & Neglect 267 (2004) (children who underwent FGC processes were referred to social services more times than were children in the control group, except for cases of neglect).
33 Lee Barnsdale & Moira Walker, Examining the Use and Impact of Family Group Conferencing (2007).
34 Tali Gal, *Children's Rights in Practice: The Participation of Children in Care and Protection Decisions, in* Ethics and Human Rights in a Globalized World: An Interdisciplinary and International Approach 323 (Klaus Hoffman-Holland ed. 2009).
35 Iris Marion Young, *Activist Challenges to Deliberative Democracy*, 29(5) Pol. Theory 670, 670–690 (2001) (defining deliberative democracy processes as such that "...bring all the potentially affected parties or their representatives into a public deliberative process. Deliberators should appeal to justice and frame the reasons for their proposals in terms they claim that others ought to accept. Doing so rules out the assertion of simple partisan interest or the attempt to compel assent by means of threats and sanctions").
36 Tali Gal, *An Ecological Model of Child and Youth Participation*, 79 Child. & Youth Serv. Rev. 57 (2017).
37 *See* Clare Huntington, *Mutual Dependency in Child Welfare*, 82 Notre Dame L. Rev. 1485 (2006).
38 *E.g.*, Tal Nir & Lotem Perry-Hazan, *The Framed Right to Participate in Municipal Youth Councils and Its Educational Impact*, 69 Child. & Youth Serv. Rev. 174 (2016) (demonstrating how urban student and youth councils eventually limit the participation of youths on issues that are, ostensibly, within the scope that is considered appropriate for their age).
39 *See* Lisa Merkel-Holguin, *Sharing Power with the People: Family Group Conferencing as a Democratic Experiment*, 31(1) J. Soc'y & Soc. Welfare 155 (2004).
40 Gal, *supra* note 36.
41 Tali Gal & Dahlia Schilli-Jerichower, *Mainstreaming Therapeutic Jurisprudence in Family Law: The Israeli Child Protection Law as a Case Study*, 55 Fam. Ct. Rev. 177 (2017).
42 John Braithwaite, *Restorative Justice & Responsive Regulation* (2002) (proposing the 'enforcement pyramid,' according to which the existence of a forceful response on

the part of the state at the top of the pyramid is a catalyst for rational players to self-regulate, leaving the use of forceful sanctions to the minority of cases, when players are unable or unwilling to do so).

43 Ravit Alfandari, *Evaluation of a National Reform in the Israeli Child Protection Practice Designed to Improve Children's Participation in Decision-Making*, 22 Child & Fam. Soc. Work 54; *See also* Oppenheim-Weller, *supra* note 24.

44 John Stuart Mill, *On Liberty* §§ 22–23 (1859) ("It is, perhaps, hardly necessary to say that this doctrine is meant to apply only to human beings in the maturity of their faculty. We are not speaking of children, or of young persons below the age which the law may fix as that of manhood or womanhood. Those who are still in a state to require being taken care of by others, must be protected against their own actions as well as against external injury").

45 Emma Uprichard, *Children as 'Being and Becomings': Children, Childhood and Temporality*, 22 Child & Fam. Soc. Work 303 (2008).

46 *See* Hillary Rodham Clinton, *It Takes A Village* (2006).

47 *See* Tali Gal, *Child Victims and Restorative Justice: A Needs-Rights Model*, Chapter 6 (2011) (proposing recommendations for RJ procedures in cases child victims of abuse).

48 *See* Schmid & Pollack, *supra* note 29.

10 The unheard voices of young girls at risk

Shiran Reichenberg

> *"All this time you took away my life and my choices..."*
> *"There is no one, no one sees, hears, listens, nothing..."*
> *"My lawyer? She didn't really practice law for me, she never visits, or calls..."*
> *"This is not justice..."*
> *"They look at you and they don't believe you."*[1]

Introduction

I was 22 years old when I first visited Messila, a locked institute for young girls removed from their home, primarily due to abuse or neglect. I have been to Messila many times since, but my first impression changed my perspective and influenced my career track. Back then, I could not imagine that one day, as part of my academic career, I would be working with these girls and training future lawyers to represent them.

That first visit encouraged me to become a clinical instructor at a children and youth at-risk rights' clinic, being a voice for children at risk and bringing their point of view to the youth court and social services. My doctoral dissertation revolved around the girls treated in Messila, interviewing them about their experience with the care proceedings processes, and their relationship with all the relevant stakeholders: social workers, youth judges, their parents, and family. The main finding of my research is that active participation in legal proceedings that concern them is a life skill we need to teach these girls. Moreover, being from a locked institute such as Messila deepens the challenges they face due to the intersectionality of their identities.

This chapter will examine whether the right to participation of at-risk adolescent girls in the framework of care and supervision proceedings is adequately incorporated into the practices used in these proceedings for an in-depth understanding of the gaps existing in this area, between law in books and law in action.

Theoretical framework – law (in)books

The convention on the rights of the child (CRC), Article 12 – participation

The CRC is the most important international document regarding children's rights. It guarantees a wide range of rights for children and imposes duties on

States to ensure them. The CRC views children as individual human beings with wishes and opinions that should be considered when making legal decisions regarding their lives. The CRC presents four main guiding principles: (1) the right to equality, (2) the right to life, survival, and development, (3) the best interest principle, and (4) the right to participate.[2] Despite the fact that the CRC was signed and ratified by almost every country, the implementation varies by country. Some jurisdictions incorporated the CRC rights into their constitutions, which means the rights upheld by the CRC can be claimed in courts, while other countries, like Israel, apply the CRC as a guideline but do not integrate it into the Israeli law.

The principle of participation in Article 12 of the CRC refers to one of the main innovations of the CRC. It requires treating children as autonomous individuals, not as human beings in the making, but rather persons that are here and now, with their own needs and abilities. The right to participate places the child's issues at the center of the discussion, expresses respect for children, diminishes the exclusion of children from society, and can be implemented at almost any age in accordance with the child's evolving capacities.[3]

Article 12 is considered "the linchpin" of the CRC because it recognizes the child as an autonomous human being with wishes and feelings who is able to take part in decisions that concern them.[4] Although there is not an explicit obligation in the CRC to appoint a legal representative for the child in legal proceedings that concern them, the CRC requires that a child's opinion be heard.[5] As scholars point out, the right to "express views" should not be limited by age or maturity. Any view or opinion should be heard and considered either directly from the child or indirectly through a representative.[6] In most cases, therefore, in order to ensure effective participation, and thereby guarantee full implementation of Article 12 of the CRC, a country needs to provide legal representation for a child in all the proceedings that concern them.

The right to participation includes three main components: (1) the right to be heard, (2) the right to speak freely, and (3) the right to have the child's opinion fully considered. This is a procedural right that contributes to the protection and promotion of other children's rights, such as the right to equality and free speech.[7] Therefore, the exclusion of children from proceedings regarding them is a violation of multiple rights: a violation of the right to participation as guaranteed by the CRC and a violation of the specific right which the proceedings are about. The right to participation can affect any aspect of the child's life, in the public sphere or the personal sphere. However, a child also has the right to waive their right to participate. Furthermore, participation does not give the child the right to make the final decision, just to be a significant part of the decision-making process.[8]

Right to participation in Israeli law

In Israel, there is no coherent legislation regarding children's rights. The laws regarding children were legislated over different years and are therefore inconsistent and not necessarily rights oriented. Many of these laws are paternalistic and include contradictory instructions for similar situations. For example, several clauses refer to representation and hearing the child in legal proceedings described in the youth law (care and supervision), such as Article 8(c), which gives the court discretion to appoint a guardian ad litem if it finds it necessary.[9] Yet, Article 3(f) guarantees lawyer representation for a child over 15 years old who objects to mental hospitalization. Meanwhile, Article 12 specifies that in cases of emergency, a court order may remove children from their home without hearing them. Article 8 determines that any decision by the youth court will be made after social services submits an expert opinion and the court will hear all the parties relevant to the proceedings. Yet, Article 9 restricts hearing the child if the court thinks that the child will not be able to understand the matter or testifying will harm the child.

There are hardly any Supreme Court or district court decisions that guarantee a child's right to participate in care and supervision proceedings. First, there is a lack of representation for the child, and therefore, few appeals. Many of these hearings are held behind closed doors and not open to the public. Finally, when there are decisions regarding the right to participation, it usually occurs in family law matters.

The right to participation of children at-risk

Several studies emphasize the importance of implementing the right to participation for children at risk.[10] The findings indicate that true child participation supports their recognition as human beings and validates their life experiences and their abilities. It allows children to take part in the decision-making process, and therefore, increases accountability for their lives. Children do not want to make the final decision on their own, but rather want to be a part of the decision-making process. When children participated in their residential care decisions, the treatment was more effective, and they collaborated more with their therapeutic process. The right to participate, according to these publications, should be applied in a way that is based on genuine inclusion, not only as "tokenism."

The Youth Law Care and Supervision (1960)

In Israel, care proceedings are usually a consequence of non-functional homes, in which a child is in danger of abuse and neglect. In such circumstances, social services intervene and demand guardianship of the child. The social service's underlying assumption is that children need protection and that their welfare and needs can be best provided by adults. Therefore, children's rights should be restricted to what adults think is in the child's best interests.

The youth law applies to minors below the age of 18. Each case is unique, involving different families, children, and circumstances. Thus, each case requires different interventions by social services. Unlike other legal proceedings, which are based on precedents and case law, every case in care proceedings is treated differently, with its own subjective, specific circumstances for each child. Different rules apply to a child who is two, six, eight, or 12 years old. Hence, legal procedures for care proceedings under the youth law are inherently different from regular legal proceedings due to the complexity of these cases and are not restrained by the formalisms of legal regulations applied to typical adult proceedings. A youth law proceeding can only be initiated by an application submitted to the court by social services.[11] It is a two-step procedure: first, the court needs to find that the child is in need as defined by Article 2,[12] then, a discussion and decision on their treatment plan occurs in accordance with Article 3.

Even though a care proceeding is based on civil law, the procedure is not subject to the Civil Proceedings Regulations, but rather a *sui generis* procedure – an application of a civil servant making a legal request to hold proceedings regarding the care of the minor. Then, the parents and the child can make different applications to the court. However, a study conducted in 2011 showed that parents rarely submit a statement of defense.[13]

There are several essential stakeholders in care proceedings: the minor, parents (or other caregivers), social workers, and the youth judges. Each party is relevant to different aspects of the legal procedure. In my research, the interviews were analyzed in association with these stakeholders, analyzing the impact they had on the way the girls coped with their care proceedings. In a significant subset of care proceedings, if there is consent of the family or the child to the treatment plan offered by social services, then a hearing may not be held in youth court, except in cases that require a court order for placement at the youth protection authority residential care.

The youth law was amended in 1995 and gave every child older than 15 a right to legal representation when he refuses psychiatric hospitalization. This is the only legal provision that gives the child a right to representation in civil proceedings, without requiring an order by the court. In 2000, another amendment to the youth law gave the court the authority to appoint a guardian ad litem for the child in care proceedings.[14] Despite those changes, a close examination of Article 8(c) demonstrates how the law remains paternalistic and does not align with rights discourse.

Article 8(c) of the youth law regulates the way the youth court addresses the child: "The court, hearing the case of a minor, may, at any time, appoint a guardian ad litem for a minor, if it finds that it is necessary for the best interest of the child." There are several problems with the terminology of this Article, preventing it from complying with true child participation in care proceedings as expressed in Article 12 of the CRC.

The court – As previously discussed, care proceedings can start by the application of social services without a court order, and if there is consent for the care plan, there may not be a court hearing at all. This fact does not, however, negate the need for legal representation in the early stages of the procedure, especially because even without court proceedings, a child can be placed in residential care. The law states that the consideration of whether to appoint a guardian ad litem for the child occurs only when a case is initiated in court, consequently leading either to a lack of representation for many children or representation that commences once the proceedings are already in progress.

May – The term "may" in Article 8 gives the court discretion as to whether to appoint a guardian ad litem for the child. The court's consideration of this matter is subject to its own views on a case-by-case basis. This can cause a violation of the right to equal protection and due process as not all children will have legal representation in similar cases.

At any time – Similarly, the term "at any time" grants discretion to the court as to when to appoint a guardian ad litem. This can lead to the violation of due process and the right to equal protection, particularly if or when representation is assigned at seemingly arbitrary points in the proceeding.

Guardian ad litem – Furthermore, there is no clear definition under Israeli law or regulations for a "guardian ad litem." The law does not describe what qualifications should be met nor what objectives will be met. In Israel, a guardian ad litem is typically a lawyer, although this is not mandatory. This is problematic because a lawyer has legal obligations and privileges that apply between lawyers and clients, such as confidentiality and representation of the client's wishes; however, it is not clear that those same obligations apply to the lawyer as a guardian ad litem. Accordingly, in the past few years, the Legal Aid at the Justice Department established a new child representation unit called "My Own Advocate." The lawyers appointed by this unit represent children in accordance with Israeli law; therefore, they are regarded as guardian ad litems. The creation of this unit marks an important change in the approach of youth judges, social workers, and the social welfare system toward care proceedings. However, in my opinion, there are several fundamental problems with the representation provided by the Justice Department. The lawyer's role in the adversarial legal system is indisputable: they examine the evidence, interview the witnesses, represent their clients' will, and are obligated to confidentiality. Yet, the role of a guardian ad litem is not clear. There is not a clear definition of their legal obligations or the scope of representation anywhere in the law. In practice, it is understood that the guardian ad litem needs to represent the child's best interests. However, this puts them in an inherent conflict with the child and their legal obligation to follow professional regulations, which may prevent them from representing the child's will when it is in conflict with the child's best interests. Hence, whether the role of guardian ad litem is more a "guardian" representing the best interests of the child or a "lawyer" advocating on behalf of the child is of utmost importance. It is not just a semantic separation since the implications can be harmful for the child.

Indeed, in an attempt to resolve any perceived tension between the child's best interests and the child's own will, the Rotlevi Sub-committee for child representation in civil proceedings (Sub-committee) determined age 12 as the legal interpretive presumption for deciding whether to represent the child's best interests or their will.[15] However, this determination is not legally binding and there is academic debate against this interpretation. Rather, others argue that each child should be represented according to the best representation suitable to them:

> [B]oth approaches (best interest and child's wishes) unfortunately oversimplify the complex nature of representing children, who range in age from the newborn to the near adult. The competing models...fail to meet most

children's needs, and fail to appropriately guide the attorney through the complex adversarial course of child protective litigation.[16]

If it finds necessary – As previously mentioned, the term "if it finds necessary" also involves court discretion and implies that appointing legal representation is not mandatory in all cases. *For the best interest of the child* – The Sub-committee defined the "best interests of a child" as a term that includes as one of the factors to be considered what the child wants, but needs to be examined in light of the child's developing capacity.

Another aspect of the critique regarding the role of guardian ad litem refers to the complexity when representing the best interests of a child.[17] First, best interests is a concept in constant change, along with the child's growth. The best interests of a 12-year-old can differ later in time. The child's best interests as presented to the court may not necessarily examine the way best interests develop over time; therefore, it is important for the lawyer to adjust their perspective on best interests accordingly.

Moreover, there is inherent hostility between the lawyer and all the other specialists who are part of care proceedings, especially as there is not a clear definition of the role of a guardian ad litem. The same stakeholders the lawyer is in conflict with provide the social information the lawyer acquires regarding the child. This information is already 'tainted' with their opinions on the child's best interests. Having a specific responsibility for each specialist and understanding the role of each person can decrease the distrust and contribute to the child in care proceedings.

Focusing on the distinction between "best interests" versus "will" restricts the role of the lawyer in care proceedings and reflects the fundamental difference between theory and practice. While in theory one can create this separation, in practice it is difficult, if not impossible, to accomplish. The dichotomy narrows the complexity needed in the discourse on child representation in care proceedings. Usually, the guardian ad litem presents to the court what they think is in the child's best interests, instead of representing the child's voice and wishes. This leads to mistrust between the guardian ad litem and the child. What is in the child's best interests? Can it be determined absolutely and objectively? Because it can only be observed in retrospect, any decision can be either a mistake or success. Therefore, one needs to be highly sensitive and look at all the available options the child has before a decision is made, a decision that has significant implications on the child's future. Such broad understanding can be in front of the youth court only if all the relevant voices, especially the voice of the child, opinions, and care plans are presented to the court. Representing just the child's best interests and accepting the care ethos without representing the child's voice puts in question the reason and the benefit for the lawyer's presence in the proceeding. In addition, what are the tools the lawyer has to determine the child's best interests? Their personal values? Conscience? Intuition? Life experience? These characteristics are not unique to lawyers and are not the reason they represent the child in court. The youth court is filled with specialists who want the best for the child and are qualified for this purpose. The lawyer is the only professional who is present to stand for the child's rights and voice. Therefore, a lawyer who advocates only the child's best interests practices contrary to their obligation to the child.[18]

Gender theories – intersectionality theory

Girlhood studies in general, and girlhood law studies in particular, are a relatively new area of research. Academic writing on young girls as a group with different characteristics from women began at the end of the 20th century.[19] There are several explanations for the absence of young girls from the public sphere. One reason is that girls were not in the public's interest mainly because girls, even at a young age, were thought of as homemakers. The academic writing about adolescents centers primarily on young boys, perhaps because male researchers conducted the research or because boys are in the delinquency system in larger numbers than girls.[20] With the growth of the feminist movement and feminist academic writing, especially by Carol Gilligan,[21] additional scholars started to distinguish between the genders and their adolescent experiences.[22] Gilligan's research criticized the concepts of Prince Charming coming to the rescue because it paralyzed young girls and made them silent and passive, waiting to be saved. In her research, she identified that women and young girls make moral choices differently – by ethics of care. Gilligan posited that women mainly referred to the specific circumstances and characteristics of those who were involved in the dilemma, understanding it is hard to make a decision without referencing its social relevance. Acting in accordance with an ethic of care meant expressing original thinking of women, which examines actions by the narrative of relationships, empathy, care, and mutual responsibility. Girls' studies emphasized those characteristics of women and young girls: the need to understand their true needs through their own eyes, gender, social status, and the dialogue they have with their family and community and through this understanding to promote their voices and rights.

Young girls at risk – "The Twilight Zone Between Normative World and Delinquency"[23]

Young girls at risk are a distinct minority group of women in general and youth at risk in particular. Young girls at risk usually come from a complex background of abuse and neglect, have experienced trauma, and are increasingly likely to drop out of school, run away from home, abuse substances, etc. The combination of young age, gender, and social status creates a unique risk situation for these girls.

A young girl at risk is defined as

> single, adolescent or young adult, from the age of 13–25. The characteristics of her behavior are, among others: self-destruction, deterioration or close to it, suffered traumatic events – emotional, social and mental, victim of social abuse or assault, incest, run away from home, school drop-out, substance abuse, addiction, depression, suicidal attempts, and eating disorders.[24]

Another common characteristic of an adolescent girl at risk is self-harming and not acting out of distress, but internalizing her problems.

Feminist theory emphasizes the terminology of girls who are in situations of risk or distress, and not a girl at risk.[25] The importance of this terminology is to separate between the girl and the situation she lives in. It is not her fault or her responsibility, but rather a consequence of her gender and sociocultural construction. Any attempt to understand and study the condition of adolescent girls out of context to their gender and the social reality of women in Israel is fundamentally wrong.[26] Adolescent girls are usually a minority in every group they are a part of: women, adolescents, marginal populations, ethnic minorities, etc. Therefore, adolescent girls face intersectionality across every experience in life: society, culture, and gender. The outcome is that even today adolescent girls are presented as either victims or pathological individuals in academic and therapeutic discourse. This perception creates a paternalistic reality of protection and judgement, which disregards the complexity of the subject and the necessity for rights discourse that emphasizes the "silent woman" perspective.

Still, girls' studies have evolved in the past years, emphasizing feminist theories and specifying young girls as a unique research area.[27] There are several national programs established based on feminist theories, such as mentoring.[28] Yet, the discourse on adolescent girls is still paternalistic, especially in care proceedings, in which the girl's behaviors are considered pathological and not as her way of coping with trauma.

Adolescent girls' right to participation

The CRC does not have specific instructions or articles on gender for young girls. The CRC applies to them as minors, but there is not a specific article referring to their unique status. As previously discussed, young girls are faced with the burden of intersectionality with regard to every aspect of their identity. Thus, implementing their right to participation will give them "a voice," making them part of society. Regarding these girls as human beings and not as human becoming is a core foundation to their adulthood.

The academic discourse focusing on the right to participate as applied to adolescent girls at risk is deficient. However, the well-being of young girls was studied in the context of their right to participate, understanding that in order to promote their well-being, there should be a development of discourse based on the young girl's opinion of her life and what she thinks is beneficial participation.[29]

Understanding the importance of the right to participation and the effects of intersectionality on young girls at risk emphasizes the value of implementing true participation in their legal and therapeutic proceedings:

> Including girls in decision-making and involving them in the process can occur within their placements, in independent living programing, and within the court setting while working with attorney and judges. Such involvement

> teaches valuable life skills and bolsters girls' confidence in themselves, the process, the court and the child welfare systems.[30]

There is still a long way to go, as a society and in academic discourse, to bring the voices of young girls at risk forward and consider their opinions without paternalism.

Law in action – their voices

> *What do you want from me? What I have done wrong? Why don't I deserve a normal place to be in?... I didn't feel safe, I felt so alone, you know? So most of the time I found myself running away, running running running to the unknown, just like that. I preferred to sleep on the streets, on a bench, to stink than to be in this institute ...*[31]

For my doctoral dissertation, I interviewed 13 adolescent girls who were in Messila.[32] My methodology combined theoretical and qualitative research, a meta-analysis of the interviews and auto-ethnography, with reflection based on my professional experience. I cannot present all their voices due to the scope of this chapter; however, my main conclusion was that the right to participation is an essential element of the right to be heard, and it is a life skill that needs to be taught if we want to encourage true participation. Additionally, I found that staying in a residential care locked facility places another intersectional burden on girls' lives.

The strongest statement that came from the girls was that they need and want to be heard. As one girl said:

> How much I felt alone, I felt that no one will help me and no one will hear me ... I can't, when I say what I feel and they look at me and through me aside, I'm no one's dog, I want to be listened to, I want someone to help me ... *But they do not really know what our souls are*, and do not know what we really think, you know?[33]

They experience this feeling of not being listened to as a frustration from the entire system and the different stakeholders surrounding them.

This "no listening – no hearing" experience makes them feel they are alone in the world and no one will help them:

> Every time I had a reason why I am in hell and nothing will be good, and that there is no way back, I need to survive, take care of myself and be responsible for me and lonely ... if it is a court order it is a court order, no one will come and listen to me, and even if they do listen they will look at me as little girl and throw me in the corner, like: Who do you think you are? Fine, even if you had hard life sit here quietly. This is how I felt, like a dog being thrown from place to place, from place to place.[34]

They described the guardians ad litem as professional figures that do not represent their voice in court. I provide a few excerpts from the interviews: "I thought my lawyer should be in my favor, but what she does – she is not, *she hears me, but her opinion is what the social services decides.*"[35] (Q) Is that what she says in court? "Yes, she does not come and say listen, but the girl is like that, and like what I'm really telling her ... I asked for something, and the welfare was against, so she was also... with them."[36] Another girl stated: "I don't know, (I would want her) to be with me, update me, because practically I don't know anything, nothing, nothing, nothing. They tell me about my legal procedure the day before, I want her (her lawyer) to be on my side."[37]

> I knew from the beginning – *I didn't have faith that the lawyer would help me* ... she didn't try to convince or argue with (the judge) in my opinion, in what I wanted ... say something, say that you object, help me, I am just a little girl... but what more could I tell her?[38]

When I asked them what they would tell their judge if they could, one said:

> I would say to the judge... to *really listen to the girl*, no... not how you look at her from the reports, because the reports are something that's written about you, she was this way and that way. *But they do not really know what our souls are*, and do not know what we really think, you know?[39]

There are two possible reasons for disregarding the child's opinion, which prevent their participation: paternalism and marginalized belonging. There are two personifications of paternalism in the context of young girls: paternalism in the way the law is written and applied, and inherent paternalism expressed by the relevant professionals. As described above, the youth law is paternalistic, applied in extreme situations when the social worker – as the state's representative – steps into the parent's shoes. The law is paternalistic in the manner in which the care procedure is conducted: the child does not take part and they can be absent from the court hearing in their matter. As a result, the girls do not understand what their role in care proceedings is and lose faith that the legal system will hear their voices or consider their views.

It is also true for the stakeholders in care proceedings. If a stakeholder wants to build a relationship that is based on trust, they cannot prejudge what is right for the child. Rotem, one of the girls I interviewed, explains:

> I can't believe them because they think about us things they don't even know or heard from the girls ... they come into conclusions on the girls without even hearing them, if someone says that she was drinking then they say she is addicted to alcohol and needs rehabilitation, and when they are jumping to conclusion they put social stigma on girls that is not necessarily true ...[40]

Most of the girls in care proceedings come from marginalized communities.[41] Their intersectionality comes from their position in relation to their gender, family, community, age, and ethnic origin. Their marginalized social positions impact the way everyone treats them, which keeps them trapped in an unbroken cycle. Many of them did not attend school; therefore, they are lacking important life skills such as participation. The way they learn to participate in order to make someone listen to them is usually by adopting extreme behaviors, such as running away. One girl said:

> Six years I am around residential care, youth court, I was shaking in front of the youth judge, I didn't know how it is working, who against who, what is going to happen, then the only thing I was able to say in front of her was take me home or take me to a different residential care, you have so much you want to tell her and explain to her why you do not want and why you runaway and why you feel so bad, you don't say anything … you understand? We are just little girls.[42]

The girls mentioned that staying in a locked institute is a stigma they will always carry, like the "mark of Cain," an obstruction from normative life. Another girl stated:

> The stigma on Messila girls is not true, each one of us is different, a world of its own … but the stigma is that Messila girls are prostitutes, alcoholics, junkies, I am a great person, don't judge me, don't judge us by the way we look …[43]

Court orders for locked residential care is for rehabilitation, and as mentioned, most of the girls there are victims of abuse and trauma. Yet we, as a society, judge them for things they did not do, morally and socially. Messila girls understand that staying in a locked residential care is another intersectionality cross they are in.

Conclusion: a work in progress

In this chapter, I spotlight the importance of true participation for young girls in care proceedings. I elaborate on the conflicts within the Youth Law, why the right to participate is a life skill, that all the stakeholders relevant in care proceedings need to carefully listen to what the girl *truly* wants and needs, and how staying in a locked residential care is another intersectionality cross for adolescent girls in care proceedings.

Therefore, if we, the system, both legal and social, lose the trust of these girls and if we want to gain it back, we need to listen to them and respect their point of view. If we want to allow these girls to undergo rehabilitation from their trauma and allow them to be "normal" adolescents, we must teach them to participate, assure them we will hear them, and give them the life skills they need to develop and grow.

Notes

1 Interviews with residents at Messila, in Jerusalem, Isr. (Mar.–Jun. 2016) (names are excluded to keep identities of the girls confidential).

2 Manfred Nowak, *Article 6: The Right to Life, Survival and Development*, in A Commentary on the United Nation Convention on the Rights of the Child (2005).
3 As guaranteed in art. 5 of the Convention on the Rights of the Child.
4 Michael Freeman, *Children's Rights: A Comparative Perspective* 3 (Aldershot et al. eds., 1996).
5 Committee on the Rights of the Child, Recommendations from the Day of General Discussion on The Right of the Child to be Heard of the Forty-Third Session of the U.N. G.A. (Sept. 29, 2006), https://www.ohchr.org/Documents/HRBodies/CRC/Discussions/Recommendations/Recommendations2006.doc.
6 Judith Masson & Maureen W. Oakley, *Out of Hearing: Representing Children in Care Proceedings* (1999); Rachel Hodgkin & Peter Newell, *Implementing Handbook for the Convention on the Rights of the Child* (2002).
7 Gary B. Melton, *Background for a General Comment on the Right to Participate: Article 12 and Related Provisions of the Convention on the Rights of the Child* (Report prepared for use by the UN Committee on the Rights of the child, Sept. 2006).
8 Ruth Sinclair, *Participation In Practice: Making it Meaningful, Effective and Sustainable*, 18 Child. & Soc'y 106–118 (2004).
9 The Youth Law (care and supervision) (1960), https://www.nevo.co.il/law_html/Law01/305_001.htm#Seif39.
10 Judith Cashmore, *Promoting the Participation of Children and Young People in Care*, 268 Child Abuse & Negl. 837–847 (2002); Judith Cashmore & Marina Paxman, NSW Dep't Cmty. Serv., Longitudinal Study of Wards Leaving Care (1996); Gerison Lansdown, UNICEF, *Promoting Children's Participation in Democratic Decision-Making of Children* (2001); Sharon Bessell, *Participation in Decision-making in Out-of-home Care in Australia: What Do Young People Say?* 33 Child & Youth Serv. Rev. 496–501 (2011); Ganna G. van Bijleveled et al., *Children's and Young People's Participation Within Child Welfare and Child Protection Services: A State-of-the-art Review*, 20 Child & Fam. Soc. Work 129–138 (2015); Sharon Bassell, *Inclusive and Respectful Relationships as the Basis for Child Inclusive Policies and Practice: The Experience of Children in Out-of-Home Care in Australia*, *in* International Perspectives and Empirical Findings on Child Participation: From Social Exclusion to Child-Inclusive Policies, 183, 191 (Tali Gal & Benedetta Faedi Duramy eds., 2015).
11 The application contains the parents and child(ren) name, the law specific articles relevant for the application and deposition specifies the facts relevant for the case.
12 The Youth Law, *supra* note 8.
13 There are several possible reasons for this, among them (1) parents agree to the application, (2) parents are not aware that they can apply a defense statement, (3) they do not have legal representation, and (4) not all the materials handed to the court by the social services are available to the parents. Tal Hasin, Bad Mom-Good Mom, Minors Being Taken Out of Their Homes by Art. 2(2) & 2(6), Youth Law (care and supervision) – 1960, an LLM. dissertation, Tel Aviv University (2011), https://law.acri.org.il/he/wp-content/uploads/2016/05/hit4044app-Hassin.pdf.
14 A guardian ad-litem is an attorney appointed to represent the best interest of the child in care proceedings. The distinction and clarification of the role of guardian ad-litem and legal advocate will be elaborated later on.
15 The Rotlevi committee was established to implement the CRC within Israeli legislation. It handed in its recommendations in 2003. There were six sub-committees of the Rotlevi committee. The Sub-committee for Representation of Children in Civil Proceedings Report, The Rotlevi Committee 6 (Jerusalem 2003), https://www.justice.gov.il/Units/YeutzVehakika/NosimMishpatim/HavaadLeZhuyot/Pages/DochKliali.aspx.
16 Merill Sobie, *The Child Client: Representing Children in Child Protective Proceedings*, 22 Touro L. Rev. 745, 756 (2006).
17 Jean Koh Peters, *The Role and Content of Best Interests in Client-Directed Lawyering for Children in Child Protective Proceedings*, 64 Fordham L. Rev. 1505, 1512 (1996).

18 Christopher N. Wu, *Conflicts of Interest in the Representation of Children in Dependency Cases*, 64 Fordham L. Rev. n.4, 1857, 1859 (1996).
19 Mary Celeste Kearney, *Coalescing: The Development of Girls' Studies*, 21 NWSA J. 1, 3 (2009).
20 *Id.* at 4.
21 Carol Gilligan, *In a Different Voice: Psychological Theory and Women's Development*, Harv. U. Press (1982).
22 Jean Baker Miller, *Towards a New Psychology of Women* (1976); Nancy Chadoraw, *The Reproduction of Mothering: Psychoanalysis and the Sociology of Gender* (1978); Meda Chensey-Lind, *Juvenile Delinquency – The Sexualisation of Female Crime*, 8 Psych. Today 43–46 (1993).
23 Miriam Golan, *The Differences Between Boys and Girls at-risk Who Stay in Residential Care*, 22 Welfare & Soc. 519, 524 (2002).
24 Ch. 17 of the social work regulation, https://www.molsa.gov.il/CommunityInfo/Regulations/SocialRegulations/pages/tas_perek_17.aspx.
25 Netta Resner & Anat Zeira, *Adolescents Girls in Difficult Situation of Stress*, 13 (2014).
26 Michal Krumer-Nevo, *Women in Poverty: Life Stories, Gender, Pain, Resistance* (2006).
27 Adva Berkowitch-Romano et al., *The Knowledge Body of Research About Girls in Distress in Israel: Literature Review from Feminist Perspective*, 33 Soc. & Welfare 7 (2013).
28 *Mentoring Program*, All Rights, Kol Zchut, https://www.kolzchut.org.il/he/%D7%AA%D7%9B%D7%A0%D7%99%D7%AA_%D7%9E%D7%A0%D7%98%D7%95%D7%A8%D7%99%D7%A0%D7%92_-_%D7%A0%D7%A2%D7%A8%D7%95%D7%AA_%D7%9C%D7%9E%D7%A2%D7%9F_%D7%A0%D7%A2%D7%A8%D7%95%D7%AA.
29 Laura Lundy, *The United Nation Convention on the Rights of the Child and Child Well-being*, *in* The Handbook of Children's Well-being: Theories, Methods and Policies in Global Perspective, 2439–2462 (Asher Ben-Arieh et al., eds., 2014); Asher Ben-Arieh, *Where are the Children? Children's Role in Measuring and Monitoring Their Well-being*, 74 Soc. Indicators Res. 573–596 (2005).
30 Karen Baynes-Dunning & Karen Worthington, *Responding to the needs of Adolescents Girls in Foster Care*, 20 Geo. J. on Poverty L. & Pol'y 321 (2013).
31 Interview, *supra* note 1.
32 My research was conducted in 2016–2017, and there has been a change in the way the care system is dealing with lawyers in care proceedings. Moreover, the 'lawyer of my own' legal aid unit had changed the amount of children being represented. Yet, many of the representation practices still appear, and they are representing as guardian ad-litem.
33 Interview, *supra* note 1.
34 *Id.*
35 *Id.*
36 *Id.*
37 *Id.*
38 *Id.*
39 *Id.*
40 Interview with Rotem at Messila, in Jerusalem, Isr. (Mar.–Jun. 2016) (a pseudonym has been used to keep interviewee's identity confidential).
41 Israel National Council for the Child, Statistic Yearbook: Children in Israel (2019), https://www.children.org.il/wp-content/uploads/2020/02/%D7%94%D7%9E%D7%95%D7%A2%D7%A6%D7%94-%D7%9C%D7%A9%D7%9C%D7%95%D7%9D-%D7%94%D7%99%D7%9C%D7%93-%D7%9C%D7%A7%D7%98-%D7%A9%D7%A0%D7%AA%D7%95%D7%9F-2019.pdf.
42 Interview, *supra* note 1.
43 *Id.*

Part III

Children's civil rights

Rights to free speech, health, religious freedom, and privacy

11 Childhood, speech, and the right to free speech

Nicholas Hatzis

In recent years, the issue of speech and childhood has attracted considerable attention, mainly in relation to the internet and social media. As the old communication barriers that made it easy to control what information a child could access or convey no longer exist, as both adults and children live in a "cosmopolis…the interconnected physical and virtual worlds,"[1] it has become necessary to reconsider how existing moral categories and legal principles can help us think about this new reality.

Some of the questions that arise in this context are: what speech and information children should be allowed to access online; who should be responsible for protecting children from harmful online speech, the government or the parents; how far can restraint of speech go when the aim is to protect children; and whether children can be liable for their own speech which is harmful to other children, as in cases of online bullying. Those are very important and complex questions about the substantive content of the right to freedom of expression and the methodology for assessing limitations on rights or resolving conflicts between them. But this chapter will not deal directly with them or propose answers. What I will try to do is take a step back and explore some of the normative assumptions underlying the debate about childhood and speech. The question I am asking is what is special, from a moral point of view, in childhood and how it affects our understanding of the right to free speech as applied to children. And in so doing, I hope to shed some light on those other important questions.

Free speech values

Human rights documents that protect the legal right to free speech do not exclude children from the range of persons who enjoy the right. For example, the European Convention on Human Rights, the International Covenant on Civil and Political Rights, and the American Convention on Human Rights all provide (in Articles 10, 19, and 13, respectively) that freedom of expression shall be enjoyed by "everyone." The same very broad approach to the issue of who are the right-holders of a free speech right is followed in national constitutional documents such as the Canadian Charter of Rights and Freedoms ("everyone" – Article 2b), the German Basic Law ("every person" – Article 5.1), the French

Declaration of the Rights of Man and of the Citizen ("any citizen" – Article 11), and the Italian Constitution ("anyone" – Article 21). The United States Supreme Court has also held that the First Amendment includes children in the scope of its protection.[2]

Also, the Convention on the Rights of the Child (CRC) explicitly provides for a right to freedom of expression in Article 13 in very clear terms:

> The child shall have the right to freedom of expression; this right shall include freedom to seek, receive and impart information and ideas of all kinds, regardless of frontiers, either orally, in writing or in print, in the form of art, or through any other media of the child's choice.

However, the practice of governments and judges appears much more ambivalent. As we will see in the following section, even in countries with very strong protection for speech, like the United States, the limitations on the right are very extensive when children are involved. To understand the difference, it might be helpful to compare freedom of expression to another right such as the right to be free from torture or inhuman and degrading treatment. This is a right where the age of the potential right-bearer is irrelevant. The moral condemnation of torture does not depend on whether the person being tortured is a minor or an adult. What triggers moral condemnation and grounds a strong right to be free from torture is the fact that a human being is being treated in a way which is incompatible with the status of being human. By contrast, when a child's speech is restricted, the assessment whether the restriction is a violation of her right to freedom of expression will depend on, among other elements, the fact that she is a child. The age of the person whose activity is restricted by the government is a criterion for the legitimacy of the restriction.[3]

Usually, four rationales are relied on to justify a robust right to freedom of expression. First, speech is indispensable for the discovery of truth about human affairs, an argument associated with John Stuart Mill.[4] Change and progress in society depend on our ability to examine different views, consider all arguments about what the right course of action is, and re-evaluate our beliefs and assumptions. This is impossible without strong protections for free communication.

Second, free expression is important because it is a precondition for democratic government and the participation of citizens in politics. As Alexander Meiklejohn, the main proponent of this view argued, speech about public matters should be fully protected because it is the medium through which the political community, "a group of free and equal men, cooperating in a common enterprise,"[5] can debate the rules for the organisation of common life and vote "wise decisions."[6] The principle covers both political speech in the strict sense and deliberation about the conduct of public affairs more generally. An argument that supplements the democratic self-government rationale is that speech functions as a check on the power of government, necessary for exposing officials who abuse their power and act in an arbitrary manner.[7]

Third, the development of our personality and our self-fulfilment as humans requires the free expression of our opinions and ideas. By communicating with others, we discover who we are, what life we want to lead, and which values and pursuits to embrace. Thus, speech is a prerequisite for our development as autonomous moral agents and an expression of our autonomy.

Fourth, we should distrust attempts by the state to regulate what can be said publicly. Governments are usually overzealous when regulating public discourse and tend to use their power to proscribe views, ideas, and forms of expression they, or a majority within society, find objectionable or upsetting.[8] The history of free speech disputes shows that this risk is serious and real and calls for a strong right as a shield against state power.

Those rationales, expressed in various forms in judicial and scholarly writings, are said to underlie a free speech principle, namely, the principle that there is something special to speech that differentiates it from other activities in which humans engage and gives it a claim for additional protection, beyond the protection from regulation that those other activities enjoy.[9] In this sense, the free speech principle is different from a general claim to be allowed to live our lives in the way we want without undue interference from the state. Liberal, democratic regimes may cast the interests involved in free speech cases in different ways, but all share the view that uninhibited communication is necessary for the flourishing of individuals and society. If speech enjoys this privileged position among activities which are protected by corresponding rights, how should we treat a child's communications?

At first sight, none of the four justifications appear to support a robust free expression right for children. This is not to say that children do not engage in activities that are instances of the right to free expression. They clearly do, in many ways. They communicate with peers and adults, express ideas, opinions, and wishes, and receive the communications of others. In this way, they explore and develop their own personality and participate in the broader public culture. Also, they participate directly in a type of political debate through student politics at school.[10] And even if children do not practice, or rarely practice, an activity which is an instance of the right to free speech, it does not follow that they don't have an interest in the existence of the right to free speech. Free expression is important as an individual right but is also a public good: it is a prerequisite for the functioning of democracy and for maintaining a lively public culture. Children have an interest in living in a democratic regime which allows for the discussion of public affairs even if they do not themselves participate in political debates.[11]

Rather, my point is that when we think of the values that justify a right to free speech and the persons whose interests the right serves, the figure that comes to mind is not, usually, a child. We are much more likely to think of adults, with their developed reasoning capacity, who participate in social and political life and make decisions about themselves. The element that explains this way of thinking is paternalism. There are different ways to define paternalism and paternalistic conduct, and fine distinctions can be drawn between different forms of paternalism, but broadly speaking, all cases involve an agent who is making decisions for another person because he (the agent) is (allegedly) better placed to serve the interests of that person rather than that person himself.[12] As the term itself suggests, the archetype for such a relationship is the one between parents and children. Thus, Joel Feinberg notes that we find paternalism objectionable because it consists in "treating adults as if they were children."[13]

On the other hand, we think that it is justified to treat children in a paternalistic manner. Children are subject to the authority of their parents, and, in some respects, the state, and decisions about their lives are made for them but not by them. An aspect of this attitude is that when children express a preference about how they want to live, we give less weight, or no weight at all, to those preferences if we think that they do not serve their best interests. Paternalism is inherent in the condition of childhood and constitutes its defining characteristic.[14]

Children as speakers and listeners

In the field of speech and communication, paternalistic decisions by adults affect children both as speakers and as listeners, restricting their power to speak and the types of speech to which they have access. Classic examples of the first type of restriction are codes of conduct in schools that require children not to use pejorative words. An example of the second type is the rating system for films: depending on the content of the film, some children, if not all children, are not allowed to watch it.

Consider the following judgments of the US Supreme Court which demonstrate how paternalism as an aspect of the moral status of childhood is relevant for judicial practice in the field of free expression. In *FCC v. Fox*,[15] the Court upheld the power of the Federal Communications Commission (FCC) to penalise even isolated instances of the use of indecent words that are uttered in broadcast media in a non-literal manner.[16] In an earlier case, *FCC v. Pacifica Foundation*,[17] the Court had decided that the FCC had authority to regulate broadcasts that included indecent words, even if they were not obscene. *Pacifica* concerned a radio broadcast of a satirical monologue called "Filthy Words," which included repeated and deliberative utterances of indecent words as a way of bringing attention to the issue of expressions that could not be used in the media. While finding for the FCC, the Court also said that its holding was narrow and it did not cover the occasional use of expletives. Thus, *Fox* went further than *Pacifica*, with the Court stating that the FCC was entitled to consider that even a single indecent word could harm children although the FCC had failed to produce any evidence to support this view.

Morse v. Frederick[18] concerned a school student who was punished because he had displayed a banner which read "Bong Hits 4 Jesus," which was interpreted by the head teacher as an indirect endorsement of drug use. The banner was displayed during the Olympic torch relay through the street outside the school. The event as such was not organised by the school and participation was optional. However, the event was approved by the head teacher and took place during teaching hours. The Supreme Court held that schoolchildren enjoy First

Amendment rights, which, though, are not the same as those of adults. The special nature of the school environment means that student speech may be limited even if it does not disrupt school life and activities and could not have been regulated if it had been expressed elsewhere.[19] In this case, the school had a compelling interest to protect children from drugs that trumped their right to speech. Justice Thomas filed a concurring opinion in which he took the view that schoolchildren have no First Amendment rights.

The asymmetry between the free speech rights of children and adults had been explored in detail in an earlier case, *Bethel School District v. Fraser*,[20] which concerned the punishment of a student for using words that implied a sexual innuendo. The student speaker was nominating another student for school president and he made a speech to the student body. He said, among other things, that the nominee is

> [F]irm – he's firm in his pants, he's firm in his shirt, his character is firm – but most of all, his belief in you the students of Bethel, is firm. [He] is a man who takes his point and pounds it in. If necessary, he'll take an issue and nail it to the wall. He doesn't attack things in spurts – he drives hard, pushing and pushing until finally – he succeeds. Jeff is a man who will go to the very end – even the climax, for each and every one of you. So please vote for Jeff Kuhlman, as he'll never come between us and the best our school can be.[21]

The Supreme Court held that his punishment did not violate the Constitution. The First Amendment protects "wide freedom in matters of adult public discourse."[22] This includes the use of words with sexual content which others may find offensive but "it does not follow that…the same latitude must be permitted to children in a public school"[23] because their rights are not "automatically coextensive"[24] with the rights enjoyed by adults. The sexual innuendo could harm the less mature students so there was an "obvious concern on the part of parents, and school authorities acting *in loco parentis* to protect children – especially in a captive audience – from exposure to sexually explicit, indecent, or lewd speech."[25]

Childhood as a special status

The first case involved the interest of the child as listener. In the second and third cases, the speech of children implicated their interests as both speakers and listeners. What the three cases have in common is the assumption that children need protection and any speech rights at stake are subordinate to this concern. In those judgments, and more generally, in legal discourse about rights, the terms "child," "minor," and "childhood" express a biological fact, but they are not merely biological concepts. They have normative content, giving us reason to act in a certain way towards the persons who are defined as children or minors. In other words, they ascribe a moral status which matters when one determines how one ought to treat those who have this status.[26]

Treating children in a paternalistic manner, and thus, deciding for them what they can say or hear, is easier to justify on utilitarian grounds. Children have not fully developed their reasoning capacity and lack the experience, knowledge, and maturity required to conduct their lives independently. If left to their own devices, they are likely to cause harm to themselves (or to others), so adult intervention serves the interests of children and maximises overall well-being. From the point of deontological ethics though, the good outcomes the paternalistic treatment of children may produce are not themselves sufficient to justify such treatment. At the root of this objection is a concern with Kantian autonomy. People are to be treated as autonomous moral agents who participate in the kingdom of ends and make choices. Even if we think that they are mistaken and undermine their own interests, we ought not to intervene because disregarding their decisions fails to accord them the respect they are due as persons.

The injunction to treat others as ends in themselves and not as means has both negative and positive aspects.[27] First, it functions as a limit on the agent's conduct: we cannot act in ways which are incompatible with others' autonomy. Second, we have a duty to acknowledge others' choices and assist in their achievement. This latter requirement flows from what Kant describes as the duty of practical love: "the maxim of *benevolence* (practical love), which results in beneficence."[28] This does not mean that we need to develop loving feelings towards others, but that we should adopt a certain kind of practical attitude towards them: "making the well-being and happiness of others my *end*."[29] Kant is not suggesting that we promote others' happiness and well-being according to what we think are valuable ends, but according to the ends they have chosen for themselves. This anti-paternalistic stance prohibits not only imposing our ends on others, but also prohibits taking over their projects and dictating the ways by which they are to pursue their ends.[30]

But isn't it obvious that this stance cannot apply when the other is a child? Children have not developed the capacity for autonomy and for making autonomous choices. Paternalistic intervention cannot be morally objectionable if one is not able to adopt and pursue ends of one's own. It seems impossible to account for the reduced capacities of childhood without supporting a very high degree of paternalism towards children. Kant says,

> I cannot do good to anyone in accordance with *my* concepts of happiness (except to young children and the insane), thinking to benefit him by forcing a gift upon him; rather I can benefit him only in accordance with *his* concept of happiness.[31]

Here, young children are placed together with mentally ill people in a group which is excluded from the anti-paternalistic attitude we are enjoined to adopt towards others. So, benevolent adults can do good to children according to what they (the adults) believe will promote the children's interest without offending the moral law. Was, then, Justice Thomas correct when he said that children have no First Amendment rights? At least with young children (however "young" is understood), should we leave it to parents, teachers, school boards, and government officials to make all the decisions about what they can hear or say, happy in the knowledge that this is the right moral attitude?

From childhood to adulthood

We started from the notion that children are more vulnerable to the harms speech may cause than adults, so it is permissible to interfere with their choices and restrict their options as both speakers and listeners. Even deontological theories allow for paternalistic treatment given that the child has not developed fully her moral agency and capacity to make autonomous choices. Does this mean that all paternalistic decisions about children's communications are morally unproblematic?

Let us go back to Kant. In his discussion of how the state is constituted, he makes a distinction between active and passive citizens and includes children in the latter category. Passive citizens are those who lack the independence to vote and thus cannot participate in decision-making on an equal footing with active citizens.[32] But this is the only incapacity entailed in the status of passive citizens. The lack of independence does not place them outside the political community as it is

> in no way opposed to their freedom and equality *as human beings*, who together make up a people; on the contrary it is only in conformity with the conditions of freedom and equality that this people can become a state and enter into a civil constitution.[33]

Passive citizens remain citizens; they are not a different kind of person or a lesser kind of citizen.[34] From this, Kant derives a further rule: that when active citizens legislate and make decisions about passive citizens, they need to make certain that those decisions do not interfere with the ability of the passive citizen to develop into an active citizen:

> [W]hatever sort of positive laws the citizens might vote for, these laws must still not be contrary to the natural laws of freedom and of the equality of everyone in the people corresponding to this freedom, namely that anyone can work his way up from this passive condition to an active one.[35]

This last proviso is important for determining which paternalistic decisions on children's speech are morally legitimate. Tamar Schapiro has argued that the best way of understanding Kant's view of the developmental process from active to passive citizenship in relation to children is that childhood is a predicament. She draws an analogy with the pre-political society in the state of nature where people lack a system of governance with a legitimate source of political authority. Kant claims that people in the state of nature are inevitably faced with the question how one ought to behave but they have not yet developed a concept of justice in accordance with the universal moral law. This is their predicament – not having the normative concepts which could guide their actions. Schapiro suggests that children face a similar predicament when compared with adults. Adults can determine their course of action by exercising their "capacity for reflective choice."[36] They can assess their conflicting desires, wishes, and motivations and reach a conclusion as to what is the right thing to do. Their reasons for acting in a particular way are their own since they result from this deliberative process, which is an expression of their autonomy. Adults resemble the politically constituted state because they are "governed by a constitution…a unified, regulative perspective which counts as the expression of [their] will".[37] Children lack this normative perspective, which is also missing from the pre-political state of nature. "[T]he condition of childhood is one in which the agent is not yet in a position to speak in her own voice because there is no voice with which counts as hers."[38]

Growing up means overcoming the predicament of not having an appropriately personal voice. Acquiring such a voice comes about gradually, as the child develops relationships, experiments with different versions of themselves, and makes provisional choices. This explains why we usually think that it is problematic to treat older children in an *entirely* paternalistic way. As a child develops, they are able to express their preference over certain domains in a way that makes them similar to an adult, while other domains remain (provisionally) beyond their normative reach. Thus, they occupy an intermediate position, being an adult in relation to certain aspects of their life and a child in relation to others.[39] In the former case, they are an active citizen with the required independence to set their own ends, so trying to promote their happiness and well-being by externally imposing other ends on them is impermissible; in the latter, paternalistic interventions are (provisionally) justified to the extent that they do not undermine their ability fully to develop their normative capacity and become an active citizen.

Under this perspective on the status of childhood, the criterion for assessing the moral legitimacy of restrictions on children's speech (regardless of their age) is whether the restrictions respect children as free and equal persons, members of the kingdom of ends, who are in the process of becoming fully autonomous and independent. As a rule, the more children grow, the less permissible it becomes to restrict their communications in circumstances where the same communications by adults would be left unrestricted. So, treating older children as if they were younger is a form of morally objectionable paternalism.[40] In relation to younger children, a greater degree of paternalistic treatment is permissible as they are more vulnerable to harm, provided it does not undermine their potential to develop into autonomous persons. For example, not allowing them any access to television or the internet in case they accidentally come across harmful material is impermissible paternalism; parental guidance and controlled access is the correct stance because although paternalistic, it does not deprive younger children of access to sources of knowledge we consider to be essential for modern life.

Developing a thinking mind

The approach in the previous section resonates with recent work on the philosophy of free speech. Seana Shiffrin has suggested a theory which places the thinking person at the centre of the justification for free speech.[41] In this view, what justifies a robust conception of the moral right to freedom of expression, and a high level of legal protection for speech, is the fact that speech and non-verbal communication is the only medium we have to access other people's minds and express the content of our own mind. This is necessary if we are to develop our moral agency and become distinctive individuals. Shiffrin writes:

> [I]t is essential to the appropriate development and regulation of the self, and of one's relation to others, that one have wide-ranging access to the opportunity to externalize one's mental contents, whatever they are, and therefore to the opportunity to make one's mental contents known to others in an unscripted and authentic way. It is equally essential to be able to receive others' representations, and to enjoy protection from unchosen interference with one's mental contents from processes that would disrupt or disable the operation of these processes.[42]

Shiffrin's theory has similarities with the autonomy rationale for free speech but takes it further by making the thinker the central figure of the right to freedom of expression. The distinction between speakers and listeners and the type of content conveyed by different forms of communication become less important because externalising the contents of our mind (as speakers) and accessing the thoughts of others (as listeners) are equally necessary for the growth of our personality and the development of our thinking capacity. Underlying all activities which involve receiving and communicating opinions, ideas, and information is a thinking mind, and it is the need to protect it from unwarranted interferences which grounds a free speech right.

I think this theory, with its emphasis on the thinking mind which develops gradually, by being part of the give and take entailed in communicating with others, is the most convincing argument for a free expression right for children. On the one hand, it does not overlook the fact that children have not yet developed their full capacities for reasoning and thinking autonomously and concedes that some regulation of speech is necessary when children are involved while regulation would not have been justified if the speech concerned adults because children are more vulnerable and there may exist no alternative to regulation for protecting them.[43] So, it accommodates that basic moral intuition mentioned at the beginning of the chapter – that we think adults do need to make decisions about children. On the other hand, it does not treat the more limited capacity of children as an exclusionary criterion, as a justification for excluding children *qua* children from the scope of a free speech right. Instead, it takes the fact that their thinking capacity is still developing as a positive reason to protect their speech.

If it is plausible to think of the condition of childhood as a predicament because children lack the normative perspective that would enable them to have an autonomous will of their own, respecting their freedom of speech is indispensable if they are to learn the requirements of morality and become fully autonomous moral agents. Recall what Kant says about decisions made by active citizens for passive citizens: they must respect them as free and equal persons and allow them to overcome their dependence on others. Of course, developing the capacity for normative judgment is only one of the aspects that make us human for which speech is necessary. Speech is also a prerequisite for developing our imagination and aesthetic sensibilities, appreciating art, establishing and enjoying friendships and other relationships, and dealing with the inevitable frustrations, disappointments, and losses. In short, it is essential for the complicated but exciting business that is living our lives by our own lights. Contrary to what is often thought, the condition of childhood is reason that does not negate or weaken but supports a free speech right for children.

This view of the moral right of freedom of speech for children has ramifications for their legal right to freedom of expression. There are two consequences that are particularly important. First, the emphasis on the child as thinker means that children have free speech rights not only against the state but also against their parents. The legal right to freedom of expression developed as a protection from state interference with speech and the state remains the most powerful actor that can limit our communications. But in the case of children, many restrictions are imposed by parents. If what justifies children's right to free speech is their interests as thinkers, then parents should not be allowed to act in ways that undermine the child's right to develop into a fully autonomous, thinking person. Rather, they have a positive duty to make decisions that assist children to grow out of the dependence and immaturity of childhood.[44]

I am not saying that this principle can provide obvious answers to specific problems about children's speech and determining how specific cases should be decided will often be controversial. Perhaps the emotional acceptance by parents of the reality that the interests of their child sometimes require them to take a step back is even more difficult. Benevolent, caring parents simply feel that they must protect their children from everything they consider dangerous or inappropriate, even if that means regularly overriding their choices. Kant captures this tension well: "The principle of mutual love admonishes [rational beings] constantly to *come closer* to one another; that of the respect they owe one another, to keep themselves *at a distance* from one another."[45] Difficult as it may be, keeping that distance during childhood is necessary if the child is ever to become an independent adult.

While facts and context will always be important for individual cases, it seems to me there is one thing that is clear: parents have an obligation towards their children to exercise their authority – their paternalistic interventions – in ways that promote the child's thinking capacity even if this means that the child is developing, or is likely to develop, opinions that are incompatible with those of the parents. The fact that the child may adopt views about, say, politics, religion or, more generally, the kind of life worth living, which parents find difficult to accept or outright reprehensible is never reason to restrict the child's speech. Thus, free speech for children functions as a very important limitation on the right of parents to raise their children in a way that is compatible with their own views.

The second ramification is that limitations on children's right to free speech are justified only if there is credible empirical evidence that the speech in question will cause them harm and there is no less restrictive alternative to obviate it. Proof of causation before a measure that restricts expression can pass constitutional muster is the norm in First Amendment law, with the Supreme Court requiring "a direct causal link between the restriction imposed and the injury to be prevented."[46] The Court has insisted on this requirement even when the regulated and, allegedly, harmful speech was addressed to children. In *Brown v. Entertainment Merchants Association*,[47] the Court dealt with a California law that restricted the sale of violent video games to minors. After noting that video games were a protected form of expression, the Court found that California had failed to "prove that violent video games *cause* minors to *act* aggressively"[48] and that the studies it relied upon showed "at best some correlation between exposure to violent entertainment and minuscule real-world effects, such as children's feeling more aggressive or making louder noises in the few minutes after playing a violent game than after playing a nonviolent game."[49] But "ambiguous proof will not suffice"[50] to justify governmental restrictions on speech because under the First Amendment, the "State must specifically identify an actual problem in need of solving and the curtailment of free speech must be actually necessary to the solution."[51]

Before *Entertainment Merchants Association*, the Supreme Court had applied the same requirement for a clear causal link between harm and speech to sexually explicit expression. *United States v. Playboy Entertainment Group*[52] concerned a federal law that required cable television providers of channels primarily dedicated to sexually explicit programmes to either scramble or otherwise block those programmes or limit transmission to hours when children were unlikely to watch television (time channelling). Cable providers already used scrambling to prevent non-subscribers from accessing their content. However, scrambling can be imprecise and sometimes parts of the scrambled programme can be heard or seen (a signal bleed); the aim of the law was to protect children from harm resulting from accidental exposure to signal bleed. As the majority of operators chose time channelling, programmes with sexual content were not available to anyone for two-thirds of the day.

The Court held that the government had a compelling interest in protecting children, but this could have been achieved by less restrictive means. The same law provided that cable operators had an obligation to provide subscribers with the option of requesting the blocking of some channels on an individual basis. Thus, each household could choose which programmes to access and parents could use this option to control the content that their children might watch, thereby ensuring that there was no accidental exposure to sexually explicit material. In response to the argument that individual blocking was an inadequate tool for protecting children, the Court noted that "there is little hard evidence of how widespread or how serious the problem of signal bleed is"[53] and that

> sanctionable signal bleed can include instances as fleeting as an image appearing on a screen for just a few seconds. The First Amendment requires a more careful assessment and characterization of an evil in order to justify a regulation as sweeping as this.[54]

In the three cases mentioned earlier in the chapter – *Fox*, *Morse* and *Fraser* – where the Court upheld restrictions on speech on the basis of the harm that might befall children, there is almost no empirical evidence of the gravity of harm or the probability of its occurring. The judgment which exemplifies this mistaken approach is *Fox*. When Justice Scalia was faced with the argument that the government had not showed that isolated utterances of indecent words can harm children, he said,

> There are some propositions for which scant empirical evidence can be marshaled, and the harmful effect of broadcast profanity on children is one of them... if enforcement [of the ban] had to be supported by empirical evidence, the ban would effectively be a nullity.

This statement cannot be reconciled with the Court's insistence in *Entertainment Merchants Association* that the government produce specific evidence showing that violent games will make children act violently, particularly as its author was Justice Scalia. As Justice Breyer noted in his dissent in *Fox*, the FCC should have been required to demonstrate why its previous policy was inadequate for the protection of children.

Morse and *Fraser* equally lacked empirical evidence linking the speech in question to the alleged harm to children. Given that both cases concerned communications at school, the Court seems to have combined the facts of childhood and educational environment as a justification for doing away with proper scrutiny of the contention that it was necessary to restrict speech because of its injurious effects. The result is very broad and unwarranted deference to the government's assessment as to what is harmful speech. This was the reason for Justice Marshall's dissent in *Fraser* (the case about a student's speech with sexual innuendo):

> [W]e may not unquestioningly accept a teacher's or administrator's assertion that certain pure speech interfered with education. Here the School District, despite a clear opportunity to do so, failed to bring in evidence sufficient to convince either of the two lower courts that education at Bethel School was disrupted by respondent's speech.[55]

Justice Stevens dissented on similar grounds in *Morse*. He found that there was nothing to corroborate the school's assertion that the statement in question (Bong Hits 4 Jesus) was an endorsement of drug use but, even if this were an arguable interpretation, "that advocacy was at best subtle and ambiguous"[56] so the scales should have come down in favour of the student speaker.

The high causation threshold usually applied in First Amendment cases should also apply where children are involved as speakers or listeners. While the argument that children are more vulnerable than adults and in need of protection is correct and explains why a paternalistic intervention with their speech activities might be justified under certain circumstances, it does not follow that the agent who acts paternalistically (the parents or state organs) should be allowed almost unlimited discretion to determine what is harmful, without, or with minimal, judicial oversight. The position in *U.S. v. Playboy* that careful characterisation of the evil is needed is preferable because it better reflects the moral standard that a child is an autonomous agent in the making.

Notes

1 Timothy Garton Ash, *Free Speech: Ten Principles For A Connected World* 19 (2016).
2 See, e.g., Brown v. Entertainment Merchants Association, 131 S. Ct. 2729 (2011) (citing *Erznoznik v Jacksonville*, 422 U.S. 205) (1975): "[M]inors are entitled to a significant measure of First Amendment protection, and only in relatively narrow and well-defined circumstances may government bar public dissemination of protected materials to them."
3 Of course, this is true of most rights typically enshrined in constitutions and human rights documents such as freedom of religion, the right to assembly, and the right to private life.
4 John Stuart Mill, *On Liberty* (1859).
5 Alexander Meiklejohn, *Free Speech and Its Relation to Self-Government* 23 (1948).
6 *Id.* at 25.
7 Vincent Blasi, *The Checking Value in First Amendment Theory*, Am. B. Found. Res. J. 521 (1977).
8 Frederick Schauer, *Free Speech: A Philosophical Inquiry* (1982).
9 Alon Harel, *Freedom of Speech, in* The Routledge Companion to Philosophy of Law 599 (Andrei Marmor ed., 2012); Eric Barendt, *Freedom of Speech* 6 (2nd ed., 2005).
10 Such debate can include broader political issues which go beyond the confines of school life. In *Tinker v. Des Moines Independent Community School District*, 393 U.S. 503 (1969) the Supreme Court ruled that a school could not punish students for refusing to remove black armbands which they had worn as a protest against the Vietnam war. The European Court of Human Rights dealt indirectly with the political expression of children in *Christian Democratic People's Party v Moldova* [2007] 45 E.H.R.R. 13. The applicant was an opposition political party whose activities were temporarily banned. One of the reasons given by the national authorities, which was accepted by the courts, was that a number of minors were present during an unauthorised demonstration of party members against the compulsory teaching of Russian at schools. The authorities claimed that this was a violation of Article 15 CRC that protects children's right of assembly and provides for its limitation on grounds of national security, public safety, public order, the protection of public health or morals, or the protection of the rights of others. The European Court of Human Rights held that this was a not a reason which could justify the ban. There was no evidence that the presence of children was arranged by the applicant and in any case

> it was rather a matter of personal choice for the parents to decide whether to allow their children to attend those gatherings and it would appear to be contrary to the parents' and children's freedom of assembly to prevent them from attending such events which, it must be recalled, were to protest against government policy on schooling.
>
> (para. 74)

This case presents the unusual situation where a government is invoking a right protected in the CRC to limit the expression of both children and adults.

11 *See* the discussion in Joseph Raz, *Free Expression and Personal Identification*, in Ethics in the Public Domain 146, 150–153 (1994).

12 It is possible for paternalistic actions to be motivated by the acting agent's self-interest. The tyrant who dictates how citizens should live their lives is acting paternalistically to perpetuate his power. This distinction does not affect my discussion here as I am assuming that parents and governmental agencies restricting children's speech are motivated by a genuine desire to protect children's well-being.

13 Joel Feinberg, *Harm to Self* 5 (1986).

14 *See* Kalle Grill, *Paternalism Towards Children, in* The Routledge Handbook of the Philosophy of Childhood and Children 123 (Anca Gheaus et al. eds., 2018).

15 129 S. Ct.1800 (2009).

16 The words at issue here were "fuck" and "shit".

17 98 S. Ct. 3026 (1978).

18 127 S. Ct. 2618 (2007).

19 *Id.* at 2627 (citing Hazelwood School District v. Kuhlmeier, 108 S. Ct. 562, 1988).

20 106 S. Ct. 3159 (1986).

21 *Id.* at 3166 (Brennan J., concurring).

22 *Id.* at 3164.

23 *Id.*

24 *Id.*

25 *Id.* at 3165.

26 Tamar Schapiro, *What is a Child?* 109 Ethics 715, 717–718 (1999).

27 Honora O'Neil, *Between Consenting Adults*, 14 Phil. & Pub. Aff. 252, 263–265 (1985).

28 Immanuel Kant, *The Metaphysics of Morals* 353, 569 (Mary J. Gregor transl., 1996), (all emphases in citations of Kant are in the original).

29 *Id.* at 571.

30 O'Neil , *supra* note 27, at 265.

31 Kant, *supra* note 28, at 573.

32 *Id.* at 457–458.

33 *Id.* at 458.

34 Schapiro, *supra* note 26, at 720.

35 Kant, *supra* note 28, at 459.

36 Schapiro, *supra* note 26, at 728.

37 *Id.* at 729.

38 *Id.*

39 *Id.* at 734.

40 Feinberg, *supra* note 13, at 5.

41 Seana Valentine Shiffrin, *Speech Matters: On Lying, Mortality, and the Law* (2014).

42 *Id.* at 91.

43 *Id.* at 105.

44 *Id.* at 104–105; Schapiro, *What is a Child?* 735.

45 Kant, *supra* note 28, at 568.

46 United States v. Alvarez, 132 S. Ct. 2537, 2549 (2012).

47 131 S. Ct. 2729 (2011).

48 *Id.* at 2739 (emphasis in the original).

49 *Id.*

50 *Id.*

51 *Id.* at 2738 (internal quotation marks and citations omitted).

52 120 S. Ct. 1878.

53 *Id.* at 1888.

54 *Id.*

55 Bethel School District v. Fraser, 106 S.Ct at 3168 (Marshall J., dissenting).

56 Morse v. Frederick, 127 S. Ct. at 2649 (Stevens J., dissenting).

12 Upholding children's civil rights as relational rights

The example of childhood circumcision

Pamela Laufer-Ukeles

Introduction

The Convention on the Rights of the Child (CRC) points to the need to uphold children's rights as a global mandate and directive.[1] The CRC crystallizes and actualizes the modern belief that children should be subjects and rights-holders and should never be treated as objects or possessions, nor punished for the sins of their parents. Parents were once entitled to use their children for labor and to collect their wages, and could punish their children harshly, even to the extent of death.[2] Children were considered the property of fathers who would retain custody as a matter of right.[3] Even when custody could be awarded to either parent, the dispute concerned the rights of two competing adults and custody of children was used as a punishment or reward for parental behavior.[4] Children were also used as a means to "punish" the sins of parents with regard to laws surrounding illegitimacy.[5] Indeed, the revolution in children's rights that has occurred over the past 30 years, signified and furthered by the passing of the CRC, is extraordinary.

However, international support for the CRC cannot mask the bitter ongoing disputes in jurisdictions worldwide regarding the nature of children's rights and how to best protect those rights. The CRC sets the basic grounding for prioritizing children's rights but does not resolve more nuanced questions of how to implement those rights, particularly when those rights are highly contested. Discord among modern approaches to children's rights creates confusion and ambiguity in advocating on behalf of children. Focus is alternately on advocacy for: (1) parental authority as the primary method to pursue children's interests based on the fundamental belief that parents should be given leeway to act on behalf of children either because they are best suited to determine what is good for their children or because children have a right to be raised by their genetic parents;[6] (2) state intervention through its *parens patriae* power in order to protect children based on the state's determination of children's "best interests" and in order to protect the state's own interests in children;[7] or (3) looking to children themselves, their voices, desires, capabilities, and lived experiences to determine what should be done for children in a manner that focuses on listening to children and furthering the potential to decipher and support children's autonomy through progressive and creative means.[8] Advocates of each of these three perspectives intend to protect children and claim the mantle of children's rights. Yet, the differences between these perspectives are significant and opposing positions are hotly debated. The discord creates uncertainty and tension where we need unison and cooperation between parents, the state, and children.

The discord between these three approaches can be found within the CRC itself. Accordingly, while the CRC provides an overall framework for the need to focus on children's rights as stakeholders granted their own Convention, there is still enormous room for differing interpretations and variations regarding how to implement the rights specified in the CRC, especially in the context of contested issues such as grandparents' visitation rights, privacy rights, rights to basic education, among others. In this chapter, I focus on the tension and discord surrounding the permissibility of childhood circumcision as a case study in the complex nature of children's civil rights. While parents steeped in certain religious and cultural traditions believe that circumcision is what is best for their children, the state has increasingly stepped in, certainly in the case of female circumcision, but also in the case of male circumcision, to curtail such practices as being against children's rights. Civil rights are personal rights, whether in the context of religious freedom or the right to vote, and thus children's own expression of their will is particularly impactful, especially when older children object to having their bodily integrity violated. Due to the complex, transitional nature of children's rights, viewing children's rights as individual rights in isolation of parents and state misses the ways children are both dependent on relationships and yet increasingly seek their own freedoms. In light of the intertwined nature of children and their parents that cannot be properly accounted for through individualism, I suggest a relational approach to further children's rights, which focuses on state obligations to support children's rights within ongoing relationships, and demonstrate how such an approach can assist in more effectively protecting children's rights in practice.

Discord in the CRC

Conflicting claims over what is "best" for children

The tension between the three different perspectives on how best to promote children's rights outlined above is represented within different provisions of the CRC itself. The CRC focuses on the importance of the family and describes the child's right to be raised with discretion and without undue state interference by one's own parents. In Article 5, the CRC provides: "States Parties shall respect the responsibilities, rights and duties of parents … to provide … appropriate direction and guidance in the exercise by the child of the rights recognized in the present Convention." Thus, the CRC gives parents, and not the state, the primary discretion to effectuate the rights of children, reflecting strong support for the perspective that parents are the best arbiters of determining what is good for children. Article 7 explains that every child has "the right to know and be cared for by his or her parents." Furthermore, when it comes to a child's right to freedom of conscience and religion, Article 14 of the CRC states that "States Parties shall respect the rights and duties of the parents and, when applicable, legal guardians, to provide direction to the child in the exercise of his or her right." Thus, the CRC seems to generally adopt the parents know best perspective on how to protect children and the CRC seems to defer to the need to allow parents' discretion in raising their children.

Yet, in other parts of the CRC, a perspective more reliant on state interference to promote children's rights can be detected. For instance, Article 19 explicitly discusses the nation-states' responsibility to prevent the abuse and neglect of children and Article 20 gives the child the right to government protection and alternative placement if taken from legal parents. As explained in Article 19, signatories commit to take "all appropriate legislative, administrative, and social and educational measures to protect the child from physical or mental violence… while in the care of parents." Article 9 underscores that separation from parents can be done in the best interests of the child but gives little further guidance. Such provisions can be understood to facilitate and rely upon state interference with parental discretion to protect children. How early the state should step in and interfere with parental actions is not clearly answered by the CRC – although the tension in the provisions is apparent: should the state wait for actual incidents of abuse and neglect to be proven or must the state interfere with parental discretion beforehand in order to protect children? Advocates for increasing state interference with parental discretion could certainly use such Articles to support the state's need to interfere as early as possible to prevent abuse.

Finally, in still other parts to the CRC, the provisions support giving children's own perspectives and experiences as much support as possible. Article 12 of the CRC assures all children

> capable of forming his or her own views the right to express those views freely in all matters affecting the child, the views of the child being given due weight in accordance with the age and maturity of the child.

The CRC discusses the child's right to identity,[9] the freedom of expression, and the right to receive information, including the right to access media, all of which can support a child-centered perspective on children's rights.[10] In Article 9, the CRC says all interested parties have a right to be heard in cases where a child is to be separated from his parents due to abuse and neglect or when parents are living separately. Presumably that includes the child's right to be heard directly, but it is not clear from what age the child has that right and whether there are limitations. The CRC goes farther than many domestic systems in trying to ensure that children's own perspectives are put at the center of children's rights inquiries. In fact, given that the three perspectives that dominate children's rights discussions can each be located within the CRC, it is not surprising that the CRC has been described, alternately, as being too tolerant of parental discretion, too focused on the potential for state interference to protect children, and inclusive of children's own voices in particularly strong ways.[11]

How tension among competing perspectives on what is best for children affects advocacy on behalf of children in the context of childhood circumcision

My analysis is not intended to deflect from the progress of the CRC in advancing children's rights. Such tensions within the document do not render the CRC unuseful in prioritizing the rights of children symbolically and practically, especially when specific provisions apply. However, the ambiguity and conflicting perspectives represented in the CRC undermine its effectiveness in two overlapping ways: (1) failing to clearly resolve hotly contested issues and (2) overreliance on imprecise "best interests" analyses. I will demonstrate these failings by engaging in an emotionally fraught test case, specifically pointing to the way the CRC contends with the volatile issue of childhood genital circumcision.

The right of parents to circumcise their children and the opposing right of children to maintain their bodily integrity and therefore to be free from circumcision is in hot debate worldwide both in the context of male and female children. Circumcision involves the religiously or culturally motivated ritualized or health-related cutting of children's genitalia. Female genital mutilation (FGM) is widely considered to be a serious human rights violation and has been deemed unlawful by the Convention of the Elimination of Discrimination of Women general committee,[12] although it is still commonly practiced in many parts of the world.[13] In contrast, male circumcision has been in common practice in Western civilization. However, more recently, male circumcision has come under more scrutiny and significant criticism.[14] Indeed, the non-therapeutic circumcision of males has been opined to be illegal or problematic by multi-country and interdisciplinary regulatory bodies,[15] has been restricted in certain Scandinavian countries and in Germany,[16] although it has not been outlawed by prohibitive regulation. While there are certainly clear differences between male and female circumcision, as will be described below, the religious and cultural significance of each is often compared, as can the physical alteration in certain instances. Thus, I believe it is more compelling to consider their differences and similarities jointly.[17] In fact, in November 2012, the Committee on Social Affairs, Health, and Sustainable Development of the Parliamentary Assembly of the Council of Europe issued a report (PACE Initiative) aimed at raising awareness and concern about "a category of violation of the physical integrity of children, which supporters of the procedures tend to present as beneficial to the children themselves despite clear evidence to the contrary."[18] Under this category, the committee includes male and female circumcision, early childhood medical intervention in the case of intersexual children, and the submission of children to piercings, tattoos, or plastic surgery.

First, the CRC itself does not resolve disputes regarding circumcision. Article 14 gives parents the autonomy to direct their children's religious and cultural upbringing only limited by "public safety, order, health or morals, or the fundamental rights and freedoms of others." This provision is understood to allow for religious freedom with regard to circumcision unless there are serious health ramifications. This provision does not explicitly indicate how to evaluate such harm, nor does it demand that children's opposition to religious rituals be heeded. On the other hand, Article 24 generally, and part 3 in particular are understood as providing support for state prohibition of female circumcision. Article 24(3) indicates, "State parties shall take all effective and appropriate measures with a view to abolishing traditional practices prejudicial to the health of children." Still, the prohibition is not explicit.

Other provisions of the CRC are also understood to push against female circumcision, in particular provisions that promote children's health at the highest levels and protect children from violence or abuse, which would seem to mediate against circumcision that causes substantial harm.[19] For instance, Article 19 of the CRC directs states to take all appropriate measures to

> [p]rotect the child from all forms of physical or mental violence, injury or abuse, neglect or negligent treatment, maltreatment or exploitation, including sexual abuse, while in the care of parent(s), legal guardian(s) or any other person who has the care of the child.

This provision is understood to obligate the state to broadly protect children's physical integrity. On the other hand, Article 30 provides specific protection for a child belonging to an ethnic or religious minority, who should "not be denied the right … to enjoy his or her own cultur[e] and, to profess and practice his or her own religion…." Therefore, it could be argued that children have a right of belonging within their familial religions and, by extension, undergo circumcision. Finally, Article 12 guarantees children old enough to voice their views the right to express those views, but that right is not deemed determinative by the CRC even in the context of bodily mutilation. Despite how frequently circumcision is practiced and how contested it is, circumcision is not prohibited or permitted explicitly, leaving a wealth of conflicting messages through which signatory states must navigate.

In 2014, the Committee on the Rights of the Child, jointly with the CEDAW Committee, issued a general comment that specifically dealt with ritual practices that may be harmful to girls and women, referencing FGM in an explicit manner, directing that all practices that are harmful be effectively eliminated.[20] This comment tacitly acknowledges the lack of clarity under the CRC. Still, many cultures do not believe that female circumcision is harmful, the General Comment does not distinguish between different kinds of FGM practiced in different cultures, and ultimately the CRC Committee provides guidance but is not binding on signatories. The issue of male circumcision is only obliquely mentioned as cause for concern and not included in the categories of harmful practices. While directive, this Comment has not effectively prevented the practice of FGM in signatory countries, nor does it explicitly deal with the issue of male circumcision, leaving openings for divisiveness and struggle. Indeed, engaging with strong cultural and religious beliefs requires sensitivity to the way prohibitions can disrupt community and family life, alienating people from progressive movements.

Second, when determinations are difficult, international law tends to lean on best interests as the governing standard both within the CRC and beyond. Articles 3 and 9 of the CRC in particular point to children's best interests as the guiding principle in making any and all determinations on behalf of children. Given the lack of clarity on the permissibility of circumcision in the CRC itself, there is a tendency to rely on the best interests standard as guiding the permissibility of circumcision. For instance, the PACE Initiative points to best interest as the applicable standard to be considered in determining whether to allow circumcision.[21] While the best interests standard appears to be a praiseworthy approach and has the benefit of being able to take into account the particularities of individual cases and the varieties of issues that may arise, the best interests analysis relies on a multiplicity of factors and is so broad and malleable that it is open to bias and varying interpretations. There are courts, scholars, and clinicians that argue that it is in the best interests of the child for male children to be circumcised to cement their belonging to their religion and community.[22] Others oppose any childhood circumcision as being against children's best interests.[23] Best interests have long been criticized as ambiguous, amorphous, and extremely difficult for judges to apply, often necessitating costly and difficult proceedings.[24] Scholars and social science studies have continually claimed that there is no scientific "best" and that efforts to optimize are expensive and largely futile.[25] The best interests standard provides authority to the state decision makers even though optimization is not possible, resulting in the application of majoritarian values and simplistic analyses, minimizing parental privacy, and the complex civil rights of children. While guidance is needed in such hot button topics as childhood circumcision, among many other contested civil rights of children, relying on the best interests standard provides a shell without impactful substantive direction.

How a relational perspective on children's rights can improve international human rights for children

The relational approach

As the preamble to the CRC acknowledges, the child is in a particularly vulnerable, yet complex place given his developing maturity.[26] Ultimately, children's rights cannot be completely subsumed to parental authority – children have rights that may be separable and in conflict with parents. Furthermore, children's rights cannot be subsumed to state control as it is usually parents who provide the needed care and too much state interference can be harmful to that relationship. Although children gradually have stronger voices of their own as they mature, they cannot be entirely relied upon themselves to effectuate their own needs as they are fundamentally dependent, although the transitional nature of childhood must be taken into account.

Perceiving children's rights as individual rights triggers the discord, tension, and uncertainty described above. It is hard to defend children's civil rights as rights that belong to individual children in a vacuum separated from parents and communities in which children are raised. Protecting children as individuals, isolated from parental care relationships, creates the specter of state interference with relationships as an oppositional dynamic. Therefore, as opposed to seeing the state as supporting them by promoting care for children, parents may perceive state enforcement of children's rights as a threat and an intrusion, undermining state efforts to advance the status of children. The civil rights of children can most effectively be defended with recognition and understanding of the nature of the relationships, families, and communities that support children, keeping in mind the transitional nature of childhood and how as children mature and become more independent, they become less reliant on relationships.

Such a relational approach to children's rights can provide further clarity when there are conflicting positions on best interests and help in implementing the rights of children.[27] The relational perspective shifts the focus of rights from the prevention of state interference in human liberty to the placement of positive duties on the state to set preconditions for healthy, beneficial relationships.[28] Jennifer Nedelsky argues that rights cannot be secured without developing autonomy through the fostering of relationships: "If we ask ourselves what actually enables people to be autonomous it is not isolation but relationships – with parents, teachers, friends, loved ones – that provide the security, education, nurturing, and support that make the development of autonomy possible."[29] Relationships are not just one factor to be weighed into an individual account of children's best interests. Rather, the overarching premise of relational rights is that individual rights can be sufficiently protected only by protecting relationships, as opposed to protecting individual freedoms in isolation from others.[30] Thus, the state's primary purpose is to support children within their functional, care relationships.

Balancing harm to relationships with harm to individual children

Accordingly, based on recognition of the nature of children's rights as fundamentally relational, in clarifying and implementing the rights of children, focus should be on balancing the harm to relationships from state interference and the harm to the individual from failing to interfere. The greater the individual harm threatened, the more the state is justified in interfering. But the more such interference would harm ongoing nurturing relationships, the more cautious the state should be. In this regard, children's rights must be understood to be transitional rights.[31] The level of maturity of the child and the extent to which the child is dependent on the relationship are directly relevant in determining whether state interference is warranted. Furthermore, generally, given that the child is likely to continue to be nurtured within the relationship, education and collaboration with parents should be preferred over coercion and punishment of parents. Although as the child matures and becomes independent, more interference can be justified.

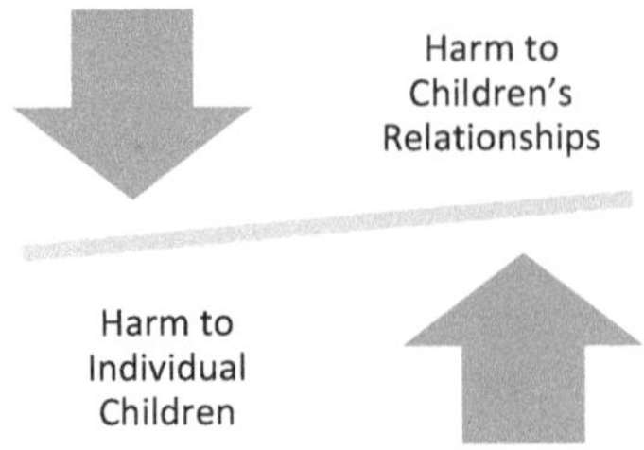

This chart demonstrates the way relational rights puts relationships at the center of the potentially competing interests of children's own desires, parental desires, and state obligations. The state must decide whether to interfere with the ongoing parental care relationship for the sake of children's personal civil rights by balancing the child's dependence on that relationship, the harm likely to result to the child if interference does not occur, and the extent of the harm to the relationship from state interference.

The rights of children to bodily integrity in the context of male and female circumcision

This relational framework can be used to clarify and support the implementation of children's rights in the context of any personal right. Here, I apply it in the context of childhood circumcision and children's right to bodily integrity as a test case. Childhood circumcision is a particularly interesting test case because of the tension between different regulatory and humanitarian approaches toward male and female circumcision and the widespread nature of the practice involving a non-medically necessitated physical alteration of a child's body.

There are several variables to keep in mind when considering whether parents have a right to perform circumcision on children based on their religious or cultural beliefs or whether, to the contrary, children have a right to be free from circumcision as a violation of their bodily integrity: (1) How would the relationship be affected by prohibiting the practice? (2) How much harm will occur to the child if the practice is permitted? and (3) How old is the child and do they object? One could also ask whether benefits of the procedure should be factored in. However, in the context of circumcision, the benefits are very subjective. Thus, I account for the benefits as part of the religious freedom of the parents and the harm to the relationship if the child does not undergo the religious procedure.

The first question is how interference with parental discretion by prohibiting the practice affects the relationship between parent caregivers on which the child is dependent for their basic needs and the child? I would not assume that a parent would punish a child for not being able to circumcise them, but if circumcision is part of religious and cultural practice, interfering in that relationship will strain parents and could strain emotional connections to children if they are not being raised within the dictates of the religious community or the cultural norms of a community. Parents may feel frustrated and alienated by the interference.

Separating child from parent with regard to important religious and cultural precepts constitutes potentially harmful interference in care relationships. For instance, under Jewish law, male circumcision is considered a precondition for being part of the Jewish community and is considered a direct obligation upon parents. To remain part of the Jewish faith, the boy would be obligated to undergo a circumcision on his own at a later age, which is much more physically difficult. Given the centrality of circumcision to Jews and Muslims, even if prohibited, one can expect illegal practice of the religious ritual, which would only compromise health and safety and potentially result in punishment of parents for deeply held religious beliefs. However, much male circumcision is not performed based on deeply held religious beliefs, but based on cultural norms. Thus, it is not as clear the extent to which interference with parental discretion would harm relationships in those contexts. If the state feels that performing male circumcision violates the rights of a child and causes that child harm, then education and doctor recommendations are likely to have significant impact on those who act due to cultural norms as opposed to religious fiat.

There are many that practice female circumcision, or FGM, based on strongly held religious or, more often, cultural beliefs. Female circumcision is considered by many to be an essential rite of passage to womanhood and failure to perform the practice can prevent acceptance into communities and alienate girls from their care relationships. Even if the harms caused by female circumcision justify prohibition, as they usually do, adherence to strongly held beliefs will lead to illegal practices likely to involve increased health risks as access to hygienic facilities and antibiotics is likely to be diminished. Thus, the state or intergovernmental body trying to minimize female circumcision should take into account why the circumcision is being performed and how directed, intensive education and health recommendations can help prevent the act in conjunction with prohibitions. Indeed, particularly in Africa, misinformation about the health impact of female circumcision has been combated by education, resulting in a decline in the practice, in particular by the Inter-African Committee on Traditional Practices. Education and dissemination of information can be more effective and less harmful to children than prohibitions that interfere with and harm care relationships. Ultimately, however, even if the harms involved justify prohibitions, education and dissemination of information are crucial to supporting children and their relationships.

Second, how much harm has the procedure been proven to cause based on documented and accepted scientific data? Even if there is great risk of harm in interfering in parental relationships, if the physical harms of the procedure are significant and substantiated, interference with parental discretion and prohibition can be justified. The harms of male circumcision are highly debated,[32] although there are some practices such as oral suction circumcision that can spread infant herpes and cause other serious complications. The physical and emotional harms of FGM are concrete and well-substantiated.[33] Women who have undergone FGM suffer physical and emotional pain and deleterious side effects, particularly during sexual intercourse, as the procedure is often intended to curb sexual pleasure, but also during urination and menstruation.

There are, however, different forms of female circumcision, ranging from removal of the hood of the clitoris to the entirety of the clitoris, labia, and narrowing of the vaginal opening. Most female circumcisions that are performed entail removing at least most or all of the clitoris and the serious and substantial health ramifications of such procedures are serious and well-substantiated. However, there are those who argue that the most "gentle" form of circumcision – just removing the clitoral hood, or merely "nicking" the hood – does not cause significant harm to the child and may even increase sexual pleasure as it is an elective procedure done for aesthetic and sensory reasons.[34] It is argued that such clitoral hoodectomies closely mirror the more accepted male circumcision and that deleterious health effects cannot be proven, although the risk of infection from any such procedure exists similar to male circumcision.

Ultimately, if female circumcision can be done in a manner that mitigates the risk of harm, and if male circumcision can do the same by eliminating risky practices, allowing such ceremonies in a modified form can facilitate engagement with communities that may otherwise feel alienated by blanket prohibitions. Such engagement can facilitate a change in practice through education and discourse, thereby substantially improving the plight of young girls and boys in accordance with the mandate of the CRC. The continued prevalence of the practice of childhood circumcision attests to the need to continue efforts to engage with communities with sensitivity and understanding. Overall, however, when relating to the more invasive ritual practices, the state is justified in interfering with parental discretion, particularly when FGM involves removal of most or all of the clitoris plus additional genitalia in which the harm to the child is widely acknowledged and overwhelmingly substantiated.

The third relevant factor is the age of the child when the circumcision is performed, and, if at an older age closer to puberty, whether the child objects. Once a child has the consciousness to object to the procedure, and does so object, forcing the procedure takes on a qualitatively different level of harm. If the child objects, the state can be less concerned of the harm it will cause to the relationships between child and parents as the willingness to object demonstrates maturity and independence from parents, at least to a certain extent. Of course, a child is easily influenced by parents, particularly a younger child, and therefore below a certain age, the level of objection may be muted. But a child's objection should be decisive, particularly when circumcision is performed near the age of puberty, common for female circumcision. Once an older child objects, the care relationship is put at risk in any event and given the potential harm, such a child should not be forced, and the state should interfere to prevent such coercion.

Conclusion: civil rights beyond the right of bodily integrity

This relational approach to children's rights and the analysis of childhood circumcision is intended to benefit understanding of the nature of children's rights and assist in the effective implementation of the CRC to children who reside and are raised within families and under parental authority. Other civil human rights of children that may conflict with parental decisions, like the right to education, the right to marriage, the right to an abortion, and the right to health care can benefit from this kind of relational analysis. As a child matures, there is more room for their own voice to prevail and less threat to the relationship due to a child's increasing independence. The younger the child, and the more interference will harm the relationship, the more the state should hesitate before interfering with a parent–child relationship and enforcing children's rights in a manner that overrides parental discretion. However, if failure to interfere will cause substantial harm to the child, then it is worthwhile to interfere despite the harm to the relationship. If the child involved is older and largely independent of their parents and does not want to act in accordance with their parents' wishes, the state can be less cautious. And, in all instances, collaboration and education with parents and efforts that support care relationships are to be preferred to coercion and prohibitions that undermine parental authority and disrupt parent–child relationships.

Notes

1 United Nations Convention on the Rights of the Child, Nov. 20, 1989, http://www.ohchr.org/en/professionalinterest/pages/crc.asp (hereinafter CRC).

2 *See* Barbara Bennett Woodhouse, *From Property to Personhood: A Child-Centered Perspective on Parents' Rights*, 5 Geo. J. on Fighting Poverty 313, 314–315 (1998).

3 Barbara Bennett Woodhouse, *Children's Rights: The Destruction and Promise of Family*, 1993 BYU L. Rev. 497, 502.

4 Modern case law has reversed the precedents punishing parents by refusing to award custody. See, e.g., Ashwell v. Ashwell, 286 P.2d 983, 987 (Cal. Dist. Ct. App. 1955) ("[I]n determining where custody of children shall lie the courts are not engaged in a disciplinary action to punish parents for their shortcomings as individuals."); Hayes v. Gallacher, 972 P.2d 1138, 1142 (Nev. 1999); Sims v. Sims, 865 P.2d 328, 330 (Nev. 1993) (holding custody determinations should be made in best interests of children, not to punish parents); *see also* Kerry Abrams, *Immigration Status and the Best Interests of the Child Standard*, 14 Va. J. Soc. Pol'y & L. 87, 97 (2006); Jane C. Murphy, *Rules, Responsibility and Commitment to Children: The New Language of Morality in Family Law*, 60 U. Pitt. L. Rev. 1111, 1187 (1999).

5 See, e.g., Taylor Gay, Comment, *All in the Family: Examining Louisiana's Faulty Birth Order-Based Discrimination*, 73 La. L. Rev. 295, 303–304 (2012); Levy v. Louisiana, 391 U.S. 68, 72 (1968) ("it is invidious to discriminate" against illegitimate children by precluding them from recovering damages for the wrongful death of their mother); Jayna Morse Cacioppo, Note, *Voluntary Acknowledgments of Paternity: Should Biology Play a Role in Determining Who Can Be a Legal Father?* 38 Ind. L. Rev. 479, 483 (2005) (reviewing the history of illegitimacy and how a child born to unwed parents had no right to child support); Browne Lewis, *Children of Men: Balancing the Inheritance Rights of Marital and Non-Marital Children*, 39 U. Tol. L. Rev. 1, 5 (2007) (illegitimate children were considered "bastards" and not entitled to inheritance rights).

6 See, e.g., Emily Buss, *"Parental" Rights*, 88 VA. L. Rev. 635, 647–650 (2002) ("Parents' strong emotional attachment to their children and considerable knowledge of their particular needs make parents the child-specific experts most qualified to assess and pursue their children's best interests in most circumstances.").

7 See, e.g., James G. Dwyer, *The Relationship Rights of Children*, 17–23 (2006) (describing children's rights to have the state protect their interests).

8 *See* Barbara Bennett Woodhouse, *Hatching the Egg: A Child-Centered Perspective on Parents' Rights*, 14 Cardozo L. Rev. 1747, 1827–1844 (1993) (suggesting different ways the law can utilize a child-centered perspective).

9 CRC, art. 8.

10 CRC, art. 13.

11 See, e.g., Barbara Bennett Woodhouse & Kathryn A. Johnson, *The United Nations Convention on the Rights of the Child: Empowering Parents to Protect their Children's Rights*, *in* What is Right for Children? 7–19 (2009) (arguing that the treatise incorporates parental rights and best interests in a manner that makes it unthreatening to parental rights advocates); Shulamit Almog & Ariel L. Bendor, *The UN Convention on the Rights of the Child Meets the American Constitution: Towards a Supreme Law of the World*, 11 Int'l J. Child. Rts. 273, 277–279 (2004) (arguing that the CRC grants rights to children that frequently conflict with both parental rights and judicial discretion, focusing on the rights of the child detached from parent or state).

12 Committee on the Elimination of Discrimination against Women, *General Recommendation No.14* (1990) (instructing signatories to take action to prevent the practice).

13 UN Children's Fund, *Female Genital Mutilation/Cutting: A Global Concern* (New York: UNICEF, 2016) (estimating that FGM is practiced in 30 countries and that three million girls are at risk of being subject to circumcision every year around the time of puberty).

14 Resolution 1952 (2013), http://www.assembly.coe.int/Committee/SOC/2013/SOC005E.pdf.

15 *See* Committee on Rights of the Child, Concluding observations on the combined second to fourth periodic reports of Switzerland, U.N. Doc. CRC/C/CHE/CO/2-4 (2014).

16 *See* Rhona Schuz, *The Dangers of Children's Rights' Discourse in the Political Arena: The Issue of Religious Male Circumcision as a Test Case*, 21 Cardozo J. L. Gender 347, 358–361 (2015).

17 *Compare* Natalie J. Friedenthal, *It's Not All Mutilation: Distinguishing Between Female Genital Mutilation and Female Circumcision*, 19 N.Y. U. Inter'l L. Rev. 111 (1996) *with* Cynthia Fernandez-Romano, *The Banning of Female Circumcision: Cultural Imperialism or A Triumph for Women's Rights?* 13 Temp. Int'l & Comp. L.J. 137, 153 (1999); and Shea Lita Bond, *State Laws Criminalizing Female Circumcision: A Violation of the Equal Protection Clause of the Fourteenth Amendment?* 32 J. Marshall L. Rev. 353 (1999).

18 Parliamentary Assembly Council of Europe, Resolution 1952, Children's Right to Physical Integrity (2013), http://assembly.coe.int/nw/xml/XRef/Xref-DocDetails-EN.asp?fileid=20174&lang=EN&search=MTk1Mnx0eXBlX3N0cl9lbjpSZXNvbHV0aW9u# (hereinafter, PACE Resolution).

19 CRC art. 19; CRC art. 24(3) ("State parties shall take all effective and appropriate measures with a view to abolishing traditional practices prejudicial to the health of children.").

20 CEDAW and CRC, Joint General Recommendation No. 31 of the Committee on The Elimination of Discrimination Against Women and General Comment No. 18 of the Committee on The Rights of The Child on Harmful Practices, U.N. Doc. CEDAW/C/GC/31/CRC/C/GC/18 (Nov. 14, 2014).

21 Pace Resolution at Sec.7.4 ("...striking a balance between rights and best interests of the child and religious freedoms of adults."); *see* J. Steven Svoboda et al., *Informed Consent for Neonatal Circumcision: An Ethical and Legal Conundrum*, 17 J. Contemp. Health L. & Pol'y 61, 83–84 (2000) (to allow children to undergo non-medically required procedures, best interests of the child must be demonstrated).

22 Andrew E. Behrns, *To Cut or Not to Cut? Addressing Proposals to Ban Circumcision Under Both A Parental Rights Theory and Child-Centered Perspective in the Specific Context of Jewish and Muslim Infants*, 21 Wm. Mary Bill Rts. J. 925 (2013) (arguing that male circumcision is in the best interest of Jewish and Muslim boys); Heli Askola, *Cut-Off Point? Regulating Male Circumcision in Finland*, 25 In't J. L. Pol'y & Fam. 100, 108 (2011) (Finish court determined that male circumcision is in the best interests of children).

23 Peter W. Adler, *Is Circumcision Legal?* 16 Rich. J. L. & Pub. Int. 439 (2013) (arguing that male circumcision violates the best interests rule); Bijan Fateh-Moghadam, *Criminalizing Male Circumcision? Case Note: Landgericht Cologne, Judgment of 7 May 2012 – No. 151 Ns 169/11*, 13 German L. J. 1131 (2012) (discussing conflicting perspectives on whether male circumcision is in the best interests of children); Svovoda, *supra* note 21 (same).

24 See, e.g., Robert H. Mnookin & Eleanor Maccoby, *Facing the Dilemmas of Child Custody*, 10 Va. J. Soc. Pol'y & L. 54, 71–72 (2002); Robert Mnookin & Lewis Kornhauser, *Bargaining in the Shadow of the Law: The Case of Divorce*, 88 Yale L.J. 950, 954–957 (1979) (discussing the effects of bargaining in the context of uncertainty and, in particularly, effects on the weaker more risk averse party).

25 Elizabeth S. Scott & Robert E. Emery, *Gender Politics and Child Custody: The Puzzling Persistence of the Best-Interests Standard*, 77 Law & Contemp. Probs. 69, 73–74 (2014).

26 "Bearing in mind that, as indicated in the Declaration of the Rights of the Child, the child by reason of his physical and mental immaturity needs special safeguards and care, including appropriate legal protection, before as well as after birth." Preamble to the CRC.

27 For more detail on the contours and implementation of the relational rights approach to children's rights, *see* Pamela Laufer-Ukeles, *The Relational Rights of Children*, 48 Conn. L. Rev. 741 (2016).

28 See Martha Minow, *Rights for the Next Generation: A Feminist Approach to Children's Rights*, 9 Harv. Women's L.J. 1, 14–21, 23–24 (1986).

29 Jennifer Nedelsky, *Law's Relations: A Relational Theory of Self, Autonomy, and Law* 124 (2011).

30 *Id.*

31 UN Committee on the Rights of the Child has admitted that CRC signatory states have not paid sufficient attention to the transitional rights of children and thus issues a comment to provide more guidance on this account:

> The Committee on the Rights of the child notes with concern that in implementing their obligations under the Convention, States parties have not given sufficient attention to the specific concerns of adolescents as rights holders and to promoting their Health and development. This has motivated the Committee to adopt the present general comment in order to raise awareness and provide States parties with guidance and support in their efforts to guarantee the respect for, protection and fulfilment of the rights of adolescents, including through the formulation of specific strategies and policies.

UN Committee on the Rights of the Child, *General Comment No. 4, Adolescent Health and Development the Context of the Convention on the Rights of the Child*, U.N. Doc. CRC/GC/2003/4 (July 1, 2003).

32 T. Hammond, *A Preliminary Poll of Men Circumcised in Infancy or Childhood*, 83 BJU Int'l., Supp. 1, at 85, 86 (1999), http://onlinelibrary.wiley.com/doi/10.1046/j.1464-410x.1999.0830s1085.x/pdf.; Am. Acad. of Pediatrics, Circumcision Policy Statement, 103 Pediatrics, no. 9, 1999, at 686, http://pediatrics.aappublications.org/content/103/3/686.full (describing pain and stress experienced by newborns who undergo circumcision without analgesia); Anna Taddio et al., *Effect of Neonatal*

Circumcision on Pain Response During Subsequent Routine Vaccination, 349 Lancet 599, 602 (1997) (indicating that infants may experience post-traumatic stress disorder from circumcision); William E. Brigman, *Circumcision as Child Abuse: The Legal and Constitutional Issues*, 23 J. Fam. L. 337, 337–338 (1984). But see, e.g., Christopher Maden et al., *History of Circumcision, Medical Conditions, and Sexual Activity and Risk of Penile Cancer*, 85 J. Nat'l Cancer Inst. 19–24 (1993); Edgar J. Schoen et al., *Report of the Task Force on Circumcision*, 84 Pediatrics 388–391 (1989); Edward C. Green, *The Circumcision and AIDS Debate*, Anthropology News, Jan. 2000, at 22 (discussing debate surrounding benefits of male circumcision in preventing the spread of AIDS).

33 See, e.g., Layli Miller Bashir, *Female Genital Mutilation in the United States: An Examination of Criminal and Asylum Law*, 4 Am. U.J. Gender & L. 415, 429 (1996).

34 *See* Natalie J. Friedenthal, *It's Not All Mutilation: Distinguishing between Female Genital Mutilation and Female Circumcision*, 19 N.Y.U. Inter'l L. Rev. 111 (1996).

13 Protection of the child's right to privacy in the Convention on the Rights of the Child, the General Data Protection Regulation and the Polish law

Agnieszka Ogrodnik-Kalita

Introduction

Passed by the United Nations 30 years ago, the Convention on the Rights of the Child (CRC) has had an enormous impact on the protection of the rights of the child.[1] The CRC expresses these rights in a comprehensive and modern way. In particular, with respect to the protection of the child's right to privacy, the CRC was years ahead of its time. Emphasizing in 1980 that a child's privacy must be guaranteed in any situation and environment,[2] the premier Polish jurist involved in the drafting of the CRC, Adam Lopatka probably did not realize how important the child's right to privacy would become. He certainly could not have forseen how many new "situations and environments" would pose a threat to this sphere of the child's life.

Children's rights have a special character because their enforcement depends largely on adults.[3] It is adults who must acknowledge the child's individuality, and it is they who should look after the child's interests.[4] It is primarily parents who should not only defend the right to privacy, but also refrain from actions that could infringe it.

The analysis of the child's right to privacy in this chapter will not be limited to the provisions of the CRC, although the CRC will be significant and provide the basis for further discussion. Nevertheless, "the Convention does not provide a full picture of the protection of the child's rights, and they should be analysed against a wider background of international and national regulations."[5] However, provisions of the CRC constitute "an important basis for the establishment of certain rules that should be followed when interpretating regulations contained in other laws."[6] The CRC is a legal act of fundamental significance for human rights protection, including family rights,[7] regulating the issue of the rights of children and parents in a comprehensive and detailed way.[8] Indeed, even though the CRC has been in force for only 30 years, its provisions are referred to not only in Polish legislation, but also in judicial decisions, which testifies to the practical impact of the CRC on Polish law.

First, I will present the treatment of the child's right to privacy within the CRC. Next, I will discuss the approach to this issue in the General Data Protection

Regulation (GDPR) and in Polish civil law. Due to its limited scope, the purpose of the chapter is not to discuss the child's right to privacy comprehensively because this issue is broad and multi-faceted. Instead, the most important and current issues pertaining to this topic will be addressed.

The child's right to privacy in the CRC

Article 16 is included in the group of the CRC's regulations that pertain to civil rights and freedoms.[9] These regulations in particular have aroused considerable controversy since the CRC came into force.[10]

The CRC explicitly grants the right of privacy to the child. According to Article 16, "No child shall be subjected to arbitrary or unlawful interference with his or her privacy, family, home or correspondence, not to unlawful attacks on his or her honour and reputation." This right can also be inferred from the words "no one" and "everyone" used in Article 12 of the Universal Declaration of Human Rights and in Article 17 of the Covenant on the Civil and Political Rights that protect private life.[11] However, it is notable that the CRC explicitly refers to the child as the subject of the right to privacy.[12] Moreover, The Convention is progressive in granting the right to privacy to children irrespective of their development level and without differentiation on the basis of their age.[13] Indeed, the wording of Article 16 of the CRC is uncompromising. It does not impose obligations on the State Parties to the CRC in order to incentivize granting the right to privacy to children, but – rather straightforwardly – stipulates that interference with the child's personal interests is prohibited.[14]

The CRC emphasizes that privacy must be ensured in all situations and environments that the child is found. Thus, the right to privacy pertains not only to family and school, but also to health care services.[15] The child's right to privacy must be guaranteed within the family, but should also be honoured in connection with other people when a child seeks advice or assistance, especially in situations when a child is allegedly harmed or is otherwise at risk.[16] Protection of the child's privacy encompasses respect for potential embarrassment, infringements of dignity, and confidentiality of contacts with other people (both family members and others). It also prohibits surveillance, eavesdropping, or searching through the child's personal belongings or documentation without permission. Moreover, it also curtails harassment of a child in a manner that disturbs his or her peace without reason.[17] Ensuring the privacy of correspondence is also directly associated with the right to privacy, which is emphasized in the prohibition on interfering unlawfully with the child's correspondence in Article 16 of the CRC.

Children's right to privacy, however, exists only within a framework that also respects parental authority. Poland issued a statement on Articles 12–16 jointly, which provides that

> The Republic of Poland claims that the child's rights specified in the Convention, especially the ones expressed in Articles 12–16, should be enforced

> with respect for parental authority and in accordance with the Polish customs and traditions pertaining to the position of the child in the family and outside.[18]

The concepts of "customs and traditions" used in this statement have vague and malleable meanings.[19] Hence, the right to privacy has become a part of the catalogue of the child's rights that should be enforced in harmony with the exercise of natural powers resulting from parental authority. Indeed, Article 18 of the CRC stipulates that it is parents who have the primary responsibility for the upbringing and development of the child,[20] which is also directly relevant to the implementation of the child's right to privacy.

Despite the importance attributed to the right to privacy in the CRC, as well as in other international legal instruments, the right to privacy has received less attention by the public in Poland. In a study carried out by students concerning the knowledge of the child's rights and a catalogue of rights the respondents would be willing to grant to children, the right to privacy ranked 11th and was mentioned by only 7.7% of the respondents. Moreover, 5% of the respondents claimed that the child's right to privacy is not respected in Poland.[21]

The child's right to privacy in the GDPR

A specialized form of privacy protection is the protection of personal data.[22] The entry into force of the European Union GDPR constituted a breakthrough in personal data protection.[23] This legal act is also critically significant to the protection of personal data of the child as an element of the child's right to privacy.

The emergence of new modern means of communication has brought not only numerous advantages but also potentially negative consequences.[24] The GDPR is supposed to prevent such a potential negative impact on the child's best interests. The EU legislator emphasizes the significance of the protection of the child's personal data at the outset in section 38 of the preamble to the GDPR:

> Children merit specific protection with regard to their personal data, as they may be less aware of the risks, consequences and safeguards concerned and their rights in relation to the processing of personal data. Such specific protection should, in particular, apply to the use of personal data of children for the purposes of marketing or creating personality or user profiles and the collection of personal data with regard to children when using services offered directly to a child. The consent of the holder of parental responsibility should not be necessary in the context of preventive or counselling services offered directly to a child.

Moreover, recital 58 of the preamble explains, "Given that children merit specific protection, any information and communication, where processing is addressed to a child, should be in such a clear and plain language that the child can easily understand." Thereby, it is required that administrators prepare special communication and information written in language readily understandable by children and young people.[25]

The principles expressed in the preamble, referring to the protection of the child's personal data and the right to privacy, are incorporated in the provisions of Article 8 of the GDPR. Article 8 provides that in the case of information services offered directly to a child, such as platforms with games for children, educational portals, or online children's magazines, it is lawful to process personal data of a child who is at least 16 years old with his or her consent. In directing member states, the EU legislator allows a decrease in this age limit, but not below 13 years old under any circumstances.[26] However, in applying the regulation in Poland, the Polish legislator did not use this opportunity to decrease the age limit, even though under Polish law, children who are at least 13 years old have limited capacity to perform legal actions. The Polish application protects the child's interests appropriately because a 16-year-old person is more aware of dangers and is more experienced in transactions. Having had limited legal capacity for three years, the 16-year-old has been able to undertake many actions on his or her own, or with the consent of a statutory representative. In the context of the more complex world of data protection, requiring this greater level of understanding and experience is appropriate.

As an additional aspect of the right to privacy, the GDPR also introduces the "right to be forgotten." According to Article 17, the data subject shall have the right to obtain from the controller the erasure of personal data concerning him or her without undue delay. The controller shall have the obligation to erase personal data without undue delay if one of the grounds indicated in this provision occurs. The simplest example may be a request to delete data available on the website if any of the conditions occurred, e.g., the personal data are no longer necessary in relation to the purposes for which they were collected. This right confers on children the right to erase their data even if they consented to its communication originally while they were still children. Recital 65 provides that

> [This] right is relevant in particular where the data subject has given his or her consent as a child and is not fully aware of the risks involved by the processing, and later wants to remove such personal data, especially on the internet. The data subject should be able to exercise that right notwithstanding the fact that he or she is no longer a child.[27]

However, these provisions of the GDPR may also raise concerns for children rights advocates because, while protecting children, these principles also emphasize the lower awareness of the child with respect to personal data processing.

As a result of the GDPR entering into effect, the child's right to privacy at school is also subject to greater and more specialized protection. The personal data of children must be protected with particular diligence in the context of recording school events, in the form of photo galleries displayed on school notice boards or websites, or medical check-ups given by a school nurse.[28] To sufficiently protect children's data, it is necessary to catalogue the collected data that implicates children's privacy, to classify the data according to specific purposes of use, and to define how the data is interconnected. Some of this data is statutorily protected, such as lists of candidates enrolled at school, while other data can be published only on the basis of consent, for example, for the purpose of publication of photos on the school website. If pictures are published on the school website without consent, they would need to be removed.[29]

The child's right to privacy under Polish civil law

Under Polish law, the right to privacy has only recently been accorded value.[30] Currently, it is regarded as a personal human right subject to protection on the basis of Articles 23 and 24 of the Civil Code.[31] Personal rights are "values, recognized by the legal system, encompassing physical and psychological integrity of a human being, his or her individuality, dignity and status in the society, which is a condition for self-fulfilment of a human."[32] Article 23 of the Civil Code, which contains a list of personal rights that belong to all individuals, does not mention the right to privacy. Nevertheless, this is an open list of rights; therefore, the judiciary and the legal doctrine are constantly expanding on the categories of these rights by creative interpretation and on the basis of evolving public opinion.[33]

Today, it is well settled that the right to privacy is a personal right. It was granted the highest recognition in Article 47 of the Constitution of the Republic of Poland of April 2, 1997, which provides that "everyone has the right to legal protection of private life." The term "everyone" used by the legislator emphasizes that the regulation pertains also to the privacy of children.[34] The provisions of Articles 23 and 24 of the Civil Code protect personal rights of every person, which refers to every human being from the time of birth.[35]

Nevertheless, under Polish civil law, the question of when a child is granted the right to privacy is contested. In particular, the question has been raised whether to grant the right to children conceived but unborn. In connection with modern technology, which makes it possible to show and record an image of a human being even before he or she is born, the question arises "to which extent it is acceptable to use and publish an image of *nasciturus* and of a very young child."[36] Clearly, the use and publication of an image is connected to the issue of privacy. This question raises significant uncertainties for several reasons. First, medical procedures administered to a child when he or she is still in the mother's womb use real-time imaging.[37] Second, users of popular social media platforms publish not only photos of newborn or very young babies but also sonograms of babies not yet born.

Joanna Haberko makes a compelling argument in favour of the protection of personal rights of an unborn child under Polish law. The regulations in Articles 23 and 24 of the Civil Code speak about a "human being" and "the one whose personal rights are threatened." In this context, the legislator does not use the term "natural person," which refers presumably to a human who has already been born as a participant of civil law relationships.[38] Nevertheless, these regulations are contained in section I of Book 1 of the Civil Code entitled "Natural Persons."[39] Still, it can be argued that the legislator is referring to an exceptional case and intends to protect personal rights of all people, including unborn children.[40] Furthermore, Article 4 of the Act on Infertility Treatment provides that infertility must be treated with respect for the right to private life.[41] In this context, privacy includes the protection of both future parents and of a baby who has been conceived and born with the help of medically assisted procreation techniques or infertility treatment in general,[42] which demonstrates a broad, subject-centred perception of the right to privacy that would include the rights of the unborn.

In the case of young children, it is parents who most often infringe children's right to privacy by sharing and distributing images of a child. An example is publication of a child's image by parents who are vloggers. On their parenting channels, they decide consciously to reveal certain areas of their own private lives and, unfortunately, of their children's private lives as well.[43] Although children may be too young to protest, whether a person posesses full or limited legal capacity – or awareness that a given personal right has even been infringed – is irrelevant to the need to protect personal rights.[44]

While there is no doubt that a child is entitled to the right to privacy, the enforcement and respect for this right is dependent on parents' actions and discretionary authority. The child's right to privacy is not absolute; rather, consideration must be given to parental authority in determining the best interests of the child.[45] Family law distinguishes three areas of parental authority: care of the child, management of the child's property, and representation of the child.[46] Care and representation of the child are the two fields of parental authority that are particularly significant to the child's right to privacy.[47]

Generally speaking, parents' duties concerning the child's right to privacy can be divided into the following three groups: (1) a duty to take care of the child's privacy as an active or a positive duty that is a duty to act; to give consent to publication of an image or to data processing, and to make sure that data is not processed excessively; (2) a passive duty to refrain from actions that may infringe on privacy, taking into account the rule of the child's best interests that can sometimes justify such actions, e.g. to refrain from reading a diary kept by the child or from uploading the child's photos in the social media, or to do this reasonably and in moderation; and (3) a duty to make the child aware of the right to privacy and the need to respect it in other people.

Certainly, the scope of these duties depends on many factors, such as the child's age, development level, or even health. For instance, in the case of very young babies, there are no duties yet connected with the upbringing of the child and education concerning the right to privacy. People close to the child or who have authority over the child can influence the child effectively, not only by sharing certain knowledge, but also by modelling specific patterns of behaviour.[48] It is important that parents, who raise the child and make the child aware of the right to protect his or her own privacy, at the same time teach the child to respect the privacy of other people.[49] Indeed, Article 5 of the CRC stipulates that parents can provide "direction and guidance in the exercise by the child of the rights recognized in the Convention." Furthermore, the level of parents' interest in the child's private life evolves as the child matures and the practices developed during childhood and youth may continue when an adult person still lives with his or her parents.[50]

Infringements of children's right to privacy frequently occur on television programmes. Such infringements happen in many different contexts, including in documentaries about children staying in educational care facilities,[51] and in talent shows in which children's performances are frequently preceded by videos presenting details from their personal life.[52] In accordance with Article 14, section 6 of the Press Law, "it is prohibited to publish information and data concerning private life without consent of the person concerned, unless they are connected directly with public activity of this person."[53] Thus, consent to disclosure of such information would have to be given by the child's parents or statutory representatives. However, in most cases, even if such consent is received, it is questionable whether publishing such private information is consistent with the child's best interests.[54] Such recurring acts can constitute the basis for interference by the guardianship court, which may issue an order prohibiting consent for disclosure of data from the child's private sphere and for dissemination of the child's image. Obviously, any interference by the guardianship court with parental authority is treated as a last resort. Moreover, not every improper exercise of parental authority may require court interference, but only those that threaten the child's welfare. The indicated manner of court interference does not completely negate parental authority. Rather, the most important goal and a characteristic feature of restricting parental authority is the elimination of a threat to the child's interests through correction of the parents' attitude. From this perspective, a limitation on parental authority can be viewed not as a penalty to parents, but as support provided to a family in crisis.[55]

It is difficult to imagine a situation in which information concerning a child's private life is connected directly to the public activity of that child. The law emphasizes that "the requirement resulting from the word 'directly' should be seriously taken into account."[56] Accordingly, a close and direct relationship between the public activity and the private life of a given person is necessary.[57] The majority of information from the private life of an individual is not connected by nature with the public activity of that person.[58] As has been pointed out by Aleksandra Sydor-Zielińska, this observation is even more relevant in the case of a child in the context of publication of a child's likeness. Sydor-Zielińska emphasizes that Article 81, section 2 of the Copyright Law,[59] which permits the dissemination of an image without consent of a person is an exception, meaning that it should not be applied extensively.[60] Consequently, if there is any doubt about whether a person is widely known "he or she should rather be excluded from the scope of the discussed notion and not the other way round."[61] This claim is also valid in the context of disclosure of information concerning one's private life, considering the similar function of both regulations. Therefore, publication of a child's personal information would almost always require parental consent.

Furthermore, when a child is at least 13 years old and, therefore, has limited legal capacity, he or she should be given a right to consent to publication of an image or information from their private lives parallel to parental consent.[62] Indeed, Article 95, section 4 of the Family and Guardianship Code[63] imposes on parents a duty to listen to a child before making decisions on more significant issues concerning the child or his or her property if this is consistent with the child's mental development, health, and maturity level. Wherever possible, parents should take into account the reasonable wishes of the child.

In sum, infringement of the child's right to privacy is governed by the provisions of the Civil Code concerning the protection of personal rights.[64] Yet, protection of the child's right to privacy in his or her relations with parents depends on the scope and manner that parental authority is exercised.[65] Any possible abuse in this area is verified and judged by the guardianship court, which can use the measures provided for in the regulations on parental authority. The court bases its decision on the best interests of the child. In extreme cases, a claim can be filed in civil law against one or both parents for the purpose of protecting the child's privacy. A lawsuit could also be filed by the state prosecutor, but this only occurs in exceptional cases.[66]

Finally, although the primary subject matter of this chapter is Polish civil law, the child's right to privacy can also be protected under criminal law. A case concerning a father who published an image of his 2-year-old son on Facebook was brought into the Regional Court in Warsaw. The photo showed a naked child touching his own private parts and holding an empty beer bottle in his hand.[67] The court decreed that the accused was guilty of a crime under Article 191(a) of the Polish Criminal Code.[68] Consequently, the perpetrator was sentenced to mandatory community service. According to the Regional Court's decision, a young child has a right to privacy.[69] Due to his age, a 2-year-old child is unable to give his consent; therefore, parents are authorized to give consent on behalf of the child. Although the mother's consent to publication of such a photo would exclude the crime from Article 191(a) of the Criminal Court and eliminate criminal liability, such consent could involve infringement of the child's best interests and result in interference of the Guardianship Court.[70] In this case, the court's limitation of parental authority is based on the child's best interests, corresponding to the notion of "best interests" used in the CRC. This decision significantly advances the protection of the child's right to privacy. First, the imposition of criminal liability cements the importance of protecting children's rights. Second, despite their lack of knowledge and self-awareness, this decision emphasizes that even young children are entitled to the right to privacy.

Conclusion

As this analysis demonstrates, the child's right to privacy is an important and developing concern in Polish law and in the CRC. The right to privacy, which is held to be fundamental for adults, is also an essential right for a child, irrespective of his or her age or level of consciousness.[71] Still, the child's awareness of his or her own right to privacy, and of the necessity to respect the privacy rights of other people, are dependent on the cooperation and actions of parents. Parents' obligation to respect and promote children's privacy rights is not only moral and social, but also legal in nature.

Notes

1 The "Polish perspective" is unique and important in discussing the impact of the CRC. Poland was the initiator of the UN Commission on Human Rights, which prepared a draft Convention. This draft was prepared by Polish lawyers associated mostly with the Institute of Legal Sciences of the Polish Academy of Sciences. *See* Leszek Wiśniewski, *The Origin of the Convention on the Rights of the Child and the Relation Between Its Regulations and Other International Law Acts, in* The Convention on the Rights of the Child: Analysis and Interpretation, 13 (Tadeusz Smyczyński ed., 1999). It has been argued that the enactment of the Convention is the greatest Polish achievement on the international arena in the sphere of protection of the child's rights. Ewelina A. Hanyś, *Poland as the Initiator and Co-founder of the Convention on the Rights of the Child*, 19 Wrocławskie Studia Politologiczne 184, 184 (2015).

2 Adam Łopatka, *The Child and the Human Rights of the Child*, 82 (2002).

3 Anna N. Schultz, *Reservations, Declarations and Objections to the Convention on the Rights of the Child, in* The Convention on the Rights of the Child: Analysis and Interpretation, 115 (Tadeusz Smyczyński ed., 1999).

4 *Id.*

5 Bożena Gronowska et al., *About the Rights of the Child*, 4 (1994).

6 Tomasz Sokołowski, *Introduction to Family Law*, 19 (2013) (Polish, translated by the author).

7 *See* Krzysztof Pietrzykowski, *Introduction, in* The Family and Guardianship Code: A Commentary, 18 (Krzysztof Pietrzykowski ed., 2010) (Polish, translated by the author).

8 Anna N. Schultz, *Contacts with the Child, Contacts of the Child – Amendments to the Family and Guardianship Code in the Light of the European Standards, in* The Amended Family and Guardianship Code, 74 (Jacek Mazurkiewicz ed., 2010).

9 Anna N. Schultz, *Reservations, Declarations and Objections to the Convention on the Rights of the Child, in* The Convention on the Rights of the Child. Analysis and Interpretation, 115 (Tadeusz Smyczyński ed., 1999).

10 *Id.*

11 Łopatka, *supra* note 2, at 82.

12 *Id.*

13 However, Leszek Wiśniewski points out: "[I]t is a pity that the Convention did not adjust its regulations to the needs of children of various ages, especially these freedoms and rights only elder children, aged 14–18, are entitled to." The author mentions here e.g., the child's right to privacy. Leszek Wiśniewski, *Freedom of Association and Freedom of Assembly of Children, in* The Convention on the Rights of the Child: Analysis and Interpretation, 250 (1999).

14 Andrzej Cisek, *Protection of the Child's Personal Interests in the Convention on the Rights of the Child*, 30 Przegląd Prawa i Administracji 45, 58 (1993).

15 Łopatka, *supra* note 2, at 83.

16 *Id.*

17 Piotr Zamelski, *The Right to Protection of Private Life, in* The Convention on the Rights of the Child: A Selection of Issues, Articles and Commentaries, 125 (S. L. Stadniczeńko ed., 2015).

18 Anna N. Schultz, *Reservations, Declarations and Objections to the Convention on the Rights of the Child*, *in* The Convention on the Rights of the Child. Analysis and Interpretation, 117 (Tadeusz Smyczyński ed., 1999).
19 *Id.*
20 *See* Piotr Kroczek, *Upbringing and Education of Children from the Perspective of Polish Law and Canon Law* 29 (2013).
21 Wiesława Walc, *The Children's Rights in the Opinions of the Students of Pedagogical Specializations*, *in* The Child's Rights: Selected Aspects, 68 (Izabela Marczykowska et al. eds., 2006).
22 Zbigniew Radwański & Adam Olejniczak, *Civil Law – The General Part*, 174 (2017).
23 Regulation (EU) 2016/679 of the European Parliament and of the Council on the protection of natural persons with regard to the processing of personal data and on the free movement of such data, repealing Directive 95/46/EC.
24 Maksymilian Pazdan, *Civil Code.* Vol I. A Commentary, 115 (Krzysztof Pietrzykowski ed., 2015).
25 Marta de Balzeairee de Rupierre, *Principles*, *in* General Data Protection Regulation. A Commentary, 177, (Marlena Sakowska-Baryła ed., 2018).
26 *See* Przemysław Polański, *Parental Consent to Profiling of the Child's Activity in Internet (Polish translated by author)*, 1 ABI – EXPERT 20 (2017). This permission was used by the following states: Belgium, Denmark, Finland, Latvia, Malta, Sweden (13 years old); Austria, Cyprus, Italy, Lithuania, Spain (14 years old); France (15 years old). *See* Milda Macenaite & Eleni Costa, *Consent for processing children's personal data in the EU: following in US footsteps? in* Informations & Communications Technology Law, 146, 153–154 (2017). *See also* Dagmara Jaroszewska-Choraś, *The Right to Protection of Children's Personal Data and Privacy in the Digital Era*, *in* The Child's Rights. A Public Law Perspective, 91 (Dagmara Jaroszewska-Choraś et al., eds., 2019).
27 *See* Zuzanna Ochońska, *Disposal of a Minor's Personal Interests*, 3 Zeszyty Naukowe Uniwersytetu Jagiellonskiego, 103, 114 (2019) (Polish, translated by author).
28 Krzysztof Dzioba, Andżelika Kosińska, *Personal Data Protection at School in Connection with the Introduction of the GDPR and the New Personal Data Protection Law*, 4 Informacja w Administracji Publicznej 17, 19 (2017).
29 *Id.*
30 Radwański & Olejniczak, *supra* note 22, at 174.
31 The Act of 23 April 1964 Civil Code (hereinafter "Civil Code").
32 *Id.* at 162 (Polish, translated by the author).
33 *Id.* at 164. Bogudar Kordasiewicz notes that:

> It is exactly due to the open character of the catalogue of protected interests that on the ground of the Polish civil law, even before the Civil Code was enacted, it was potentially easy to accept the private life sphere as a protected interest. It was only a matter of time to recognize this interest formally in doctrine or jurisdiction.

Bogudar Kordasiewicz, *The Right to Privacy – Civil Law Aspects*, *in* The Right to Privacy – Legal and Psychological Aspects, 50–51 (Krzysztof Motyka ed., 2010).
34 Marek Andrzejewski, *Houses on Sand: Children's Homes. From Care of a Child to Support for a Family* 39 (2007).
35 Andrzej Cisek, *A Duty to Obey Parents vs. Protection of the Child's Personal Interests* clxxxvi Acta Universitatis Wratislaviensis: Prawo 36, 36 (1990).
36 Joanna Haberko, *Availability and Publication of a Picture of a Nasciturus, a Newborn Baby, an Infant and a Child in Light of the Child Welfare Principle*, 3 Ruch Prawniczy, Ekonomiczny i Socjologiczny 59 (2013) (Polish, translated by author).
37 *Id.* at 60. As emphasized by the Author:

> nowadays, not only ultrasound technologies (X-ray) but also magnetic resonance make it possible to observe *nasciturus* on the monitor and to record the image of

a conceived child, presenting the child's features and often movements and gestures, in a photo or a video.

38 Radwański & Olejniczak, *supra* note 22, at 142.
39 Haberko, *supra* note 36, at 59, 61.
40 *Id.*
41 The Act of June 25, 2015 on Infertility Treatment, Journal of Laws of 2020, item 442.
42 Joanna Haberko, *The Act on Infertility Treatment. A Commentary*, 76 (2016).
43 Mateusz Kot, *Privacy of the Child on the Internet and the Dissemination of His Image by Parents Leading Video Blogs*, 3 Kwartalnik Nauk o Mediach (2016), http://knm.uksw.edu.pl/prywatnosc-dziecka-internecie-a-rozpowszechnienie-wizerunku-rodzicow-prowadzacych-wideoblogi/ (last visited Oct. 7, 2020).
44 Haberko, *supra* note 36, at 59, 61.
45 *Id.*
46 Jerzy Ignatowicz & Mirosław Nazar, Family Law, 513 (2016).
47 The duty to protect the child's right to privacy may also appear in matters connected with management of the child's property and is connected to distributing the minor's personal information.
48 Wiesława Walc, *The Children's Rights in the Opinions of the Students of Pedagogical Specializations*, *in* The Child's Rights: Selected Aspects, 62 (Izabela Marczykowska et al. eds., 2006).
49 This duty is presented in an accessible and vivid way by 12-year-old Marta Chudzik in a story "Respect My Privacy" in which one sister reads a diary of the other sister. This was a brochure by children and printed for children in 2010. *See* My Rights and my Duties: About the Convention on the Rights of the Child with Children.
50 Piotr Zamelski, *The Right to Protection of Private Life*, *in* The Convention on the Rights of the Child: A Selection of Issues. Articles and Commentaries, 125 (Stanisław L. Stadniczeńko ed., 2015).
51 *See* Marek Andrzejewski, *Houses on Sand. Children's Homes. From Care of a Child to Support for a Family*, 39 (2007); Marek Andrzejewski, *The Child's Rights – Discussion of the Sense of the Idea and Its Devaluation*, in The Child's Rights. Legal and Pedagogical Contexts, 54 (Marek Andrzejewski ed., 2012).
52 In the context of election campaigns where the image of politicians' children is used, Aleksandra Sydor-Zielińska points out that

> it raises serious doubts whether exposing a minor child to judgement of more or less favourable public opinion for the purpose of building a positive image in the media of a politician as a model loving father is consistent with the child's best interests.

Aleksandra Sydor-Zielińska, *Dissemination of the Image of a Minor under Art. 81 (2) of the Polish Act on Copyright and Related Rights*, 4 Zeszyty Naukowe Uniwersytetu Jagiellońskiego 79, 89 (2017).
53 Ustawa z dnia 26 stycznia 1984 r. Prawo prasowe [Press Law Act of January 26, 1984], Internetowy System Aktów Prawnych [The Online Legal Database], http://isap.sejm.gov.pl/Download?id=WDU19840050024&type=3.
54 Roman Nowosielski & Michał Sowiński, *Child's Interest. Protection of Children's Rights in the Mass Media*, 1–2 PALESTRA 110, 116 (2007).
55 Marek Andrzejewski, *Relations Between Parents / Other Adults and Children in the Light of New Articles of the Family and the Guardianship Code As Well as Other Laws (Selected Problems)*, 821 Zeszyty Naukowe Uniwersytetu Szczecińskiego: Acta Iuris Stetinensis 371, 383–384 (2014).
56 Maksymilian Pazdan, [commentary on Article 23], *in Civil Code. Vol I. A Commentary*, 130 (Krzysztof Pietrzykowski ed., 2015) (Polish, translated by the author).
57 Joanna Braciak, *The Right to Privacy*, 200 (2004).

58 *Id.* However, the Court of Appeals in Gdańsk in its judgement of June 24, 2014 r. (I ACa 206/14) pointed to a possible interesting example of such a connection, claiming that

> the sphere of any extramarital relationships of public figures can be regarded as a sphere of information that can be relevant to the society with respect to evaluation of activity of a public figure in the context of his or her conduct in private life juxtaposed with the opinions and moral and ethical worldview presented publicly by this person. This is significant for perception of this person by citizens, their election preferences and credibility of a given public figure.

For obvious reasons, such a relationship does not exist in the case of a child.

59 The Act of February 4, 1994 on Copyright and Related Rights (Journal of Laws of 2019, item 1231).

60 Aleksandra Sydor-Zielińska, *Dissemination of the Image of a Minor under Art. 81 (2) of the Polish Act on Copyright and Related Rights*, 4 Zeszyty Naukowe Uniwersytetu Jagiellońskiego 79, 82 (2017).

61 *Id.* (Polish, translated by the author).

62 Katarzyna Badźmirowska-Masłowska, *Image of the Child on the Internet vs. Threats to the Right to Privacy*, *in* Right to Privacy as a Principle of the Information Society, 60 (Katarzyna Chałubińska-Jentkiewicz, Ksenia Kakareko, and Jacek Sobczak eds., 2017); *see also* Krystyna Święcka, *The Right to Publication of Information About the Sphere of Privacy in Polish Law* 2 Studia Prawnicze 59, 70–71 (2011).

63 The Act of Februrary 25, 1964, Family and Guardianship Code.

64 Tadeusz Smyczyński, *The Child's Personal Rights*, *in* The Convention on the Rights of the Child and the Polish Law, 109 (Adam Łopatka, 1991). In Polish civil law, the measures to protect personal rights include declaratory action; demand to give up actions which threat or infringe on personal rights, removal of the consequences of an infringement, and financial compensation or payment for a social purpose. *See* Radwański & Olejniczak, *supra* note 22, at 182–186.

65 Smyczyński, *supra* note 64.

66 *Id.* Andrzej Cisek points to the fact that an opportunity for filing certain claims against parents is hypothetical to a large extent, because it is the parents who are the statutory representatives of the child and are authorized to represent him or her. A need to establish a guardian by the court would rather entail the application of measures based on Article 109 of the Family and Guardianship Code. Andrzej Cisek, *A Duty to Obey Parents vs. Protection of the Child's Personal Interests*, Clxxxvi Acta Universitatis Wratislaviensis: Prawo 36, 36 (1990).

67 Judgement of the Regional Court Warszawa – Praga of 25 January 2017, VI Ka 1206/16, after: Zuzanna Ochońska, *Disposal of a Minor's Personal Interests*, 3 Zeszyty Naukowe Uniwersytetu Jagiellońskiego 103, 117 (2019).

68 The Act of June 6, 1997 – Criminal Law (Journal of Laws of 2019, item 1950).

69 Zuzanna Ochońska, *Disposal of a Minor's Personal Interests*, 3 Zeszyty Naukowe Uniwersytetu Jagiellońskiego 103, 117 (2019).

70 *See also* Joanna Haberko, *Availability and Publication of a Picture of a Nasciturus, a Newborn Baby, an Infant and a Child in Light of the Child Welfare Principle*, 3 Ruch Prawniczy, Ekonomiczny i Socjologiczny 59, 70 (2013).

71 Janusz Barta & Ryszard Markiewicz, *Technical Progress in the Media*, *in* Media vs. Personal Interests, 78 (Janusz Barta & Ryszard Markiewicz eds., 2009); Aleksandra Sydor-Zielińska, *Acting in the Defence of a Legitimate Public Interest as a Circumstance Precluding the Unlawfulness of Violating a Child's Privacy*, 4 Państw: Prawo 111, 111 (2019).

14 Children's digital rights

Realizing the potential of the CRC

Katharina Kaesling

Online social interface and digital youth cultures

Constant technological innovation over the last 30 years has placed communication and sociality onto new foundations. Following the appearance of the IBM personal computer and the Apple Macintosh in the 1980s, the World Wide Web was launched in the 1990s and social networks emerged in the 2000s. By now, most of the world population has access to the internet,[1] with one in three internet users estimated to be a child.[2] The wording of the United Nations Convention on the Rights of the Child (CRC) of 1989 has remained unchanged despite these fundamental societal changes, leading to calls to update this instrument of public international law.[3] However, even in its current format, the CRC – the only nearly globally ratified instrument for the protection of children's rights – has considerable, and to this date still unrealized, potential for dealing with children's participation and protection in digitalized contexts.

Childhood experiences differ from generation to generation, with concerned parents evaluating the risks of emerging forms of media and communication.[4] Keeping up with fast-developing environments online is a challenge for both adults and children. While it is not helpful to focus on the dichotomy of children as digital natives versus parents and lawmakers as digital immigrants,[5] childhood in the digital age is influenced by opportunities and risks surpassing those presented by dime novels, comic books, and television. Risks associated with online activities are manifold, ranging from cyberbullying and damage to one's reputation to exposure to sexual predators. Known data breaches have affected children at the youngest ages,[6] even in the context of educational platforms,[7] which is exacerbated by the fact that toymakers are recording more and more data.

At the same time, children's opportunities are also enhanced in countless ways by digital means. Digital tools can foster the development of creativity just like analogue play, depending on the way tools are used rather than on their digital nature.[8] Children's "digital playgrounds" include digital (social) media, mobile apps, and the "internet of toys."[9] Social media are used for communication, self-representation, and information. A new sociality online has emerged[10] – one that children generally have a right to be a part of and that contributes to them becoming citizens in the digital age.[11] The realization of children's rights in the digital environment is therefore essential to the realization of children's rights in general.[12]

As both risks and opportunities are enhanced,[13] children's rights are a natural part of the discourse on children's participation online. Their full range of rights is impacted in both positive and negative ways.[14] Accordingly, the Committee on the Rights of the Child is preparing a General Comment on children's rights in relation to the digital environment[15] that provides an overview of how the CRC should be understood and implemented in relation to the digital environment.[16] This chapter will focus on children's digital rights in the context of user-generated content (UGC) online, as its creation and consumption is a vital part of children's social life.

The CRC and the borderless nature of social media

Successful social media platforms are part of global digital transformations. TikTok and Facebook, for example, are active in over 150 countries.[17] The short (music) video application TikTok is currently popular among young people in particular.[18] One can therefore speak of a near-global dissemination of social media content, which is accompanied by a transnational youth culture, as demonstrated by new forms of user creativity and online manners. The borderless nature of the internet is, however, generally not reflected in the law since legal norms continue to be set primarily by each nation-state. The CRC, on the other hand, contemplates a space beyond borders, comparable to international social media environments, which is demonstrated by several provisions. For instance, Article 17 of the CRC on access to appropriate information explicitly recognizes the importance of access to information and material from a diversity of national and international sources. This access also serves as a condition for the exercise of other fundamental rights, most importantly the right to freedom of expression referenced in Article 13 of the CRC.[19] It also expressly includes the freedom to seek, receive, and impart information and ideas of all kinds, regardless of frontiers. While Article 17 of the CRC focuses on mass media, Article 13 declares that the choice of media is not restricted to traditional forms, but, rather, can be selected by the child. Thus, the CRC demonstrates a remarkable openness to emerging technologies and changes in the media landscape, such as those that have emerged from recent digital transformations.

UGC can be shared with the public at large, people with whom links were formed (e.g., "friends" on Facebook), smaller groups of people chosen for that specific exchange (e.g., WhatsApp groups), or singular people via messaging features. In all these respects, social media have become an integral part of young people's daily life.[20] Children share UGC with personal details as part of self-presentation and the promotion of social relationships.[21] Ephemeral spoken words have been replaced by records and data assemblages; communication that used to be private has become public by default.[22] While social media are widely used to uphold existing relations in the real world, social media communities and communication partners can be from all over the world.

Children as subjects in the digital world

Online environments are spaces where children can exercise their rights to participation in particularly effective ways as independent actors with their own agency.[23] Social media does not only hold great potential for accessing information,[24] but as part of the Web 2.0, social media allows end-users to interact and become content creators themselves, making them their own "media authorities."[25] These opportunities correspond to the CRC's understanding of children as rights-holders with individual agency.[26] Under the CRC, the child is no longer reduced to an object of law and of parental authority. Parental rights are not self-serving, but rather granted in the interest of the child.[27] While children may be protected by means of parental responsibility, children's rights are not a pure reflex of parental rights.[28] Thus, there is an inherent possibility of conflicting parental and children's interests and (fundamental) rights.

Children's right to privacy is a prime example of the potential for forward-thinking that the CRC holds. While the first general privacy[29] and data protection[30] laws were adopted in the 1970s in response to increasing data collection, privacy only became a priority for children in the 21st century.[31] Today, children's privacy is specifically addressed with the Children's Online Privacy Protection Act in the United States[32] and the General Data Protection Regulation[33] in the European Union (EU), though with important limitations.[34] Article 16 of the CRC, on the other hand, has guaranteed the specific area of individual existence and self-determination for children since 1989.[35] It has since influenced the protection of privacy in numerous legal orders.[36]

Article 18 of the CRC describes the classic triangular relationship between the state, parents, and children, focusing on the state's obligation to respect and legally establish the parents' primary responsibility for the children's upbringing and development. While the CRC does not spell out specific standards for (digital) parental care, the children's standing as independent rights-holders provides for a certain harmonization of state and parental responsibilities. As it emphasizes children's opportunities and sets robust limits for their legal restriction,[37] parental and state actions must not be guided by efforts to protect children alone. Instead, the best interests of the child – taking into account personal context, situation, and needs – must serve as the guiding principle.[38] Consumption and creation of UGC touches all dimension of children's rights, often framed as provision, protection, and participation in the context of the CRC.[39] In view of potentially harmful content and contact, such as defamation, cyberbullying, violence, grooming, and child pornography,[40] balancing children's rights to protection and participation is particularly challenging.[41] The CRC has the potential to prevent both the state and parents from overreaching and safeguard children's claims to take part in sociality online.

The triangular relationship between children, parents, and the state has been altered by the appearance of nearly globally operating social media platforms. In addition to enforcing existing provisions in virtual realms, novel dynamics must be considered. Dangers can be countered by design elements and filtering technology; the EU Audiovisual Media Services Directive, for example, requires that video-sharing platform providers take appropriate measures to protect children from user-generated videos that may impair their physical, mental, or moral development.[42] While such protective measures can be particularly effective, they are only permissible to the extent that they are compatible with the CRC, including children's participative rights.

Joining social media: parental responsibility and children's autonomy

While the consumption of some UGC does not necessarily presuppose the creation of a user account, active participation generally does. Joining a social media platform such as Facebook or TikTok requires a contractual agreement, for which applicable laws determine the capacity of children. Furthermore, consent to process children's data is necessary under the applicable privacy or data protection laws. The disclosure of data may also constitute contractual consideration.[43] Therefore, the applicable laws determine the extent to which parents are gatekeepers to sociality online and how much of a say children have. Because the far-reaching guarantees of the CRC are, in principle, available to both younger children and adolescents (Article 1 CRC), their evolving capacities must be taken into account (Article 5 CRC) and their voices heard (Article 12 CRC).[44] Children's voices carry particular weight for questions touching on their fundamental rights,[45] in particular if children are able to understand the consequences of joining social media and assess the corresponding risks accordingly.

A number of risks connected to joining a social media network are related to the disclosure of data. Once divulged, the data is accessible to a sizeable, albeit undefinable, audience by legal and illegal means, with no effective remedy in case of data breaches. Data is combined in order to create personality profiles for individual children.[46] The nature of the data also determines the extent to which each child's development may be harmed by its exposure online. Long-term effects hinge on a number of factors that are difficult to determine, such as the long-term retention of data on the internet and the duration of storage on international servers. Furthermore, potential future uses are difficult to assess for both parents and children.[47]

Just like their counterparts in other legal orders, the EU GDPR and the Children's Online Privacy Protection Act (COPPA) provide consent-based mechanisms for dealing with the disclosure of data.[48] COPPA regulates the gathering and disclosure of online data pertaining to children under the age of 13.[49] While the GDPR covers adults and children, its declared goal is to offer special protection to the latter.[50] Under Article 8 of the GDPR, the processing of children's personal data generally requires parental consent for children under 16. Member States may provide for a lower age, as young as 13. Thus, there is no uniform EU approach to children's autonomy in questions relating to their personal data.[51] Instead, Member States can opt to align the capacity to contract and to consent to data processing provided that the first does not set in later than age 16. All of these legal norms thereby rely on lawmakers' abstract but diverging assessments of children's abilities. The effectiveness of these regulations rests on the verifiability of age and consent.[52]

As it is literally "child's play" to enter a fake birthdate or open an email account in a parent's name, children should be offered effective participation so that they do not have to rely on circumventing safeguarding measures. Despite the right to voice opinions established in Articles 5 and 12 of the CRC, children's voices are not always heard when it comes to their inclusion in social activity online. Should parents fail to include them in their decision-making regarding their capacities and the permissibility of access to online content, children do not have any legal recourse available to them.[53] Children of a certain age, e.g., 14,[54] should be given the right to appeal to a family court or another state institution to ensure their point of view and their arguments are taken into account if a conflict with their parents over a matter of considerable importance to the child arises.[55] Disagreements between children and parents could thereby allow a decision based on the best interests of the child in the case at hand – just like disagreements between separated parents with joint parental responsibility. It is sensible to limit state intervention to disagreements on important matters,[56] such as whether to join a social network. Social media participation is indeed an activity associated with considerable dangers and opportunities. The number of CRC rights impacted by the decision to join or not to join a social network alone illustrate that this is a matter of fundamental importance. While differences of opinion are to be settled primarily within the family, state resources, as a subsidiary means of intervention, promote the recognition of the rights and interests of all parties and can foster a more balanced intrafamilial decision-making process.

Parental monitoring and children's privacy

Once children join social networks, parents have to mind their children's activities as part of their parental responsibility. Legal standards for digital parental care do not only vary according to domestic family laws, but also with regard to the applicable copyright law, general personal rights, and data protection law.[57] German courts have imposed parental obligations to control access in order to prevent violations of third-party rights, such as copyright on filesharing platforms and privacy rights on WhatsApp,[58] as parents did not ensure consent of the child's contacts before installing WhatsApp. In the context of UGC, the use of proprietary images, text, music, and videos by children can lead to the violation of personality rights and copyrights of third parties, especially in jurisdictions without fair-use doctrines. Children may also engage in defamation, cyberbullying, and other forms of illegal behaviour. Parents can certainly be obligated to inform children about possible unlawful uses[59] and set parental rules in accordance with the age and insights of the respective child.[60] A general duty to control children's social media activities, however, conflicts with Article 5 of the CRC, as well as children's participation rights. Infringing on children's right to privacy and personal identity (Articles 8, 16 CRC) can harm their capacities for future relationships, as privacy is fundamentally linked to trust, specifically in adolescent–parent relationships.[61]

Accompanying the new possibilities for children in the digital era are unprecedented capacities for monitoring children.[62] Parents increasingly use so-called "parental control apps,"[63] allowing them not only to block content deemed particularly dangerous, but also learn about their child's behaviour.[64] Monitoring functions generally allow parents to check the content of the child's mobile device, which makes saved media, posts, and messages on social media or other messenger providers accessible to parents. Some applications also let parents monitor their child's activities in real time, such as by linking the microphone and camera of the child's mobile device to their own smartphones. Against the background of online risks, monitoring children's activities online has become widely accepted as "good parenting" to keep children safe.[65] While children also recognize various risks flowing from digital environments,[66] a study referencing 37 mobile online safety apps revealed that parents' ratings of monitoring apps were significantly higher than those of the children concerned, who labelled the apps as overly restrictive and invasive of their personal privacy.[67]

The use of monitoring functions has a negative impact on children's participation rights, as described in Article 13 of the CRC and must therefore be justified. Live monitoring and full access to the child's social media accounts will only be justifiable with regard to concrete circumstances, e.g., in cases of repeated offenses by the child in question. It follows from the CRC that children's voices regarding their access to media, their ability to express themselves online, and the interference with their privacy must be heard. The right to be heard is a fundamental principle[68] which influences the interpretation and implementation of rights under the CRC.[69] As the use of covert surveillance mechanisms by parents represents a particularly serious encroachment on children's privacy,[70] the monitoring of social media activities by parents should be generally reserved for cases in which the child consents to such measures. The capacities of the individual child in question are to be considered when determining the necessity of such a measure and when asking for consent. Such monitoring is intrinsically connected to the right to privacy, given that the protection of privacy creates a space for reflection and exchange without any form of surveillance.[71]

Even though Articles 8 and 16 of the CRC protect children against infringements of privacy, data protection laws are often not applicable in family contexts. The GDPR, for example, does not apply to the processing of personal data by a natural person in the course of a purely personal or household activity.[72] In these circumstances, parents do not need consent to process their child's data in the first place, even if the child is deemed old enough to decide autonomously according to the data protection regime. The Court of Justice of the European Union has not yet had the opportunity to clarify whether online activities such as "sharenting," parental sharing of information about children online usually in the form of photos or videos of their children and family on social media, still fall under that household exemption.[73] In any case, consent of children in relation to information society service is generally given by the holder of parental responsibility when the child is younger than 16.[74] Children retain only general legal remedies, which often do not include a right for subsidiary judicial or other state intervention.[75] Respecting children's rights is therefore contingent on the respective family dynamics. Power imbalances within families thus determine the limits to children's rights.

"Sharenting" and the evolving capacities of children

Power imbalances within the family also dominate the practice of "sharenting." While the term "sharenting" has a negative connotation,[76] parents also have legitimate interests when creating their UGC. Their activities are protected by fundamental rights, such as the freedom of expression, which need to be balanced against the rights of the children concerned. *Inter alia*, parents aim to connect with friends and family,[77] as well as receive (validating) feedback,[78] and social support.[79] Parents are also aware of a number of risks associated with sharenting and often times try to respond to them, especially when confronted with their children's criticism for sharing certain images.[80] The case of sharenting thus represents a conflict of parental and children's rights.

Images touch on a number of aspects of personality rights. They may generally only be distributed or publicly displayed with the consent of the person depicted. If that person is a child, the consent of the parents, as legal representatives, is generally required. The German right to one's own image entails that not only the parents,[81] but also the child's consent is required, if the child is able to understand the meaning and scope of the issue in question.[82] Generally, these capacities are presumed for children aged 14 and older. Younger children are dependent on involvement in the parental decision as it is part of their parental responsibility.

In cases of disagreements between separated parents with joint parental responsibility, courts generally determine whose decision best realizes the best interests of the child. In such circumstances, one parent asked the Dutch District Court of The Hague to remove images from the daily life of their children, aged two and four, that were posted by the other parent on social media.[83] The court ordered the mother to remove all visual material of the children and – as the father had asked – to refrain from posting such content on social media, unless access was limited to 250 known and authorized users. The Court considered that the minor's privacy was at stake and stressed the potential long-term effects on the children, such as future bullying because of certain shared videos and photos. Emphasizing the risks for sexual exploitation and other crimes arising from the disclosure of photos of and information on children on social networks, the Portuguese Court of Appeal of Évora made it part of a custody arrangement that both parents should refrain from posting photos or information that allows their child to be identified on social networks.[84]

Children's agency can be lost in these circumstances. Their rights, as guaranteed by the CRC, are not respected if they have no say in the publication of their own image regardless of their age. Studies show that children form opinions on the publication of images in different contexts from a young age.[85] Instead of imposing bans on the publication of all images of children, participatory rights could be ensured and be a part of each child's social media education.

Pictures of children are also personal data, thus triggering the application of data protection laws, which, regrettably, do not foresee safeguards for children's participation rights. Focusing on parental consent and control, privacy and data protection laws do not sufficiently respect children's rights as articulated in the CRC, in particular its Article 8.[86] Privacy laws do not provide sufficient protection of children's privacy from their parents.[87] This does not only concern cases in which a child's and parents' opinions on its best interests differ, but also instances where parents have no interest in safeguarding them. Furthermore, parents striving to act in their child's best interests may encounter significant hurdles, as they might not fully comprehend social media environments, the number of third parties with which information will be shared, and the durability of their posts. While the first cases can be addressed by introducing enforceable, participatory rights for children,[88] the latter concerns can only be dealt with in a larger framework encompassing media literacy initiatives for parents and children.

Realizing this potential

Children's digital rights, although not explicitly named, are well-protected by the CRC in its current form. Due to the CRC's near worldwide validity, it has the potential to influence how children's rights are respected in ways that diverse national approaches cannot. Fundamentally (near) global actors, such as social networks and regulatory frameworks, can use the CRC guarantees as guiding principles. Especially with regard to the UGC, it is important to recognize children as subjects in the digital world, whose access and active participation have to be safeguarded just as much as they have to be protected from harmful content and contacts.

Realizing the potential of the CRC for children in the digital age also means that countries must reevaluate existing legislation and measures with children's rights in mind.[89] Facing considerable challenges to enforcing the law and learning about new dangers connected to children's activities online can lead to a risk-based approach. The CRC, which acknowledges the vast range of children's fundamental rights, suggests a balanced, rights-based approach overall.[90] Requirements for the lawful restriction of participation rights, such as the freedom of expression, are high, as their function is central to children's position both in analog and digital environments. With children's rights to personal identity and privacy, the CRC pioneered developments that have become key for children's lives in the 21st century. The General Comment on Children's Rights in Relation to the Digital Environment will certainly contribute to an understanding of the CRC as a fundamental but future-oriented international legal instrument and provide guidance on legislative policy and other appropriate measures.[91]

Maximizing this potential presupposes a wide range of implementing measures. Implementing an instrument of public international law is an arduous process which entails further steps after the initial adoption. The interplay between different legal orders, including international and supranational ones, can lead to a hybridization of legal orders.[92] The CRC has influenced the jurisprudence of supranational and international bodies, notably with the interpretation of the EU Charter and the European Court of Human Rights (ECHR).[93] State parties fulfil their obligations under the CRC in accordance with their respective domestic laws. Domestic laws also govern the question of direct applicability of public international law instruments in the respective legal order, ranging from classical, monistic approaches to dualistic ones. The fundamental principle of the best interests of the child has influenced legislative practice and the application of the law in a range of legal areas[94] and it will certainly continue to do so in the digital era. Children must be understood as independent legal subjects worthy of their own rights in national legal systems and not only as a barrier to parental rights.[95] The creation of the possibility for individual complaint before the United Nations Committee on the Rights of the Child[96] filled the void[97] of jurisdictional scrutiny on the international level.

Parents, children, and social media platforms, as part of civil society, can benefit from the CRC's provisions. Especially with regard to digital environments, comprehensive policies and strategies, including raising awareness and training, are essential.[98] As part of programs to develop children's digital skills and access to opportunities recommended by the draft General Comment,[99] awareness should not only be raised for risks, but also for the significance of participation in sociality online and digital youth cultures. Impact assessments of children's rights can inform the legislative process[100] and, especially if carried out by businesses,[101] can play an important role in conceiving online environments with children's needs in mind. Following comic books and television, the Web 2.0 marks an important step in digital transformation for children's rights, but certainly it will not be the last milestone. Rather, realizing the potential of the CRC and the importance of children's rights in the digital environment will become all the more important.

Notes

1 *Internet Usage and World Population Statistics Estimates for July 20, 2020*, Internet World Stats https://www.internetworldstats.com/stats.htm (last visited Aug. 28, 2020).
2 Sonia Livingstone et al., *One in Three: Internet Governance and Children's Rights*, Innocenti Discussion Papers no. 2016-01 (UNICEF Office of Research, 2016).
3 Tim Baillie, *Incorporating Children's Digital Rights into the UNCRC*, Children and Young People's Commissioner Scotland (2020), https://cypcs.org.uk/resource_tag/human-rights-act/ (last visited Aug. 28, 2020); Sonia Livingstone, *An Updated UNCRC for the Digital Age*, LSE Media (Jan. 19, 2017), https://blogs.lse.ac.uk/medialse/2017/01/19/an-updated-uncrc-for-the-digital-age/ (last visited Aug. 28, 2020).
4 Stewart Hoover & Lynn Hoover, *Children and Media in the Context of the Home and Family*, *in* The International Handbook of Children, Media and Culture, 105 (Kirsten Drotner & Sonia Livingstone eds., 2008).
5 Contrary to what the terms suggest, both children and parents need to learn media literacy.

6 Andrea Peterson, Toymakers Are Tracking More Data About Kids – Leaving Them Exposed to Hackers, Wash. Post (Nov. 30, 2015), www.washingtonpost.com/news/theswitch/wp/2015/11/30/toymakers-are-tracking-more-data-about-kids-leaving-them-exposed-tohackers/ (last visited Aug. 28, 2020).

7 Natasha Singer, *Uncovering Security Flaws in Digital Education Products for Schoolchildren*, N.Y. Times (Feb. 9, 2015).

8 Beverley Barnaby & Victoria Burghardt, *Creativity in a Digital Age*, *in* Young Children in a Digital Age: Supporting Learning and Development with Technology in Early, 101 (Lorraine Kaye ed., 2016); Shirley Allen, *Play in a Digital Age*, *in* Young Children in a Digital Age: Supporting Learning and Development with Technology in Early, 101 (Lorraine Kaye ed., 2016).

9 Donell Holloway & Lelia Green, *The Internet of Toys*, Communication Research and Practice, doi:10.1080/22041451.2016.1266124, 1–2 (2016); Karen Louise Smith & Leslie Regan Shade, *Children's Digital Playgrounds as Data Assemblages: Problematics of Privacy, Personalization, and Promotional Culture*, 5 Big Data & Soc'y 1, 1–2 (2018).

10 Caja Thimm, *Digitale Werteordnung: Kommentieren, kritisieren, debattieren im Netz*, Forschung und Lehre, at 1062–1063 (Dec. 2017), https://www.wissenschafts-management-online.de/beitrag/digitale-werteordnung-kommentieren-kritisieren-debattieren-im-netz-8506.

11 Cees J. Hamelink, *Children's Communication Rights: Beyond Intentions*, *in* The International Handbook of Children, Media and Culture, 509 (Kirsten Drotner & Sonia Livingstone eds., 2008).

12 Cf. German comments to the concept note of the General Comment on children's rights in relation to the digital environment, https://www.ohchr.org/EN/HR-Bodies/CRC/Pages/Submissions_Concept_GC_Digital_Environment.aspx (last visited Aug. 28, 2020).

13 Sonia Livingstone et al., *Children's Data and Privacy Online: Growing Up in A Digital Age*, LSE Media & Commc'n 11 (2018), http://www.lse.ac.uk/media-and-communications/assets/documents/research/projects/childrens-privacy-online/Evidence-review-final.pdf.

14 Including, but not limited to art. 13, 17, 28, 30, 31 UNCRC.

15 U.N. Convention on the Rights of the Child (CRC), *Draft General Comment No. 25 On Children's Rights in Relation to the Digital Environment*, U.N. Doc CRC/C/GC/25, Aug. 13, 2020 [hereinafter Draft CRC/C/GC/25].

16 *Id.* at para. 7.

17 *Facebook Users by Country 2020*, World Population Rev. (2020), https://worldpopulationreview.com/country-rankings/facebook-users-by-country (last visited Aug. 28, 2020); J. Clement, *TikTok- Statistics & Facts*, Statista (Sep. 10, 2020), https://www.statista.com/topics/6077/tiktok/ (last visited Aug. 28, 2020).

18 *Id.*

19 Stan Meuwese et al., *Handboek Internationaal Jeugdrecht* [*Handbook International Youth Law*] 144 (2005).

20 *See* Bernadette Kneidinger, *Facebook und Co.Eine Soziologische Analyse Von Interaktionsformen in Online Social Networks* [*Facebook and Co. A Sociological Analysis of Forms of Interaction in Online Social Networks*] 129 (2010) (Identifying new patterns of interaction in social networks on the basis of an empirical survey of Facebook users).

21 *Id.*

22 Sonia Livingstone et al., *supra* note 14, at 11.

23 Laurène Graziani, *Les Enfants et Internet: La Participation des Jeunes à Travers les Reseaux Sociaux.* [*Children and the internet: Youth participation through social networks*] 317 Journal du droit des jeunes 36, 45 (2012).

24 Draft CRC/C/GC/25, *supra* note 16, at para. 51.

25 Thimm, *supra* note 11, at 1062 f.
26 Nina Dethloff & Alexandra Maschwitz, *Kinderrechte in Europa – wo stehen wir? (Children's rights in Europe- where do we stand?)* Familie, Partnerschaft, Recht, 190, 191 (2012).
27 Bundesverfassungsgericht, [Federal Constitutional Court], BVerfGE 24, 119, Neue Juristische Wochenzeitschrift [NJW] 2233 (1968) (Ger.).
28 Barbara Bennett Woodhouse, *Hatching the Egg: A Child-Centered Perspective on Parent's Rights*, 14 Cardozo L. Rev. 1747, 1755 (1993).
29 U.S. Privacy Act of 1974, 5 U.S.C.A. § 552a (West 2013).
30 Hessen Data Protection Act of 1970, GVBl I 1970, 625, http://starweb.hessen.de/starweb/LIS/amtsblaetter.htm.
31 Ayelet Blecher-Prigat, *Children's Right to Privacy*, *in* The Oxford Handbook of Children and the Law, 1 (James G. Dwyer ed., 2019).
32 Children's Online Privacy Protection Act of 1998, 15 U.S.C. §§ 6501–6505 (West).
33 Regulation (EU) 2016/679, of the European Parliament and of the Council of Apr. 27, 2016 on the protection of natural persons with regard to the processing of personal data and on the free movement of such data and repealing Directive 95/46/EC, 2016, 2016 O.J. (L 119) 1 [hereinafter *GDPR*].
34 *See below*, para 11–23.
35 Stefanie Schmahl, Kinderrechtskonvention (Convention on the Rights of the Child) art. 16 CRC (221), art.17 CRC (225) (Baden-Baden, 2d. ed., 2013).
36 See, e.g., *Nunez v. Norway* No. 55587/09, 28 July 2011; *see also, Avilkina et al. v. Russia* No. - 1585/09- 6 June 2013; *Söderman v. Schweden*, No. 5786/08, 12 November 2013.
37 Cf., e.g., art. 13 CRC.
38 U.N. CRC, *General comment No. 14 on the right of the child to have his or her best interests taken as a primary consideration*, art. 3, para. 1, U.N. Doc. CRC/C/GC/14, para. 1 (2013); Draft CRC/C/GC/25, *supra* note 16.
39 Ann Quennerstedt, *Children, But Not Really Humans? Critical Reflections on the Hampering Effect of the "3 p's,"* 18.4 Int'l J. of Children's Rts. 619–635 (2010).
40 Simone van der Hof, *'Online Grooming – een geval van technopaniek?'* Strafblad maart, 19–25 (2014); U.N. CRC, *General comment No. 13* (2011): The right of the child to freedom from all forms of violence, U.N. Doc. CRC/C/GC/13, para.13 (2011); Kimberly A. Svevo-Cianci et al., *The New UN CRC General Comment 13*, 35 Child Abuse & Neglect 979–989 (2011).
41 Adam Thierer, *Kids, Privacy, Free Speech and the Internet: Finding the Right Balance* (Mercatus Centre, Working Paper 11, 2011).
42 Art. 28b, Directive (EU) 2018/1808, 2018 O.J. (L 303) 69.
43 *See* Directive (EU) 2019/770, 2019 O.J (L 136) 1.
44 Draft CRC/C/GC/25, *supra* note 16, at para. 20.
45 Katrin Lack, *Grenzen der elterlichen Entscheidungsbefugnis (Limits to parental decision-making)*, Zeitschrift für das gesamte Familienrecht – Ehe und Familie im privaten und öffentlichen Recht (FamRZ), 1730, 1731 (2017).
46 *Id.* at 1732.
47 Benjamin Shmueli & Ayelet Blecher-Prigat, *Privacy for Children*, 42 Colum. Hum. Rts. L. Rev. 759 (2011).
48 15 U.S.C. § 6501 (2012); GDPR, *supra* note 33, at art. 8.
49 15 U.S.C. §§ 6501–6506 (2012).
50 Cf. art. 8 and 12, Recitals 38 and 58 GDPR.
51 Bart Custers et al., *A Comparison of Data Protection Legislation and Policies Across the EU*, 34 Comput. L. Sec. Rev. 234–243 (2018); Ingrida Milkaite & E. Lievens, The GDPR Child's Age of Consent for Data Processing Across the EU – One Year Later (July 2019), Biblio.ugent.be (2020), https://biblio.ugent.be/publication/8621651 (last visited Aug. 28, 2020).

52 Draft CRC/C/GC/25, *supra* note 16, para. 122; Victoria Nash et al., Oxford Internet Institute, Effective Age Verification Techniques: Lessons to be Learnt from the Online Gambling Industry – Final Report (2013), https://www.oii.ox.ac.uk/archive/downloads/publications/Effective-Age-Verification-Techniques.pdf.

53 Cf. Reform Propositions by the German Jurist Association, Verhandlungen des 72. Deutschen Juristentages [Proceedings of the 72nd German Jurist Association Day], Vol. II/1, Thesis 13 b (2019).

54 Marina Wellenhofer, *Gemeinsam getragene Elternverantwortung nach Trennung und Scheidung* [*Joint Parental Responsibility After Separation and Divorce*], Neue Juristische Wochenzeitschrift [NJW] 2758, 2761 (2018) (Ger.).

55 *Id.*

56 For disagreements between parents, *see* Bürgerliches Gesetzbuch [BGB] [Civil Code], § 1687, para. 1, http://www.gesetze-im-internet.de/englisch_bgb/index .html (Ger.).

57 Katharina Kaesling, *Protection and Participation of Children online: A Rights-based Approach*, *in* Digital Transformation of Law and Society, Comparative Perspectives on Families and New Media (Nina Dethloff et al., eds., forthcoming 2021).

58 Bundesgerichtshof [BGH] [Federal Supreme Court] (Nov. 15, 2012), Neue Juristische Wochenschrift [NJW] 1441 (2013) (Ger.); AG Bad Hersfeld, BeckRS 2017, 112602.

59 Oberlandesgericht [OLG] Köln (Jan. 15, 2013), Zeitschrift für Urheber- und Medienrecht [ZUM] 497 (2013) (Ger.); Landgericht [LG] Berlin (Jan. 24, 2014), ZUM 821 (2014) (Ger.).

60 NJW 1441 (2013) (Ger.); BGH, June 11, 2015, NJW 28 (2015) (Ger.); ZUM 821 (2014) (Ger.).

61 Judith G. Smetana, *The Role of Trust in Adolescent–Parent Relationships: To Trust You is to Tell You*, *in* Interpersonal Trust During Childhood and Adolescence, 223 (2010).

62 Deborah Lupton & Ben Williamson, *The Datafied Child: The Dataveillance of Children and Implications for their Rights*, 19 New Media & Society 783 (K.J. Rotenberg ed., 2017).

63 Monica Anderson, *Parents, Teens and Digital Monitoring*, Pew Rsch. Ctr.: Internet, Sci. & Tech. (2016).

64 Álvaro Feal et al., *Angel or Devil? A Privacy Study of Mobile Parental Control*, 2 Proc. on Priv. Enhancing Technologies 314, 315 (2020).

65 Valerie Steeves, *Hide and Seek: Surveillance of Young People on the Internet*, *in* Routledge Handbook of Surveillance Studies, 352 at 356 (David Lyon et al., eds., 2012); Ayelet Blecher-Prigat, *Children's Right to Privacy*, *in* The Oxford Handbook of Children and the Law, 3.1 (James G. Dwyer ed., 2019).

66 Christa Gebel, *Online-Risiken aus der Sicht von Jugendlichen* [*Online risks from the perspective of young people*], 65 Recht der Jugend und des Bildungswesens, 314 ff. (2017).

67 Arup Kumar Ghosh et al., *Safety vs. Surveillance: What Children Have to Say about Mobile Apps for Parental Control*, 6 (Proceedings of the 2018 Conference on Human Factors in Computing Systems, Paper 124, 2018).

68 U.N. CRC, *General comment no. 5* (2003): *General Measures of Implementation of the Convention on the Rights of the Child*, U.N. Doc. CRC/GC/2003/5, para. 6 (2003).

69 Aisling Parkes, *Children and International Human Rights Law/The Right of the Child to be Heard*, 482–487 (2015); Draft CRC/C/GC/25, *supra* note 16, at para 9, 18–19 ("guide for determining the measures needed to guarantee the realization of children's rights").

70 Louisa Specht, Urheberrechtsgesetz [Copyright Act], § 23 KUG para. 48 (Thomas Dreier & Gernot Schulze eds., 6th ed., 2018).

71 Simone van der Hof, *I Agree, or Do I: A Rights-Based Analysis of the Law on Children's Consent in the Digital World*, 34 Wis. Int'l L.J. 409, 427 (2016).
72 GDPR, *supra* note 33, art. 2, para 2, subpara c, Recital 18; *see also* Canada John Lawford, Public Interest Advocacy Center, All in the Data Family: Children's Privacy Online (2008), http://www.piac.ca/wp-content/uploads/2014/11/children_final_small_fixed.pdf (last visited Aug. 28, 2020).
73 *See* Schantz andWolff, Die unterschiedlichen Kodifikationen des Datenschutzrechts, in Das neue Datenschutzrecht, para. 316 (Auflage 2017); for the previous directive 95/46/EC see CJEU, Nov. 6, 2003, C-101/01 – Lindquist, ECLI:EU:C:2003:596.
74 Member States may provide by law for a lower age for those purposes provided that such lower age is not below 13 years.
75 *See infra* para 19–23.
76 Alicia Blum-Ross & Sonia Livingstone, *Sharenting: Parent Blogging and the Boundaries of the Digital Self*, 15 Popular Commc'n 110–125 (2017).
77 Brandon T. McDaniel et al., *New Mothers and Media Use: Associations Between Blogging, Social Networking, and Maternal Well-Being*, 16 Maternal and Child Health J. 1509–1517 (2012).
78 Stacey B. Steinberg, *Sharenting: Children's Privacy in the Age of Social Media*, 66 Emory L.J. 839, 846 (2017).
79 Meredith R. Morris, *Social Networking Site Use by Mothers of Young Children*, *in* Proceedings of the 17th ACM conference on Computer Supported Cooperative Work & Social Computing, 1272–1282 (2014).
80 Ulla Autenrieth, *Family Photography in a Networked Age. Anti-sharenting as a Reaction to Risk Assessment and Behaviour Adaption*, *in* Digital Parenting, 219–231 (Giovanna Mascheroni et al., eds., 2018).
81 OLG Oldenburg, May 25, 2018, NJW 3261 (2018) (Ger.); BGH [Federal Court of Justice] Sept. 28, 2004, NJW 56 (2005) (Ger.).
82 Norbert Dasch, *Die Einwilligung zum Eingriff in das Recht am eigenen Bild* [*Consent to Encroach on the Right to One's Own Image*], 103 (1990); Götting, *Persönlichkeitsrechte als Vermögensrechte* [*Personality Rights as Economic Rights*], 154 (1995); Klass, AfP 2005, 507, 515.
83 Rechtbank Den Haag [District Court of The Hague], Oct. 1, 2018, ECLI: NL: RBDHA: 2018: 13105 (Dutch).
84 Court of Appeal of Évora, June 25, 2015, 789/13.7TMSTB-B.E1 (Por).
85 Nadia Kutscher & Ramona Bouillon, Kinder. Bilder. Rechte. Persönlichkeitsrechte von Kindern im Kontext der digitalen Mediennutzung in der Familie [Children. Pictures. Rights. Personal rights of children in the context of digital media use in the family] 53 ff, 62 f (Deutsches Kinderhilfswerk ed., 2018).
86 Sheila Donovan, *'Sharenting': The Forgotten Children of the GDPR*, 4 Peace Hum. Rts. Governance 35–59 (2020); for the UK *See* Marion Oswald et al., *The Not-So-Secret Life of Five-Year-Olds: Legal and Ethical Issues Relating to Disclosure of Information and the Depiction of Children on Broadcast and Social Media*, 8 J. Media L. 198, 209 (2016).
87 Steinberg, *supra* note 78, at 862.
88 Cf. para 15–18.
89 Cf. Draft CRC/C/GC/25, *supra* note 16, at para. 25.
90 Sonia Livingstone, *Reframing Media Effects in Terms of Children's Rights in the Digital Age*, 10 J. Child. & Media 4–12 (2016); van der Hof, *supra* note 71; Kaesling, *supra* note 57.
91 *See* Draft CRC/C/GC/25, *supra* note 16, at para. 8.
92 Nina Dethloff, *Zusammenspiel der Rechtsquellen aus privatrechtlicher Sicht* [*Interplay of Legal Sources from a Private Law Perspective*], *in* Internationales, nationales und privates Recht: Hybridisierung der Rechtsordnungen? 47–86 (Andreas L. Paulus et al., eds., 2014).

93 Ursula Kilkelly, *The Best of Both Worlds for Children's Rights? Interpreting the European Convention on Human Rights in the Light of the UN Convention on the Rights of the Child*, 23 Hum. Rts. Q. 308–326 (2001).

94 Holger Fahl, *§ 1626a BGB und das Kindeswohl – Reformbedarf wegen Verstoßes gegen die UN-Kinderrechtskonvention [§ 1626a BGB and the Welfare of the Child – Need for Reform Due to Violation of the UN Convention on the Rights of the Child*], Neue Zeitschrift für Familienrecht (NZFam) (Ger.) 155, 157 (2014).

95 Schmahl, *supra* note 35, at art. 16 CRC, para. 22.

96 Optional Protocol to the Convention on the Rights of the Child on a Communications Procedure, A/ RES/66/138, adopted and opened for signature, ratification and accession by General Assembly resolution A/RES/66/138 of Dec. 19, 2011, entered into force on Apr. 14, 2014.

97 Hamelink, *supra* note 11.

98 Draft CRC/C/CG/25, *supra* note 16, at para. 25 ff and 33 ff.

99 Draft CRC/C/CG/25, *supra* note 16, at para. 26.

100 U.N. CRC, *General Comment* No. 5 on General measures of implementation of the Convention on the Rights of the Child (arts. 4, 242 and 44, para. 6), U.N. Doc. CRC/GC/2003/5, para. 45 (Nov. 2003); U.N. Doc. CRC/C/GC/14, *supra* note 38, para. 99; U.N. CRC, *General comment* No. 16 (2013) on State obligations regarding the impact of the business sector on children's rights, U.N. Doc. CRC/C/GC/16, para. 78–81; CRC/C/CG/25, *supra* note 16, at para. 24.

101 U.N. Doc. CRC/C/GC/16, para. 62-63; Draft CRC/C/GC/25, *supra* note 16, at para. 38.

Part IV

Children's right to identity

15 The child's right to know their biological origin in comparative European law

Consequences for parentage law

Gordana Kovaček Stanić

Introduction

In the doctrine and practice of family law, special attention has been paid to the issue of the child's right to know their biological origin, after the adoption of the UN Convention on the Rights of the Child (CRC).[1] The inclusion of the right of child to know, that is, to maintain their family identity, was motivated by political reasons, primarily by the large-scale "disappearance" of children in Argentina in the 1970s; the children's identity papers were deliberately falsified and family ties were arbitrarily severed.[2] The motives behind the inclusion of this right into the text of the CRC indicate that the basic aim was to protect the natural, biological origin. The question of biological origin is also of great importance in Spain, as during the Franco dictatorship there was also a number of similar cases to those in Argentina.[3] In Serbia, the issue of "missing" babies is a current problem. An act recently adopted in March 2020 established the inclusion of facts pertaining to the status of newborn children that are currently missing from maternity hospitals in Serbia (hereinafter, "the Act").[4] The aim of this Act is to establish facts for finding the truth on the status of these newborn children and to exercise the obligation of the Serbian government that arises from the judgment of the European Court for Human Rights (ECHR) in *Jovanović v. Serbia.*[5]

The lack of correlation between legal and biological parentage may occur in families where children have been naturally born, but also as a consequence of artificial reproduction technologies (ART), and as a consequence of adoption. Contrary to most other personal rights, the right to know one's biological origin generally concerns the rights of other people as well, particularly the rights of the genetic and/or social parents and their right to privacy and family stability.

The child's right to know their biological origin

There are three basic interests of an individual to know his genetic origin: psychological need to identity, desire to know medical history, and a material interest connected to the bloodline.[6] The psychological interest is expressed in the desire and need to know one's parentage. Such interest is the most pronounced during adolescence, when a person's identity is formed. The medical interest often occurs when starting a family because of potential genetic defects that may be inherited by the future child of a particular person. The medical interest gains importance with the realization that adopting a certain lifestyle can possibly prevent or delay the occurrence of hereditary diseases or the disease may occur in a less aggravated form. The material interest is expressed by the child's right to receive maintenance and inherit property from the parents and other relatives. It may be said that the medical and material interests are by nature practical, while the psychological interest is predominantly abstract and conceptual.

The provisions of the CRC guarantee the right of the child to an identity, both under Article 7, which states that a child is to be registered after birth, and has a right to a name, nationality, and to be cared for by their parents, and Article 8, which provides a child with the right to preservation of their identity. The CRC was ratified by former Yugoslavia in 1990, and it is in force today in the Republic of Serbia.[7]

Under comparative European law, the right to know one's biological origin is sometimes found in the country's constitution. For example, in Switzerland, the constitution has a provision which guarantees the right for everyone to know their origin.[8] In Germany, the Constitutional Court in a case of a child contesting parentage, expressed the opinion that the child has a right to know the identities of their parents.[9] The 2006 Constitution of the Republic of Serbia stipulates that all children have a right to know their origin.[10] Other countries guarantee the right to know one's origin in their statutes. In Sweden, the amendments to the 1994 Secrecy Act permit adult children to obtain access to information for determining who are their biological parents.[11] In Serbia, in addition to the Constitution, the Family Act stipulates that a child, independent of their age, has the right to know who their parents are and that this right may only be limited by the Act. A child who has reached the age of 15 and who is able to reason has the right under Article 59 of the Family Act to inspect the register of births and other documentation related to his or her origin.[12] However, prior to the age of 15, only the parent or guardian can exercise the right of the child to know their origin.

The right to know one's biological origin is a subjective right of the child. The term "child" in this context denotes a family and blood relationship between a certain person and their parents, especially of a child whose origin is at issue, has reached a certain age, and has legal capacity to bring such an action. As with other subjective rights, the exercise of this right depends on the will of its holders. Children acquire an independent right to exercise the right to know their origin at the time of maturity, or earlier depending on the particular law. The enforcement of the right to know their origin may depend on the will of third parties, particularly the people who are the child's legal parents. Moreover, in contemporary family law, the forming of parent-child relationships could depend on the potential parent's will, creating the possibility for the exercise of family autonomy.[13]

The right to know one's biological origin is a personal right and, thus, subject to limitations. Civil law often balances values and interests, and oftentimes law makers will limit the rights of enjoyment of personal values, recognizing that values and interests of society are more important than the realization of a particular personal value or right.[14] The balancing of different interests becomes complicated when the right to know one's biological origin is exercised. In a number of situations, the right to know one's biological origin is either limited or completely denied when balancing it against the other person's right to privacy, the biological parent's right to remain anonymous, and the interest in family stability. The question is whether these limitations are justified and whether the rights of other persons are stronger and more important than the right of children seeking their biological origin. Furthermore, the right may be viewed from the perspective of different parent-child configurations: natural birth, ART, and adoption.[15]

Natural birth

The laws of France, Luxemburg, Italy, and the Czech Republic discuss the question of children's right to know their biological origin in the context of anonymous birth.[16] The right of a woman to give birth anonymously was introduced in the French Civil Code in 1993, which provides a basis for the rejection of an action to determine maternity.[17] This solution already existed under Article 47 of the French Civil Code: the *Code de la famille et de l'aide sociale*. The possibility to give birth anonymously is a controversial provision in French theory. Jacqueline Rubellin-Devichi explains:

> Some justifiably consider this freedom is of benefit to both mother and child, for it avoids abortion, infanticide and abuse. Others invoke the need for the individual, at the time he is developing his personality, to know genetic parents, without recognizing that the individual in question will have largely passed the age of development when he starts his search for his origins.[18]

She is of the opinion that

> it is wrong to allege that this text is contrary to Article 7 of the United Nations Convention on the Rights of the Child. In fact, the mother's right to remain anonymous makes it specifically impossible for the child to know his parents.[19]

In 2002, the child's ability to find out about their biological origins improved slightly due to the law on access to origins for adopted persons and wards of the state, which

> … does not allow access to identity of a mother who has required secrecy, but facilitates the lifting of secrecy by encouraging the mother to give information which could be passed on to the child and by setting up the National Council for Access to Origins, whose aim is to assist with the provision of information to origins, when a case arises.[20]

In the UK, the child's right to know their identity was recognized in *Re H (Paternity: Blood Tests)*, but conditioned on the welfare of the child.[21] As Ward LJ stated:

> Every child has a right to know the truth unless his welfare clearly justifies the cover-up. The right to know is acknowledged in the UN Convention on the Rights of the Child … and in particular article 7 [where] … the clear intent of the article is that there are two separate rights, the one to know and the other to be cared for by one's parents.[22]

Sometimes in order to establish and contest paternity under the law, it will depend on the family situation. For example, a biological father has a limited, if any, right to contest the paternity if another man is considered the legal father. In Germany, a biological father was first granted statutory right to challenge fatherhood in 2004, after a ruling of the Federal Constitutional Court in 2003. As authors Detlehoff and Ramser have explained:

> The man must state in a statutory declaration that he had intercourse with the mother during the conception time (s. 1600, para. 1 no. 2 of the German Civil Code). There must be no "socio-familial" relationship (s. 1600, para. 2 of the German Civil Code) between the child and the father previously attributed to him/her. In accordance with the legal definition contained in s. 1600, pare 3. sent 1 of the German Civil Code, a "socio-familial" relationship is considered to exist if the legal father bears "responsibility in practise" for the child, or did so at the time of his death. Such responsibility shall, as a rule, be assumed in accordance with s. 1600, pare 3. sent 2 of the German Civil Code if the legal father is married to mother or has lived with the child in the same household over a long period of time. Finally, the challenger must prove to be the biological father of the child.[23]

In Serbia, the possibility of establishing and contesting maternity and paternity in court proceedings is a right given to all persons involved. Since the Family Act of 2005, the man claiming to be the biological father has the right to contest paternity no matter the family situation. Thus, it is possible for the man claiming to be the biological father to contest paternity of the mother's husband, even if mother and her husband live together in an existing marriage. He is obliged to request the establishment of his paternity by the same action to insure the child has a legal father.[24] The Family Act sets no time limit on the child to initiate the proceedings to establish and contest maternity and paternity. In these proceedings, the court is obliged to determine the biological truth, which may be based on DNA and other biomedical evidence. These provisions are clearly in favour of the right of the child to know their biological origin.[25]

Adoption

The right to know information about one's natural parents has been introduced in a number of European adoption (Family Law) acts, including the United

Kingdom, Sweden, Norway, Finland, Switzerland, Poland, Israel, Serbia, Croatia, and Slovenia. In Germany, this right is subject to a preliminary approval.

On the other hand, adoption is done in secret in some countries. For instance, in Russia, it is possible to change the place of birth and the date of birth of the adoptee.[26] The date of birth of the adoptee is not to be changed more than three months from the original date, and only if the child who is being adopted is not more than one year old. This article was amended in 2004, and now reads, "The court may order to change date of birth even if a child is one year old or older for a valid excuse."[27]

The adoptee's right to know their origin and to inspect the birth register could be limited in practice. It depends on whether the adoptee knows that they are adopted or not. In most cases, adoption acts recommend adopters to tell the truth and inform the adoptee that they are adopted, but this is rarely an obligation that is enforced. Thus, in practice, the right to know one's origin depends on the adopter's will to tell the truth or to keep it a secret. In Serbia, there is an obligation for the official of the guardianship authority to advise future adopters to tell the child the truth of their origin as soon as possible.[28] Before the ruling on adoption is delivered, while preparing adopters for the adoption, one of the issues discussed is the right of the adoptee to know their origin and how and when the truth about their origin should be presented to the adoptee.[29] After the adoption, the child and the child's adopters have the right to view the register of births. It is stipulated that before allowing the child to view the register of births, the registrar is under obligation to refer the child to psycho-social counselling.[30] A child who has reached the age of 15 and who is able to reason has the right to inspect the register of births and other documentation related to their origin.[31]

Artificial reproductive technologies (ART)[32]

The Act on Insemination in Sweden from 1984 introduced the right of a child whose conception was a result of artificial insemination by donor sperm to know the identity of the donor.[33] The provision of this right was a departure from the principle of donor anonymity, and, as such, it may be called revolutionary in its approach to ART. In Sweden, donation of ova was introduced in 2002, and in accordance with this law as well, the child has the right to know the identity of an ova donor. The United Kingdom, Austria, Netherlands, and Switzerland have also introduced the right of a child to know the identity of a donor.[34]

The age when a child has the right to get information on their donor identity varies from country to country. In Sweden, it is when a child reaches the necessary level of maturity, in Austria, it is 14, and in the Netherlands, it is 16. In Switzerland, a child of 18 can receive that information without any other showing, but can find out the donor before 18 if they show a material interest. In the Netherlands and Switzerland, the data on the donor should be kept for 80 years from the birth of a child.

There are a number of countries that have been steadfast in keeping the information on the donor a secret, including Serbia,[35] Russia, Slovenia, and France.[36] In Russia, the Federal Law on the Basics of Health Protection of the Citizens in

Russian Federation stipulates that in the usage of donor reproductive cells and embryos, citizens have the right to get information on medical data of the donor, medical-genetic examination of the donor, his race, nationality, and outward appearance only.[37] In Serbia, Slovenia, and Croatia, the child has the right to obtain only medical data of the donor. Article 57 of the Serbian Law on biomedically assisted fertilization states:

> The child conceived by biomedically assisted fertilization (BMAF) with reproductive cells of the donor has a right to ask to get data on the donor, for medical reasons, from the Board of Directors for Biomedicine kept in the State Registry. This right is obtained when the child reaches 15 years of age and is able to reason.
>
> The data obtainable is not of a personal nature of the donor, but only of medical importance for the child, their future spouse or partner, or their future offspring.
>
> The legal representative or guardian of the child may ask for the data from the Board of Directors for Biomedicine on permission from the court in an extra civil procedure, if justifiable medical reasons exist. The medical doctor of the child may ask, for medical reasons, information from the State registry to prevent risk to the child's health.

The child's rights in parentage law

The CRC stipulates in Article 18 the obligation of States' Parties to "use their best efforts to ensure recognition of the principle that **both parents** have common responsibilities for the upbringing and development of the child."[38] It could be said that the CRC recognizes the interest of the child to be cared for by two parents. In some situations, the child has only one legal parent. This may be as a result of ART, in particular, artificial insemination by donor (if a single woman is concerned) or surrogate motherhood (if a single man is concerned).[39] In comparative family law, there are different approaches regarding the permissibility of ART and if it is permitted to a single person. A single person has access to ART in the UK, Spain, the US, and Sweden, but not in France, Austria, Italy, and Switzerland. In the legislation of former Yugoslav countries, including Serbia, Croatia, Montenegro, and North Macedonia, single women have access to ART, but only as an exceptional option. On the other hand, in Slovenia, single women do not have access to ART.[40]

The main reason why some countries do not allow a single person access to ART is the belief that children need two parents. It could be said there are three particular interests a child has in having two parents: the interest of the child to know their biological origin, psychological (developmental) need, and material interest (maintenance, inheritance). These interests could be met by specific legal solutions if the child has just one legal parent. The interest of the child to know their biological origin could be met if the principle of donor anonymity is abandoned.

The interest of a child to have more than one person involved in child rearing (the psychological need) is recognized in the UK by requiring supportive parenting as a condition that single women must meet to have access to ART.[41] For implementing this requirement, the guideline states that "[w]here the child will have no legal father, the centre should assess the prospective mother's ability to meet the child's/children's needs and the ability of other persons within the family or social circle willing to share responsibility for those needs."[42] The Model of Direction on ART of 2006, amended in 2017, (Directions) indicate that a child's material interest is of importance to ART practice in Germany by limiting access to ART to those who have spouses and partners. However, it is the practice of some clinics, whose medical boards have the authority to enforce legal access to ask single women to name a person who will pay maintenance to the child. In most cases, these are the woman's parents.[43]

There is a form of ART where a child does have two legal parents, but *de facto* only one parent – posthumous fertilization. In comparative family law, there are different approaches concerning posthumous fertilization. It is permitted in the UK, but it is forbidden in France, Switzerland, and Italy. In Serbia, there is no explicit rule that would forbid posthumous fertilization.[44] However, one of the conditions for ART is that spouses or partners live together when performing the procedure.[45] This condition excludes posthumous fertilization. In the UK legislation, according to amendments to Human Fertilization and Embryology Act (HFEA), it is stipulated that the husband is the legal father, despite the fact that he is not alive, but only if no one else is to be treated as the legal father. It is allowed only if consent to posthumous fertilization was not withdrawn.[46]

Keeping in mind the child's interests in having two parents, it could be said that some of the particular interests in posthumous fertilization are met, while some are not. The interest of the child to know their biological origin is met, but psychological (developmental) need and material interest in the form of maintenance are not.

Right of a child to respect for their private life: identity and parentage

In decisions involving children born as a result of surrogate motherhood, the ECHR examined the interest of the child to identity as an element of a child's right to respect for their private life, which is stipulated in Article 8 of the Convention for the Protection of Human Rights and Fundamental Freedoms (ECHR).

In 2014, in *Case of Mennesson v. France*, the Court found that the refusal to grant legal recognition in France to parent-child relationships established overseas was in violation of Article 8 of the ECHR (children's right to private life).[47]

As the ECHR observed, respect for private life requires that everyone should be able to establish details of their identity as individual human beings, which includes the legal parent-child relationship:

> ...an essential aspect of the identity of individuals is at stake where the legal parent-child relationship is concerned...[A]lthough aware that the children have been identified in another country as the children of the first and

> second applicants (*commisioning parents*), France nonetheless denies them that status under French law. The court considers that a contradiction of that nature undermines the children's identity, nationality and their inheritance rights...The court considers, having regard to the consequences of this serious restriction on the identity and right to respect for private life of the third and fourth applicants, that by thereby preventing both the recognition and establishment under domestic law of their legal relationship with their biological father, the respondent State overstepped the permissible limits of its margin of appreciation.[48]

In the *Case of Paradiso and Campanelli v. Italy*,[49] the Court decided that there is no violation of Article 8 of the ECHR (right to private life) when a child born abroad as a result of a surrogacy arrangement is then removed by the couple who has no biological link with the child. The Court accepts that

> [t]he Italian courts, having assessed that the child would not suffer grave or irreparable harm from the separation, had struck a fair balance between the different interests at stake, while remaining within the wide margin of appreciation available to them in the present case.[50]

In its reasoning, the ECHR stated:

> In respect of the child's interests, the [Italian] minor's court had had regard to the fact that there was no biological link between the applicants and the child and had held that a suitable couple should be identified as soon as possible to take care of him. Given the child's young age and the short period spent with the applicants, the court had not agreed with the psychologist's report submitted by the applicants, suggesting that the separation would have devastating consequences for the child. It had concluded that the trauma caused by the separation would not be irreparable...
>
> The Court did not underestimate the impact which the immediate and irreversible separation from the child must have had on the applicants' private life. While the Convention did not recognise a right to become a parent, the Court could not ignore the emotional hardship suffered by those whose desire to become parents had not been or could not be be fulfilled. However, the public interests at stake weigh heavily in the balance, while comparatively less weight was to be attached to the applicants' interest in their personal development by continuing their relationship with the child. Agreeing to let the child stay with the applicants, possibly with a view to becoming his adoptive parents, would have been tantamount to legalising the situation created by them in breach of important rules of Italian law.[51]

The biological origin did, however, have a substantial impact in establishing a parent-child relationship in court practice in other cases brought before the ECHR. As seen above, in the *Case of Mennesson v. France*, the biological origin was one of the facts that led to the conclusion that there was a violation of Article

8 of the CRC, as the parent-child relationship was not established between the child and the biological father, who was part of the commissioning couple. In contrast, in the *Case of Paradiso and Campanelli v. Italy*, the lack of biological origin was one of the facts supporting the court's opinion that there was no violation of Article 8 of the CRC although the parent-child relationship was not established between commissioning parents and the child.

Conclusion

The right of the child to know their biological origin and rights of family members to privacy and family stability, as well as the right of the donor to be anonymous, could be considered conflicting rights. The legal choice of the overriding right will determine whether the possibilities for enforcement of the right of the child to know their biological origin will be broader or narrower.

In the legislation that stipulates the solution of anonymous birth, the interest of the mother to remain anonymous prevailed over the interest of the child to know one's biological origin. In the legislation stipulating donor anonymity, the interest of the donor to remain anonymous prevailed over the interest of the child to know one's biological origin. In the legislation that stipulates secrecy of adoption, the interest of the biological parents to remain anonymous and the interest of adopters to be seen as the "only" parents prevailed over the interest of the child to know their biological origin.

The other possible approach to this problem would be to attempt to eliminate the existing conflict of rights. Such a solution supposes a radical change to the social and individual attitude to parentage, such that it would be culturally acceptable that the child may have more than two parents with different roles: biological parents, social parents, and legal parents.

The conflict between reproductive freedom of the potential parents and interests of the potential child could be solved in different ways. Concerning the right of the single person to access ART and the need of the child to have two parents, there are some solutions that could meet the particular interests of the child to know their origin, psychological developmental need, and material interest. This can happen by abandoning donor anonymity, having supportive parenting, and naming the additional person (in lieu of a second parent) who will be obliged to pay maintenance to the child.

The biological origin of the child is an important fact in the opinion for establishing the parent-child relationship in the court practice of the ECHR. In cases of surrogate motherhood, the existence of the blood relation between child and commissioning couple resulted in a finding that there was a violation of a child's right to private life because the parent-child relationship was not established in *Case of Mennesson v France*. However, the lack of blood relation led another court to find that there was no violation of the child's right as no parent-child relationship was established in *Case of Paradiso and Campanelli v Italy*. The court came to different conclusions in these two cases of surrogate motherhood as the facts of the cases were different.

Notes

1 United Nations Convention on the Rights of the Child, Nov. 20, 1989, http://www.ohchr.org/en/professionalinterest/pages/crc.asp (hereinafter CRC).
2 See more about this in Gordana Kovaček Stanić, *Pravo Deteta Da Zna Svoje Poreklo [Right of the Child to Know His or Her Origins]* 13 (1997).
3 For a fictionalized account of this issue, *see* Ruta Sepetis, *The Fountains of Silence* (2019).
4 Zakon o utvrđivanju činjenica o statusu novorođene dece za koju se sumnja da su nestala iz porodilišta u Republici Srbiji [Law on Determining the Facts on the Status of Newborn Children Suspected of Missing from Maternity Hospitals in the Republic of Serbia] (Official Gazette of the Republic of Serbia, No. 18/2020).
5 *Jovanović v. Serbia*, No. 21794/09, § 2, 26 March 2013; *see also*, *supra* note 4.
6 *See* Katherine O'Donovan, *A Right to Know One's Parentage*, 2 Int'l J. L. & Fam. 27 (1988).
7 CRC Signatories, Nov. 7, 1995, 1577 U.N.T.S. 3 n. 55; Official Journal of Yugoslavia, *International Contracts*, No. 15/90 (1990).
8 *See* Olivier Guillod, *Switzerland: Everyone Has the Right to Know His or Her Origins*, 32 U. Louisville J. Fam. L. 465 (1993).
9 *See* Rainer Frank, *Germany: Blood Versus Mere Social Ties*, 32 U. Louisville J. Fam. L. 335 (1993) (citing BVerfGE 79, 256 = NJW 1989, 881 = FamRZ 1989, 255).
10 Ustav Republike Srbije (Constitution of the Republic of Serbia, Official Gazette of the Republic of Serbia, No. 98/06, art. 64/2).
11 Ake Saldeen, *Sweeden—The Rights of Children to Speak for Themselves and Obtain Access to Information Concerning Their Biological Origins ETC.*, *in* The International Survey of Family Law, 441 (Andrew Bainham ed., 1994).
12 Family Act (Official Gazette of the Republic of Serbia, No. 18/05).
13 Gordana Kovaček Stanić, *Family Autonomy in Contemporary Parent-Child Relations*, 1 Int'l. J. Juris. Fam. 147 (2010).
14 Obren Stankovic & Vladimir V. Vodlinelic, *Uvod u Građansko Pravo*, 120–123 (1996).
15 The expression natural birth may be criticized because its antonymous are words "unnatural" and "artificial." It is by no means the intention of the author to treat the families created by ART or adoption as unnatural or artificial, or in any way abnormal. The expression is used here only for the lack of a more suitable one, and it means the creation of the family without assistance of medicine (ART) or law (adoption).
16 On Italy and Luxemburg law in: Jacqueline Rubellin-Devichi, *La recherche des origines personnelles et le droit a l'accouchement sous X dans la loi du 22 janvier*, Dr. famille chr. No. 11, art 7. (2002), on Czech law in: Zdenka Kralickova, *Czech Family Law: The Right Time for Re-codification*, *in* The International Survey of Family Law, 163–165 (Bill Atkin ed., 2009).
17 Art. 341-1 of Act 93-22 of January 1993.
18 Jacqueline Rubellin-Devichi, *Reforms and Controversies*, *in* The International Survey of Family Law, 251 (Andrew Bainham ed., 1994).
19 *Id.*
20 Sylvie Ferré-André et al., *Work in Hand for the Reform of French Family Law*, *in* The International Survey of Family Law, 178 (Andrew Bainham ed., 2003).
21 *Re H (Paternity: Blood Tests)* (1996) 2 FLR 65.
22 *Id.*
23 Nina Detlehoff & Claudia Ramser, *Tension Between Legal, Biological and Social Conceptions of Parentage*, 182 (Ingebor Schwenzer ed., 2007).
24 Family Act, *supra* note 12, at art. 56, sec. 2.
25 Stanić, *supra* note 13.
26 Family Code of the Russian Federation No. 223-FZ, art. 135. (1995)

27 *Id.* at No. 185-FZ.
28 Family Act, *supra* note 12, at art. 322.
29 Regulations on Program for Preparing for Adoption, (Official Gazette of the Republic of Serbia, No. 60/05, art. 8).
30 Family Act, *supra* note 12, at art. 326.
31 *Id.* at art. 59.
32 *See* Gordana Kovaček Stanić & Sandra Samardžić, *Assisted Reproductive Technologies: New Family Forms and Welfare of Offspring in Comparative Family Law, in* Family Law and Family Realities, 235 (Carol Rogerson et al., eds., 2019).
33 Act on Insemination of Sweden, SFS 1984:1140 (1985). The IVF Act was repealed by the Genetic Integrity Act on June 1, 2006. The right to identifying information about the donor in Chapters 6 and 7 Genetic Integrity Act. *See* Jane Stoll, *Swedish Donor Offspring and Their Legal Right to Information* (2008).
34 UK Human Fertilization and Embryology Act 1990, 1990 c. 37, replaced by UK Fertilization and Embryology Act 2008, 2008 c. 22, http://www.legislation.gov.uk/ukpga/2008/22; *see also* Erwin Bernat & Erich Vranes, *The Austrian Act on Procreative Medicine: Scope, Impacts and Inconsistencies, in* Creating the Child: The Ethics, Law & Practice of Assisted Procreation, 325 (Donald Evans ed., 1996); Caroline Forder, *Opening up Marriage to Same Sex Partners and Providing for Adoption by Same Sex Couples, Managing Information on Sperm Donors, and Lots of Private International Law, in* The International Survey of Family Law, 256–261 (Andrew Bainham ed., 2000) (discussing the Act on artificial insemination [information on donor] of Netherlands 2002); Olivier Guillod, *A New Divorce Law for the New Millenium, in* The International Survey of Family Law 365 (Andrew Bainham ed., 2000) (discussing the Act on medically assisted procreation of Switzerland 1998).
35 Law on Biomedically Assisted Fertilization, (Official Gazette of the Republic of Serbia, No. 40/2017, art. 25(1)).
36 *See* France: Bioethical Laws 1994, 2004, 2011; *see also* Laurence Francoz Terminal, *The Changing Concept of "Family" and Challenges for Family Law in France, in* European Family Law Vol. II: The Changing Concept of "Family" and Challenges for Domestic Family Law 39 (Jens M. Scherpe ed., 2016); Act on Treatment of Infertility and Fertilization Procedures by Biomedical Assistance, (Official Gazette of the Republic of Slovenia, Nos. 70/2000 and 15/2017); Act on the Basic Health Protection of the Citizens in Russian Federation Federal Law No. 323-FZ of Nov. 21, 2011 (author translation to English), http://www.consultant.ru/document/cons_doc_LAW_121895/3b0e0cbbd6f1b1a07c0b0b3d4df406a2ecf108a1/.
37 Federal Law No. 323-FZ of November 21, 2011 on Basics of Health Protection of the Citizens in the Russian Federation as amended to December 29, 2015.
38 CRC art. 18 (emphasis added).
39 The media have cited the case of the famous football player Cristiano Ronaldo, who has three children born through surrogacy. However, no woman is regarded as the legal mother of these children.
40 Stanić, *supra* note 32.
41 Human Fertilisation and Embryology Authority, Code of Practice § 14(2)(b) (8th ed. 2017).
42 *Id.*
43 Access to ART is regulated by directions of medical boards in the different provinces, as well (*Landesärztekammern*). Practice however differs from existing rules as some clinics allow access to single women.
44 ESHRE, Comparative Analysis of Medically Assisted Reproduction in the EU: Regulation and Technologies 18, SANCO/2008/C6/051, https://ec.europa.eu/health//sites/health/files/blood_tissues_organs/docs/study_eshre_en.pdf.

45 Zakon o biomedicinski potpomognutoj oplodnji (Law on Bio-Medically Assisted Fertilization), art. 25 (2017), https://www.paragraf.rs/propisi/zakon_o_biomedicinski_potpomognutoj_oplodnji.html&prev=search&pto=aue.
46 HFEA, sec. 39(1) (2008), https://www.legislation.gov.uk/ukpga/2008/22/section/39.
47 Mennesson v. France, No. 65192/11, E.C.H.R. [Section V], (2014), https://www.globalhealthrights.org/wp-content/uploads/2018/06/CASE-OF-MENNESSON-v.-FRANCE-Extracts-1.pdf.
48 *Id.* at 20, 24, 26.
49 Paradiso and Campanelli v. Italy, no. 25358/12, E.C.H.R. [G.C], (2017); Information Note on the Court's case-law 203 (2017), https://www.echr.coe.int/Documents/CLIN_2017_01_203_ENG.pdf.
50 *Id.* at 17.
51 *Id.* at 16–17.

16 Québec's (out)law concerning medically assisted procreation

A plea for access to origins

Johanne Clouet and Valérie P. Costanzo

Introduction

For several years, medical advancements have made it possible, for a couple or a single person, to have a child through medically assisted procreation. In Québec, this method of reproduction is legally regulated by the Assisted Human Reproduction Act,[1] by the Act Respecting Clinical and Research Activities Related to Assisted Procreation,[2] and by the Civil Code of Québec (CCQ). While the first act sets out prohibited activities related to assisted human reproduction, the second regulates clinical and research activities relating to assisted procreation in order to ensure high-quality, safe, and ethical practices. As for the CCQ, it provides a definition and rules for establishing the filiation of children born by medically assisted procreation. In this regard, the general rule is that no filiation can be established between the child and a gamete donor; the latter's personal information is required to remain confidential.

This chapter explores the absence of the right of the child to know his or her origins in the Province of Québec. The first part of the chapter presents the current state of Québec's laws on assisted procreation, emphasizing the legal definition of assisted procreation and the filiation of children born by this method of reproduction. This will shed light on the justifications behind the principle of confidentiality and the psychological factors that promote the right of the child to know his or her origins.

Next, the chapter provides an overview of the legal factors that have been used as arguments in favor of lifting the confidentiality of personal information of gamete donors in the context of medically assisted procreation, which are echoed in the Convention on the Rights of the Child (CRC): the right of the child to know his or her parent, the best interests of the child, and the right to equality. The chapter concludes with a discussion on the conflicting rights of the child and of the parents – legal and biological – to privacy.

Assisted procreation in the Province of Québec

As a federal state, Canada has a political regime that implies the division of legislative powers contained in Articles 91 and 92 of the Constitution Act, 1867,[3] between the Federal Parliament (central government) and Provincial Legislatures.

While some areas of legislative authority, such as agriculture and immigration, are shared by the provinces and the Federal Parliament (concurrent jurisdiction), others are exclusively assigned to the federal or provincial legislatures. According to Article 92(16), all matters of a private nature – such as the issue of assisted procreation – fall under the province's legislative authority. The following paragraphs present the current state of Québec's laws on assisted procreation by focusing on the legal definition of assisted procreation and on the filiation of children born of this method of reproduction.

Québec's laws on assisted procreation

The Québec Legislature adopted the first legal framework for medically assisted procreation in 1994 by introducing in the Civil Code a new section entitled "Medically Assisted Procreation."[4] In 2002, the Civil Code was amended to recognize three different types of assisted procreation: (1) Medically Assisted Procreation, (2) "Amicable Assisted Procreation," in which an individual provides the potential mother with genetic material via sexual intercourse, and (3) "Artisanal Assisted Procreation," meaning that the sperm is injected into the uterine cavity of the potential mother with a syringe, without medical intervention or sexual intercourse.[5] The new chapter added in 2002 revolves around the parental project involving assisted procreation. According to Article 538 of the Civil Code, a parental project exists from the moment that "a person or spouses decide, by mutual consent, in order to have a child, to resort to the genetic material of a person who is not party to the parental project."

This disposition raises three important comments.

First, the "person" to whom this Article refers is inevitably a woman, since surrogacy agreements are absolutely null in Québec according to the Civil Code.[6] Québec is the only province in Canada that does not recognize surrogacy contracts.

Second, regarding the "spouses," they may be of the same or of opposite sex, married or not.[7] For the reason mentioned above for a sole person, the term "same-sex couple" refers to a lesbian couple. In other words, a sole man and same-sex male partners can register as a child's parents only by adoption. Moreover, as the definition refers to "spouses," two individuals who do not form a couple – for example, a single woman and her best friend – cannot consent to a parental project involving assisted procreation.

Finally, the genetic contribution of the third party consists of a donation of gametes. It can be a donation of sperm and/or ovum as nothing excludes the possibility of a single parental project involving the contribution of genetic material from both male and female donors.

Filiation of children conceived by assisted procreation

The filiation of a child born of assisted procreation will generally be established between the child and the intended parent(s), defined as the people who consented to the parental project prior to the conception of the child. In fact, contributing genetic material for the purpose of a third-party parental project does not create a bond of filiation between the contributor and the child born, except if the genetic material is provided by way of sexual intercourse. In this specific case, a bond of filiation may be established, in the year following the birth, between the contributor and the child.[8]

The use of medically assisted procreation technologies raises the question of the confidentiality of the personal information of the donor.[9] According to Article 542 of the Civil Code, "Personal information relating to medically assisted procreation is confidential."[10] The sole exception is the provision of medical history if failure to provide the information could endanger the life of the child or of any of their descendants. In this specific case, the personal information of the donor can be confidentially transmitted to the medical authority.

According to the comments of the Minister of Justice, the anonymity of the egg donor "[translation] promotes respect for the right to privacy of those directly affected by medically assisted procreation of a child."[11] It is therefore in the interests of the adult parties to the parental plan – which are the donor and the intended parent(s) – that the principle of confidentiality has been adopted, while children's rights and best interests have been completely ignored.

One may wonder why the legislator chose to maintain the confidentiality of personal information relating to medically assisted procreation when the Civil Code was amended in June 2017 relaxing the confidentiality of the files concerning the adoption of a child.[12] Indeed, the right of children to know their origins in the context of adoption and of medically assisted reproduction was often compared, considering that until the recent legislative modification, access to origins was denied to children in both scenarios. The amending law operates a paradigm shift: the adopted child can now have access to the content of his or her adoption file unless a parent of origin registers an identity disclosure veto in the year following the birth of the child.[13]

Why were children born of medically assisted procreation left out? The Journal of Debates of Québec's National Assembly provides no answer.[14] In fact, no question was made by parliamentarians with regard to maintaining the confidentiality of origins in cases of medically assisted procreation in contradiction with the recognition of the adopted children to have access to their origins. The question was only raised during the public commission on the bill.[15] The interrogations were, however, never answered by the Minister of Justice.

Some intellectuals argue that the analogy between the situation of children born of medically assisted procreation and adopted children is inappropriate.[16] According to them, at the center of adoption lies the trauma of abandonment – justifying the quest for origins – compared with children born of medically assisted procreation, for whom there is no empirical data to confirm that the fact of not having information on the identity of the donor is necessarily a source of prejudice. As Bureau and Guilhermont state, "[translation] If the sufferings related to the secrecy of the origins can exist and be real, the argument in itself is not enough to infer that being born of medically assisted procreation constitutes harm for the child."[17]

Others, including the French sociologist Irène Théry, reject this argument with a new perspective. If adopted children, whose beginnings have been traumatic and scarred by abandonment can access their origins, why couldn't children – whose births are in no way traumatic, but desired, planned, and even organized by the institutions of our society with the cooperation of a donor – also have the right to know their origins? Even if it is true to say that children born from reproductive technology do not suffer the same suffering as adopted children, it is nonetheless false to pretend that they do not suffer at all. According to Théry, the suffering comes from the ideological and legal arrangements that make a child believe they are born from an "interchangeable material of reproduction,"[18] symbolically depicting the child as the *origin of himself or herself*.[19]

Moreover, many experts are of the opinion that access to one's biological origins is necessary to one's development as an individual, regardless of the child being adopted or being born of medically adopted procreation. Vardit Ravitsky, an ethicist and professor at the Public Health Department of University of Montréal, argues that the provision of information on biological origins makes it possible to avoid harm to children born of medically assisted procreation, who, without this data, would be deprived of the possibility to realize their full development both physically and psychologically.[20] As mentioned by a child born of medically assisted procreation, "[translation] The desire to know our origins goes far beyond the practical aspects; it is something visceral, a need to anchor in a universal human reality."[21]

Legal factors to promote the right of origins

Psychological factors have been used as arguments in favor of lifting the confidentiality of medically assisted procreation, but there are also legal factors that should be considered. This section focuses on the legal arguments, which are echoed in the CRC,[22] ratified by the Federal government of Canada in December 1991.[23]

The CRC presents the legal framework that anchors children's rights to know their origins in Articles 7 and 8, the children's best interests in Article 3, and their right to equality in the preamble. In addition to the provisions of the CRC, we will also demonstrate how the right to privacy can also be used to argue in favor of a child's right to know his or her origins.

Articles 7 and 8 of the CRC: The Child's Right to Know His or Her Parents and to Preserve His or Her Identity

The first legal factor that promotes access to the origins of the child born of medically assisted procreation is provided by Articles 7 and 8 of the CRC, which are among the basic provisions of the treaty:

Article 7

1 The child shall be registered immediately after birth and shall have the right from birth to a name, the right to acquire a nationality and, as far as possible, the right to know and be cared for by his or her parents.
2 States Parties shall ensure the implementation of these rights in accordance with their national law and their obligations under the relevant international instruments in this field, in particular where the child would otherwise be stateless.

Article 8

1 States Parties undertake to respect the right of the child to preserve his or her identity, including nationality, name and family relations as recognized by law without unlawful interference.
2 Where a child is illegally deprived of some or all of the elements of his or her identity, States Parties shall provide appropriate assistance and protection, with a view to re-establishing speedily his or her identity.

In 2001, the Court of Appeal of Québec used Article 7 of the CRC to interpret Québec's legislation and forced a child's presumed biological father to undergo DNA testing: "[translation] the right of the child to know his parents, provided for in Article 7 of the Convention on the Rights of the Child, fits perfectly within the framework of the Article 33 of the Civil Code of Québec,"[24] which provides all decisions concerning a child should be made in his or her best interests. The Court ruled in favor of the child's best interests to know his origins over the presumed father's right to bodily integrity. Although this decision is related to a case of biological filiation, its principles could justify challenging the rule of confidentiality that applies to medically assisted procreation.[25]

In another decision rendered in 2012, in a case where the plaintiff – who had been conceived by medically assisted procreation – contested the unwavering rule of confidentiality in such cases, the British Columbia Court of Appeal (BCCA) dismissed the request to recognize the existence of a right to know one's origins.[26]

In dismissing the request for acknowledgment of a right to know one's origins, the BCCA does not refer to the prior decision rendered by the Court of Appeal of Québec, not even to dismiss its findings or consider them irrelevant. What impact does such a decision have across Canada, and more specifically in the Province of Québec? In terms of governing rules in Canada, the Supreme Court of Canada established that

> a provincial appellate court is not obliged, as a matter either of law or of practice, to follow a decision of the appellate court of another province unless it is persuaded that it should do so on its merits or for other independent reasons.[27]

That is to say that if faced with a similar case to the one heard by the BCCA concerning the nonexistence of a right to one's origins, the Court of Appeal of Québec could come to different findings. Until then, it can be said that the CRC can be a source of interpretation of national law, but according to the BCCA, it cannot be viewed as a source of a right of a child to know his or her origins, at least when the child is born of assisted procreation.[28]

It is, however, important to mention that the wording of Articles 7 and 8 of the CRC is open to interpretation, consequently weakening the foundations of the right to know one's origins. For instance, in Article 7, the expression "parents" does not refer specifically to "biological parents," and "as far as possible" does not necessarily imply both legal and practical measures.[29] Such space for interpretation could be used to deny the existence of the right to know one's origin in specific cases like medically assisted procreation. Nonetheless, the United Nations (UN) Committee on the Rights of the Child has commented – as early as 1994 – on Norway's law protecting the sperm donor's anonymity in medically assisted procreation, noting, "the possible contradiction between this provision of the Convention with the policy of the State party in relation to artificial insemination."[30]

Article 3 of the CRC: The Best Interests of the Child

The second legal factor which promotes the right of a child born of medically assisted procreation to know his or her origins is contained in Article 3 of the CRC:

1 In all actions concerning children, whether undertaken by public or private social welfare institutions, courts of law, administrative authorities or legislative bodies, the best interests of the child shall be a primary consideration.
2 States Parties undertake to ensure the child such protection and care as is necessary for his or her well-being, taking into account the rights and duties of his or her parents, legal guardians, or other individuals legally responsible for him or her, and, to this end, shall take all appropriate legislative and administrative measures.
3 States Parties shall ensure that the institutions, services and facilities responsible for the care or protection of children shall conform with the standards established by competent authorities, particularly in the areas of safety, health, in the number and suitability of their staff, as well as competent supervision.

A similar legal provision existed in Québec's legislation about a decade prior to its adoption in the CRC.[31] This presents the question: is the rule of confidentiality in medically assisted procreation in the child's best interests?

As adults, children born of medically assisted procreation are making their voices heard regarding the pain of living without knowing their biological origins. In the 2011 case of Olivia Pratten, she made an application to the Supreme

Court of British Columbia to know the sperm donor who participated in her conception.[32] With the support of several testimonials on the trauma of being a child born of medically assisted procreation with no access to their biological origins, she convinced the tribunal that:

> Not knowing, and not being able to know, are sources of great frustration, anger, depression, anxiety and sadness. They [children born of medically assisted procreation] worry about the implications for their health, and the health of their own children. They mourn the loss of half-siblings, but also fear unknowingly developing romantic relationships with a half-sibling.[33]

These are among the psychological arguments referred to earlier: to know one's biological origins is in the best interests of the child, since such knowledge is necessary to one's development as an individual.[34] Pratten was granted authorization to obtain information relating to her origins at the first instance but was denied that right on appeal.[35] In fact, although the BCCA recognized the pain and suffering of children born of medically assisted procreation, Pratten's complaint was dismissed on other grounds, such as the aforementioned absence of a right to know one's origins and the absence of a violation of the right to equality of children born of medically assisted procreation.[36]

Right to equality: The CRC and the Canadian Charter of Rights

The third legal argument is based on the right to equality. The preamble of the CRC contains "the inherent dignity and of the equal and inalienable rights of all members of the human family is the foundation of freedom, justice and peace in the world."[37] Within Canada, Article 15 of the Canadian Charter of Rights and Freedoms provides that every individual is equal before the law.

As mentioned above, the legitimacy of adopted children's aspirations to gain access to their identity was recently recognized in Quebec, and they can have access to the content of their adoption files unless their biological parents vetoed their anonymity. This right previously existed in other provinces of the country, such as British Columbia. According to Olivia Pratten, the Adoption Act of British Columbia,[38] which was amended in 1996 to allow adoptees, once adults, to have access to information about their origins, but provides no such right for children born of medically assisted procreation, is therefore discriminatory. Indeed, based on the recognition of the legitimacy of one's identity aspirations in the context of adoption,[39] one can argue for the same right of a child born of medically assisted procreation.[40] The Supreme Court of British Columbia also recognized such wrongful discrimination in the Pratten case, but that decision was overruled by the Court of Appeal.[41]

Rather than viewing the difference of treatment as a violation of the fundamental right to equality, the BCCA drew the conclusion that adopted children were subject to a positive discrimination within the meaning of section 15(2) of the Canadian Charter, which provides that equality before and under the law mentioned in subsection 1

> does not preclude any law, program or activity that has as its object the amelioration of conditions of disadvantaged individuals or groups including those that are disadvantaged because of race, national or ethnic origin, colour, religion, sex, age or mental or physical disability.

The Court concedes that children born of medically assisted procreation are in the same situation as adopted children: their sense of identity is equally affected. However, the Court of Appeal considered the difference of treatment as legitimate.[42]

Given that adoption breaks the ties of filiation between children and their biological family and gives them a new identity, the purpose of the Adoption Act of 1996 was to allow children whose identity was changed through adoption access to data on their origins.[43] This is a critical element of the Court's decision, which found that a law may legitimately allow adoptees to have access to their origins, without having to provide similar benefits to all people who wish to obtain the same right without having been adopted, especially those whose legal status has never changed.

Pratten's application for leave to appeal from the judgment of the BCCA was dismissed by the Supreme Court of Canada.[44] However, such dismissal, which provides no reason for the decision, is not an indication whether the Supreme Court supports the judgment being appealed or not. One could then argue that the battle is not yet over.[45]

Beyond the CRC's provisions: conflicting rights to privacy

Beyond the specific provisions of the CRC, the right to know one's origins has been sought in the context of the right to privacy guaranteed by several international conventions, such as the European Convention of Human Rights.[46] The European Court of Human Rights has shown openness to concede to such a right on several occasions, without regard specifically to the case of medically assisted procreation.[47] Nonetheless, the child's right to privacy must be proportionally balanced with the right to privacy of the child's biological parents.[48]

The Canadian Charter of Rights and Freedoms does not provide for a specific right to privacy,[49] although it is somewhat implied in the right to life, liberty, and security of person (section 7). As the Supreme Court of Canada declares: "Society has come to realize that privacy is at the heart of liberty in a modern state."[50] In Québec's Charter of Human Rights and Freedoms,[51] section 5 provides specifically that "every person has a right to respect for his private life." The right to privacy comprises several elements, among which "*a right to autonomy in structuring one's personal and family life* and a right to secrecy and confidentiality."[52]

Again, the right to privacy can be used in favor of children seeking their biological origins, but also in favor of the biological parents to remain anonymous, and in favor of the right of a child's legal parents to autonomously structure their personal and family life. While the privacy of biological parents appears to be obvious, the privacy of legal parents implies the control of the information given to the child about his or her origins – or the right moment to discuss such matter – and guarantees the absence of intrusion from the biological parents in the legal parents' or the child's lives.[53] In the Province of Québec, the choice was to favor the said right of the parents, both biological and legal, over the child's right to privacy in knowing his or her origins.[54]

While such a position is commonly acknowledged, the rigidity of the rule of confidentiality can nonetheless be questioned. Are such rights to privacy consistently contradictory? Some legal parents could be open to allowing their child to have access to the information of the donor; some biological parents could be open to being known by their offspring. Yet even with the consent of the stakeholders, the Québec legislature does not allow the possibility to lift the confidentiality. Is such rigidity justified? We do not believe so. As it is now the case for adoption, we believe that the confidentiality should be the exception and not the other way around.

Conclusion

In recent years, many Western states have modified their laws to recognize the right to origins of children born from a gamete donation, but some resistance to this right exists. Such is the case in the Province of Québec, which, to this day, maintains the anonymity of the donor in terms of medically assisted procreation.

In its report to the minister of Justice in 2015, the Québec Advisory Committee[55] recommends to "[translation] formally recognize the right to know one's origins in the Charter of Human Rights and Freedoms."[56] In the eventuality that this recommendation is followed by the government, a child born of medically assisted procreation who wishes to know their origins could obtain any information allowing them to identify the person(s) who is (are) at the origin of their existence.

As mentioned by the Québec Advisory Committee's Report,

> [translation] It is simply a question of allowing the child … born of medically assisted procreation who wishes it to take power on all the parts of his or her history, without making moral judgment on the legitimacy of his or her quest for identity.[57]

No legislative progress has been made on this issue since the tabling of the report. And the position of the Québec government on this matter remains unknown.

We are perfectly aware that the recognition of children's right to their origins can be in contradiction with the right of the parents and of the donors to their privacy. However, considering the major importance in the development of children to have access to information allowing them to build their identity and given their best interests, which, according to Article 3 of the CRC, shall be a primary consideration in all laws concerning children, we believe the rules need to be reviewed.

Notes

1 Assisted Human Reproduction Act, SC, c. 2 (2004).
2 Act Respecting Clinical and Research Activities Relating to Assisted Procreation, CQLR, c. A-5.01 (2009).
3 Constitution Act, (UK), 30 & 31 Vict., c. 3 (1867).
4 Civil Code of Québec, CQLR, c. CCQ-1991, https://www.canlii.org/en/qc/laws/stat/cqlr-c-ccq-1991/latest/cqlr-c-ccq-1991.html.
5 An Act Instituting Civil Unions and Establishing New Rules of Filiation, SQ, c. 6 (2002).
6 *CCQ, supra note 4, at § 541.*
7 According to art. 61.1 of the Interpretation Act, CQLR, c. I-16, the word "spouse" means a married or civil union spouse. It also includes a *de facto* spouse unless the context indicates otherwise, which it is not the case in assisted procreation, https://www.canlii.org/en/qc/laws/stat/cqlr-c-i-16/latest/cqlr-c-i-16.html?searchUrlHash=AAAAAQAOaW50ZXJwcmV0YXRpb24AAAAAAQ&resultIndex=1.
8 *Id.* at § 538.2.
9 Intended parent(s) can also have a child using insemination from a known donor. This scenario remains an exception.
10 "Personal information" is any information which relates to a natural person and allows that person to be identified. *See* Act Respecting the Protection of Personal Information in the Private Sector, CQLR, c. P-39.1, § 2, and Act Respecting Access to Documents Held by Public Bodies and the Protection of Personal Information, CQLR, c. A-2.1, § 54.
11 Québec – Ministry Of Justice, *Comments of the Minister of Justice*, t. II, (1993), § 542. The right to privacy is protected by the Charter of Human Rights and Freedoms, CQLR, c. C-12, § 5, and by the Canadian Charter of Rights and Freedoms, Part I of the Constitution Act, being Schedule B to the Canada Act (UK), c. 11, § 7.
12 An Act to Amend the Civil Code and Other Legislative Provisions as Regards Adoption and the Disclosure of Information, SQ, c. 12 (2017, entry into force in 2018). The opportunity to interrogate the relevance of donor anonymity also arose in 2010, when the Act Respecting Clinical and Research Activities Relating to Assisted Procreation, *supra* footnote 2, was adopted. However, no public or political debate took place on the question, the Québec legislator maintaining purely and simply the principle of anonymity. *See* § 44.
13 Civil Code of Québec, CQLR, c. CCQ-1991, § 583.4.
14 Public hearing on Bill 13, An Act to Amend the Civil Code and Other Legislative Provisions as Regards Adoption and the Disclosure of Information, 1st Sess., 41st Leg., Québec (Nov. 23, 2016).
15 Public hearing before the Standing Committee on Institutions, Bill 113, An Act to Amend the Civil Code and Other Legislative Provisions as Regards Adoption and the Disclosure of Information, 1st Sess., 41st Leg., Québec (Nov. 23, 2016) at 12h17 (Association of Family Lawyers) and at 15h04 (Professor Alain Roy).
16 Marie-France Bureau & Édith Guilhermont, *Le droit de connaître ses origines: chronique d'une réforme annoncée*, 73 R. du B. 599 (2014); Marie Pratte, *Le nouveau Code civil du Québec: Quelques retouches en matière de filiation*, *in* Mélanges Germain Brière, 283, 299 (Wilson & Lafleur, 1993); Sonia LeBris, *Procréation médicalement assistée et parentalité à l'aube du 21e siècle*, 1 C.P. du N. 133, 144 (1994).

17 Bureau & Guilhermont, *supra* note 15, at 621.

18 France. Direction générale de l'action sociale et al., *Filiation, origines, parentalité. Le droit face aux nouvelles valeurs de responsabilité générationnelle*: Rapport remis à la ministre déléguée chargée de la famille, Ministère des Affaires sociales et de la Santé, 220 (O. Jacob, 2014), http://www.justice.gouv.fr/include_htm/etat_des_savoirs/eds_thery-rapport-filiation-origines-parentalite-2014.pdf.

19 *Id.*

20 Vardit Ravitsky, *Knowing Where You Come From: The Rights of Donor-Conceived Individuals and the Meaning of Genetic Relatedness*, 11 Minn. J. L. Sci. & Tech 655 (2010).

21 Andréane Letendre, *Testimony Made at the Citizens Commission on Family Law* (June 2018).

22 United Nations Convention on the Rights of the Child, Nov. 20, 1989, http://www.ohchr.org/en/professionalinterestpages/crc.asp (hereinafter CRC).

23 In Canada, the negotiation, the signature, and ratification of international treaties are controlled by the executive branch of the federal government. Despite its ratification from Canada, the CRC does not have force of law in the Province of Québec, considering that it has not been incorporated through domestic law to be enforceable at the national level. However, the Supreme Court of Canada – which is the highest tribunal of the country – recognized that the CRC can be used in a contextual approach to interpret Canadian laws.

24 A.P. v L.D., [2001] RJQ. 16 at para 37 (C.A.).

25 Laurence Le Guillou, *La procréation médicalement assistée et le droit des enfants qui en sont issus à la connaissance de leurs origines*, Essay, Sherbrooke, Faculty of Law, Sherbrooke University, 38 (2014); Michelle Giroux, *Le droit fondamental de connaître ses origines biologiques: impact des droits fondamentaux sur le droit de la filiation*, R. DU B. 255, 290–293 (2006); Michelle Giroux, *Le droit fondamental de connaître ses origines biologiques*, *in* Rights of The Child: Proceedings of the International Conference, 355, 384–385 (Wilson & Lafleur, 2008).

26 Pratten v. British Columbia (Attorney General), BCCA 480 (2012).

27 Wolf v. The Queen, 2 SCR 107, 109 (1975).

28 The decision goes on to consider that such a right cannot be anchored in the Canadian Charter of Rights and Freedoms either.

29 Julie Cousineau, *L'anonymat des dons de gamètes et d'embryons au Québec et au Canada*, Thesis, Montréal, Faculty of Law, McGill University, 239–243 (McGill University Libraries, 2011).

30 U.N. CRC Commitee, *Concluding observations of the Committee on the Rights of the Child: Norway*, U.N. Doc. CRC/C/15/Add.23, at para. 10 (Apr. 25, 1994). *See also* Ineta Ziemele, *Article 7: The Right to Birth Registration, Name and Nationality, and the Right to Know and Being Cared for by Parents*, *in* A Commentary on the United Nations Convention on the Rights of the Child (Martinus Nijhoff Publishers, 2007).

31 *Civil Code of Québec, CQLR c. CCQ-1991, § 33. At the time of its adoption such principle was provided by section 30 (1980).*

32 Pratten v. British Columbia (Attorney General), BCSC 656 (2011).

33 *Id.* at para. 50.

34 *Id.*

35 *Pratten*, *supra* note 26.

36 Pratten also argued that her right to security provided by Article 7 of the Canadian Charter of Freedoms and Rights was denied by not being allowed access to sensitive information that could impact her health, or the health of a child born from relationship with a half-sibling. BCSC, *supra* note 31, at para. 42. That argument was also dismissed, since both courts were not convinced by the existence of a true correlation between the right to security provided by section 7 and the said right to know one's origins. BCCS., *supra* note 31, at para. 49 and BCCA, *supra* note 25, at para. 50.

37 Beyond the CRC, the right to equality of all children is rooted in United Nations' 1948 Universal Declaration of Human Rights, which provides that "all children, whether born in or out of wedlock, shall enjoy the same social protection." Res. 217 A (III), Doc. Off. A.G.N.U., 3rd Sess., suppl. n° 13, p. 17, Doc. N.U. A/810 § 25(2), (1948). *See also* European Convention on Human Rights, Council of Europe, PA, The European Convention on Human Rights 4.XI, § 14 (1950).
38 Adoption Act, RSBC 1996 c. 5, § 6, 8, 9, 32, 48, 56, 58–71.
39 Cousineau, *supra*, note 29, at 231–232.
40 Marie-Christine Kirouak, *Le projet parental et les nouvelles règles relatives à la filiation: une avancée ou un recul quant à la stabilité de la filiation? in* S.F.P.B.Q., Développements récents en droit familial, Cowansville, Éditions Yvon Blais, 369 at 481 (2005); Carmen Lavallée & Michelle Giroux, *Le droit de l'enfant québécois à la connaissance de ses origines évalué à l'aune de la Convention internationale relative aux droits de l'enfant*, 72 R. DU B. 147, 170–171 (2013). *See also* Commission De L'éthique De La Science Et De La Technologie, *Avis éthique et procréation assistée: des orientations pour le don de gamètes et d'embryons, la gestation pour autrui et le diagnostic préimplantatoire*, xxii, recommandation 2 (2009), https://www.ethique.gouv.qc.ca/media/1101/pa-avis-et-errata-en.pdf.
41 *Pratten*, *supra* note 26, at paras 41–43 (2012).
42 Referring to a previous judgment from the Court of Appeal of Ontario. Marchand v. Ontario, ON O.A.C. 787 (2007).
43 *Pratten*, *supra* note 26, at paras 41–43 (2012).
44 Pratten v. Attorney General of British Columbia, CanLII 30404 (CSC, 2013).
45 Supreme Court Of Canada, https://www.scc-csc.ca/unrep-nonrep/res-int/guide-eng.aspx. (last visited Aug. 2, 2020).
46 Nov. 4, 1950, S.T.E. n° 5 § 8 (1953, entry into force Sept. 3, 1953).
47 Odièvre c. France [GC], n° 42326/98, CEDH 2003-III; Jäggi c. Suisse, n° 58757/00, CEDH 2006-X; Bensaïd c. Royaume-Uni, n° 44599/98, CEDH 2001-I; Gaskin c. Roy/aume-Uni, série A, n° 160 (1989); Mikulić c. Croatie, n° 53176/99, § 54 et 65, CEDH 2002-I; Godelli c. Italie, n° 33783/09, CEDH 2012; Pascaud c. France, n° 19539/08, CEDH 2011 et Anayo c. Allemagne, n° 20578/07, CEDH 2010.
48 Odièvre, *supra* note 47.
49 Canadian Charter of Rights and Freedoms, *supra* note 10, § 7.
50 R. v. Dyment, 2 SCR 417, at para. 17 (1988).
51 Charter of Human Rights and Freedoms, *supra* note 10.
52 Godbout v. Longueuil (Ville), 3 SCR 844, at paras. 97–98 (1997) (quoting The Gazette (Division Southam Inc. v. Valiquette [1997] RJQ. 30, at 36) (C.A.) (emphasis in the original text). *See also* R. v. Morgantaler, [1988] 1 SCR 30.
53 Commission De Réforme Du Droit Du Canada, *La Procréation Médicalement Assistée* 169 (1992); Le Guillou, *supra* note 25, at 51 (2014); Cousineau, *supra* note 28, at 198 (2011).
54 Le Guillou, *supra* note 25, at 41 & 47 (2014); Giroux, *supra* note 25, at 290.
55 The Committee was created by the Government of Québec in 2013. Its mandate was to assess the advisability of reviewing family law and, if so, to make recommendations.
56 Recommandation 3.33.
57 QUÉBEC (PROVINCE). Comité Consultatif Sur Le Droit De La Famille, *Pour un droit de la famille adapté aux nouvelles réalités conjugales et familiales* (Éditions Thémis, 2015).

Part V

Protecting children at risk

17 Suffering at the hands of caregivers

The mandatory duty of caregivers to report child abuse and neglect from a South African perspective

Mildred Bekink

Introduction

Many children across the world bear both the physical and psychological scars of maltreatment by those who are supposed to protect them.[1] According to the World Health Organization (WHO), it is globally estimated that up to one billion children between the ages of two and seventeen have endured physical, sexual, or emotional violence or neglect in the past year.[2] Governments throughout the world are increasingly involved with the challenge of detecting cases of maltreatment at an early stage to allow for an early intervention and treatment. As a central approach in this endeavor, many countries have enacted legislation commonly known as mandatory reporting laws, requiring designated persons to report known or suspected cases of abuse or neglect.[3] The motivation for the creation of such statutory laws is to respond to the problems that take place in private settings that result in severe child maltreatment.[4]

On enacting mandatory reporting laws, these countries comply with the provisions of the United Nations Convention on the Rights of the Child (CRC).[5] The United Nations and its signatories to the CRC acknowledge that children are a vulnerable group and should be afforded special protection. Article 19 of the CRC compels signatory states, such as South Africa, to take:

> all appropriate legislative, administrative, social and educational measures to protect the child from all forms of physical or mental violence, injury or abuse, neglect or negligent treatment, maltreatment or exploitation, including sexual abuse, while in the care of parent(s), legal guardian(s) or any other person who has the care of the child.[6]

Furthermore, Article 19(2) of the CRC stipulates that both protective and preventative measures should be implemented, including reporting, referral, investigation, treatment, and follow-up of instances of child abuse, maltreatment, and/or neglect.

In line with the CRC, the South African Constitution explicitly affords children protection against abuse and maltreatment.[7] Section 28(1)(d) of the Constitution guarantees every child the right "to be protected from maltreatment, neglect, abuse or degradation."[8] Section 110 of the Children's Act, as amended, further provides for the mandatory reporting of abused or neglected children in that it compels certain designated persons to report any suspected child abuse or deliberate neglect to the relevant authorities.[9] In addition, section 54 of the South African Criminal Law (Sexual Offences and Related Matters) Amendment Act (SORMA) compels a person who knows that a sexual offense has been committed against a child to report it to a police official.[10]

In April 2019, it was widely reported by the media that a woman who filmed her colleague abusing children at a crèche in Gauteng in South Africa was arrested and would appear in court.[11] In the videos, the caregiver can be seen repeatedly beating three different toddlers in three respective incidents. It is alleged that the videographer failed to protect the children when she saw her colleague assaulting the toddlers but, instead, chose to film her. After being dismissed from the crèche for another matter, the videographer allegedly tried to bribe the owner of the crèche by showing her the videos. The owner failed to act on the information.[12] The crèche was closed and the necessary arrests were made after the videos of the recorded abuse went viral on social media.[13] This arrest of a fellow caregiver who filmed the incidents of abuse is believed to be the first of its kind in South Africa. A later report produced by the media reported the South African Police Service's (SAPS) denial of an earlier confirmation of the videographer's arrest.[14]

The circumstances once again raise awareness of the importance of the duty not only to protect children but also to report incidents of abuse. Given the staggering evidence of the escalation of violence and abuse directed against South African children, it is appropriate to investigate whether South African law currently complies with the protection principles of the CRC and adequately provides for the liability of those who are compelled to report child abuse but fail to do so. In addition, a comparative legal study to determine whether lessons can be learned from other jurisdictions is beneficial.

South Africa

Many South African children suffer severe abuse and neglect.[15] A 2018 national prevalence study showed that 9.9% of boys and 14.6% of girls between the ages of 15 and 17 have experienced lifetime sexual victimization.[16] Physical abuse, emotional abuse, neglect, family violence, and other forms of victimization were also strongly associated with the sexual victimization.[17]

Consequently, following the 1960 reporting laws of the United States (US), South Africa adopted mandatory reporting legislation in section 42(1) of the Child Care Act of 1983.[18] The mandatory reporting law was also included in the subsequent Children's Act[19] in section 110 and came into effect on April 1,

2010. Section 110(1) of the Children's Act, like its predecessor, places a mandatory obligation on certain professions:

> (1) Any correctional official, dentist, homeopath, immigration official, labour inspector, legal practitioner, medical practitioner, midwife, minister of religion, nurse, occupational therapist, physiotherapist, psychologist, religious leader, social service professional, social worker, speech therapist, teacher, traditional health practitioner, traditional leader or member of staff or volunteer worker at a partial care facility, drop-in centre or child and youth care centre who on reasonable grounds concludes that a child has been abused in a manner causing physical injury, sexually abused or deliberately neglected, must report that conclusion in the prescribed form to a designated child protection organisation, the provincial department of social development or a police official.

Apart from the obligatory reporters, members of the general public or so-called "community reporters" are given the discretion in terms of section 110(2) of the Children's Act to report a belief that "a child is in need of care and protection," but are not compelled to do so.[20]

In addition to the Children's Act, section 54 of SORMA mandates "[a] person who has knowledge that a sexual offence has been committed against a child must report such knowledge immediately to a police official."[21] SORMA accordingly follows a blanket approach by placing a mandatory reporting obligation on "a person." In other words, all citizens who are aware of the sexual exploitation of children must report it. This appears not to tolerate any exceptions.[22]

A fundamental issue in reporting statutes is the level of certainty that must be reached for a valid reporting obligation to arise. The reporting obligation in the Children's Act is triggered by a conclusion on reasonable grounds that the child has been abused or deliberately neglected. This inevitably implies that some minimum investigation must have taken place for the potential reporter weighing up the "evidence" to come to the required conclusion. A mere suspicion will not suffice.[23]

Community reporters who choose to report child abuse only have to believe on *reasonable grounds* that the child is in need of care and protection.[24] Reports made in good faith by both the obligatory reporters and the community reporters in terms of section 110 of the Children's Act will exempt reporters from civil liability.[25] However, failure to report child abuse or neglect when legally obligated to do so can give rise to such a person being guilty of an offense.[26] A person who violates section 110(1) of the Children's Act is liable for a fine or imprisonment for a period not exceeding ten years, or both.[27]

In contrast, section 54 of SORMA determines that a person who has *knowledge* of sexual offenses directed against children must report such knowledge immediately to a police official.[28] A person who fails to report such knowledge is guilty of an offense and liable, on conviction, to a fine or imprisonment for a period not exceeding five years, or both.[29] SORMA accordingly sets a much higher reporting standard than that of the Children's Act. Furthermore, section 54 of

SORMA makes no provision for an exemption from criminal or civil liability due to unfounded reporting of sexual offenses against a child.[30] According to Sloth-Nielsen, the high standard of knowledge is to be welcomed, given that no exemption from criminal and civil liability has been created for erroneous reporting.[31]

In 2019, the Department of Social Development drafted a Children's Amendment Bill. The purpose of the Bill is to amend the Children's Act to further promote and protect certain children's rights as well as to align the Children's Act with SORMA. The Bill also includes a proposal to amend section 110 of the Children's Act. This proposed amendment intends to broaden the pool of obligatory reporters further by adding any officer of the court, any official working for Home Affairs, any person working with children, and ward counselors.[32]

The Bill also proposes to amend the level of certainty for a valid reporting obligation arising from a *conclusion* on reasonable grounds that the child has been abused or deliberately neglected to that one *suspects* that a child has been abused to report that *suspicion* in the prescribed form.[33] This accordingly proposes a lower threshold than what is currently required.

An evaluation of the scenario given in the introduction of the videographer *prima facie* places her within the ambit of section 110(1) of the Children's Act. The videographer, a member of the staff working at the care facility, had first-hand knowledge of the incidents and a conclusion on reasonable grounds of abuse could have been reached by the videographer. Instead of acting in the children's best interest by protecting them or reporting the matter to the designated authorities, the videographer chose to disseminate the video on social media. An argument could accordingly be made that she had failed to comply with section 110(1) of the Children's Act.

However, no arrest was made. An investigation into whether any similar arrests for failure to report child maltreatment were made by the SAPS in the past revealed that no body of knowledge exists of any similar arrests. Thus, it seems there have been no prosecutions for withholding information relating to child protection concerns in terms of the provisions of section 110 of the Children's Act. Taking the abovementioned discussion of the South African mandatory laws as well as the example of the crèche into account, it seems that although South Africa's mandatory reporting laws are quite extensive, no criminal action has been taken for failure of reported incidents of child abuse. This raises the question whether this position is unique to South Africa or whether similar difficulties are also experienced in other countries. In the following section, the process of other jurisdictions will be evaluated to ascertain whether their reporting laws may be implemented to develop the South African practice.

Other jurisdictions

Many countries in the world have enacted mandatory reporting laws, although the approaches differ among jurisdictions.[34] The three early adopters, the US, Canada, and Australia have given detailed attention to the development of these laws over several decades.[35] This section will focus on arrangements from the US and Canada.

United States

The US has a strong and well-established culture of mandated reporting, with the first laws being drafted in 1963. These laws were initially limited to requiring medical professionals to report suspected physical abuse. The scope of this legislation expanded with the enactment of the Federal Child Abuse Prevention and Treatment Act (CAPTA) that requires each state to have procedures for requiring certain individuals to report known or suspected instances of child abuse and neglect.[36] Mandatory reporting has become an important feature of the US child abuse system. Although the specifics may vary between states in the US, all 50 states have mandatory reporting statutes.[37]

Forty-seven states have designated professionals as mandated reporters.[38] The most commonly mandated professionals include: social workers; teachers, principals, and other school personnel; physicians, nurses, and other healthcare workers; counselors, therapists, and other mental health professionals; childcare providers; and law enforcement officers.[39]

Nineteen states have universal mandatory reporting laws that state any person who suspects child abuse or neglect is required to report it.[40] Of these 19 states, 16 specify certain professionals who must report, but also require all persons to report suspected abuse and neglect, regardless of their profession.[41] The other three states – Indiana, New Jersey, and Wyoming – require all persons to report child abuse or neglect without specifying any professions. In all other states, any person is permitted to report child abuse or neglect. These voluntary reporters of child maltreatment are often referred to as permissive reporters.[42]

The circumstances under which a mandatory reporter must make the report also vary from state to state. Typically, a report must be made when the reporter suspects or has reason to believe that the child has been abused or neglected. Another common requirement is to report in situations in which the reporter has knowledge of, or observes the child being subjected to, conditions that would reasonably result in harm to the child.[43]

All 50 states have some form of immunity for reporting child abuse or neglect, provided the report is made in good faith. This immunity extends to both mandatory and voluntary reporters. Seventeen of these states follow a "presumption of good faith," meaning that the good faith of the reporter is presumed unless it can be proven otherwise.[44]

Approximately 49 states[45] impose penalties on mandatory reporters who knowingly and willingly fail to submit a report when they suspect that a child is being abused or neglected.[46] Penalties range from small fine misdemeanors to felony charges, which include the possibility of imprisonment.[47]

Florida has the most stringent monetary penalty that imposes a fine of up to $1,000,000 on any institution of higher learning, including any state university or non-public college that fails to report or prevents any person from reporting an instance of abuse committed on the property of the institution or at any point when sponsored by the institution.[48] This penalty has accordingly been described as the "most comprehensive child abuse reporting law in the nation."[49]

This penalty was passed in the wake of the Sandusky scandal.[50] The Sandusky scandal happened in November 2011, and concerned allegations of child sexual abuse committed by Jerry Sandusky, the assistant football coach for Pennsylvania State University. He served in this position for over 15 years. In June 2012, Sandusky was convicted on 45 counts of child sexual abuse and was sentenced to a minimum of 30 years and a maximum of 60 years in prison.[51]

One of these incidents of abuse was witnessed in 2002 by a graduate assistant who informed the football head coach. The head coach, in turn, informed the athletic director, who shared this with the vice president of the University. In the aftermath of the controversy in 2011, the vice president and athletic director were charged with the failure to report the suspected child abuse to the proper authorities.[52]

A preliminary investigation of the US mandatory reporting legislation indicates that the US legislation is quite extensive and became more stringent after the Sandusky scandal. However, Hogelin calls attention to the fact that apart from the Sandusky scandal, there are very few cases where actual criminal action has been taken for failure to report child abuse.[53] He finds it alarming that there are not more cases filed when it is known that many instances of suspected or known child abuse cases go unreported.[54]

Canada

Like in the US, mandatory reporting has been an important feature in Canadian child laws for some time.[55] All jurisdictions in Canada have some kind of universal mandatory reporting legislation. Although the law varies between jurisdictions, all require that reports are to be made by *anyone* aware of a child being maltreated and in need of protection.[56] Professionals working with children and youth have an added responsibility to report child maltreatment and are specifically mentioned in the mandatory legislation of most jurisdictions.[57] The most commonly mandated professionals or officials assumed to have such a special awareness include healthcare professionals, teachers, school principals, social workers, family counselors, religious officials, operators and employees of childcare centers or home childcare agencies, youth and recreation workers, and peace officers.[58]

Though subtle differences exist between the different jurisdictions of Canada, reporting must typically be made when the reporter reasonably believes or has reasonable grounds to suspect that the child has been abused or neglected. This means that the reporter's suspicion is supported by information that an average person, using normal or honest judgement, would rely on. This standard has been recognized by the courts as creating a low threshold for the reporting of child maltreatment.[59]

Notwithstanding these differences, some similarities exist between the respective jurisdictions. Immunity from criminal and civil liability is granted in all the jurisdictions to any person giving information about a child in need of protection, provided the report is made in good faith. Furthermore, all the jurisdictions impose penalties on a person who fails to report a reasonable suspicion of abuse or neglect,[60] although the jurisdictions differ in the maximum amount imposed. For example, penalties vary between a fine of up to $50,000 and/or imprisonment for up to two years[61] and a fine of $10,000 and/or imprisonment for up to six months.[62]

Despite what seems to be quite extensive mandatory reporting legislation, in her discussion of the shortcomings of mandated reporting for child maltreatment under healthcare professionals in Canada, Gordon highlights that very little case law exists dealing with reporter liability.[63] This is surprising considering the high liability for failing to report and the low threshold created by Canadian legislation that focuses on suspicion of risk of harm rather than actual knowledge.[64]

Analysis and conclusion

The above analysis of the three countries' respective mandatory legislation reveals that all three have a wide-ranging pool of mandatory reporters. While South Africa and the US follow a combination of universal and designated mandatory reporting, Canada has extended this duty to everyone within all jurisdictions. The reporting standard required by all three countries is that of reasonable grounds, while Canada makes allowances for a suspicion of child abuse or neglect. Notably, in South Africa, SORMA requires reporters of sexual offenses committed against children to have knowledge of the offense, thus setting a high standard for the reporting of sexual abuse.

Despite these differences, some similarities exist among the three countries. Specifically, immunity is granted from criminal and civil liability in all three countries, provided the report is made in good faith. Moreover, although the severity varies, all three countries impose penalties on a person who fails to report a reasonable suspicion of abuse or neglect. This ranges from a mere fine to imprisonment or both.

Despite the development of mandatory reporting laws in all three countries, there is very little case law regarding reporter liability for failure to report. This raises two serious questions: (1) What are the reasons for the lack of prosecution and for not enforcing statutory reporting requirements?, and (2) Are mandatory reporting rules in fact effective and serving their purpose? Reasons given for the lack of reporting include the lack of understanding reporting legislation, lack of "hard" evidence, concerns regarding the legal consequences of reporting, lack of faith in child protection services, and accompanying concern for the safety of the child, as well as a lack of effective and comprehensive training.[65] This raises the question whether the aforementioned reasons may also contribute to a lack of prosecution.

One of the barriers to reporting child abuse is often a lack of indication of clear evidence. Research has indicated that, where clear definitions are not given, the decision to report depends on the reporter's subjective interpretation of what constitutes abuse.[66] A study conducted by Jamieson et al. of the Cape Town

Children's Institute showed that physical abuse is severely underreported.[67] The study indicated that even when physical abuse is in fact reported, it is often regarded as "justifiable" punishment under the guise of discipline despite evidence suggesting a pattern of violence. Moreover, the report highlighted that none of the cases reported to the social services were reported to the police, and that those cases reported directly to the police were withdrawn soon afterward. Professionals dismissed these incidents as not serious enough or regarded the perpetrator's actions as justifiable discipline.[68]

Related to the issue of clear evidence is the concept of reasonable grounds to suspect, believe, or to conclude that abuse exists. Research has shown that the interpretation and application of these terms is variable and inconsistent,[69] and may even lead to inaction.[70] In order to assist those involved in the prosecution of child abuse cases, specific forms and protocols have been developed from the interpretation of reported cases. In South Africa, a Form 22 or a SAPS 581(b) must be completed for each child presumed to be abused. However, the study conducted by Jamieson et al. revealed that only 5% of the reports were recorded on the prescribed form. Consequently, critical information was not recorded.[71] Police and social workers were also found not to be adequately trained on the Children's Act.[72] This phenomenon is not unique to South Africa. Studies conducted in the US and other countries suggest that professionals are not adhering to policies, citing a lack of adequate training on the policies regarding mandatory reporting and the indicators of child abuse as the cause.[73]

Another frequently identified reason for the ineffectiveness of mandatory reporting legislation is that child protection and law enforcement authorities are already overburdened and unable to meaningfully address the increased reports.[74] In the University of Cape Town Children's Institute's 2018 Annual Report, it is highlighted that South African social and health service providers face many work-related challenges including poor infrastructure, staff shortages, long working hours, low morale, and even a lack of trust between professionals.[75] Jamieson et al. also signified a lack of inter-sectional collaboration. They alluded to the fact that although the Children's Act is based on a co-operative implementation model that obliges social workers and police officials to work together, only 8% of reported cases were cross-referred and none were jointly managed.[76] In countries where law enforcement authorities are overwhelmed with crime in general, such as South Africa, the lack of prosecution of those failing to report abuse may be attributed to a want of prominence. The arrest and prosecution of perpetrators is most likely perceived as more deserving of scarce resources. This may also contribute to the fact that, for most individuals, the threat of prosecution is not a major factor in their decision to report child abuse or neglect.[77] Coupled with this may be a perception that the penalties for failure to report are enacted as an encouragement to report maltreatment rather than for policing.[78] It thus seems, as was evident with the Sandusky case, that the prosecution for failure to report is only ignited in serious instances of child abuse or where society demands it. In the scenario given of the crèche, society is still calling for the arrest of the videographer.[79]

As indicated above, this raises the second serious question: Is South Africa's mandatory reporting legislation in fact serving its purpose? Many countries in the world have enacted mandatory reporting laws. Other countries, such as England and New Zealand, have chosen not to enact mandatory reporting laws. The reasons given include the perceived danger of over-reporting of innocent cases, which may divert resources from already known deserving cases.[80] The primary fear being that mandatory reporting overloads the system and results in children in need of protection losing out.[81]

In contrast, countries such as the US, Canada, and Australia acknowledge a litany of concerns that may outweigh problems or resource allocation. For example, mandatory reporting reflects a consideration of more than just the immediate protection of children in danger, but recognizes the broader seriousness of child abuse. It also prevents the revictimization of children, reinforces moral responsibility of community members, and increases the number of identified child abuse cases. All of this enables the criminal justice system to respond to child abuse.[82]

This has led to a controversial debate about the advantages and disadvantages of having mandatory reporting laws.[83] Though the scope of this chapter does not lend itself to an in-depth discussion of the debate, there is a consensus that mandatory reporting has consistently produced an increase in the number of both substantiated and un-substantiated reports made to governments.[84] Nevertheless, these reports reflect a positive outcome if it leads to early notification and intervention. This depends on whether the system can cope with the many referrals and provide the necessary resources needed. However, research about mandatory reporting indicates that most of the reaction time is not spent on investigations, but on addressing the needs of children and families. Also, that the investigations that lead to un-substantiated abuse still frequently uncover problems that require help for the child and/or the family.[85]

As highlighted by Jamieson et al. in their report and illustrated by the incident discussed in the introduction, the mandatory reporting of child abuse in South Africa is far from perfect. A recent report by the media indicates that the caregiver has been found to be guilty of two charges of common assault, as well as one account of assault with the intention to do grievous bodily harm. Unfortunately, no indication is given as to what charges, if any, the videographer will face while the case against the owner of the crèche is still proceeding.[86] Though South Africa's mandatory reporting system may be open to question, it does have the potential to play an important role in protecting children from further maltreatment. It may thus be ill-advised to reverse the mandatory provisions that are currently in place and not to hold those accountable that blatantly disregard it. However, there can be no doubt that mandatory reporting is not the panacea for child abuse but it is part of a broader solution aimed at comprehensively addressing the issue. The challenge seems to be how to realize mandatory reporting's protective potential.

A golden thread that runs through research in this field is the importance of understanding and reporting abuse and the significant role training plays in this regard. South Africa's government should invest in the training of all stakeholders regarding the relevant mandatory legislation. Linked information sharing between agencies working with children is also necessary. The government needs to invest in proper resources and a coordinated, national child protection system where social services, police, and health professionals can share information and jointly manage complex cases. In this regard, it is hoped that the recently established Inter-Ministerial Committee on Gender Based Violence and Femicide (GBVF) in South Africa tasked, among others, with overseeing a national coordinated response to the eradication of GBVF (including violence directed against children) will make a difference.[87] Likewise, the government should continue its effort of assessing the legal framework and evidence to ensure the most effective approach. Laws that are adapted to provide for co-ordination between relevant stakeholders have proven to be the most successful.

Being a signatory to the CRC, South Africa must continue in its efforts to ensure that protective and preventative measures, which include the reporting of child abuse and/or neglect, are in place. For, in the words of former President Nelson Mandela, "[t]here can be no keener revelation of a society's soul than the way in which it treats its children." Hopefully the abovementioned measures will act as a "voice" against the silence of child abuse and/or neglect as we owe it to our most vulnerable citizens, namely children, to protect them against all odds.

Notes

1 *See* Kayla Gordon, *Good Intentions, Questionable Results: The Shortcomings of Mandated Reporting for Child Maltreatment*, 9 W.J. Legal Stud. 1 (2019).
2 World Health Organization, Global Status Report on Preventing Violence Against Children 2 (2020).
3 Ben Mathews, *Mandatory Reporting Laws and Identification of Child Abuse and Neglect: Consideration of Different Maltreatment Types, and a Cross-Jurisdictional Analysis of Child Sexual Abuse Reports*, 3 Soc. Sci. 460, 461 (2014).
4 *Id.* at 464.
5 United Nations Convention on the Rights of the Child, Nov. 20, 1989, http://www.ohchr.org/en/professionalinterest/pages/crc.asp (hereinafter CRC) (South Africa ratified the CRC on June 16, 1995).
6 CRC, *supra* note 5, at art. 19.
7 S. Afr. Const. (1996), ch. 2, § 28(1).
8 *Id.*
9 *See* Children's Act, 35 of 2005 as amended by Children's Amendment Act, 41 (2007).
10 Criminal Law (Sexual Offences and Related Matters) Amendment Act, 32 (2007).
11 *See Woman Who Filmed Child Abuse Arrested and Charged*, News 24 (Apr. 30, 2019), https://www.politicsweb.co.za/news-and-analysis/woman-who-filmed-child-abuse-arrested-and-charged.
12 This is another aspect for which the videographer could be charged. No indication of such a charge could be established.
13 *Id.*
14 Ntwaagae Seleka, *Gauteng Cops Deny Earlier Confirmation of Second Arrest in Carletonville Crèche Abuse Case*, News 24 (Apr. 30, 2019), https://www.news24.com/SouthAfrica/News/woman-accused-of-filming-alleged-abuse-at-carletonville-creche-arrested-and-charged-20190430.

15 Tammy Petersen, *Child Protection Week: Status of Children in SA Bleak – NGO Network*, News 24 (June 9, 2019), https://www.news24.com/SouthAfrica/News/child-protection-week-status-of-children-in-sa-bleak-ngo-network-20190609.
16 Catherine L. Ward et al., *Sexual Violence Against Children in South Africa: A Nationally Representative Cross-Sectional Study of Prevalence and Correlates*, 6 The Lancet Glob. Health e460–e468 (2018).
17 *Id.*
18 Child Care Act, 74 (1983).
19 Children's Act, 35 of 2005 as amended by Children's Amendment Act, 41 (2007).
20 Julia Sloth-Nielsen, *Protection of Children* as printed in C.J. Davel & A.M. Skelton (eds.) *Commentary on the Children's Act* (Juta Revision Service 8 2018) 7-1 at 7-22.
21 SORMA, § 54.
22 However, section 56(5) of SORMA provides that a person may not be convicted of an offence in terms of section 54 if that person is a child and, in addition, is not a person contemplated in sections 17 (1) and (2) or 23 (1) and (2) as the case may be. *See also* Julia Sloth-Nielsen, *Section 54: Obligation to Report Commission of Sexual Offences against Children or Persons Who are Mentally Disabled*, *in Sexual Offences Commentary Act 32 of 2007* (P. Pithey & D. Smythe eds.) (Juta 2011) 18-4–18-6 (highlighting some of the anomalies that may arise due to the blanket approach by the legislature.)
23 Sloth-Nielson, *supra* note 20 at 7–22.
24 *See* the Children's Act, 38 of 2005, § 110(2).
25 Children's Act, 38 of 2005 § 110(3)(b).
26 *Id.* at § 305(1)(c).
27 *Id.* at 305(6).
28 Reference must also be made to section 54(2) of SORMA that compels a person who has knowledge, *reasonable belief or suspicion* that a sexual offence has been committed against a *person who is mentally disabled* to report it to a police officer.
29 SORMA, § 54(1)(a).
30 Note that an exemption is only given in subsection 54(2) relating to the mandatory reporting of sexual offences committed against a person who is mentally disabled. No similar provision is found in section 54(1) of SORMA.
31 Sloth-Nielson, *supra* note 22, at 18–26.
32 Children's Amendment Bill (Feb. 22, 2019).
33 Children's Amendment Bill (2019).
34 Ben Mathews and Maureen C. Kenny, *Mandatory Reporting Legislation in the United States, Canada, and Australia: A Cross Jurisdictional Review of Key Features, Differences, and Issues*, 13 Child Maltr. 50, 50 (2008).
35 *Id.*
36 Child Welfare Information Gateway, *Mandatory Reporters of Child Abuse and Neglect* (Washington, DC: U.S. Department of Health & Human Services, Children's Bureau, 2019).
37 *Id.* at 2.
38 As of April 2019, Indiana, New Jersey, and Wyoming are the only States that do not innumerate specific professional groups as mandated reporters but require all persons to report. See *Id.*
39 *Id.*
40 This include Delaware, Florida, Idaho, Indiana, Kentucky, Louisiana, Maryland, Mississippi, Nebraska, New Hampshire, New Jersey, North Carolina, Oklahoma, Rhode Island, Tennessee, Texas, Utah, and Wyoming.
41 These include Delaware, Florida, Idaho, Kentucky, Maryland, Mississippi, Nebraska, New Hampshire, New Mexico, North Carolina, Oklahoma, Rhode Island, Tennessee, Texas, and Utah.
42 *See id.* at 3.

43 Child Welfare Information Gateway, *supra* note 36, *Immunity for Reporters of Child Abuse and Neglect.*
44 *Id.* at 2.
45 The state of Wyoming has no professional mandatory reporting laws.
46 Child Welfare Information Gateway, *supra* note 36, *Penalties for Failure to Report and False Reporting of Abuse and Neglect.*
47 *Id.* at 2.
48 *Id.*
49 Leonard G. Brown III and Kevin Gallagher, *Mandatory Reporting of Abuse: A Historical Perspective on the Evolution of State's Current Mandatory Reporting Laws with a Review of the Laws in the Commonwealth of Pennsylvania*, 59 Vill. L. Rev. 9, 55, 64 (2014).
50 *Id.*
51 Jon M. Hogelin, *To Prevent and to Protect: The Reporting of Child Abuse by Educators*, BYU Educ. & L. J. 225, 230–232 (2013).
52 *Id.*
53 *Id.* at 65.
54 *Id.*
55 Mandatory reporting has been in effect in Alberta, for example since 1966. *See* The Child Welfare Act, RSA c.13, s. 39 (1966).
56 Isla Wallace and Lisa Bunting, *An Examination of Local, National and International Arrangements for the Mandatory Reporting of Child Abuse: Implications for Ireland*, NSPCC, 11 (2007); Child, Youth and Family Services Act, SO c. 14. Sch 1, s. 125(5)–(9) (2017).
57 Wallace, *supra* note 56.
58 Child, Youth and Family Services Act, SO c. 14. Sch 1, s. 125(8) (2017).
59 Gordon, *supra* note 1, at 6.
60 *Id.* at 11.
61 Child and Family Services Act S.M. c. 33, s. 3 (2014).
62 Child, Family and Community Service Act, RSBC, (1996), s14.
63 Gordon, *supra* note 1, at 10.
64 Gordon, *supra* note 1, at 5.
65 Hogelin, *supra* note 51, at 246–249 (2013); Gordon, *supra* note 1, at 5–11.
66 Matthews, *supra* note 34, at 58.
67 Lucy Jamieson et al., *Out of Harm's Way? Tracking Child Abuse Cases through the Child Protection System in Five Selected Sites in South Africa*, The Child. Inst., Cape Town U. 1, 23 (2017).
68 *Id.* at 53.
69 Gordon, *supra* note 1, at 7.
70 Commw. Austl., *Improving Institutional Responding and Reporting*, Royal Commission into Institutional Responses to Child Sexual Abuse, Vol. 7, 44, https://www.royalcommission.gov.au/royal-commission-institutional-responses-child-sexual-abuse/child-safe-institutions.
71 Jamieson, *supra* note 67, at 24.
72 *Id.* at 55.
73 Beverley Chia Chi Liu & Michael S Vaughn, *Legal and Policy Issues from the United States and Internationally About Mandatory Reporting of Child Abuse*, 64 Int'l J.L. & Psychiatry 219, 222 (2019).
74 Natalie A MacCormick, *To Mandate Or Not to Mandate: A Review of Mandatory Reporting of Suspected Child Abuse and Neglect*, 26 Am. J.L. & Med. 334, 334–340 (2018).
75 The Children's Institute, University of Cape Town, *Annual Report* (2018), http://www.ci.uct.ac.za/sites/default/files/image_tool/images/367/CI_Annual%20Report%202018_lowres%20%28cropped%29.pdf.

76 Jamieson, *supra* note 67, at 55.
77 Gordon, *supra* note 1, at 13–21.
78 Matthews, *supra* note 34, at 52.
79 *Woman Who Allegedly Took Carletonville Creche 'Abuse' Videos Arrested*, The Citizen (Apr. 30, 2019), https://citizen.co.za/news/south-africa/education/2124830/woman-who-allegedly-took-carletonville-creche-abuse-videos-arrested/.
80 Matthews, *supra* note 34, at 52.
81 Emma Davies et al., *Mandatory Reporting? Issues to Consider when Developing Legislation and Policy to Improve Discovery of Child Abuse*, 2 ISLRev 9, 20 (2014).
82 Liu, *supra* note 73, at 219–229.
83 Matthews, *supra* note 34, at 50.
84 Wallace, *supra* note 56, at 5.
85 Davies, *supra* note 81, at 21.
86 Tankiso Makheta, *Carletonville Crèche Caregiver Found Guilty of Assault*, Sowetan (July 8, 2020), https://www.sowetanlive.co.za/news/south-africa/2020-07-08-carletonville-creche-caregiver-found-guilty-of-assault/ (Despite numerous attempts, no further information could be obtained on the position of the videographer).
87 Minister Maite Nkoana-Mashabane, *Establishing an Inter-Ministerial Committee Council to Eradicate Gender-Based Violence and Femicide* (June 8, 2020), https://www.gov.za/speeches/inter-ministerial-committee-resolves-fast-track-establishment-council-eradicate-gender.

18 The journey from ignorance to acknowledgement of child sexual abuse in India

Namrata Mishra

Introduction

It is true that life's aspirations come in the guise of children. India is amply blessed with this valuable natural resource for it is home to approximately 440 million children,[1] almost one in five total children in the world. Unfortunately, in recent years, India has become infamous for being home to the largest number of sexually abused children in the world.[2] Just like many other countries, child abuse in India is a phenomenon which is widespread and cuts across social, cultural, and pecuniary borders. It is disheartening to point out, despite India being a signatory to the United Nations (UN) Convention on the Rights of Child (CRC),[3] and having ratified it 28 years ago, many Indians do not regard a child as an individual, with their own rights and interests, entitled to protection. Millions of children face staggering challenges from the time of birth.[4] Children are sexually abused by relatives at home, by people in their neighbourhoods, at school, and in residential facilities for orphans and other at-risk children.[5] Many cases go unreported. Recently, it has become more common for children to share their experiences of abuse with members of their family or caregivers, and yet, such cases are grossly underreported.[6] Although the well-being of our children is imperative for our nation's growth, it should also be deemed necessary as an end in itself.[7] Under the Constitution of India, it is an obligation to provide a safe environment for the holistic growth and development of children.[8]

Existence of child sexual abuse (CSA) in India and related studies

India has been in denial of the occurrence of child exploitation for decades. Sexual abuse of children first became a public issue in the 1970s and 1980s. Still, it is not until after the ratification of the CRC that India conducted its first study on the existence of CSA. The study was conducted in 1998 by Recovery and Healing from Incest, an Indian NGO, that found that a majority (76%) of the participants reported were abused during childhood or adolescence.[9] In 2006, the international organization, Save the Children, and the Tulir – Centre for Healing and Prevention of Child Sexual Abuse, an Indian NGO, conducted another study that surveyed 2,211 schoolchildren in Chennai. The results indicated about 48% and 39% of the boys and girls, respectively, reported being sexually abused, and 15% of the participants stated having faced severe forms of sexual abuse.[10] The problem extends to the tourism industry. A study on tourism-related commercial sexual exploitation of children on the eastern coast of India found that out of a sample of 150 children, 60% had come to the tourist area after being promised a better job, accompanied by a "neighbourhood uncle."[11] It also found that 40% of the children interviewed mentioned "force" as the means used. For example, moneylenders would force parents to sell their children to repay debts.

It was not until the Ministry of Women and Child Development conducted a study on "Child Abuse in India 2007," that the government officially accepted child abuse as a problem. The study found that about 53% of children surveyed reported having faced one or more forms of sexual abuse.[12] In most cases, the offender was a family member, near relative, or an acquaintance. Generally, the child victim in such cases does not report these incidents that may occur repeatedly over a period of time. Sexual abuse scars the psyche of the affected child for their entire life.[13] According to the latest government figures, a child is sexually violated every 15 minutes in India.[14] In India, one out of two children are exposed to a form of sexual abuse and one out of five children are exposed to a critical form of such abuse.[15] Between 2005 and 2015, total crime against children increased 529% in India and the incidence of "child rape" and "penetrative sexual assault," including "aggravated penetrative sexual assault," increased by 408%.[16] In 2018, the National Crime Record Bureau (NCRB), which is an Indian government agency responsible for collection and analysation of crime statistics, reported child rape as the main crime committed against children at 34.7%.[17] Crime rate within per lakh child population in 2018 was reported at 31.8% in comparison with 28.9% in 2017.[18] Such reports have exposed the indignity of young children being subjected to sexual vehemence. In a few hapless cases, the sufferers of abuse were as young as infants.[19]

A close glance at crime against children committed in different states reveals that the five largest states, i.e., Uttar Pradesh, Madhya Pradesh, Maharashtra, Delhi, and Bihar account for 51% of all crime in the country.[20] According to a recent report released by the NCRB, 32,608 cases were reported in 2017, whereas 39,827 cases were reported in 2018 under the Protection of Children from Sexual Offences Act (POCSO Act).[21] The highest number of child rapes was recorded in Maharashtra at 2,832, followed by Uttar Pradesh at 2,023, and Tamil Nadu at 1,457.

According to official records, the majority of these abuses are committed by people known to the survivors, such as relatives, neighbours, and employers.[22] These statistics are a grim aide-mémoire of the fact that the government lacks effective implementation of preventive mechanism to address severe violations of children's rights. Our child protection budget is more service absorbed when additional investment is required for prevention, rehabilitation, and restoration of child safekeeping. Numerous attempts to create empathetic environments and premeditated multi-sectoral intervention plans for abused children's relief have not yielded results as anticipated.

Why the high numbers and underreporting?

A major reason behind this shrouded silence is the fact that India is a conservative society where most girls are hesitant to discuss simple topics like menstruation with their mothers. Parents are uncomfortable speaking about puberty, the physical and emotional changes that take place during their growing years, with their children. Hence, it's highly unlikely that a child would feel comfortable discussing sexual abuse that involves being touched in inappropriate places. It is necessary for India to move in the direction of the Netherlands, which has a comprehensive sex education curriculum in schools.[23] Beginning at age four, all children in Dutch schools receive compulsory age-appropriate sexuality education classes. And these classes are not just about the nuts and bolts, so to speak, of sex. The main emphasis is on building respect for one's own and others' sexuality.

Underreporting may also be exacerbated by the socio-cultural norms to not speak unless spoken to. In most conventional families, it is a cultural norm for children to obey their elders and remain silent or "talk less." The socio-cultural milieu of parental rights prevalent in India, involving closely knit patriarchal families, often does not recognize that children are individuals with their own rights and neglects reports by the child on sexual and other forms of abuse.[24] As a serious repercussion of this culture, most forms of sexual abuse that a child undergoes fail to be reported. This silence not only aggravates the distress of abuse survivors and their families, but also emboldens the abusers to continue the abuse and to press their advantage to subject the child to more severe forms of sexual abuse.[25] The survivor and their families are even discouraged to seek redress owing to the fear of indignity, denial from the community, social stigma, not being able to trust government bodies, and gaps in communication between parents and children about this issue.

Another cultural norm predominant in India is that society shields the accused and shifts the blame onto survivors. There is stigmatization towards survivors of abuse and their families, which continues to pressure them into silence. Abuse survivors are socially isolated and forced to drop out of school or to change their school and shift their home. This culture of shame follows survivors into law enforcement, the court system, and hospitals, further silencing survivors' voices.[26]

All too often, if the accused is an influential political or religious leader or has the backing of powerful individuals, even the justice system looks away.[27] This is especially true if the accuser is one who is already marginalized within society, leaving them particularly vulnerable to sexual violence. The "Chennai Horror" case is one such harrowing incident where the parents and the abused child were held accountable for the gruesome gang rape of their 11-year-old "hearing impaired" daughter. She had been repeatedly raped by an entire community of workers between the ages of 23 and 66 years. This incident took place in Chennai at a gated, safe, and secured residential premises.[28]

One of the worst consequences of any sexual assault is when the survivor is blamed by the community instead of ostracizing the perpetrators of such heinous crimes. The parents in this case were blamed for failure to read the red flags and were branded negligent by society. Though 15 of the 18 accused were convicted, the outraged society failed to take into account that the alleged rapists drugged, molested, raped, and threatened the differently abled child of dire consequences if she opened her mouth. Thus, the child and her family suffered collateral consequences of community shame as the community deviated the blame away from their sexually aggressive behaviour. When society behaves in this manner, we are sending the wrong message that rapists will not be held accountable for their actions and that victims are responsible for the abhorrent behaviour of others, which would further fail to deter sexual predators from committing such crimes.

As more child rape cases enter India's criminal justice system, the courts are clogged with pending cases, delaying justice. Furthermore, while the POCSO Act requires Special Courts to try child sexual abuse cases, in practice these courts are either overburdened because they also handle other types of cases or they are not fully functional as a child-friendly court. According to the data of the NCRB, 95% of the rapes are committed by family members. The conviction rate in cases of rape of children is 20% under the POCSO Act.[29] Conviction rates are low because police and prosecutors are susceptible to outside pressures. Long delays in litigation increase the likelihood of threats and intimidation against survivors and their families. This also keeps survivors from moving forward with their lives, quiets them, and even makes them hostile towards the justice system.

The resulting silence around CSA creates situations where children do not even realize that they have been violated unless somebody intervenes. Even more distressing is that once a child musters up the courage to voice their ordeal, they are disbelieved, and the child is deprived of support and immediate medical intervention that is critical for their healing. Such obstructive behaviour augments two or three layers of trauma on top of the abuse of such children. Wracked with guilt and shame, these dejected children often end up becoming terrified, anxious, withdrawn, or belligerent; they become affected with a host of psychological and emotional disorders that some children and adolescents might never overcome.[30] Helping them cope with trauma requires skilled intervention and support from family and society. Rehabilitation of children is the weakest component of the POCSO Act, and poor implementation of services combined with the lack of necessary convergence and coordination make things worse for children.[31]

Actions to decrease CSA in India

India's efforts to prevent the sexual exploitation of children came years after it ratified the CRC; however, rising public consciousness and media reporting has demanded justice and prevention of CSA over the years. In compliance with the global standards of care and protection of children, the National Commission for the Protection of Child Rights (NCPCR) was established in 2005,[32] the Prohibition of Child Marriage Act in 2006,[33] and the Right of Children to Free and Compulsory Education Act in 2009.[34]

Path-breaking legislation for children's protection: POCSO Act

The POCSO Act, which was enacted in 2012,[35] is India's first child-friendly and gender-neutral regulation. It is a legislative shield for protection of children against sexual offences and aims to create a robust legal framework for different agencies to work together as state collaborators to secure justice for sexually abused children. The POCSO Act defines a child as any person below the age of 18 and provides protection to all children from offences such as sexual assault, penetrative sexual assault, and sexual harassment. It also penalizes a person for using a child for pornographic purposes. This comprehensive legislation is a special enactment by the Indian government in compliance with the international standards established by the CRC[36] to protect children from offences of sexual assault, sexual harassment, and pornography.[37] It further sought to safeguard the interests of the child at every stage of the judicial process through child-friendly mechanisms for reporting, recording of evidence, investigation, and speedy trial of offences through special designated Courts.[38]

A positive effect of the POCSO Act is an increase in the reporting of cases.[39] In one such case, an audit was conducted by the Tata Institute of Social Sciences, volunteers of the Muzaffarpur Institutional Home in Bihar, in May 2018. Although this audit, investigation, and charges occurred several years after the enactment of the POCSO Act mandating reporting of CSA,[40] it uncovered a sordid sexual abuse scandal of 40 shelter home girls. The audit triggered a political storm and prompted the state government to bring in the Central Bureau of Investigation.[41] Although the accused, Brajesh Thakur, was there to provide protection to orphaned children, he inflicted scars upon the children that would last for a lifetime. The prolonged silence of the neighbours and members of the child welfare committee due to their fear of Brajesh Thakur's political power made the screams, cries, and misfortunes of these children go unheard and unnoticed for many years.

Stumbling blocks for the effective enactment of the POCSO legislation

Criminalization of consensual sexual acts between minors

Even well-meaning laws can have unintended negative consequences. Consented sex between minors had been a grey area even before the POCSO Act was enforced. For instance, the Supreme Court of India, in the case of *State of Madhya Pradesh v. Balu*[42] held that consent given by a minor is invalid in the eyes of the law. This verdict has been reiterated in many cases of the Supreme Court and subordinate courts over the years. Hence the minor's consent has no bearing under the POCSO Act as well. Accordingly, all adolescent sexual activities, including those that are consensual, are now criminalized. Questions arise as to whether interdiction of consensual adolescent sexual activities has an adverse impact on reproductive and sexual health rights of adolescents. This concern is further intensified by sections 19 and 21 of the POCSO Act, which require that a person, including a health-care provider, who knows or has reason to believe that an offence under the POCSO Act has been or is likely to be committed, must report the same to the police.[43]

In *Sabari v Inspector of Police*,[44] the Madras High Court noted the blanket criminalization of consensual underage sexual acts. It suggested that the POCSO Act be amended to reduce the age of consent from 18 to 16 years. It also recommended the introduction of an age-proximity clause, wherein if the parties were in the same age group, they would be treated differently. Since it was said as *obiter dicta*, it cannot be enforced as law, but it has added persuasive value for future judicial and legislative decisions. The Court considered this a reasonable conclusion after contemplation of the ground realities and post-modern moralities of society. In an analogous context, it is also appropriate to note that the Justice Verma Committee on Amendments to Criminal Law had in fact recommended that the age of consent under the Indian Penal Code (IPC), which is the official criminal code of India, be fixed at 16, and that the POCSO Act be accordingly amended.[45]

Mandatory reporting under the POCSO Act

Section 19(1) of the POCSO Act requires a person who has the knowledge or an apprehension that an offence punishable under the Act has been committed or is likely to be committed to report the same to the police.[46] Failure to report the commission of an offence is a punishable offence under section 21 of the POCSO Act.

In *Kamal Prasad v State of Chhattisgarh*,[47] the interpretation of sections 19 and 21 arose before the Chhattisgarh High Court. A charge sheet had been filed against the headmaster of a school for not reporting an offence of penetrative sexual assault committed against a student by an employee of the school. The grandmother of the child had informed the petitioner around two and a half hours before she filed a complaint against the employee. The High Court held that a prosecution under section 21 cannot be initiated unless the main offence, the unreported penetrative sexual assault in this case, is proved before a criminal court. Hence, it mandated that conviction of the original offender under the POCSO Act is a prerequisite for initiation of an action against a person for not reporting the act once it comes to their knowledge. The Court also advised prosecution agencies to be watchful before initiating prosecutions under section 21.

Although the intent behind mandatory reporting provisions is praiseworthy, this requirement may have an adverse impact on the reproductive and sexual health rights of adolescents and young girls. Since reporting is a prerequisite of section 19, access to contraceptive services for young girls may be undermined. This might compel girls to resort to unsafe abortions, thus endangering their lives. Further, mandatory reporting provisions under the POCSO Act are also in conflict with confidentiality requirements in the Rules under the Medical Termination of Pregnancy Act, 1971.[48]

Marital sex

Exception two to section 375 of the IPC contravened the Convention on the Rights of Child (CRC) and Convention on the Elimination of Discrimination Against Women (CEDAW)[49] by creating an exception to the offence of rape in cases of forced sexual intercourse by a man with his own wife if she is 15 years or older. The exception has not been amended. This resulted in an anomalous situation in which forced sexual intercourse by a husband with a minor wife between the ages of 15 and 18 was permitted.[50] This had adverse repercussions on young girls above the age of 15, who couldn't file a claim of rape against their husbands, as consent was assumed within marriage. However, any sexual act with an unmarried girl under 18 would still be regarded as rape, regardless of whether it was consensual under the POCSO Act. This issue of rape within child marriages, and the contradiction between the IPC and the POCSO Act, was dealt with by the Supreme Court in *Independent Thought v. Union of India*,[51] by a division bench of the Supreme Court of India. In this decision, the Supreme Court interpreted Exception two to section 375 of the IPC as violating Articles 14 and 21 of the Constitution of India, and thereby deemed it unconstitutional, increasing the age of consent to 18, regardless of marital status. This brought the law in line with all other statutes where a child is recognized as a person below the age of 18.[52]

Factors leading to death penalty for child rapists

There has always been a disagreement in both legal circles and civil society about whether the death penalty should be exercised and whether it really acts as a deterrent, especially in child abuse cases. Historically, exercising the death penalty by a court of law in India occurs only in the rarest of cases, where the crime committed is so heinous that it shocks the collective conscience of society. While clemency in sentencing is seen as a specific benefit flowing from a judge-centric approach to justice, severity is unvaryingly in the name of society.

For example, the Indian Supreme Court in *Bachan Singh* held that the death penalty must be awarded only in "*the rarest of the rare*" cases, where "aggravating circumstances" exist, and thus acknowledged the need for proportionate punishment for crimes of varying degrees.[53] The Apex Court in this landmark case laid down that life imprisonment is the rule and death sentence an exception. In yet another case, *Macchi Singh v. State of Punjab*,[54] the Supreme Court condensed the guidelines for applying the doctrine of "rarest of rare" to cases involving death penalty. These guidelines include the manner of commission of a murder, motive, socially abhorrent nature of a crime, magnitude of crime, and the personality of the victim of murder. Since then, the courts balance a variety of infuriating and vindicating situations to determine whether the accused should be given the death penalty or not. The sentencing policy, therefore, needs to strike a balance between the "twin factors" – the deterrent effect and the possibility of reformation of the offender in civil society.

In recent years, horrendous child sexual abuse cases like the *Unnao* and *Kathua* gang rapes emerged, where minor victims were not only brutally gangraped but also callously murdered by the perpetrators of the crime. These cases are just precursors to a surge of child rapes, which jolted people's collective conscience and shook their faith in humanity. The fact that the culprits accused in the most outrageous rapes in the history of the Indian subcontinent "Nirbhaya"[55] were escaping from the death penalty, infuriated the civil society.[56] The rationale for capital punishment has been stated in *Ravi v. State of Maharashtra*,[57] which held that in a criminal trial, the criminal is punished according to the nature and gravity of the crime. If for heinous crimes the most deterring punishment is not given, then concern arises that ultimately there will be no deterrence left in society.

When considering death penalty in India, we must remember that there is a significant population, hence it is challenging to settle whether the death penalty is acting as a deterrent or not. There are many people who might refrain from committing such crimes due to the severity of punishment, but there are many others, who would be encouraged to kill the victim to escape from getting caught. The ugly truth is that children are still getting raped, society is increasingly enraged, and immediate steps to address this aggravating issue have to be taken. Hence, legitimate amendments to the POCSO Act were carried out in 2019, which now require the investigation and trial of child rape cases to be completed in 90 days. The government allows capital punishment for anyone convicted of raping children under the age of 12.[58] India also voted against the UN General Assembly's draft resolution proposing a ban on the death penalty embargo,[59] as it goes against the statutory law of the country in which an execution is carried out in the "rarest of rare" cases. By doing so, India became the 13th nation in the world to impose the death penalty for child rapists.

Although welcomed by many, the new amendment has also been criticized by a number of academics, NGOs, judges, and legal practitioners, who have questioned whether the death penalty is really an effective deterrent or likely to worsen the plight of victims of CSA. In its 262 report,[60] the Law Commission of India concluded that there was no evidence to suggest that the deterrent effect of the death penalty was any better than that of life imprisonment. In its 2016 report,[61] titled *Crime in India*, the NCRB revealed that the conviction rate under the POCSO Act is an abysmal 28.9% and pendency in cases of child rape was 89.6%. *The Death Penalty in India: Annual Statistics 2018* report, released by the Delhi-based National Law University's research group Project 39A, revealed that Maharashtra accounted for the second highest number of death penalty verdicts, 16, while courts in Karnataka and Uttar Pradesh handed out 15 each. As of December 31, 2018, the report points out that 426 convicts were on death row. Of these, 46%, i.e., 198 convicts, were from three states – Madhya Pradesh, Uttar Pradesh, and Maharashtra – each of which had 66 death row prisoners.

However, we cannot overlook the fact that a large number of child rape cases still go unreported, coupled with poor case disposal and lower conviction rates. Moreover, there are no witness and victim protection programmes[62] in place, and no probe has been made into the functioning of Child Welfare Committees[63] set up by the government. This situation often ends in embitterment as victims must wait years before they get justice. What we actually need is child-friendly investigation and court procedures in letter and spirit, robust victim protection programmes, an efficient criminal justice system, sensitized police officers, and an environment that encourages children to report sexual abuse. Imposing stringent punishments become meaningless if the law remains a mere dead letter. In the long run, only time will tell whether death penalty will act as deterrence.

To summarize, the verdict in *Ravi v. State of Maharashtra*[64] suggests a path that India must follow. It states:

> One cannot argue about the abolition of death sentence citing violation of human rights of the offenders; doing away with the penalty harms the interests of the society. Hence, neither should the Court recklessly hand out death sentences nor should it follow the "reverence for life" principle by the book. The punishment before all things must be befitting the nature of crime and deterrent with an explicit aim to make an example out of the evil-doer and a warning to those who are still innocent.

Additional measures to harmonize and reinforce child protection procedures

Ensure child participation

We cannot see things from our perspective and our sense of justice; rather, we need to look at it from the child's perspective. The best way to determine what is right for children is by making them part of the conversation and listening to them. It is now well-established that any intervention for children also needs to recognize age-appropriateness and their evolving capacity along with what would be in their best interests.

Increase financial investments on children

Sufficient funds in health, nutrition, education (early grade learning and elementary), and protection systems should be invested to help in the growth and development of all deprived and marginalized children.

Capture disaggregated and issue-based data on children

The government and civil society should make greater investments to create reliable multiple data sources, by using a comprehensive surveillance system, which would enhance the scope of accurate monitoring of incidents of sexual abuse and prudent steps required to address them adequately.

Facilitate multi-stakeholders approach

A long-term, sustainable, synchronized, and inclusive approach is required to ensure child protection and the onus lies with the state governments, police departments, the judicial system, medical fraternity, civil society, and private sector to work collectively and create a supportive environment full of empathy, kindness, and compassion for the holistic development of children.

Strengthen online abuse prevention mechanism

While many nations have already taken the plunge into the depths of the digital world, India is still grappling with Child Sexual Abuse Materials (CSAM) invading the digital platform like they never have. Of the overall internet population, 433 million are of age 12 years and above, and 71 million are of age 5–11 years, who access the internet on the devices of family members, as per the *Internet & Mobile Association of India*'s (IAMAI) *Digital in India* report.[65] Data from Pornhub, the world's largest pornography website in the world, revealed that during lockdown, traffic from India has increased by 95% between March 24 and 26, 2020, as compared with their average traffic, pre-COVID-19.[66] Pitifully, Indian enforcement authorities struggle with minimal tools, tracking resources, and expertise to locate online offenders. What is more worrisome is that India neither has a ministry of internet safety nor e-Safety Commissioners that are crucial to crack down on offensive websites steering a multi-million market that trades in children's dignity. The Government of India must urgently crack down on child pornography and also initiate a global dialogue for an international convention against child sexual abuse material. India must show urgency to develop a robust framework for the protection of children from online abuse and ensure privacy, safety, and confidentiality of data.

Conclusion

From being ignorant to hesitant, and from officially acknowledging to bravely addressing the vortex of sexual exploitation of our children, India has come a long way and still has a long way to go. Celebrating the 30th Anniversary of the UN CRC, India has not only made its official mandate to ensure the best interests of the child, but also has taken pragmatic steps to curb abuse. It is also true that government and law alone cannot bring about desirable social change in any society. Robust laws would hold limited bearing in reducing crimes against children unless they are accompanied by a change in the attitudes of the police, government officers, and members of the judiciary and of society at large. Education initiatives, mass awareness drives, sensitization of all stakeholders, inclusion of skilled intervention experts, effective audit processes, scientific investigations, better policing, and gender sensitization of youth are also necessary. Let us act now! Tomorrow may be too late!

Notes

1 Mannat Mohanjeet Singh et al., *An Epidemiological Overview of Child Sexual Abuse*, 3(4) J. Fam. Med. Prim. Care 430–435 (2014). doi:10.4103/2249-4863.148139.
2 *Id.*
3 United Nations Convention on the Rights of the Child, Nov. 20, 1989, http://www.ohchr.org/en/professionalinterest/pages/crc.asp (hereinafter CRC).
4 Ministry of Women and Child Development, *Report of the Working Group on Child Rights for the 12th Five Year Plan* (2012–2017).
5 Human Rights Watch, *Breaking the Silence. Child Sexual Abuse in India* (2013).
6 Vikas Choudhry et al., *Child Sexual Abuse in India: A Systematic Review*, 13 PLoS ONE e0205086–e0205086 (2018), https://pubmed.ncbi.nlm.nih.gov/30300379.
7 Inter-Parliamentary Union and UNICEF, *Child Protection: A Handbook for Parliamentarians* (2004).
8 Deepti Susan George, *Children's Rights Under the Constitution*, Legal Serv. India http://www.legalservicesindia.com/article/285/Children-Rights-under-the-Constitution.html (last visited on Aug. 25, 2020).
9 Hum. Rts. Watch, *supra* note 5.
10 Ministry of women and Child Dev., *Study on Child Abuse: India* (2007). wcd.nic.in/childabuse.pdf.
11 P.M. Nair & S. Sen, *Trafficking in women and children in India* (Orient Blackswan, 2005).
12 Ministry of women and Child Development, *supra* note 10.
13 A.K. Shrivastava, S.B. Karia, S.S. Sonavane, A.A. De Sousa, Child Sexual Abuse and the Development of Psychiatric Disorders: A Neurobiological Trajectory of Pathogenesis, 26(1) Ind. Psychiatry J. 4–12 (2017 Jan–Jun).
14 *India Sexual Abuse: 'Four Child Victims Every Hour'*, BBC (Dec. 1, 2017) https://www.bbc.com/news/world-asia-india-42193533.
15 P.B. Behere et al., *Sexual Abuse in Women with Special Reference to Children: Barriers, Boundaries and Beyond*. 55(4) Ind. J. Psychiatry 316 (2013). doi:10.4103/0019-5545.120535.
16 Bharti Ali et al., *Implementation of the POCSO Act-Goals, Gaps and Challenges: Study of Cases of Special Courts in Delhi & Mumbai* (2012–2015) (HAQ: Center for Child Rights, 2017).
17 *Crime up by 1.3% as 50 lakh New Cases Filed: NCRB*, New Indian Express (Jan. 9, 2020), https://www.newindianexpress.com.
18 Nat'l Crime Records Bureau, *Crime in India* (2018), www.https.ncrb.gov.in.
19 *4 Month Baby Raped and Murdered in Indore: Madhya Pradesh Hangs its Head in Shame*, Times of India (Apr. 21, 2018). https://www.timesofindia.indiatimes.com.
20 *Indian Children Remain as Unprotected as Ever; NCRB records 388 Crimes against Them Each Day*, India Educ. Diary (Jan. 14, 2020), https://www.indiaeducationdiary.in.
21 Nat'l Crime Records Bureau, *supra* note 18.
22 *Child Sexual Abuse*, Vikaspedia, https://vikaspedia.in/social-welfare/women-and-child-development/child-development-1/resources-on-safe-childhood-for-panchayat-members/child-sexual-abuse-1 (last visited Sep. 24, 2020).
23 Laurel Avery, *Sex Education in the Netherlands-Dutch Review*, Dutch Rev. (Dec. 2, 2019), https://dutchreview.com/expat/education/sex-education-in-the-netherlands/.
24 *Id.* at 2.
25 *Id.* at 12.
26 *Sexual Violence in India*, Equality Now, https://www.equalitynow.org/learn_more_sexual_violence_in_india (Last visited on Sep. 24, 2020).
27 Meenakshi Ganguly, *South Asia Failing to Address Its Child Rape Problem*, Hum. Rts. Watch (Feb. 11, 2020), https://www.hrw.org/news/2020/02/11/south-asia-failing-address-its-child-rape-problem.

28 *Chennai Horror Hearing Impaired 11-year-old Girl Raped by over 20 Men for 7 Months 18 Nabbed* (July 17, 2018), https://www.india.com/news/india/chennai-horror-hearing-impaired-11-year-old-girl-raped-by-over-20-men-for-seven-months-18-nabbed-3170542/.

29 *Less Than 20 per cent of POCSO Cases End in Conviction, Reveals Data*, DT Next (Sep. 25, 2018) https://www.dtnext.in/News/City/2018/09/25005027/1089738/Less-than-20-per-cent-of-POCSO-cases-end-in-conviction-.vpf.

30 David Carson et al., *Child Sexual Abuse in India: Current Issues and Research*, Psych. Stud. 318 (2013).

31 Bharti Ali, *Rehabilitation and Victim Compensation for Child Victims of Sexual Abuse* (Jan. 5, 2020) (HAQ Centre for Child Rights presented for the Nat'l Jud. Acad., Bhopal).

32 Commissions for the Protection of Child Rts. (CPCR) Act 2005.

33 Prohibition of Child Marriage Act, 2006.

34 Right of Child. to Free & Compulsory Educ. Act, 2009.

35 Protection of Child. from Sexual Offences Act (POCSO), 2012.

36 CRC, *supra* note 3.

37 POCSO, *supra* note 35.

38 POCSO, *supra* note 35, at § 39.

39 Nat'l Crime Records Bureau, *Crime in India* (2015), https://www.ncrb.gov.in.

40 POCSO, *supra* note 35, at § 39.

41 Aman Sharma, *How TISS Team Blew the Lid off Bihar Sexual Abuse Case*, Econ. Times (Jul. 31, 2018), https://economictimes.indiatimes.com/news/politics-and-nation/how-tiss-team-blew-the-lid-off-bihar-sexual-abuse-case/articleshow/65219173.cms?from=mdr.

42 State of Madhya Pradesh v. Balu, SC Appeal (Crl.) 1273 of 2004.

43 POCSO, *supra* note 35, at §§ 19, 20.

44 *Sabari v. Inspector of Police*, AIR 2018 SC 490.

45 Justice Verma et al., *Report of the Committee on Amendments to Criminal Law*, 444 (2013).

46 POCSO, *supra* note 35, at § 19(1).

47 Writ Petition (Criminal) No. 8/2016, High Court of Chhattisgarh.

48 Dipika Jain, *Conflicting Abortion Laws in India: Unintended Barriers to Safe Abortion for Adolescent Girls*, 4 Indian J. Med. Ethics 4 (2019).

49 Convention on the Elimination of All Form of Discrimination Against Women (CEDAW) G.A. Res. 34/180, 34 U.N. GAOR, Supp. No. 46, U.N. Doc. A/34/46, at 193 (Dec. 18, 1979).

50 *Exception to Rape within Child Marriages*, Supreme Court Observer (Sep. 11, 2017).

51 *Id.*

52 *Supra* note 33; *supra* note 34; *supra* note 35.

53 *Bachan Singh v State of Punjab* (1980) 2 SCC 684.

54 *Machhi Singh v. State of Punjab* (1983) 3 SCC 470.

55 *Nirbhaya Case: Chronology of Events and How the Case Unfolded*, Free Press J. (May 5, 2017), https://www.freepressjournal.in/cmcm/nirbhaya-case-chronology-of-events-and-how-the-case-unfolded.

56 Out of six accused in Nirbhaya case, one committed suicide in prison, four were hung on March 20, 2020 after seven and a half years of trial in fast-track Court and the juvenile who committed maximum atrocity on the victim, served only three years imprisonment.

57 Ravi v. State of Maharashtra (2019) 9 SCC 622.

58 *India Introduces Death Penalty for Child Rapists*, BBC (Apr. 21, 2018).

59 Athit Perawongmetha, *India Votes Against UN General Assembly Draft Resolution on Death Penalty Embargo*, Reuters (Nov. 14, 2018), https://scroll.in/latest/902079/india-votes-against-un-general-assembly-draft-resolution-on-death-penalty-embargo.

60 Law Commission of India Report 262, http://lawcommissionofindia.nic.in/reports/report262.pdf.
61 Nat'l Crime Records Bureau, *Crime in India* (2016).
62 *Asaram Case Highlights Need Witness and Victim Protection in India*, https://www.hrw.org/news/2018/.
63 Kavita Kishore, *Child Welfare Committee Kept in Dark over Child Sexual Abuse* (May 11, 2013), https://www.thehindu.com/news/national/other-states/child-welfare-committee-kept-in-dark-over-child-sexual-abuse/article4706795.ece.
64 Ravi v. State of Maharashtra (2019) 9 SCC 622.
65 India Has Over 500 Million Active Internet Users, 14% 5–11 years: IMAI, *Internet & Mobile Association of India's* (IAMAI) *Digital in India* (May 5, 2020), https://www.business-standard.com/article/technology/india-has-over-500-million-active-internet-users-14-in-5-11-yrs-iamai.
66 IANS, *Demand for Child Pornography in India Spiked since Lockdown: ICPF* (Apr. 14, 2020), https://ciso.economictimes.indiatimes.com/news/demand-for-child-pornography-in-india-spiked-since-lockdown-icpf/75127959.

19 Dutch strategies for combating child poverty

A child rights-based approach

Merel Jonker, Jet Tigchelaar, Catrin Finkenauer, Kirsten Visser, and Gonneke Stevens

Introduction

The Netherlands is one of the wealthiest countries in the world.[1] Nevertheless, according to the Netherlands Institute for Social Research (SCP), the poverty rate amongst children had increased from 8% in 2007 to approximately 11% in 2014.[2] In 2015, the Committee on the Rights of the Child had expressed its concern with regard to "the substantial increase in poverty among children in the Netherlands, in particular children in single-parent families and children in welfare dependent families."[3] Although the current figures show a decrease in poverty, approximately 8% of the children in the Netherlands lived in poverty in 2018.[4] Living in poverty affects children's emotional and social development, and may lead to health problems and social exclusion.[5] Furthermore, children who grow up in poverty are more likely to experience poverty as adults.[6]

As a state party to the United Nations Convention of the Rights of the Child (CRC), the Dutch government is obliged to follow the mandate of Article 27 to "recognize the right of every child to a standard of living adequate for the child's physical, mental, spiritual, moral, and social development." This right has to be considered in connection with Article 6(2) of the CRC, which obliges state parties to ensure the survival and development of the child to the maximum extent possible.[7] Furthermore, the right to an adequate standard of living is laid down in several other international conventions,[8] which the Netherlands has signed and ratified. In other words, the Dutch government is obliged to take measures to combat child poverty. As a result of the above-mentioned concerns, combating child poverty was one of the aims of the Dutch Government Agreement (*regeerakkoord*) in 2017.[9] The governmental strategy to reach this aim was published in 2018.[10]

For many years, economists and social security specialists examined (child) poverty from a predominantly material approach, in which income was taken as a key factor to define poverty and children were not seen as individuals, but as a member of their family or household.[11] As such, child poverty was seen as a consequence of family poverty.[12] Therefore, measures to reduce child poverty were, and still are, often aimed at parents, i.e., measures aimed to increase the involvement of parents in paid labour.[13] Furthermore, social security for families functions as a safety net for children. However, since the signing of the CRC, children are more often recognized by legislators as individuals with their own rights. Moreover, child poverty is understood as more than a lack of income, and includes deprivation of social services. As a result, the understanding of how to address child poverty has changed over the years from a more material approach to a more child rights-based approach.[14] According to UNICEF, this focus on the child rights-based approach resulted from a "growing recognition that needs-based or service-delivery approaches have failed to substantially reduce child poverty."[15]

A child rights-based approach is derived from the more general human rights-based approach, which is a normative framework to promote and protect human rights. Applying a human rights-based approach means that the norms, standards, and principles of international human rights are integrated in the process of policies and strategies.[16] There is no single human/child rights-based approach. However, common features of most approaches are the linkage to human rights – both in their interrelatedness and interdependency – and the principles of participation, non-discrimination, empowerment, and accountability.[17] Of course, with regard to children, the linkage to children's human rights and integration of the four main principles of the CRC – the right to life, survival, and development, the right to participate, non-discrimination, and adherence to the best interests of the child – are of importance.[18] Combining a general human rights and more specific child rights approach in a broadly conceived child rights-based approach allows for the implementation of holistic policies that takes children's rights, the four core principles of the CRC, and empowerment and accountability into account.

The question arises whether the measures taken by the Dutch government to combat child poverty are in line with this broad child rights-based approach. This chapter evaluates the strategies of the Dutch state for combating child poverty in light of a child rights-based approach.

The introductory section describes the international general human rights and specific children's rights provisions on the right to an adequate standard of living and related rights. This enables a linkage of a poverty policy to children's rights and to the right to life, survival, and development as fundamental to the CRC. The next section examines the way the principles of participation, non-discrimination, adherence to the best interests of the child, empowerment, and accountability play a role in the human and child rights-based approach. The combination of these two sections provides the criteria for a child rights-based approach to assess poverty reduction policies in the Netherlands. In order to gain some insight into the implementation of the right to an adequate standard of living in the Netherlands, the next section addresses the Dutch legal context and policy aims of the past five years. In the final section, we apply the assessment criteria in order to evaluate the extent to which the Netherlands follows a child rights-based approach concerning the implementation of the right to an adequate standard of living.

International rights on an adequate standard of living for a child

Having an adequate standard of living is a prerequisite for a child's development. The right to an adequate standard of living is laid down in, among others, the following human right documents: Article 25 of the Universal Declaration of Human Rights (UDHR), Article 11 in the International Covenant on Economic, Social and Cultural Rights (ICESCR), Article 34 in the Charter of Fundamental Rights of the EU (CFR), Articles 12–14, 16–17 and 30 of the European Social Charter (ESC), and Articles 26–27 in the CRC.

While the UDHR, the ICESCR, and the CFR generally protect the human rights of every person, Article 17 of the ESC also includes specific provisions to guarantee the rights of children and young persons to social, legal, and economic protection. The main aim of this provision is to "ensure the effective exercise of the right of children and young persons to grow up in an environment which encourages the full development of their personality and of their physical and mental capacities." In addition, Article 30 of the ESC provides for a right to protection against poverty and social exclusion. This right encompasses more than a material safeguard (e.g., through social security), since it includes the positive obligation for states to take measures against social exclusion.[19]

Two other main provisions that apply specifically to children are Articles 26 and 27 of the CRC. The right of every child to benefit from social security, including social insurance, is laid down in Article 26 of the CRC. Article 27, paragraph 1 of the CRC recognizes the right of every child to a standard of living adequate for the child's physical, mental, spiritual, moral, and social development. While there is an overlap between Articles 26 and 27 of the CRC and other human rights instruments with regard to the right to an adequate standard of living, it is clear that these provisions of the CRC translate general human rights to the specific circumstances of children. Article 27 of the CRC, for example, explicitly connects the right to an adequate standard of living as instrumental to the child's broadly formulated development, thus not only including a specific child's right, but relating it also to the fundamental principle of the development of the child.

It is unclear what the right to social security in Article 26 of the CRC entails. The CRC Committee has not yet adopted a General Comment on this right and the *travaux préparatoires* provide little guidance. It only indicates that this Article should be interpreted in line with Article 9 of the ICESCR.[20] The latter describes this right as follows:

> The right to social security encompasses the right to access and maintain benefits, whether in cash or in kind, without discrimination in order to secure protection, *inter alia*, from (a) lack of work-related income caused by sickness, disability, maternity, employment injury, unemployment, old age, or death of a family member; (b) unaffordable access to health care; (c) insufficient family support, particularly for children and adult dependents.[21]

Interestingly, Article 26 of the CRC implies that children have a direct right to social security, while children are rarely the direct beneficiaries of social security benefits.[22] The right of every child to a standard of living adequate for the child's physical, mental, spiritual, moral, and social development provided in Article 27 means that children should not only have a right to a minimum standard of living necessary for a child's physical development, but that they should also have enough means to be able to develop "to the maximum extent"[23] and to their "fullest potential,"[24] also with regard to the other aspects of development.[25] UNICEF mentions that all kinds of children's rights – like the freedom of expression, the right to information, their rights to enjoy their culture and religion, and rights regarding education – contribute to children's social, moral, mental, and spiritual development.[26] Consequently, the adequate standard of living is more than material welfare and an assessment of the implementation of this right "should not be reduced to exclusively economic indicators," but additionally has to identify the conditions that are of importance to the child's development in a holistic sense.[27] This includes a safe and healthy local environment, opportunities for forming and maintaining friendships and supportive key adults.[28] The broad approach to the child's development right requires the involvement of different parts of government in order to develop an integrated approach of the relevant children's rights.

Although the parent(s) or others responsible for the child have the primary responsibility to secure, within their abilities and financial capacities, the conditions of living necessary for the child's development,[29] the state has to take appropriate measures to assist parents and others responsible for the child to implement this right and, in case of need, provide material assistance and support programmes.[30] These elements of Article 27 indicate that the assistance of the state should not be limited to financial resources, but should also empower parents or other caretakers with the skills, tools, and information necessary to take responsibility.[31] Furthermore, the Committee states that the interpretation of Article 27 of the CRC is not limited to measures to assist parents or others responsible for the child, but should be interpreted as to assist children directly.[32]

The right to an adequate standard of living is a socio-economic right. Article 4 of the CRC indicates that with regard to economic, social, and cultural rights, states' parties shall undertake all appropriate legislative, administrative, and other measures for implementation to the maximum extent of their available resources and, where needed, within the framework of international cooperation. The CRC Committee has clarified that "regressive measures may only be considered after assessing all other options and ensuring that children are the last to be affected, especially children in vulnerable situations."[33] States must demonstrate that such regressive measures "are necessary, reasonable, proportionate, non-discriminatory, and temporary and that any rights thus affected will be restored as soon as possible."[34] The state may choose what measures it takes, so it has some discretion, but these measures should be appropriate and effective to secure the enjoyment of the rights of the child. States need to have a national strategy for the implementation of these rights.[35]

In summary, in order to provide an adequate standard of living for the child's development, states should have a national strategy that combines appropriate and effective legislative, administrative, and other measures that provide children with more than positive economic indicators. These measures should provide a broad and holistic approach to children's development with a supportive environment that allows for social inclusion and direct assistance to parents and children.

We have focused on two principles of a human/child rights-based approach: an explicit linkage to interrelated human and child rights, with a focus on Article 27 of the CRC and the right to development of the child. In the next section, the remaining principles of a human/child rights-based approach will complement these two principles.

A child rights-based approach

In this section, the principles of participation, empowerment, accountability, non-discrimination, and the best interests of the child will be translated to the context of children and child poverty. In this way, these principles (in addition to the ones discussed in the Introduction) of a child rights-based approach can be used as a framework for the implementation of an anti-child poverty strategy, more specifically of the right to an adequate standard of living of children.

Participation, in the context of Article 12 of the CRC, can be understood as the right of children to express their views freely in all matters that affect them. This right can extend to policy matters, and consequently, children should be involved in the decision-making processes concerning a child poverty strategy.

Closely related to participation is *empowerment*. In terms of empowerment, states have the obligation to take appropriate measures for children who are affected by policies, and to encourage children and others who may have knowledge about children's situations, to participate in the decision-making process related to such policies[36] and to provide for effective legal remedies to redress violations of children's rights.[37] Such effective remedies relate to the principle of *accountability*, which aims to ensure that the obligations of policymakers are anchored in an accountable relationship with children. States need to safeguard the effective exercise of the rights of the child. Accountability requires mechanisms to ensure the fulfilment of entitlements as well as opportunities to address denials and violations: creating formal (political, administrative, and quasi-judicial) and informal accountability of the state as a duty bearer to children for children's rights.[38] This already plays a role in the decision-making processes and may entail, among others, monitoring mechanisms, complaint procedures, civil society organizations that mobilize and empower the demand for accountability, and independent oversight bodies.[39]

It is often legally impossible for children to claim their rights before the court,[40] and even if possible, not easy for a child to access justice and enforce the right to an adequate standard of living before the court. However, the CRC Committee has emphasized that states have to ensure "effective, child sensitive procedures for children and their representatives."[41] Therefore, Sedletzki argues that independent human rights institutions for children constitute a major instrument to strengthen accountability.[42] In addition, Graziani states that if "their representatives" is interpreted broadly, a children's rights NGO could start litigation, although this may have its limitations,[43] or file a complaint in the name of children in order to claim their rights.[44]

Relevant for ***non-discrimination*** in the context of child poverty is that these processes can reinforce each other: discrimination can cause poverty and living in poverty can cause discrimination. This reciprocity should be considered when formulating an anti-poverty strategy. Therefore, stigmatization needs to be prevented. In addition, an anti-poverty strategy must pay special attention to identifying and giving priority to marginalized and disadvantaged groups, such as children with disabilities and refugee children.[45] Thus, the implementation of non-discrimination requires an "active" approach of the government to create equal chances for children and to eliminate discrimination against certain groups of children.[46]

One of the core principles of the CRC is adherence to *the best interests of the child*. This principle aims to ensure "both the full and effective enjoyment of all the rights recognized in the Convention and the holistic development of the child."[47] The concept of the child's best interests is a threefold concept: it is a substantive right, a fundamental interpretative legal principle, and a rule of procedure. The substantive right entails the right of the child

> to have his or her best interests assessed and taken as a primary consideration when different interests are being considered in order to reach a decision on the issue at stake, and the guarantee that this right will be implemented whenever a decision is to be made concerning a child, a group of identified or unidentified children, or children in general.[48]

The legal interpretative principle seems to be included in the child rights-based approach, as these interdependent rights provide the framework for interpretation. For a policy on child poverty and, more specifically, for the implementation of the right to an adequate standard of living, the procedural aspect of the best interests of the child seems to have most relevance. After all, the decision-making process regarding such an implementation policy must include an evaluation of the possible impact – positive or negative – of the decision on the child or children concerned. Furthermore, the justification for a decision should include explicit insight to the fact that the substantive right of the best interests of the child is taken into account and how this is done. According to the CRC Committee, the latter entails that the state explains "what has been considered to be in the child's best interests; what criteria it is based on; and how the child's interests have been weighed against other considerations."[49]

We have discussed a child rights-based approach to a child poverty reduction policy that considers the best interest of the child explicitly and includes the principles of participation, empowerment, accountability and non-discrimination. To summarize, such an approach must evaluate the possible impact on children, must facilitate children and their representatives to participate in the decision-making process and in child-sensitive procedures, must provide for effective legal redress for violations of children's rights and should give priority to marginalized and disadvantaged groups of children. In order to examine the extent to which these elements of a child rights-based approach are recognizable in the Dutch policy of child poverty reduction, we will first describe the existing Dutch policy and analyse it in light of this child rights-based approach.

National context: The Netherlands

In the Netherlands, the fundamental right to an adequate standard of living is laid down in Article 20 of the Dutch Constitution. Several acts aim to safeguard this right.[50] However, at the legislative level, children seem to have an indirect right to an adequate standard of living, as a member of a family. The right to social security and the amount of this benefit, for example, depend on the household they are living in. Minors do not have an individual right to social security. The Netherlands made an important reservation towards Article 26 of the CRC, in that the Dutch law shall not imply an independent entitlement of children to social security, including social insurance. The Dutch government states that, in the Netherlands, the right of children to social benefits is adequately safeguarded through their parents or other caretakers.

At the same time, child poverty has a prominent place on the political agenda, both at a national and local level. Due to decentralization, municipalities have a growing responsibility (and discretion) regarding their local poverty strategy. At a national level, combating child poverty was one of the main aims of the Dutch Government Agreement (*regeerakkoord*) in 2017.[51] In the same year, two important advisory reports on child poverty were published in the Netherlands. The first report, *Growing Up Without Poverty* (*Opgroeien zonder armoede*) was presented by the Social and Economic Council of the Netherlands (SER) and the second report *Creating Opportunities for All Children to Succeed* (*Alle kinderen kansrijk*) was initiated by the Netherlands' Ombudsman for Children.[52] As a reaction to the two reports, the government explained its national strategy extensively in a letter to the parliament in 2018[53] and examined possibilities to develop qualitative and quantitative poverty-reduction aims. In its letter, the government explicitly refers to its international obligations based on the human rights framework. It aims at reducing child poverty by tackling the structural causes of poverty and announces measures to reduce the negative consequences of poverty, thereby explicitly recognizing the importance of eliminating poverty for the child's development and to enable the child's participation in society.

First, according to the government, the most effective and appropriate strategy is to combat the *structural causes* of child poverty. Therefore, measures are taken to increase parental labour market participation.[54] The government intends, for example, to increase the difference between receiving the minimum wage and social benefits, which would stimulate parents to work. Furthermore, measures are taken to minimalize the number of parents in debt and to prevent debt. Interestingly, the government hardly mentions the possibility of changing the child benefit policies. It only states that parents with a low income will profit from the increased general child benefit and childcare benefit. However, it is not indicated why other child benefit policies are not considered. This might change in the near future. In 2020, the Netherlands Bureau for Economic Policy Analysis (CPB) published a report in which it describes and analyses approximately 60 policy measures to reduce poverty. In regard to child poverty, not only are there several options to directly increase child benefits, but there are also other policy measures that may reduce child poverty, such as increasing the budget for preschool education and investing in additional language, grammar, and mathematics education for children who lag behind. Furthermore, the CPB analysed the possibility to invest in physical and mental health of children.

Second, the government aims at preventing negative consequences of growing up in a low-income family. It is stressed that children should not be the victim of their parents' financial situation. The primary responsibility to ensure this lies with the Dutch municipalities with the central government supporting them. The focus of the central government is primarily investing in child development and education.

To further the development of children, the government has provided an extra €85 million to municipalities since 2017, specifically for children living in poverty. These resources are intended to provide "child packages," in-kind facilities to children (e.g., sports gear, musical instruments, school equipment, clothing, or transportation) who are currently unable to participate in school, sports, cultural, and social activities due to poverty. The central government has made administrative agreements with the municipalities on how these funds are to be spent. The midterm evaluation in 2018 of this programme showed that nine out of ten municipalities had used the allocated budget.[55] In 92% of the municipalities, at least part of the budget was spent on the child poverty policy. However, in 55% of the municipalities, part of the funds was also used for more general poverty policies not specifically aimed at children and for other general domains, such as education, sports, or culture. Furthermore, municipalities invested, although indirectly, in the reduction of intergenerational transmission of poverty by providing information and prevention strategies, like healthy lifestyle programmes, debt-prevention courses, and organizing connections with supportive families and buddies in the neighbourhood. While the in-kind services are meant to increase the inclusion of children in fighting poverty, the government also stresses the importance of giving children the opportunity to contribute and discuss anti-poverty policy matters that concern them. The ministry financially supported several projects that actively involve children in the shaping of their local poverty strategy.[56]

Additionally, the national government focuses on education to alleviate poverty. More budget is available to create equal chances through pre-school education. Schools are also viewed as an important place to identify children living in poverty and can play an important role in improving the accessibility of the target group for poverty reduction. The Secretary of State, together with the Minister for Primary and Secondary Education and Media, will explore how schools, municipalities, and possibly other parties can receive specific support for issues related to poverty that are identified in schools. The government also subsidizes educational projects that focus on promoting the financial skills of children and young people.

Qualitative and quantitative reduction aims

Besides the policy aims mentioned above, the government has developed qualitative and quantitative poverty reduction aims. In April 2019, four aims were formulated:[57]

1 All children who live in poverty should be able to participate in social activities in order to develop and to prevent social exclusion. The aim of the government is to reach 100% of the children in families who receive social assistance and 70% of the children who live in a low-income family by 2021 in order to offer them the possibility to apply for a "child package" as mentioned above.
2 Reducing the number of low-income households by reducing income taxes and increasing tax credits.
3 Providing insight periodically in how children experience poverty, focusing on the obstacles to a promising upbringing, like psychological health, societal isolation, and low literacy.
4 Sharing best practices between municipalities on how to combat child poverty and the negative consequences of poverty.

The described aims of the Dutch government give an insight into the priorities and plans, which will be reflected from a child rights-based approach in the following.

A child rights-based approach in the Netherlands

Based on the international child rights provision of Article 27 of the CRC, children have a right to an adequate standard of living, which encompasses the opportunity of children to develop to their full potential. While parents have a primary responsibility towards children, states have a secondary responsibility to respect, protect, and fulfill this right by ensuring an effective anti-poverty strategy. This means that the Dutch government is obliged to take appropriate and effective legislative, administrative, and other measures for implementation of the right of the child to an adequate standard of living. This chapter does not aim at answering the question of whether the measures taken by the central government are effective; however, it is possible to reflect on the question of whether the announced measures are appropriate in the sense that they adhere to the main features of a child rights-based approach. Based on a child rights-based approach, the implementation of policies should take into account an integrated approach of child rights, the four principles of the CRC – non-discrimination; adherence to the best interests of the child; the right to life, survival, and development; and the right to participate – and the principles of empowerment and accountability.

The Dutch strategy should include an integrated approach to safeguard not only financial welfare, but also the development of the child. The emphasis of the current strategy lies on the structural causes of poverty, aiming at the income positions of parents, and is not directly targeted at children, as should be the case based on Article 26 of the CRC. Since the Netherlands has made a reservation to this Article, the Dutch government is not obliged to safeguard a direct right on social security. Nevertheless, this gives rise to a lot of debate in the Netherlands;[58] would it make a difference if the Dutch government were to withdraw its reservation? NGOs argue that in certain situations, for example, in the case of children of undocumented residents or children of parents who are evicted, it should be possible for children to have a direct right to social security. At the same time, children are directly addressed in the anti-poverty strategy when it comes to reducing the consequences of living in poverty. The Dutch government seems aware of the fact that living in poverty may affect children's development. Measures are implemented to ensure that all children can participate in social activities, which enables them to experience their environment as safe, supportive, and socially inclusive. Providing for in-kind items for children who are living in poverty might reduce their social exclusion immediately. One must keep in mind, however, that these measures may reduce some of the consequences of poverty but are not a structural solution to prevent poverty. Investing in pre-school education can be regarded as a preventive measure that illustrates both an integrated approach of child's rights in relation to the development of the child and an attempt to create equal chances for children, safeguarding the non-discrimination principle. Educating children of marginalized and disadvantaged groups before the age of four might narrow down the differences between children when they start primary school.

Furthermore, a child rights-based approach would facilitate children and others who are knowledgeable of their situation to participate in the decision-making process. The government documents show an awareness of the rights of children to participate in matters that concern them, including anti-poverty policies. At a central level, a budget is reserved for projects that involve children in shaping local poverty strategies. Municipalities, however, have discretion on how to design their local strategy, and only a limited number of municipalities have children participate in and offer opinions on local poverty strategies.[59] Nevertheless, as was the case before the new anti-poverty strategy, children might be represented indirectly through organizations like the Dutch Children's Ombudsman or the Dutch National Youth Council (Nationale Jeugdraad) that advise the government on the child anti-poverty strategy. It can be concluded that the Dutch government is at least aware of the fact that children should participate in the policymaking process. More research, however, is needed to evaluate the initiatives that are taken. Do all children have the opportunity to participate? How are their opinions included in the strategies?

As previously mentioned, other important and closely related features of a child rights-based approach are creating accountability and empowerment. In their anti-poverty strategy, no provisions are provided for changing complaint procedures or independent oversight bodies. Nevertheless, several independent oversight bodies exist in the Netherlands that pay attention to the position of children who are living in poverty, such as Children's Ombudsman and The Netherlands Institute for Human Rights. For instance, the report of the Ombudsman was one of the reasons the anti-poverty strategy was intensified. Interestingly, the central government has recently formulated poverty reduction aims,[60] which could serve as a monitoring mechanism and increase the accountability in the future. However, the question remains how this will work out in practice. Could the government be held legally accountable by others, for example an NGO, for the achievement of the formulated goals? Most probably, the reduction aims serve as a monitoring feature, giving members of parliament and NGOs the opportunity to address the political accountability if the aims are not reached. This could force the government to react and accelerate the process.

To conclude, in the Netherlands the emphasis on governmental anti-poverty strategies still focuses on material welfare by tackling the structural causes of child poverty. Furthermore, money is provided to allow for in-kind items that allow children to participate in society activities which are important for their development. However, it is not clear what effects such measures have on reducing child poverty. More empirical research is needed to evaluate these measures. At the same time, the latest child poverty strategy shows some awareness of the importance of a more holistic and integrated approach of the child's development and the best interests of the child, although the best interests of the child are not considered explicitly in anti-poverty measures. Concrete steps are taken to enhance the participation of children in the policy process and first steps towards accountability are taken by introducing reduction aims. Hopefully, this encourages NGOs to follow up with the aims formulated and take further political, and maybe judicial action, if the aims are not reached. In addition, the government itself should invest in proper monitoring and evaluation of their policies. Only then, can it be determined whether the measures taken are effective in combating child poverty and are in the best interests of the child.

Notes

1 Kathrin Brandmeir et al., *Allianz Global Wealth Report*, 55 (2017).

2 Measured according to the "modest but adequate" criterion, which means that in addition to a minimum budget to necessary expenditure on unavoidable basis needs, a budget is required for participation, Stella Hoff & Bart Van Hulst, *Armoede bij kinderen en volwassenen in Armoede In Kaart*, 24 (2019).

3 UN Committee on the Rights of the Child (CRC), *Concluding Observations on the Fourth Periodic Report of the Netherlands*, U.N. Doc. CRC/C/NDL/CO/4 (2015); UN Committee on Economic, Social and Cultural Rights (CESCR), *Consideration*

of reports submitted by States Parties under articles 16 and 17 of the Covenant, U.N. Doc. E/C.12/NDL/CO/4-5 (2010); *see also*, Organisation for Economic Co-operation and Development (OECD), Poor Children in Rich Countries: Why We Need Policy Action (2018) (suggesting the Netherlands has an intermediate range of child poverty).

4 CBS, *Child Poverty Stable in 2018, Less Long-term Poverty* (Oct. 12, 2019), https://www.cbs.nl/en-gb/news/2019/50/child-poverty-stable-in-2018-less-long-term-poverty.

5 Sociaal-Economische Raad (SER), *Opgroeien Zonder Armoede*, 33 (2017).

6 Stella Hoff, *Armoede Onder Kinderen – Een Probleemschets* (2020); Josje den Ridder et al., *De Sociale Staat Van Nederland*, 25 (2020).

7 Asbjørn Eide, *Article 27: The Right to an Adequate Standard of Living*, 17 (Martinus Nijhoff Publishers, 2006); Rachel Hodgkin & Peter Newell, *Implementation Handbook for the Convention on the Rights of the Child*, 93 (2007).

8 *See supra* par. 2.

9 Regeerakkoord, VVD, CDA, D66 & ChristenUnie, *Vertrouwen In De Toekomst (2017–2021)* 27 (2017).

10 *Kamerstukken II*, 24515, nr. 430 (2017–2018).

11 Virginia Morrow, *Child Poverty, Social Exclusion and Children's Rights: A View from the Sociology of Childhood*, *in* Why Care? Children's Rights and Child Poverty, 36–37 (Wouter Vendenhole et al., eds., 2010).

12 Rita Maria Sousa Fernandes, *A Child Rights Approach to Child Poverty*, 3 (Eurochild, Discussion Paper 2007).

13 Morrow *supra* note 11, at 37.

14 UNICEF, *A Human Rights-based Approach to Education for All*, 9 (2007); College voor de rechten van de mens, *Jaarlijkse Rapportage Mensenrechten in Nederland 2016: armoede, sociale uitsluiting en mensenrechten*, 10–11 (2016).

15 UNICEF, *supra* note 14, at 9.

16 Wouter Vandenhole et al., *Why Care? Children's Rights and Child Poverty*, 23 (2010).

17 *Id*; *see also* Office of the United Nations High Commissioner for Human Rights, Principles and Guidelines for a Human Rights Approach to Poverty Reduction Strategies, 4–6 (2006).

18 U.N. CRC, *General Comment No. 5 General Measures of Implementation of the Convention on the Rights of the Child*, U.N. Doc. CRC/GC/2003/5 (2003).

19 Eur. Treaty Series No. 163 *Explanatory Report to European Social Charter* (Revised), 12–13 (1996).

20 *See* U.N. CESCR, *General Comment No. 19 The Right to Social Security (Art. 9 of the Covenant)*, U.N. Doc. E/C.12/GC/19 (2008); Malcolm Langford, *The Right to Social Security*, *in* The UN Convention on the Rights of the Child: A Commentary, 988–989 (John Tobin ed., 2019); Wouter Vandenhole, *A Commentary on the United Nations Convention on the Rights of the Child, Article 26, The Right to Benefit from Social Security* (2007).

21 *General Comment No. 19, supra* note 20, at § 2. n. 14.

22 Langford, *supra* note 20, at 987.

23 U.N. CRC, art. 6, Nov. 20, 1989, http://www.ohchr.org/en/professionalinterest/pages/crc.aspx (hereinafter CRC).

24 *Id.* at art. 29.

25 U.N. CRC, *General Comment No. 20 on the Implementation of the Rights of the Child During Adolescence*, U.N. Doc. CRC/C/GC/20 (2016); Eide, *supra* note 7; Hodgkin *supra* note 7, at 393; *see also* Noam Peleg, *The Child's Right to Development* (2019).

26 Hodgkin, *supra* note 7, at 395.

27 Aoife Nolan, *Art. 27 The Right to a Standard of Living Adequate for the Child's Development*, *in* The UN Convention on the Rights of the Child: A Commentary, 1028 (John Tobin ed., 2019).

28 *See also General Comment No. 20*, *supra* note 25, at § 17.
29 *Id.* at art. 27, par. 2.
30 *Id.* at art. 27, par. 3.
31 U.N. CRC, *General Comment No. 4 on Adolescent Health and Development in the Context of the Convention on the Rights of the Child*, U.N. Doc. CRC/GC/2003/4 §12 (2003); Nolan, *supra* note 27, at 1045.
32 U.N. CRC, *General Comment No. 21 on Children in Street Situations*, U.N. Doc. CRC/C/GC/21 § 49 (2017).
33 *General Comment No. 19*, *supra* note 20.
34 *Id.* at §28.
35 Nolan, *supra* note 27, at 1034.
36 *General Comment No. 19*, *supra* note 20, at §31.
37 *General Comment No. 5*, *supra* note 18.
38 UNICEF, *supra* note 14, at 11.
39 The Committee places great importance on accountable, transparent, inclusive, and participative decision-making processes (GC *No. 9*, §33). Compare for accountability instruments: Vanessa Sedletzki, *Closing the Gap between Social and Formal Accountability: Exploring the Role of Independent Human Rights Institutions for Children*, *in* The United Nations Convention on the Rights of the Child: Taking Stock After 25 Years and Looking Ahead, 169–171 (Ton Liefaard & Julia Sloth-Nielsen eds., 2016); Fernandes, *supra* note 12, at 7.
40 Because of their lack of legal capability. According to the Committee on the Rights of the Child, the character of a socioeconomic right (like art. 26 and 27 CRC) does not imply that the right is non-justiciable. UN Committee on the Rights of the Child, *General Comment No. 5*, *supra* note 18 at §25.
41 *General Comment No. 5*, *supra* note 18 at §24.
42 Sedletzki, *supra* note 39, at 183.
43 John Tobin, *The UN Convention on the Rights of the Child: A Commentary*, 117 (2019) ("It tends to be reactive rather than preventive, adversarial rather than conciliatory, excessively legalistic, invariably resource intensive, and often has a focus on addressing individual grievances rather than systemic change.").
44 Laurene Graziani, *Access to Justice: A Fundamental Right for all Children*, *in* The United Nations Convention on the Rights of the Child: Taking Stock after 25 years and Looking Ahead, 125–141(Ton Liefaard & Julia Sloth-Nielsen eds., 2016). Graziani pays specific attention (on pages 137–138) to the helpful role of NGOs in international human rights law proceedings, e.g., before the European Committee on Social Rights.
45 *General Comment No. 5*, *supra* note 18 at § 30.
46 Hodgkin, *supra* note 7, at 21.
47 U.N. CRC, *General Comment No. 14 On the Right of the Child to Have His or Her Best Interests Taken as a Primary Consideration (art. 3, para. 1)*, U.N. Doc. CRC/C/GC/14, §25 (2013).
48 *Id.* at §5.
49 *Id.*; *see also id.* at § 99 for a Child-rights impact assessment.
50 E.g., The Dutch Participation Act and the Social Support Act.
51 Regeerakkoord, *supra* note 9.
52 SER, *supra* note 5; de Kinderombudsman, Alle kinderen kansrijk, *Van De Ontwikkelingskansen Van Kinderen In Armoede* (2017).
53 *Kamerstukken II*, *supra* note 10.
54 E.g., measures to strengthen the infrastructure of the labour market regions, which means that municipalities have to work closely together with amongst other employers, employees, educational institutions, and sheltered employment companies.
55 Bureau Bartels, *Eerste Evaluatie Van De Bestuurlijke Afspraken Tussen Szw En Vng Over Kinderen In Armoede*, 43 (2018).

56 speaking minds, https://speakingminds.nl/.
57 *Kamerstukken II*, 24515, nr. 484 (2018–2019).
58 Tamara van Ark, *Beantwoording Kamervragen* (Jun. 13, 2019).
59 Speaking minds has already consulted children in 43 municipalities (Aug. 28, 2020).
60 *See supra* par. 3, Qualitative and quantitative reduction aims.

Index

Note: Page numbers followed by "n" denote endnotes.

abuse: "Child Abuse in India 2007" 239; online abuse prevention mechanism 247; physical 229, 232; sexual 90; *see also* child abuse; child sexual abuse (CSA)
academic writing 116, 134
accountability 255; in anti-poverty strategy 261
ACERWC *see* African Committee of Experts on the Rights and Welfare of the Child (ACERWC)
ACRWC *see* African Charter on the Rights and Welfare of the Child (ACRWC)
active citizen 149, 150, 152
Act on Insemination of Sweden 203, 209n33
Act Respecting Clinical and Research Activities Related to Assisted Procreation 211
"adequate standard of living" 74
ad hoc 24, 67, 69
administrative justice system 104
adolescent girls' right to participation 135–136
adoption 202–203; of CRC 199; intercountry 36–37; in Russia 203
Adoption Act of British Columbia 217, 218
Africa: ACRWC 37–38; child participation and access to justice 34–35; child population 30; child-sensitive social protection 37; family and urbanisation reconfiguration 39; impact of CRC 32–40; intercountry adoption 36–37; law reform 32–33; monitoring and enforcement 38; pluralistic legal systems and restorative justice 39–40; population growth 30–31; role of non-state actors 38–39; sexual and reproductive health rights 39; specialised institutions, personnel, and courts 35–36; systems strengthening for child protection 33–34
African Charter on the Rights and Welfare of the Child (ACRWC) 37–38
African Child Policy Forum 34, 41n12, 42n40
African Committee of Experts on the Rights and Welfare of the Child (ACERWC) 38, 39
African Committee of Experts Report on Agenda 37
age-appropriate sexuality education classes 240
Age of Enlightenment 116
American Convention on Human Rights 143
anti-poverty strategy 256, 259–261
Arbel (Justice) 50
Argentina, disappearance of children in 199
artificial reproduction technologies (ART) 199, 203–205
Assisted Human Reproduction Act 211
assisted procreation 211–212; artificial reproduction technologies 199, 203–205; filiation of children conceived by 212–214; laws on 212
assisted reproductive technologies 10
at risk: liberal implementation of right to participation 119–120; right to participation of 130; young girls 134–135

attorney-client relationship 93
Audio-Visual Media Services Directive into Member States law 22–23

Beinisch, Dorit 47
best interests of the child 132, 133, 157, 162, 163, 178; Article 3 of CRC 216–217; biological origins in 217; principle of 23, 50–51, 110, 191, 256
Bethel School District v. Fraser 147, 154
biomedically assisted fertilization (BMAF) 204
bodily integrity 158; civil rights beyond right of 166–167; rights of children to 164–166
breadth of participation 121–122
Breyer (Justice) 154
British Columbia Court of Appeal (BCCA) 215–218
Brown v. Entertainment Merchants Association 153, 154
Brown, Wendy 73
Bucharest EU Children's Declaration 25
Bureau, Marie-France 213

Canada: abuse and neglect 230–231; governing rules in 215; Province of Québec (*see* Province of Québec); Universal Child Care Benefit 75
Canadian Charter of Rights and Freedoms 143
caregiver 69, 92, 233; abusing children 226
care proceedings: Israel 130, 132; stakeholders in 131, 137
CARES Act 78
Case of Mennesson v. France 205–207
Case of Paradiso and Campanelli v. Italy 206, 207
C.E. v. Belgium 8
Charter of Fundamental Rights of the EU (CFR) 253
Charter of Human Rights and Freedoms 217–219; Article 7 of 221n36; Article 15 of 217
"Chennai Horror" case 240
child abuse: in Canada 230–231; in India 238; in South Africa 226–228; in United States 229–230
"Child Abuse in India 2007" 239
Child Care Act, section 42(1) of 226
child-centered justice 105
child focused justice 105
child-friendly justice 99n15, 103, 109–112; interdisciplinarity at heart of 105–107; lofty goals and real consequences 107–109; origin and core of 103–105; professional ethics, moral advocacy, and human rights 112–113
childhood: to adulthood 149–150; condition as predicament 152; experiences from generation to generation 183; issue of 143; moral status of 146; perspective on status 149
childhood circumcision 164–166
Child Justice Act 75 (2008) 32
child marriage 35
"child packages" 258, 259
child participation 9; and access to justice 34–35
child poverty 76–78, 251, 252; non-discrimination 255, 256, 260; policy measures reduce 258; qualitative and quantitative reduction aims 259; structural causes of 257
child protection: capture disaggregated and issue-based data on 246; ensure child participation 246; financial investments 246; multi-stakeholders approach 247; online abuse prevention mechanism 247; path-breaking legislation for 242; procedure 122; systems strengthening for 33–34
child rape: cases of 241; factors leading to death penalty 244–246
children: corporal punishment of 52; decision-making process 91; development of 258; education of 79–82; filiation of 212–214; financial investments on 246; framework for representation of 92–97; legal empowerment of 112; mortality rates of 30; to participate in community, and society 74; personal data of 174; pictures of 190; role and impact of armed conflict on 31; sempiternal adult-centric perception of 111; sharenting and evolving capacities of 189–190; as speakers and listeners 146–147; as special status 147–149; transitional rights of 169n31; used as means to "punish" sins of parents 157
Children Act 1982 33
Children Amendment Act 2020 32–33
children at-risk, right to participation of 130

children filed communications 9
Children in Street Situations 7
Children's Act 232; section 110(1) of 227, 228
Children's Amendment Bill 228
children's digital rights 190–191
Children's Legal Protection Center 42n40
Children's Ombudsman 261
Children's Online Privacy Protection Act (COPPA) 185, 186
children's privacy 187–189
children's rights: on adequate standard of living 253–255; adoption 202–203; ART 203–204; Articles 7 and 8 of CRC 214–216; to bodily integrity, of male and female circumcision 164–166; child-centered perspective on 159; in digital environment 10; discourse on 117; identity and parentage 205–207; to know biological origin 199–207; legal framework for 5; natural birth 201–202; in parentage law 204–205; relational approach to 162–163; relational perspective on 162–166; respect for private life 205–207; revolution in 157
"children's rights actor" 18
Children's Rights Committee 65
children's rights discourse: communitarian paradigm and effect on 118–119; liberal paradigm and effect on 116–118
Children's Rights in the Child Justice System 7
children's rights jurisprudence 35
children's voices 25, 40, 92, 97, 186–188
child representation 89, 102n60, 132, 133
child rights-based approach 252, 255–257, 259–261
child rights culture 23–24
child-sensitive 37, 105
child sexual abuse (CSA) 238–239; actions to decrease 241–242; high numbers and underreporting 240–241
Child Sexual Abuse Materials (CSAM) 247
child's right to an adequate standard of living 75–76
child's right to health 74–75
child's right to privacy 185; analysis of 171; in CRC 172–173; in GDPR 173–175; infringements of 177; under Polish civil law 175–178
A Child's Right to Respect (Korczak) 11
Child Welfare Committees 245–246
Christian Democratic People's Party v. Moldova 155n10
circumcision, childhood 164–166
Civil Code 176; Article 33 of 215; Article 538 of 212; Article 542 of 213; Articles 23 of 175; Articles 24 of 175; provisions of 178
Civil Code of Québec (CCQ) 211
civil justice system 104, 105
Civil Proceedings Regulations 131
civil rights 158
Committee on the Rights of the Child 184
communication: barriers 143; emergence of new modern 173; non-verbal 151
communication procedure 8; Optional Protocol on 9, 14n49
communitarian approach 121–124
communitarian paradigm 124; and effect on children's rights discourse 118–119; liberal paradigm and 122–123
community reporters 227
Concluding Observations 5–6
consensual sexual acts, criminalization of 242–243
Constitution Act, Articles 91 and 92 of 211–212
Constitution of India 238, 244
Constitution of the Republic of Poland, Article 47 of 175
Convention for the Protection of Human Rights and Fundamental Freedoms, Article 8 of 205, 206
Convention on the Elimination of Discrimination Against Women (CEDAW) 160, 244; CEDAW Committee 161
conviction rates 241
COPPA *see* Children's Online Privacy Protection Act (COPPA)
Copyright Law 177
Council of Europe 103–104
Council of Europe Guidelines 104–108
Covenant on the Civil and Political Rights, Article 17 of 172
CRC Committee 10, 48, 54, 75, 76, 79, 169n31, 191, 216, 254, 256; child participation 9; child's best interests 50–51; communication procedure 8; mandate of 4–7; right to participation defined by 49; Rules of Procedure 6
CRC-compliant law reform 32
crime rate 239
criminal justice system 104, 105
CSA *see* child sexual abuse (CSA)

CSAM *see* Child Sexual Abuse Materials (CSAM)
custody 91, 92, 97

data protection laws 186–188, 190
death penalty, child rape 244–246
decision-making 91, 98
decision-making process 117, 119, 122, 124, 130, 256
Defence for Child International (DCI) 34
Democratic Republic of Congo 32
depth of participation 121
Detlehoff, Nina 202
"developmental equality" 78
digital media 10
digital parental care, legal standards for 187
digital playgrounds 183
digital tools 183
digital youth cultures 183–184
diversion 42n38, 42n39
Dolinsky, Anna 80
Dowd, Nancy 78
Dutch Children's Ombudsman 261
Dutch Constitution, Article 20 of 257
Dutch Government Agreement 251, 257
Dutch National Youth Council 261

education 6, 79–80; heart of CRC 80–81; "minimum standards as may be laid down by the state" 81–82; right to education 82
employment equality legislation 18
empowerment 255; in anti-poverty strategy 261
equality principle 53
equal protection rights 69
Ethiopia 36; criminal justice policy of 42n40; laws on operation of non-profit organisations 38–39
EU Charter of Fundamental Rights (CFR) 19; Article 24 of 19
EU child-protective measures 22
EU child rights strategy 17, 18; incorporating UNCRC at EU level 24–25
EU free movement laws 18
European adoption (Family Law) acts 202–203
European Child Guarantee scheme 17, 25
European Commission 23
European Convention on Human Rights 67, 143, 218
European Court for Human Rights (ECHR) 155n10, 199, 207, 218; Article 8 of 205, 206
European Court of Justice (ECJ) 20, 23
European law 200
European Social Charter (ESC): Article 17 of 253; Article 30 of 253
European Union (EU): challenges in making children's rights concrete 22–23; children's rights protection, before and after Lisbon Treaty 18–20; children's rights protection in 17–20; child rights culture 23–24; Court of Justice of 188; General Data Protection Regulation 185, 186, 188; laws and policies, incorporation of CRC 20–22
European Union Agency for Fundamental Rights 99n15, 111
European Union GDPR 173
Europe 2020 strategy 21–22
ex ante integration of children's rights 24
ex post enforcement of children's rights 24
extended family members 117, 118

Facebook 184, 186
Family Act 202; Article 59 of 200
Family and Guardianship Code 178
Family Group Conference (FGC) model 115, 120; *vs.* PTACs 120–123
family law 176; doctrine and practice of 199
family, need human rights: child poverty 77–78; child's right to an adequate standard of living 75–76; child's right to health 74–75; infant mortality 77; maternal mortality 77
family obligations: complicated relationship between 73; and human rights conflict 79–82
family, reconfiguration of 39
FCC *see* Federal Communications Commission (FCC)
FCC v. Fox 146, 154
FCC v. Pacifica Foundation 146
Federal Child Abuse Prevention and Treatment Act (CAPTA) 229
Federal Communications Commission (FCC) 146
Federal Law on the Basics of Health Protection of the Citizens in Russian Federation 203–204
Feinberg, Joel 146
female circumcision 164–166

female genital mutilation (FGM) 160, 161; physical and emotional harms of 165
financial investments 246
Fineman, Martha 81
First Amendment 144, 147, 148, 153–155
forced sexual intercourse 244
For Every Child, Every Right 11n5
formal accountability 255
formal justice systems 39–40
Frattini, Franco 19
free expression 144–145
Freeman, Michael 11n6
free speech: autonomy rationale for 151; values 143–146
French Civil Code 201
French Declaration of the Rights of Man and of the Citizen 143–144
Fruits, Salads, and Smoothies: A Working Definition of Interdisciplinarity (Nissani) 106

gender-based violence 36
Gender Based Violence and Femicide (GBVF) 234
Gender Based Violence Courts 36
gender theories 134; adolescent girls' right to participation 135–136; young girls at risk 134–135
General Comments 6–7, 191
General Data Protection Regulation (GDPR) 171–172, 185, 186, 188; Article 8 of 174; child's right to privacy in 173–175
genetic origin 199–200
German Basic Law 143
Germany 203; ART practice in 205; Constitutional Court 200
Getting Girls Equal 31, 41n12
Ghana: child-friendly court in 36; surrogacy in 37
Gilligan, Carol 134
global capitalism 73
global inequality 76
Graham v. Florida 91
Graziani, Laurene 256
guardians ad litem 92, 132, 133, 137
Guidelines on Children in Contact with the Justice System 105
Guilhermont, Édith 213

Haberko, Joanna 175
Hague Convention on Intercountry Adoption (1993) 36, 67
Hague Convention on the Civil Aspects of International Child Abduction 43n57
Henkin, Louis 81
Human Fertilization and Embryology Act (HFEA) 205
human rights 112–113; on adequate standard of living 253–255; legal right to free speech 143
human rights-based approach 252
human rights, need families 78; on ground 78–79; teaching children about 79
human rights treaties, network of 82n4

IFSW *see* International Federation of Social Workers (IFSW)
impermissible paternalism 150
Independent Thought v. Union of India 244
India, child sexual abuse in *see* child sexual abuse (CSA)
Indian Penal Code (IPC) 243; section 375 of 244
inequality 76
infant mortality 77
informal accountability 255
informal justice system 40
Information Communication Technologies (ICTs) 10
Inter-African Committee on Traditional Practices 165
intercountry adoption 36–37
international adoption 64–67, 70n10
International Association of Youth and Family Judges and Magistrates 105
International Code of Ethics 94
International Covenant on Civil and Political Rights (ICCPR) 65, 67, 68, 143
International Covenant on Economic, Social and Cultural Rights (ICESCR) 68; Article 9 of 253
International Federation of Social Workers (IFSW) 94
international human rights for children: balancing harm to relationships with individual children 163–164; childhood circumcision 164–166; relational approach 162–163
international human rights instruments 20
International Labour Organization (ILO) convention 38
International Society of Family Law's 30th Anniversary Celebration 6
Interpretation Act 220n7

intersectionality theory 134–136
Israel: best interests of the child principle 50–51; CRC recognition, as conceptual basis for laws on children 47–48; Family Group Conference model 120; guardian ad litem 132; legislation and case law in 47–48; life and survival and development principle 52–53; non-discrimination principle 53–54; participation principle 48–50; PTACs operating in 123
Israeli case law 50, 54, 55n11
Israeli law: care proceedings 130, 132; right to participation in 129–130
Israeli National Council for the Child 46
Italian Constitution 143–144

Jamieson, Lucy 231–233
Jovanović v. Serbia 199
judicial proceeding 105, 107, 111
Judicial Service of Ghana 36
justice, access to 34–35
justice sector reform 40
juvenile justice laws 32

kafalah 8, 14n52
Kamal Prasad v. State of Chhattisgarh 243
Kant, Immanuel 148, 149, 152
Kathua gang rape case 245
Kennedy (Justice) 91
Kenya 35, 36
Korczak, Janusz: *A Child's Right to Respect* 11
Krugman, Paul 75

Lagarde, Christine 76
law (in)books: CRC, Article 12 128–129; right to participation in Israeli law 129–130; right to participation of children at-risk 130; youth law care and supervision 130–134
Law Commission of India 245
law in action 136–138
law-making function 33
Law of the Marriage Act 35
Law on Children's Foster Care 52
Law on Foster Care for Children 47
Law on Information about the Influence of Legislation on Children's Rights 47
Law on the Rights of Students 47
Law on the Rules of Evidence 49
Law on Working Youths (1953) 49
lawyer: educational process for 97; framework for representation 92–97
legal proceedings: active participation in 128; participation in 135–136
von der Leyen, Ursula 17
liberalism 116, 117, 124n4
liberal paradigm 119; and communitarian paradigm 122–123; and effect on children's rights discourse 116–118; participation in 123
liberal theory 116
life and survival and development principle 52–53
Lisbon Treaty 18, 25; phases of children's rights protection in EU 18–20
Locke, John 124n4
Lopatka, Adam 171

Macchi Singh v. State of Punjab 244
Madzhuru v. Minister of Justice, Parliamentary and Constitutional Affairs 35
mainstream children 106
Making Children's Rights Widely Known (Todres) 12n20
male circumcision 164–166
mandated professionals 229, 230
mandatory reporting laws 225, 228, 229, 231, 233
mandatory reporting, under POCSO Act 243
Mandela, Nelson 234
Mann, Jonathan 113n12
marginalized communities 137–138
marital sex 244
Marshall (Justice) 154
maternal mortality 77
Mauritania 36
medically assisted procreation 211, 212; compared with children born of 213–214; Olivia Pratten case 217; use of 213
Medical Termination of Pregnancy Act (1971) 243
Millennium Development Goals (MDG) 30, 37
Mill, John Stuart 144
Model Rules of Professional Conduct (MRPC) 93
moral advocacy 112–113
Morse v. Frederick 146–147, 154
mortality rates 30
Mozambique 32–33

multi-stakeholders approach 247
Muslim faith 30–31
MWK v. Attorney General 35
"My Own Advocate" 132

National Association of Counsel for Children (NACC) 102n62
National Association of Social Workers (NASW) Code of Ethics 102n51; Section 1.02 of 94
National Commission for the Protection of Child Rights (NCPCR) 241
national constitutional documents 143
National Council for Juvenile and Family Court Judges (NCJFCJ) 97, 102n61
National Crime Record Bureau (NCRB) 239
national human rights institutions (NHRIs) 6
National Organization of Forensic Social Work (NOFSW) 102n62
natural birth 201–202, 208n15
natural person 175–176
Nedelsky, Jennifer 163
neglect: in Canada 230–231; in South Africa 226–228; in United States 229–230
neoliberalism 73
Netherlands: child rights-based approach 259–261; national context 257–259; poverty rate in 251; poverty reduction policies in 252; qualitative and quantitative reduction aims 259
Netherlands Bureau for Economic Policy Analysis (CPB) 258
The Netherlands Institute for Human Rights 261
Netherlands Institute for Social Research (SCP) 251
Netherlands' Ombudsman for Children 257
Nissani, Moti: *Fruits, Salads, and Smoothies: A Working Definition of Interdisciplinarity* 106
non-discrimination 255, 256, 260
non-discrimination principle 53–54
non-governmental organisations (NGOs) 4, 5, 7–10, 38, 261
non-state actors, role of 38–39
non-verbal communication 151
notion of dignity 108

Ombudsperson for Children Act of Mauritius 2003 44n67
online abuse prevention mechanism 247
online environment 185–186
online social interface 183–184
Optional Protocol 8, 9, 12n12; on communication procedure 9, 14n49
Optional Protocol to the Convention on the Rights of the Child on a Communications Procedure 196n96
Organization for Economic Cooperation and Development (OECD) 76

PACE Initiative 160, 162
Palermo Protocol 38
Pandemic Electronic Benefit Transfer 78
parens patriae 60, 61, 157
parentage law, child's right in 204–205
parental authority 157, 162, 167, 172, 173, 176–178, 185
parental control apps 187
parental monitoring 187–189
parental responsibility, social media 186–187
parental rights, socio-cultural milieu of 240
parent-child relationship 200, 205–207
participation principle 48–50, 255
participation rights 115–116, 122, 187, 190; in Article 13 of CRC 188; communitarian implementation of 120
partnership 120, 121; principles of 119
passive citizen 149, 152
paternalism 137, 145–146
paternalistic intervention 148, 150, 152, 155
penalty 229–232
personal information 211, 213, 220n10
physical abuse 229, 232
Piketty, Thomas 76
Plan International 41n12
Planning, Treatment, and Assessment Committees (PTACs) 115, 119–120; conceptualization of 123; *vs.* FGC model 120–123
pluralistic legal systems 39–40
POCSO Act *see* Protection of Children from Sexual Offences Act (POCSO Act)
Poland: regulation in 174; statement on Articles 12–16 172–173
Polish civil law 172, 178; child's right to privacy under 175–178
Polish Criminal Code, Article 191(a) of 178

"Polish perspective" 179n1
pornography 247
Portuguese Court of Appeal of Évora 189
posthumous fertilization 205
poverty 22
poverty rate, in Netherlands 251
Pratten, Olivia 216–218, 221n36
Press Law 177
principle of confidentiality 211, 213
principle of participation 116, 129
privacy laws 190
"Procedural Safeguards Directive" 22
professional ethics 112–113
"Protection and Empowering Children as Human Rights Defenders" 9
Protection of Children from Sexual Offences Act (POCSO Act) 239, 241, 242, 245; criminalization of consensual sexual acts between minors 242–243; mandatory reporting under 243; marital sex 244; section 19(1) of 243
Province of Québec: assisted procreation 211–214; legal factors to promote right of origins 214–219
public hearing 220n14, 220n15
public international law 183, 190–191

Québec Advisory Committee 219

RAINN 98n5
Ramser, Claudia 202
rape: cases of 241; factors leading to death penalty 244–246; *Kathua* gang rape case 245; *Unnao* gang rape case 245
ratification 74; of CRC 97
Ravitsky, Vardit 214
Ravi v. State of Maharashtra 245, 246
relational approach 162–163
"reporting cycle" 12n11
reporting requirements 231
restorative justice 39–40
Rifqa's case 89–90; framework for representation 92–97; in US and CRC 91–92
Right of Children to Free and Compulsory Education Act (2009) 241
right of freedom of speech 152
right of origins, legal factors to promote 214–219
right of parents 160
rights to participation, online environment 185
rights to privacy 218–219
right to education 82
right to equality 129; CRC and Canadian Charter of Rights 217–218
right to freedom of expression 144, 152; right to express 91
right to free speech 129
right to know biological parenthood: adoption 202–203; ART 203–204; identity and parentage 205–207; natural birth 201–202; in parentage law 204–205; respect for private life 205–207
right to participation 49, 115–116; adolescent girls 135–136; of children at-risk 130; communitarian implementation of risk 120; components of 129; in Israeli law 129–130; liberal implementation of risk 119–120
Roper v. Simmons 91
Rotlevi committee 139n15
Rotlevi, Savyona 46
Rubellin-Devichi, Jacqueline 201
Russia: adoption in 203; Federal Law on the Basics of Health Protection of the Citizens in Russian Federation 203–204

Sabari v. Inspector of Police 243
San Antonio Independent School District v. Rodriguez 80, 82
Sandusky scandal 230, 232
Save the Children 76
Scalia (Justice) 154
Schapiro, Tamar 149
Schmit, Nicolas 17
"second wave" law reform 32
Secrecy Act (1994) 200
Sedletzki, Vanessa 256
Serbia: disappearance of children in 199; Family Act 200; maternity and paternity in court proceedings 202; posthumous fertilization 205
Serbian Law, Article 57 of 204
sex-trade rackets 65
sexual abuse 90
sexual and reproductive health rights (SRHR) 39
sexual assault 240–243
sexual offenses 227, 228, 231
sexual violence 36
Shamgar, Meir 47
sharenting 189–190
Shiffrin, Seana 151
Skivenes, Marit 111, 112
Sloth-Nielsen, Julia 228

Smolin, David 81
smoothie 103, 105, 106
Social and Economic Council of the Netherlands (SER) 257
social cash transfer schemes 37
social media 183, 185, 189; nature of 184; parental responsibility and children's autonomy 186–187; participation in 187
social security 251, 252
social worker 102n51; educational process for 97; framework for representation 92–97; inter-professional team of 95
socio-economic rights: child's right to an adequate standard of living 75–76; child's right to health 74–75; right to education 82
South Africa 35; abuse and neglect 226–228, 233; Article 19 of CRC 225; mandatory reporting system 233; rules for child witnesses 36; social and health service providers 232; surrogacy in 37
South African Constitution 226
South African Criminal Law (Sexual Offences and Related Matters) Amendment Act (SORMA) 226, 231; section 54 of 227–228; section 56(5) of 235n22
South African Police Service (SAPS) 226
special rights fallacy 59–60
speech: free speech values 143–146; issue of 143; legal protection for 151
"Spot-lighting the Invisible: Access to Justice for Children in Africa" 34
Stalford, Helen 112
state intervention 79, 157, 187, 189
State of Madhya Pradesh v. Balu 242–243
States Parties 3, 48, 53, 110, 215; concluding observations 5–6; general comments 6–7; obligations under CRC 4–7
Stevens (Justice) 154
sub-Saharan Africa 30, 31
substantive due process rights 68
Šuica, Dubravka 17
sui generis 67
surrogacy 37
Sustainable Development Goals 37, 107
Sydor-Zielińska, Aleksandra 177, 181n52
systems strengthening, for child protection 33–34

Tanzania 35
Thakur, Brajesh 242
Théry, Irène 214
thinking mind 151–155
third-party parental project 213
Third Protocol 67–68
Thomas (Justice) 148
threshold conditions 122
TikTok 184, 186
Tinker v. Des Moines Independent Community School District 155n10
Todres, Jonathan: *Making Children's Rights Widely Known* 12n20
tourism-related commercial sexual exploitation 239
trafficking 65
transversal human rights program 104
Treaty on European Union (TEU) 26n13
Treaty on the Functioning of the European Union (TFEU) 26n13; Article 216 of 25

UN Committee on the Protection of the Rights of All Migrant Workers and Members of Their Families (CMW) 7, 13n32
UN Committee on the Rights of the Child *see* CRC Committee
UN Convention on the Rights of Persons with Disabilities 25
underreporting 240–241
UN Economic and Social Council Guidelines on Justice in Matters Involving Child Victims and Witnesses of Crime 105
UNICEF 4, 31, 36, 64, 65, 76
United Nations Children's Fund 42n42
United Nations Convention on the Rights of the Child (CRC) 3, 17, 59; adoption of 199; on African continent 30; Article 2 of 79, 82; Article 3 of 110, 162, 216–217; Article 3(1) of 60; Article 3(2) of 61; Article 5 of 21, 176–177, 187; Article 6(2) of 251; Article 7 of 21, 215; Article 8 of 188, 215–216; Article 9 of 159, 162; Article 12 of 9, 48, 91, 110, 128–129, 159, 187, 255; Article 13 of 144, 188; Article 14 of 159, 160; Article 14(2) of 61; Article 16 of 172, 188; Article 17 of 184; Article 18 of 173, 185, 204; Article 19 of 161, 225; Article 24 of 30, 73, 74, 161; Article 26 of 253, 254, 257, 260; Article 27 of 37, 253, 254, 259; Article 27.1 of 75; Article 29.1 of 79–81; Article 29.2 of

80; Article 42 of 12n20; and borderless nature of social media 184; and Canadian Charter of Rights 217–218; claims over best for children 158–159; context of childhood circumcision 160–162; Dutch government 251; false notion citizenship 64; Israel ratification 46; rights to communities 63; rights to extended family 63; and right to participation 115–116; section 2 of 53; States' obligations under 4–7; strengthen US legal system 89
United States: abuse and neglect 229–230; Children's Online Privacy Protection Act 185, 186; and CRC 91–92; CRC's harmful impact 64–68; family need human rights 74–78; family obligations and human rights conflict 79–82; homeschooled in 74; human rights need families 78–79; legal proceedings in 91; rejection of CRC affects children 76–78; special rights fallacy 59–60; specific deficiencies in CRC 60–64
United States v. Playboy Entertainment Group 153
Universal Child Care Benefit (UCCB) 75
Universal Declaration of Human Rights (UDHR) 68, 253; Article 12 of 172
Unnao gang rape case 245
UN Special Rapporteur on Violence Against Children 31
UN Treaty bodies 6–8
urbanisation 39
US Constitution, Article 6 of 82
user-generated content (UGC) 184, 185, 187, 190
US legal system, CRC strengthen 89
U.S. v. Playboy 155

violence against children 31
visitation 90–94, 97

Ward (Justice) 202
Web 2.0 185, 191
WhatsApp 187
Woodhouse, Barbara Bennett 77, 81
World Economic Outlook (WEO) 76
World Health Organization (WHO) 225
Worst Forms of Child Labour 38

young girls at risk 134–135
youth law: Article 8 of 130–132; Article 9 of 130; care and supervision 130–134

Zimbabwe, Constitutional Court 35

Kolibri 360 GmbH
Ferdinand-Jühlke-Straße 7
99095 Erfurt, Deutschland
produktsicherheit@kolibri360.de